My Name is Freida Sima

Judith Tydor Baumel-Schwartz

My Name is Freida Sima

The American-Jewish Women's Immigrant Experience Through the Eyes of a Young Girl from the Bukovina

PETER LANG

Bern · Berlin · Bruxelles · Frankfurt am Main · New York · Oxford · Wien

Bibliographic information published by die Deutsche Nationalbibliothek
Die Deutsche Nationalbibliothek lists this publication in the Deutsche
Nationalbibliografie; detailed bibliographic data is available on the Internet
at ‹http://dnb.d-nb.de›.

British Library Cataloguing-in-Publication Data: A catalogue record for this book is
available from The British Library, Great Britain.

Library of Congress Cataloguing-in-Publication Data: A catalogue record for this
book is available.

This book was produced with the generous assistance of the Fanya Gottesfeld Heller
Center for the Study of Women in Judaism, Bar-Ilan University, Ramat Gan, Israel.

ISBN 978-3-0343-2193-8 pb.   ISBN 978-3-0343-2411-3 eBook
ISBN 978-3-0343-2413-7 MOBI   ISBN 978-3-0343-2412-0 EPUB

© Peter Lang AG, International Academic Publishers, Bern 2017
Wabernstrasse 40, CH-3007 Bern, Switzerland
info@peterlang.com, www.peterlang.com

Printed in Switzerland

Contents

Chapter 1 How it all began – Ramat Gan 1975

Introduction

It had truly been a joyous evening. For hours, the entire family sat around the dining room table, eating and celebrating. An unending array of food had streamed out of the kitchen: strips of lightly fried schnitzel, paper-thin potato pancakes with apple sauce and finally, more substantial fare, meat patties smothered in fried onions. Throughout the evening, platters of delicacies were passed around, especially the apple-matzo meal latkes that were my grandmother's specialty. "Come sit down Ma", my mother called out to her, still in the kitchen, "it's your day, enough cooking." "Just one more batch", was the expected answer. Although it was still two months until Chanukah, these latkes had nothing to do with the season. In my grandmother's family, apple pancakes were a tradition, and no celebration was held without them.

And what a celebration it was! Not only was it my grandmother's eightieth birthday, but it was also one of those rare occasions when a good part of her extended family could gather under one roof. Of course it wasn't her entire family; four of her siblings lived in New York and her four stepsons lived in California, ten time zones away. But she was with her daughter, son-in-law and granddaughter, with whom she had moved to Israel a year earlier. "Another move across the sea", she had said, musing over how much had changed since her first overseas journey, sixty-four years ago. Then, she had been a young girl of fifteen who had left home alone to get an education in America. Now she was a very senior citizen, but her sense of adventure remained undiminished. "Who knows what this journey will lead to? Be positive!" she admonished me, when I, at fifteen, had expressed uncertainty coping in a new country.

The crowd at the table included some of my grandmother's brothers and sisters-in-law who had gathered for the occasion: her oldest brother Abie and his wife Minnie, who were in Israel on a visit from America, and two middle brothers, Srul and Leibish, along with their wives, Anna and Frieda. She still thought of Srul and Leibish as "the boys" as they had been five and three when she had left Europe. The next time she saw them, they were already in their mid-forties, having been separated from her by three geographical upheavals, two World Wars and one Holocaust which they had experienced in Europe while she was already in the United States. Now they were in their late sixties, and she was trying to bridge the gap of years and experiences which separated them. Above all, she had to remember not to pepper her Yiddish with English expressions which they, having come directly to Israel from post-war Europe, could barely understand.

"Time for cake and presents", I called out, as I brought in a round birthday cake ablaze with candles. By the time my own mother would celebrate her eightieth birthday more than three decades later, we would be using a large sheet cake onto which we could easily fit the requisite eighty candles. Then, however, Israeli stove pans were smaller. Looking at the size of the cake earlier in the day, my mother and I had wordlessly decided to stop at eighteen candles – the numerical equivalent of the Hebrew word *chai* – "life". One by one those sitting around the table presented my grandmother with birthday gifts: a scarf, a bottle of cologne, a book of Yiddish poetry, a sweater, a pair of warm slippers, a rhinestone pin, and finally, a curiously shaped package which appeared to be some kind of large square glass bottle.

"How many *einiklach* (grandchildren) give their Baba apricots in liquor for her eightieth birthday?!" she laughed as she handed out tiny glasses into which she poured the spirits. "This is what you give the woman who has everything!" Each of the guests lifted a small tumbler containing some of the clear liquid, raising the glass and calling out *lechaim* – to life. "Boytee, you have some granddaughter", said Abie. "And she has some grandmother!" my grandmother answered back. "*Shvester* (sister) Babaleh, is this how they raise them in America?" asked Srul, using her childhood nickname, and shaking his head at the notion that a sixteen-year-old girl would give her octogenarian grandmother a bottle of schnapps for her birthday. "Why not? It tastes good", she answered him, shrugging her shoulders and looking towards me in the kitchen doorway. "*Lechaim*" she called out with a smile, raising her glass high and blowing me a kiss.

Towards midnight, the crowd began to take their leave from the "birthday girl", giving her final blessings for a long and healthy life. "So Ma, how did you enjoy your party?" my mother asked, after closing the door behind the last guest. "It was wonderful", my grandmother answered in her customary tongue-in-cheek manner. "The best eightieth birthday party I ever had." "Just wait until you are ninety," I countered, "then we'll even top this one." Little did I know that she would be gone a year and four months short of her ninetieth birthday.

"Just explain one thing Baba," I asked her in a more serious vein. "Why do your brothers in America call you by one name, while your brothers in Israel call you by another?" "And why do my older cousins in Israel call me by a third?" she replied, "It's a long story and it's the story of my life, the places that I have lived and the people that I have known. Everyone gives you a different name," she said, "but the only important thing is the name that you eventually give yourself. That's the one that people remember."

Who was Freida Sima?

My grandmother was a woman of many names and many talents, each of which corresponded with a different period in her life. Like numerous women of her generation. she was able to whip up a three course meal out of nothing, and make a one week Depression salary last for six months. But she could also milk a cow with her eyes closed and ride a horse bareback, legacies of her childhood on an Eastern European farm, in one of the few areas where Jews were permitted to own land by 1860. Used to living creatures of all kinds, she was fearless, picking up live cockroaches and throwing them out the window, laughing when I would shudder to see her holding them with her bare hands.

Although she only became a mother when she was thirty-three, she became "Baba", meaning grandmother, when she was less than a year old. As her granddaughter I called her "Baba", but she had first been called that more than sixty years before my birth. This was how her older cousins referred to her, treating it as a nickname and calling her "Babaleh" in diminutive. On her immigration papers from 1911 she is listed as Babe, the immigration official's phonetic equivalent of what he heard when he asked her name, and she automatically answered what everyone had called her for the previous fifteen years, "Babeh".

The story of how she received that nickname was a central tale in our family lore. When her parents married, her mother Devorah had long fiery-red braids that almost reached the ground. Enamored with his young wife's hair, her husband Nachman forbade her to cut it after marriage, as was the custom. Instead, she pinned up her flowing locks under her marriage wig, to the dismay of her relatives and neighbors who had come to shave her head the morning after her wedding. What's more, it appears that she used to pull out pieces of her own beautiful hair from under the wig and wrap it around her head to make the wig look more lifelike. Nachman was obviously happy with the results and so, one presumes, was seventeen-year-old Devorah, but the same was not true for the women of Mihowa, as we will soon see. Refusing to heed their warnings about where such immodesty could lead, she and her tall, strapping Nachman lived happily together, soon delighting in the news that she was going to bear their first child.

Soon after, my grandmother entered the world and was named Freida Sima. Sima after a neighbor who had recently died childless, and Freida, the Yiddish equivalent of *Simcha* – "happiness" in Hebrew, in honor of Simchat Torah, one of Judaism's most joyous festivals which was celebrated on the previous day. But that happiness was soon threatened. Several months later little Freida Sima fell ill with diphtheria. Seeing her baby convulsed with fever, the terrified eighteen-year-old Devorah ran to a neighbor for assistance.

This was the moment that the local women had waited for. Admonishing Devorah that her baby daughter's illness was the Lord's punishment for her misdeeds, they coerced her into shaving her head in the hope of appeasing the Almighty. When Nachman returned home and saw his wife's denuded scalp, he bellowed with rage, running out of their cottage, and swinging an axe at anyone and everything in sight. But it was too late. The deed had been done, and Devorah never grew her beautiful hair again.

At the same time, in order to "cheat the devil" it was customary to change a sick child's name to that of an elderly person, so that they would be spared the evil eye. Boys would often receive the name *Alter* ("The old one") or *Zeide* (grandfather), and girls would be called "old lady" or grandmother. Thus, little Freida Sima was re-named "Baba", or "Babaleh", "little grandmother", a name which stuck for close to ninety years, almost wiping out the memory of what she had been called at birth. All of her future names would be based on the sound of this one. Her aunts in America gave her the English name "Bertha", which was the closest one they could find to "Babaleh". After joining her in America, her younger siblings transposed it to "Boytee" which was easier for them to pronounce. A decade later, Max, her Russian-born husband, would call her "Bert" or "Bertie", glossing over the "th" sound which was so difficult for immigrants to enunciate. Maybe that was why my grandmother was always careful to stress the "th" in "the", pronouncing it with a pure American accent, and not slurring it, as did so many of the people in New York, her adopted city.

Only when old age began creeping up on her did she begin to refer to her birth name, reminding us of its existence. At her eightieth birthday party, after everyone had toasted her with good health and long life, she turned to my mother and said "Just remember one thing. My name is Freida Sima. That's what I want you to put on my tombstone. Remember. Freida Sima", she repeated a second time.

One of my grandmother's favorite expressions was "I was Jewish before you were born", and indeed her almost automatic reactions to various situations were deeply rooted in Jewish traditions, customs, beliefs, and even superstitions. Happiness is transient, an illusion. Every moment of joy has its flip side lurking in the shadows. Traditionally, Jews dilute even the greatest happiness with a brief mention of sorrow. Ashes are placed on a bridegroom's forehead; a glass is broken during the wedding ceremony, in memory of the destruction of the Temple. Here too, there could be no absolute celebration or undiluted joy. Even when drinking a birthday *lechayim* and celebrating life, in a corner of your mind, you should always think of the grave.

Freida Sima and the Immigrant Generation

Our Sages have taught us that every person has a number of names: the one that parents give, the one that people use, and the one a person earns by themselves, through their unique talents and abilities. That name, as my grandmother used to say, echoing the Midrash, is the most important name of all.[1] Each name expresses a different one of a person's attributes. Each contributes an essential component to that person's essence. My grandmother was indeed a woman of many talents, and almost as many names; obviously her essence was just as complex.

Unlike many of my friends who had lost all their grandparents in the Holocaust, I was lucky enough to have one set of live grandparents who lived with us throughout most of my formative years. Both of my

---

1   *Midrash Tanhuma*, Exodus, Vayakhel.

grandparents, Freida Sima (Bertha) Eisenberg Kraus and Max Kraus, were among the two million Jewish men, women and children who emigrated from Europe to the United States during the Great Wave of Immigration (1881–1914). From as early as I could remember, my grandmother would tell me stories about her life as in Europe, and her experiences as a young girl in America. She was a walking history book. From her I learned about the Triangle Shirtwaist Factory fire of March 1911 that occurred seven weeks after she arrived in New York, the largest industrial disaster in the city's history, in which 146 garment workers, mostly young immigrants, died from the fire or jumped to their death. The fire was the impetus for the creation of the American Society of Safety Engineers, the oldest and largest professional safety organization in the United States.

Then, there was the sinking of the Titanic in 1912, or the funeral of the famous Jewish author, Sholem Aleichem, in 1916, one of the largest funerals in New York City history, where she joined the estimated 100,000 mourners lining the streets, including my grandfather, who she would only meet twelve years later. At a time when Harlem was an Afro-American or Hispanic neighborhood, she spoke to me nostalgically about the days when Harlem had been Jewish, her first real home, two weeks after getting off the boat from Europe.

In many respects, her story was representative of an entire generation of young women who came to America during those years. Like so many of them, she eventually worked in a sweatshop, which she always referred to as "the factory". Not having a bathtub at her disposal, once a week she availed herself of the New York Public Baths, usually late on a Friday afternoon. During the 1920s, she and her cousins, also immigrants, imitated the "flappers" by wearing shorter skirts than the older generation, and bobbing their hair. Few, however dared to emulate those bold women in more than fashion.

During the years that followed, she, like so many young immigrants at that time, became exceedingly patriotic, viewing America as her true homeland. One of the proudest moments of her life was the day she received her Certificate of Naturalization, officially marking her status as an American citizen. Like so many of those immigrants who perceived America as the country that saved them from poverty, persecution or worse, her love of the United States was a lifelong affair that never underwent any disillusion. Her story was not only that of a generation of immigrant women, but it was also the story of America of that generation, the period to which American immigration historian Oscar Handlin referred when he wrote:

"Once I thought to write a history of the immigrants in America. Then I discovered that the immigrants *were* American history".[2]

In certain ways, however, her story was unique. Her initial reasons for immigrating were somewhat different than the norm, as were a number of personal choices that she made during her formative years in America. She married at what was then considered to be a rather advanced age for a woman from a traditional background. And in view of that background, her choice of spouse was also somewhat extraordinary, as were the circumstances leading to her sudden marriage. While she may have stretched the limits of propriety in her youth, she never once crossed over into territory that would have marked her as an overt rebel. My grandmother was the embodiment of a generation of young women immigrants who lived in a different world than their parents, not just figuratively, but in many cases, such as hers, also literally. Her story is certainly hers, but in some ways, it is also theirs, a micro-history that allows us a glimpse into the lives and inner worlds of an entire generation.

The Challenges of Micro History and Grandmothers

What can we learn from the story of a particular person or a family that can shed light upon the history of an entire generation? While preparing some of the articles upon which this book was based, I discussed that concept with a number of cousins, one of whom succinctly summed it up by stating: "There is really nothing illustrious about our family; they were little people in the large scheme of things, and this kind of micro-history shows the importance of even those who did not do earth-shattering things. They represent a large swath of humankind. And they certainly made a difference in the lives of their families and in the lives of future generations."[3]

Even while conceptualizing the idea of this book, I grappled with the issue of how to best write a micro-history. For an experienced historian, writing a micro-history is a fascinating challenge, requiring one to walk a fine line

---

2   Oscar Handlin, *The Uprooted: The Epic Story of the Great Migrations that Made the American People,* Boston: Little Brown and Co., 1951: xii.

3   Author's correspondence with Dr. Dora Polachek, December 23, 2015.

between the individual tale being told and the broader narrative of a society at large. Throughout the process of creating this book I tried to remain aware of the various methodological pitfalls of dealing with micro-history of this sort, particularly the fear of trivialization which turns a historical enquiry into a series of anecdotes without a broader conceptual basis. Carlo Ginzburg, one of the world's foremost micro-historians, reminds us that to write a successful micro-history, one should constantly switch back and forth between macro and micro components, first presenting the "text" within the "context" and then switching to the influence of the "context" upon the "text".[4] I have tried to do so by going back and forth between examining Freida Sima's life as part of a broader story of mass Jewish immigration from Europe to the United States at the beginning of the 20th century, and then examining how what was going on in the broader story affected the individual, in other words, Freida Sima.

A second methodological issue concerns micro-history being a form of cultural history. A historian of cultural history deals with a number of historical discourses that require different tools and methodologies: intellectual history and its discourse, popular history and its discourse, daily life of various subgroups and the like.[5] Although this is a study of cultural history, I have also drawn heavily on studies of economics, education, linguistics, geography, social welfare, psychology and other fields, in order to better understand the world of the immigrants, their issues of identity, culture, belief and praxis.

As I began to make headway through the literature about women immigrants to the United States during the Great Wave of Immigration, I was fascinated to see how many of the authors began their books or articles with descriptions of their immigrant grandmothers. Elizabeth Ewen opens her study of Italian and Jewish women in the Lower East Side with a description of her Italian grandmother who had been a milliner when she came to America.[6] Sydney Stahl Weinberg's opening paragraph of her study of the *World of Our Mothers*, evokes the memory of her "slight, wrinkled

---

4   Carlo Ginzburg, "Microhistory: Two or Three Things That I Know About It", *Critical Inquiry* 20:1 (1993): 10–35. Ginzburg writes about employing a technique that is common in the film industry, Sigfried Kracauer, *From Hitler to Caligari: A Psychological History of the German Film*, Princeton: Princeton UP, 1971.

5   Raymond Williams, *The Sociology of Culture*, Chicago: University of Chicago Press, 1999; Roger Chartier, *Cultural History: Between Practices and Representations*, Ithaca: Cornell UP, 1988.

6   Elizabeth Ewen, *Immigrant Women in the Land of Dollars: Life and Culture on the Lower East Side 1890–1925*, New York: Monthly Review Press, 1985: 11–13.

bubbe's" immigrant sense of Jewishness.[7] It seems, therefore, that my choice to examine the history of an entire generation of Jewish immigrants in America through my grandmother's story, is not unique.

The English historian, diplomat and journalist Edward Hallett Carr, reminds us that the history of a generation can often best be perceived through the story of the individual.[8] The danger of doing so, he continues, is only if the individual in question is chosen by a power group wishing to use his or her story to promote their own beliefs or values. When that is the case, the result is often a two-dimensional figure lacking depth and complexity. I have tried to avoid this pitfall by portraying my grandmother and her contemporaries as they were, human beings who did not always fit the mold of the "typical immigrant" of the time, if there even was such a mold. By doing so, I hope to have made a small step in returning a bit of the complexity and depth to the story of the immigrant generation.

Identity and Immigration

The focus of our story is the history of an entire generation of Jewish immigrants to America, as seen through the experiences of one immigrant, my grandmother Freida Sima. At the same time it is also the story of immigration and identity, or more precisely, the dynamics by which immigration and acculturation during adolescence affected her emerging identity. Erik H. Erikson (1902–1994) was among the foremost theoreticians who studied the formation of human identity, claiming that a person's identity is formed during the fifth out of eight stages that one undergoes during one's life. Erikson calls this stage "identity versus identity confusion" and places it in adolescence, when a teenager forms a sense of personal identity and feels singularity while still trying to adjust to the conditions of surrounding society.[9]

The process of identity formation is central to Freida Sima's story, in view of the fact that she immigrated to America at fifteen, encountering a

---

7   Sydney Stahl Weinberg, *The World of Our Mothers: The Lives of Jewish Immigrant Women,* Chapel Hill and London: The University of North Carolina Press, 1988: xiii.

8   E.H. Carr, *What is History?* Cambridge: Cambridge UP, 1961, 31–32.

9   Erik H. Erikson, *Childhood and Society,* New York: W.W. Norton and Company, 1993.

new country, a new family, and a new culture. According to Erikson, identity is formed during adolescence not only by identifying with a group and accepting its norms, but also by the adolescent's experimenting with different roles during this difficult transition between childhood and adulthood. Unlike today, when adolescents are given a period of moratorium during which they do not yet have to function as adults, this was not yet the case at the time that Freida Sima immigrated to America.[10] The moment she left her parents' home she became an adult, with adult responsibilities and challenges. How did this affect her burgeoning identity? That is one of the major themes of our story as we will see in the following chapters.

Under normal conditions adolescents shape their identity through four basic issues: forming a professional identity, delineating their relationship with parents and family, creating a sense of social belonging, and determining their relationship with members of the opposite sex. Erikson claims that the best way to deal successfully with these issues is for an adolescent to create a continuum with his or her past to help them answer the question "Who am I?" This is difficult enough for an adolescent in a familiar environment and within the confines of family, but how does one do this as an immigrant adolescent whose parents are thousands of miles away? This, too, is a dilemma that I will examine throughout our story.

What composes an immigrant adolescent's identity? Leon and Rivka Grinberg, psychoanalysts who have deal in depth with this phenomenon, claim that a person's identity is formed by three interacting factors: spatial integration, temporal integration and social integration. Spatial integration is what gives a person their sense of being "different" than others. Temporal integration, connected to the changes taking place within the adolescent's identity, gives them the sense of "self" and of being "similar" to others. Social integration includes the relationships formed through identification, and assists in creating the feeling of "belonging".[11]

These processes are even more complex when dealing with adolescent immigrants. Their spatial integration can be confused by a meeting of cultures, causing internal dissonance during which an immigrant adolescent has difficult in merging the different parts of their identity. While these cultural tensions may ostensibly resolve, they often continue to exist out of sight, only surfacing later, such as during a crisis. I will examine this issue by probing

---

10   Erik H. Erikson, *Identity, Youth and Crisis,* New York: W. W. Norton and Company, 1994.

11   Leon and Rebeca Grinberg, *Psychoanalytic Perspectives on Migration and Exile*, New Haven and London: Yale, 1989: 130–132.

various watershed events and crises during Freida Sima's life, seeing what affect, if any, they had on her changing identity.

Interference in an adolescent immigrants' temporal integration creates confusion about place and language, and many solve this problem by integrating languages, articles or significant values from their past lives into their present ones. By doing so they create a sense of continuity that helps them consolidate their old-new identity. But what happens when a new society encourages or even requires an immigrant to adopt a different name, language, culture, form of dress or values in order to integrate successfully? I will examine this issue by exploring Freida Sima's transition from an Eastern European to an American-Jewish culture, albeit with Eastern European overtones, but one that is nevertheless different than her original culture in many respects.

Interference in one's social integration, which is the most difficult type of impediment to identity formation, is caused by role change or role reversal when an immigrant loses their defined place in society after immigration. This instability can only be solved by building new roles enabling one's cultural and practical integration into a new society. Throughout this book I will probe Freida Sima's social integration into her new culture, and the means by which she created new roles for herself both within the family and in the professional world.

Gender and identity are always interrelated in one form or another. Sociologist Nancy Chodorov has shown us the connection between motherhood and gendered identity, and how the initial base of constructing one's identity is a connection to and imitation of a mother figure.[12] While boys transfer their identity to a male figure during adolescence, girls can continue to construct their identity based on a connection to their mothers. What, however, happens to an adolescent female who constructs her identity far away from her mother, in a different country and a different culture? This is another factor that I explore while examining the process by which Freida Sima constructed her teenage identity.

A final component of identity is "ethnic identity", which is closely connected to cultural identity. Most forms of identity are created through a power struggle and do not delineate a homogenous entity.[13] That struggle

12   Nancy Chodorow, *The Reproduction of Mothering: Psychoanalysis and the Sociology of Gender*, Berkeley, 1978.
13   Stuart Hall, "Who Needs Identity?", in: Stuart Hall and Paul du Gay, eds., *Questions of Cultural Identity*, London: Sage Publications, 1996: 1–17; Floya Anthias, "New

can be almost imperceptible when one's culture of origin is similar to the new culture in which they are living. In Freida Sima's case, the culture in which she found herself as an older adolescent was somewhat different than her culture of origin. Part of understanding her story, therefore, requires mapping out her changing cultural identity as she made the transition from the Eastern European cultural world of the Bukovina to the American Jewish cultural world of the first decades of the 20th century.

The starting point of our journey is therefore an attempt to understand the process of building a new identity among an entire generation of Jewish immigrants from Eastern Europe who came to America during the end of the 19th and beginning of the 20th century. This includes building a new identity and a sense of "self" among immigrant adolescents, constructing a gendered identity among female immigrant adolescents, and finally, the struggle to create a cultural and ethnic identity among immigrant minorities who are similar, but not identical, to the majority in their adopted country.

Sources and Methodology

The stories that my grandmother told me throughout the years are the basis of this book, augmented by a plethora of additional sources. These include written and oral family memoirs and recollections, Holocaust testimonies from the USC Shoa Foundation – Institute for Visual History and Education,[14] documents from various archival collections, Benevolent Society archives, cemetery archives, online historical databases such as the Statue of Liberty – Ellis Island Foundation passenger search,[15] and my grandparents' personal documents which came into my possession after my mother's death in 2014.

The passenger search on the Ellis Island Foundation website is a veritable treasure trove of information if one knows how to use it correctly, and is capable of cross- referencing the material it provides. There are, of course deviations and diversities in the spelling of names which often makes it

Hybridities, Old Concepts: The Limits of 'Culture'", *Ethnic and Racial Studies* 24:4 (2001): 619–641.

14   <https://sfi.usc.edu/vha/about> (retrieved Dec. 1, 2015).

15   <http://www.libertyellisfoundation.org/passenger> (retrieved Dec. 1, 2015).

difficult to find specific people, and one must bear in mind that the website material was copied, at times incorrectly, from passenger manifests of the various vessels bringing immigrants to America. But all in all if used correctly it can provide information that is often unavailable elsewhere.

The material listed on the website is based on information that the passenger gave the shipping company when leaving their port of origin. The amount of information was usually a factor of when the immigrant came to the United States. During the end of the 19th and beginning of the 20th century the passenger record usually included the passenger's original name, age, gender, marital status, ethnicity, date of arrival, ship of arrival and port of departure. If one goes into the ship's manifest, however, there is often additional information listed that can give us a fascinating look into the lives of the immigrants. This includes not only physical characteristics and distinguishing marks, but also their citizenship, calling or occupation, how much money they had upon arrival, whether they were literate and if so, in what languages, by whom was their passage paid, whether they were going to a relative or friend and if so, their full name and address, their last address in their country of origin, the name and complete address of closest friend or relative in the country from which they came, and their final destination.

It was through the ship's manifest listings of various relatives who came to America during the early 20th century that I began to truly understand the dynamics of immigration of that time. Almost all of these relatives had travelled to America with what looked at first glance as half of my grandmother's hometown, Mihowa!

Going up and down the manifest's pages I noted various Jewish Mihowians travelling together on each ship, sometimes as many as fifteen at a time! When checking who had paid the passage of all these Jewish Mihowians, and to whom they were traveling, it appears that many of them were either close friends or, if one takes into account their last name, then even related. I then looked up when the people they were traveling to immigrated to America, and lo and behold, they led me to other family members of whom I had never heard, also from Mihowa. Interestingly enough, despite her young age, my grandmother was one of the few family members who travelled alone, possibly because she did not emigrate directly from Mihowa, but rather from Eastern Galician where they family was then living.

By diligently sitting for hours with the information from various ships manifests, I managed to put together a mosaic of when various near and distant family members and their friends (who often later became family members by marrying into the Schaf-Eisenberg clan), immigrated to America. I also discovered who their close relatives were in Europe, or to whom they were traveling in America, and saw that some of them later married each other and married into the family. Often the material was not available by doing a regular "passenger search" as the website instructs, but only by painstakingly going through page after page of ships manifests, looking for familiar names which were sometimes written or copied incorrectly into the data base.

Depending on the penmanship of the clerk writing up the ship's manifest and the paleographic abilities of the website's transcriber, "Scharf" appeard as "Schirf", "Sciarf" and "Scarf". "Leib" was turned into "Leile" and "Mihowa" into "Milawa", "Malawa" and "Myhev". At times, the only way to identify who travellers really were was to examine who their closest relatives were in Europe or their original European address. All in all, it was a fascinating source through which I was able to reconstruct the immigration history of many Mihowians at the end of the 19th and beginning of the 20th century, including my own family.

Other sources were painful in their absence. What could have been an important documentary corpus – the numerous letters that my grandmother wrote to her family in Europe over an almost thirty-year period from her arrival in America in early 1911 until the outbreak of the Second World War – were destroyed in the Holocaust. In her conversations with me over the years, she occasionally mentioned specific incidents that she had written about to her parents, which only whet my sense of historical and personal loss even more. The only other reference to these letters came through a secondhand source, my mother, who had heard about them from my grandmother's youngest sister.

As for the letters that my grandmother received from her parents, brothers and sisters in Europe, for whatever reason, she kept only two that her father had written during the 1930s, and which I later found among her personal documents. "Why didn't you keep any more of them, Baba?" I wanted to ask her, "and why specifically these two?" But there is no longer anyone to ask. Maybe that is why I kept every letter, note or scrap of paper that my own mother wrote me from my teenage years onward, subconsciously aware of the fact that one day, they might become the last tangible evidence that I once had a mother, and the props of my memories. Or, as a cousin to whom I mentioned this, remarked to me, the basis of my next book.

An unexpected source of information about my grandmother's life, giving me a new perspective, was my parents' correspondence, which also came into my possession after my mother's death. There I found letters and cards that my father had written to my grandparents on various occasions, notes from my grandmother written when she visited California with my grandfather during the 1950s and 60s, my mother's correspondence with my grandmother's cousins about their mothers, and documents pertaining to my grandmother's latter years.

To enhance the readers' understanding of the lives of that generation of young Jewish women immigrants, I have added historical descriptions about the various places where my grandmother lived, and analyses of some of the major incidents which she experienced or recalled. As the book is written primarily from her perspective, in many of the chapters she is both participant and narrator, other than those sections dealing with events in which she was not present, such as those occurring before her birth, or her European family's ordeals during the Second World War. An exception is the chapter dealing with her mother's trip to America during the early 1930s, during which she was present. Nevertheless, a portion of that chapter is written from her mother's perspective, taken from stories that my great-grandmother told her children in Europe when she returned in 1933 and which they, in turn, told me years later.

Trying to reconstruct a person's life is a complex task, particularly when relying heavily on oral history, and even more so, when one is a family member of the person in question.[16] As I collected material about my grandmother's life, I was constantly reminded of the delicate nature of oral documentation, experiencing firsthand the "Rashomon" phenomenon of everyone viewing an incident from his or her perspective.[17] Events described by their participants years after they occurred, could become blurred or embellished, details forgotten or changed, with interpretation replacing narration. Episodes described by third parties who were not participants but

---

16   Regarding the need for caution with oral documentation see: John Miles Foley, *The Theory of Oral Composition: History and Methodology*, Bloomington: University of Indiana Press, 1988; David Henige, *Oral Historiography*, London: Longman, 1982; Valery Raleigh Yow, *Recording Oral History: A Practical Guide for Social Scientists*, Thousand Oaks, CA: Sage, 1994.

17   Rashomon was the Japanese period film from 1950, directed by Akira Kurosawa, involving various characters who provide alternative, self-serving and contradictory versions of the same incident.

bystanders, or who had heard about them from their parents, decades later, were an additional challenge. There I was dealing with not one, but two filters through which an episode had passed before reaching me, and determining its veracity became an even more complex undertaking.

It was at those times that I blessed my extended family, my wonderful cousins who were able and willing to assist me in my reconstruction efforts. For months I bombarded them with phone calls and emails about this or that incident, spending hours, and sometimes days, trying to cross-reference everything, from basic chronology to minute details of stories I had been told. Not only did I certainly try their patience, but I challenged their own memories of both my grandmother and their own parents and grandparents, causing them to reconstruct their own past. Without exception, they accepted my prodding with good grace; over and over they made special efforts to help me in my quest for information, even at the cost of their own nerves.

Sometimes it took weeks to get a simple story straight, such as my grandfather's siblings' birth order, a question my mother could have answered in sixty seconds, had I thought of asking her two years earlier when she was still alive. Reconstructing the chronology of my grandmother's first trip to Israel during the 1950s was an operation stretching across two continents, involving cousins on all sides of my family. If only I had listened closer to my grandmother's stories about that trip! If only she had dated her pictures from that trip on the back, or written a word or two about where they were taken!

At moments like that I was sharply reminded of how timing is everything in life, and that one should ask questions while one still has whom to ask. I blessed my mother for noting names and dates on the back of most of her own pictures, so that one day her descendants would be able to identify the people, place or event in question. How lucky I was that my extended family never got tired of my endless questions about pictures, persons or events! Or if they did, they were kind enough never to show it to me.

When I began writing this book, I also hadn't envisaged the geographical challenges that it would raise. One example was finding the final resting places of various family members who were not buried in the Scharf-Eisenberg Family Circle Plot at Wellwood Cemetery in Farmingdale, Long Island. Historians are well aware that tombstones are not only monuments to the dead, but texts to be read and interpreted that can provide a wealth of information about their lives and even the perceptions of their family members who designed the inscriptions. In various cases, even the location of a grave is the key to the history of the person lying under the tombstone. In some cases locating a family grave turned into an enterprise that involved synchronized efforts of friends, relatives, burial society employees and cemetery supervisors spanning different cities, States, and even continents. In each case everyone was extremely helpful, and went far beyond the call of duty to assist me.

Another challenge was navigating the waters of what I called being a "Compassionate Historian" as opposed to being one who keeps to the "letter of the law". How much should one write about unpleasant family incidents? How deep should one dwell on the less complimentary traits of respected and beloved family members who are no longer alive? What happens when different family members have different a different and even diametrically opposed perspective on their ancestor's actions? What if some object to having a particular story told, as it paints an ancestor in an uncomplimentary light, even if this was the story which I had heard directly from my grandmother and which she insisted was true?

Grappling with these dilemmas, I discussed them with a number of colleagues, and also with a few family members. My cousin David Eisenberg, in particular, succinctly and thoughtfully summed up the matter: "Few, if any, would be comfortable with the less than pleasant things about them and their families being revealed…the book conceived as a beautiful memorial could then become anathema, and you would be remembered by posterity as its author; exactly the opposite of what you're trying to do. It's not worth the risk. There's so much you can write about real people without making anyone a plaster saint."[18]

Taking David's words to heart, I continuously walked the tightrope of that fine line of interpretation between telling the truth, the whole truth, and nothing but the truth. Although this book is written primarily from my grandmother's perspective, I always remained aware that her parents and grandparents had other living descendants, and gave great weight to their opinions about what to include and what to omit, what to stress and what to blur. My primary goal was to remain true to my grandmother's stories, but at the same time I attempted to examine her narrative with a critical eye, in order to understand not only the text but the context, both what she said, and why she said it.

---

18   Correspondence with Dr. David Eisenberg, Nov. 15, 2015.

I hope that I have succeeded in presenting things pretty much as they were. As I often told my cousins, this project was a family effort and they deserve credit for any if its success; all mistakes, however are mine alone. I hope that I will be judged favorably for my role in this endeavor. If one day it is included in my final judgment, I hope that my ancestors will speak up on my behalf, as even during the worst arguments among the Scharf-Eisenberg clan, they would lay down their lives for each other when necessary, as we will soon see.

And Finally, Acknowledgement and Thanks

Throughout this project I received love and support from all sides. From my Zeide Max's family, I thank Michelle Atias, Mona Luchans, and Sylvia Weintraub for the special help they gave me as we reconstructed the basics of the Kraus family. On my Baba Freida Sima's side, the revived Scharf-Eisenberg Family Circle, which functions until today, was an incredible source of love, support, and information. Once having dwindled to barely a burial society, almost eighty years after it was first conceived, its new president Norman Eisenberg revitalized the Family Circle, opened a family tree on the genealogical site "Geni" which today lists over a thousand interrelated persons connected to the Scharf-Eisenberg clan, and began a Scharf-Eisenberg Family facebook page. Yigal Arens took on the job of creating and administrating a Scharf-Eisenberg internet discussion group which allows the family to communicate as a group, sharing past memories and current experiences and events. As a result of these steps, the Scharf-Eisenberg Family Circle is now a thriving group of relatives, some closely and some more distantly related, who remain in contact through Family Circle parties, online groups and social media.

One of the wonderful traits of our family is that when someone marries into the family, they, too, become family. And so it has been in our generation. The wives and husbands of our cousins have in so many cases become as close, if not more, than those relatives related by blood. They have all become the mainstay of the Family Circle which has recently been joined by members of the third and even fourth generation of Scharf and Eisenberg descendants, hopefully ensuring its continuation.

I would like to thank the Fanya Gottesfeld Heller Center for the Study of Women in Judaism at Bar-Ilan University for supporting this project, and to particularly thank Fanya Gottesfeld Heller for being a personal example to Jewish women everywhere. Special thanks to Adrian Stähli of Peter Lang Publishers for his support and expert assistance in the preparation and publication of this book and to Marina Essig overseeing the typesetting of this book.

So many people assisted me as I researched and wrote this book, that it would be impossible to mention them all, but I would nevertheless like to mention a number of people who were central in making this book what it is. Years ago, Prof. Jonathan Sarna, a good friend and colleague, who is one of the foremost experts today on American Jewish history, planted the idea in my mind to write about my grandmother's *Techina*, which eventually germinated into one of the seeds of this book. Another longtime dear friend and colleague, Prof. William B. Helmreich, unstintingly helped me with leads about the history and demography of New York City far beyond what he included in his fascinating book *The New York Nobody Knows*.[19] My former student and research assistant, Aliza Haiman, now Director of the Archives of Religious Zionism at Bar-Ilan University, encouraged me with her enthusiasm from the onset of this project. What began as her looking for a map of the Bukovina for me, ended up putting me in touch with an entire new branch of cousins from the Enzenberg side of the family. Jason Maoz, the dedicated and innovative editor of *The Jewish Press*, gave me a chance to publish the Freida Sima series over the period of a year in *The Jewish Press*, describing various episodes in my grandmother's life, which later became the basis for this book. His willingness to help had no bounds, not only regarding the series of articles, but also as I grappled with phrasings in the book. Thank you Jason for giving me the continuous encouragement I needed to finish a wonderful, but at times exhausting project.

I am also especially grateful to two people who helped me with the technical side of finding information about family members. John Nolan, Vice President of Wellwood Cemetery and Beth Moses Cemetery, went beyond the call of duty again and again, providing me with important information, documents and photographs of the Scharf-Eisenberg Family Plot, and helping me check out leads about where various family members, not found in the Family Plot at Wellwood, were actually buried. Roy Singh

---

19   William B. Helmreich, *The New York Nobody Knows: Walking 6,000 Miles in the City,* Princeton: Princeton University Press, 2013.

of Riverside Cemetery provided me with information about and photographs of Israel Nachman Handel's grave at Riverside Cemetery in Saddle Brook, New Jersey.

I would like to especially thank those Family Circle members who stepped out of their comfort zone again and again on two continents, separated by ten time zones, in order to assist me with support and information. Muriel Arens, Moshe Arens, Yigal Arens, Shelly Burlon, Baila Cohen, Daniel Eisenberg, David Eisenberg, Max Eisenberg, Moshe Eisenberg, Norman Eisenberg, Gail Eisenberg, Nute Eisenberg, Steven Eisenberg, Thomas Enzenberg, Bernice Finkelstein, Bob Friedman, Gary M. Gorran, Bernard Handel, Dora Hildenbrand, Techiya Hildenbrand, Phil Hirsch, Carol Scharf Hoffer, Nancy Gorran Horowitz, Avraham Iwanir, Irving Levine, Marta Lowy, Dora Polachek, Moshe Rosenberg, Uri Rosenheck, Moishe Rosman, Stephanie Rosman, Sheila Saltzman, Jeffrey Sanders, Goldie Storch, and Marina Lowy Vebman. My special thanks go to cousin Jonathan Gottfried, vice president of the Scharf-Eisenberg Family Circle, who photographed each tombstone in the Scharf-Eisenberg Family plot at Wellwood Cemetery and sent me the pictures, so that I could use the information in the book. During the months I wrote the book, I referred to the pictures constantly, as they provided me with important information about our family that would have been difficult, if not impossible, to find elsewhere. In the twenty-first century, Freida Sima's dreams of reuniting her family that I write about in this book, have taken a different turn, but that same family feeling of love among the cousins, is still there. Thank you, my cousins, for being there for me!

During the days and nights when I wrote the series of articles appearing in *The Jewish Press* upon which this book is based, and later, as I wrote the book, I often felt enveloped by my extended family; those who are here and mentioned above, and those who are no longer with us, and who I was describing. By doing so, I sensed that I was making them come alive once again, even for a short while. Some, such as my grandmother's brothers and youngest sister, or some of my mother's first cousins, I had known well. Others, such as my great grandparents, Nachman and Devorah, I had never met. But having heard so much about them since my childhood and growing up with their pictures, I had little difficulty imagining them as living, breathing people.

It was surprising to see how important pictures were in turning someone from a story character into a flesh and blood figure. Two examples were my grandmother's Baba Malka who raised her until she was five, and my grandmother's sister Marium who died in Transnistria during the war. I had heard many stories about both of them, but could never imagine their faces. To my delight, I discovered their pictures while researching this project, at which point they suddenly became vibrant and beautiful young women to me. This discovery spurred me to include as many pictures as possible in this book of the characters I mention. By doing so, I hope to help readers who had never known them, perceive them as real people, with particular facial features, hair styles, and fashion choices. As for those readers who had known and loved them, I hope that the pictures will revive the memory of their loved ones, granting them a bit more life, at least virtually.

The family that envelops me with love on a daily basis was, as usual, my main source of encouragement as I dedicated my days and nights to this project. My beloved husband, Joshua Jay Schwartz, gave me the original inspiration to write this book. More than once he reminded me how family is the most important thing in my world, and if so, why not write a book about my family? His children and their families – Laya, Alon, Eviatar, Uriah and Talia; Chaim, Ayelet, Halleli and Roni; Yoni and Keren, have shown me the blessing of being the third generation of blended families, following the tradition started by my Baba Freida Sima and her husband, my Zeide Max, and his four sons, Herbert, Stewart, Ben and Harry, and continued by my mother and father, Shirley and Chaskel Tydor, and his children, Manfred and Camilla.

My wonderful daughters, Beki and Rina never had the privilege of knowing their great-grandmother, as Beki was born nine weeks before my Baba's death and Rina was named after her. But they grew up knowing what she looked like, hearing countless stories about her, and becoming familiar with her aphorisms that were constantly used in our home. I hope that, at times, I succeeded in conveying her essence to them, even though it was diluted by three generations, just as I hope that after reading this book they will have a better sense of who their Baba Devorah and Baba Malka were, and can envision them as they had been, close to a century and a half ago: young, energetic, strong, and beautiful women, just as my daughters are today. It is to my precious daughters that I have dedicated this book, with love. It is my story, it is their story and above all, it is Freida Sima's story.

Chapter 2 The Education of Freida Sima – Mihowa-Eastern Galicia (1895–1911)

Introduction

What makes a ten-year-old girl from a Viznitzer Hassidic family decide that her life's dream is to get an education? What drives the oldest daughter of a large family, to face down her very traditional father, enabling both her and her sister to continue their schooling when he wanted them to stay home and help with the younger children? How did she manage, even before she was fifteen, to convince her parents to let her postpone marriage, leave home and travel close to 5,000 miles to a place where she hoped she could fulfill this dream? And finally, what happened when after her arrival she found out that all of her plans had to be revised as nothing was as she thought it would be?

The girl in question was my grandmother, Freida Sima, the oldest daughter of Devorah Scharf and Nachman Enzenberg, who was one of more than two million Jews leaving Eastern Europe for America during the "Great Wave of Immigration" (1881–1914). Each immigrant had their own story, their own reasons for immigrating, their own dreams of a new life. Most came for economic betterment, many as refugees from pogroms, some just wanting adventure. Freida Sima's reasons were not the usual ones one would have expected from a fifteen-year-old Hassidic girl who had been brought up in a rural Bukovinian enclave, but then again, her life, even before emigration, was somewhat different than that of her contemporaries.

This is the story of a Jewish farm girl who at seven could milk a cow faster than an experienced milkmaid, and at ten could outrace local boys bareback on her father's horse. It is also the story of a girl who adored the schoolroom and chose geography books over the *Tzena-U'Re'ena,* the Yiddish compendium of commentaries, parables and stories that most Eastern-European Jewish girls read at the time.[20] This is the story of a teenage girl

---

20   Chava Turniansky, "A Haskala Interpretation of the Cene-rene", *Hasifrut* 2 (1971): 835–841; Khone Shmeruk, "The East European Versions of the 'Tsene-Rene'"

who preferred education to marriage and was willing to leave everything dear to her, in order to achieve this burning desire. This is the story of how my grandmother, even before she was fifteen, decided to move to America.

Mihowa

Our story begins in Mihowa,[21] a small town in the Bukovina where my grandmother's family lived since in the early 1800s. For years, when asked to fill in her mother's country of birth on various forms, my mother was stumped. What should she write? When my grandmother was born, it was part of the Austro-Hungarian Empire, belonged to the Wiznitz district, and its name was written in the German form – Mihowa. Between the two World Wars it was part of Romania, belonged to the Strojinet district, and was written as "Mihova". After the Second World War it was annexed to the Soviet Union and called Migovoye, and since the dissolution of the Soviet Union it is part of the Ukraine, and its name is written Myhove. For purposes of consistency I have chosen to use the German spelling, used during my grandmother's formative years "at home" in Europe, and in the language that she learned in school.

Mihowa is part of the Bukovina, located on the northern slopes of the central Eastern Carpathian mountains and the adjoining plains. Historically part of Moldavia, from 1775 it became an administrative district of the Habsburg Monarchy, later, the Austrian Empire, and finally, Austro-Hungary. Taking its name from the abundant beech forests characterizing the area (the Slavic form of beech being *buk*), the Bukovina of Freida Sima's childhood was indeed a wonderous woodland with numerous waterfalls, rivers and streams. All of them, she would remind me, recalling the geography lessons of her youth, end up in the Danube and empty into the Black Sea.

(Yiddish). *For Max Weinreich on His Seventieth Birthday,* London, The Hague, Paris, 1964: 319–336. See also: *The Weekly Midrash Tz'ena Ur'enah: The Classic Anthology of Torah Lore and Midrashic Commentary,* translated by Miriam Stark Zakon. New York, 1994; *Sefer Tzena urena,* translated from the Yiddish into the Holy Tongue by Rabbi. S. A. Hershkovitz, Bnai Brak, 1974.

21   Also spelled Myhove (Ukranian), Migovoye (Russian), Mihova (Rumanian), Mihowo, Mikhova, Mikova, and Migovo.

Austria developed the Bukovina as a strategic link between Transylvania and Galicia, turning Czernowitz,[22] the "Black City" that took its name from the oak and dirt walls of the original fortress city, into the area's capital. In 1778 the city began to flourish when Knight Karl von Enzenberg was appointed the chief of the military administration, and invited merchants and craftsmen to develop trade in the area. Although the Ukranian natives of the area spoke a dialect colloquially known as Ruthenian, German eventually became the official local language for commerce and schooling. Like all the Jews in the area, Freida Sima spoke Yiddish to her family and Ruthenian (which she referred to as "Goyish") to the locals Gentiles, but her secular schooling took place in German, and she continued to count in that language for the rest of her life.

The origins of the family name appear to be connected to the aforementioned von Enzenberg. According to one version of the story, the tall strapping ancestors of my great-grandfather Nachman, went to work at his estate, adopting his surname as a natural step when the area's inhabitants were required to list themselves by more than a patronym. A second, less positive version that Freida Sima recounted, was that the local authorities forced the family to adopt the surname of the biggest anti-semitic landowner of the area, another Count von Enzenberg, possibly related to the Knight, a common tactic used to mock and denigrate Jews at that time.

Under the Austrians, the Bukovina was an ethnically diverse area with Rumanians in the south, Ukranians, known as Ruthenians, in the north, and Germans, Poles and Jews in the towns. In 1802 there were 3,286 Jews living in the Bukovina, and by 1846 their number had risen to 11,581 out of a total population of 371,131. After the 1848 revolution, economic and political discrimination against the Jews gradually declined, particularly after the Bukovina was officially separated from Galicia a year later. For the next twelve years the Bukovina underwent bureaucratic and administrative changes until 1861, when it was finally made permanently into an autonomous Duchy. As the Jews of the Bukovina had taken an active part in the struggle to make it autonomous from Galicia, they also reaped the benefits of that step, and with the success of that endeavor, the Jewish population of the area grew, outpacing the general population growth.[23]

---

22   Also known as Cernauti (Romanian), Cernivci (Serbian), Chernivtsi (Ukranian), Chernovtsi (Russian), Csernyivci (Hungarian).

23   Between 1850 and 1880, the general population of the Bukovina grew by 50% while the Jewish population quadrupled. This growth can be attributed to birth and hygiene, but

In 1867, the Jews of the Bukovina received full emancipation. By 1880 they were 11.79% of the total population (67,418) and by 1910 they had grown to 12.9% (102,919). The Jewish population of the area continued to expand and four years later, at the outbreak of the First World War, there were close to 120,000 Jews living in the Bukovina.[24]

Czernowitz, where a number of Freida Sima's brothers eventually resided, continued to be the province's administrative capital. It also became the center of national movements, including the first Yiddish Language Conference, coordinated by Nathan Birnbaum in 1908. A city of Jewish and non-Jewish cultural and educational institutions, Czernowitz was one of the five university centers of interwar Rumania, boasting a population of 112,400 in 1930, 37.9% of whom were Jews.[25] Czernowitz was also a major economic center of the Bukovina, and the Jews played a central role in this sphere as well. Since the emancipation, Jewish entrepreneurs were central to the area's economic development, and by 1906, almost half the provinces tax revenues in the Bukovina came from Jews.[26]

From the way Freida Sima described the Mihowa of her youth, one might have thought it to be a minor Czernowitz, a Jewish metropolis. In her eyes as a child, it was the center of her life, containing everything that her family needed. But in truth, it was a small farming community on the banks of the Mihowa river, a tributary of the Sereth, boasting a Jewish population of 336 in 1880.[27] Allowed to own land in the area since the emancipation in 1867, the Jews earned their living as farmers, in lumber transportation, as cattle dealers and merchants. Food was abundant and there were several houses of Jewish worship. Jews owned the industrial enterprises in Mihowa – two steam powered sawmills, two distilleries and a yeast factory.[28]

---

also to immigration from Russian, Rumania and Galicia, where the Jews faced greater discrimination and in some areas, much more overt persecution, than in the Bukovina.

24 Andrei Corbea-Hoisie, „Bucovina", The YIVO Encyclopedia of Jews in Eastern Europe, <http://www.yivoencyclopedia.org/article.aspx/Bucovina>, retrieved Dec. 4, 2015.

25 <http://czernowitz.blogspot.co.il/2014/05/census-of-romania-for-year-1930.html>, retrieved Dec. 2, 2015.

26 Andrei Corbea-Hoisie, „Bucovina", The YIVO Encyclopedia of Jews in Eastern Europe, <http://www.yivoencyclopedia.org/article.aspx/Bucovina>, retrieved Dec. 4, 2015.

27 <http://data.jewishgen.org/wconnect/wc.dll?jg~jgsys~community~-1046548>, retrieved Dec. 2, 2015.

28 Jakob Enzenberg, „Mihowa", in: Hugo Gold (ed.), *Geschichte der Juden in der Bukowina*, vol. II, Tel-Aviv: Olameinu, 1962.

Louis Handel, five years younger than Freida Sima, a distant cousin who would eventually be related to her a second time by marriage, described what a Mihowa farm was like at the turn of the century when he was born: "We lived on a farm – a very large farm – with cows, horses, sheep and chickens. We had everything growing on our farm or "Plantation", as they call it in the USA. We had melons, coffee trees, plums, apples, strawberries and mushrooms all over the valley."[29]

On the Mihowa scale, the Enzenberg family was considered "comfortable". They owned a farm where they grew their own crops. They raised milk-cows and horses, one of which can be seen in a family picture taken during the late 1920s. The only well in the area was on their land, and they had an arrangement with their non-Jewish neighbors who were permitted to use the well whenever they wanted and as much as they needed, except for the eight days of Passover when the well was off limits to non-Jews who might accidently drop crumbs of leaven near or into the water.

In addition, Freida Sima's father Nachman worked in the lumber industry, as had his father, Israel Enzenberg. Freida Sima spoke of Mihowa being populated during her childhood by fifty Jewish families, most of whom were related to each other in some way. Bearing in mind that a family could easily consist of eight to ten children, it appears that at the turn of the twentieth century there were approximately 500 Jews living in the town, but they bore only a few different last names!

The large size of the Enzenberg and Scharf families was part of a modern demographic transition that had evinced itself in Europe throughout the 19th century and that has been described as a "population explosion". Until the middle of the 18th century, extremely high death rates were quite frequent in Europe. During the latter part of that century, new concepts about the importance of hygiene, and the development of a better transportation infrastructure, were among the reasons that crisis mortality became less frequent. The smallpox vaccine led to the eradication of the disease, with the last European pandemic occurring in 1871. In addition, throughout the 19th century, child survival began to improve. Consequently, the average death rate decreased from thirty deaths per 1000 inhabitants at the beginning of the 19th century, to fifteen deaths per 1000 inhabitants by the beginning of the 20th century. And as the birth rate stayed at its previously high rate of

29   Louis Handel, "The Story of My Life", Correspondence Louis Handel to Lauren Gold, 1975, in the possession of Bernard Handel.

thirty to thirty-five births per 1000 inhabitants, the result was an overall and continuous growth in European population throughout the century.[30]

The Jews in Eastern Europe were no exception to this phenomenon. While the average Jewish family in late 18th century Eastern Europe appears to have consisted of a husband, wife, and two to three children, by the end of the 19th century the number of children had risen greatly, and it was common to find Jewish families with between six to ten children who reached adulthood.[31] Although my grandmother once told me that women in Mihova usually knew what herbs to take if they did not want to bear children, it is commonly accepted that traditional Jews of 19th century Eastern Europe did not practice birth control, and considered large families to be either a blessing or at least God's will. Only after coming to America did the immigrants from such families become westernized enough to put into effect what was euphemistically known as "family planning", with very few choosing to have families as large as those into which they had been born. Often, however, they continued the accepted Eastern European tradition of marrying "within the family", as can be seen within Freida Sima's own family.

The phenomenon of marrying relatives was not unique to Mihowa or to the Scharf and Enzenberg families, but a look at our family does show this to be a fairly common practice. My grandmother's grandparents, Avrum (Abraham) and Malka (Haller) Scharf, were cousins, and two of their ten children married Scharf cousins as well. Their firstborn child Devorah, my great-grandmother, did not marry a cousin, but between the two World Wars, two of Devorah's ten children also married Scharf cousins, who themselves were children of cousins. Nachman's brother, Meier Moses, married Gittel Haller, a cousin of Malka. Additional cousins married cousins on the Enzenberg side as well, and when such matches were offered and turned down, it caused bad blood in the family for years.[32] Looking back, it is amazing that all this inbreeding did not lead to any known serious physical or

---

30   Jay van Bavel, "The World Population Explosion: Causes, Backgrounds and Projections for the Future", in: *Facts, Views and Visions, Issues in Obstetrics, Gynaecology and Reproductive Health* 5:4 (2013): 281–291.

31   Andrejs Plakans and Joel M. Halpern, "An Historical Perspective on Eighteenth Century Jewish Family Households in Eastern Europe", in: Paul Ritterband (ed.), *Modern Jewish Fertility*, Leiden: Brill, 1981: 18–32.

32   Author's telephone interview with Abraham Iwanir, great-nephew of Nachman Enzenberg, Jan. 28, 2016.

mental infirmities. On the contrary, the Scharfs and Enzenbergs were known for their good looks and intelligence, which seemed to be passed down from generation to generation.

Nachman Enzenberg and Devorah Scharf may not have been cousins, and physically they looked totally different from each other, but it seems that they had more than one personality trait in common. In their younger days they were both willful, stubborn, and fun-loving, which is how my grandmother remembered her parents when she was a small child. One of her earliest memories was of her father coming home and picking up her mother, swinging her around the room and dancing first with her and then with his two little daughters. "The *Tateh* dancing the *Mameh* around the room? Impossible!" remarked my grandmother's youngest sister Sheindl in disbelief when she heard the story from her older sister decades later. But that was indeed the difference that the twenty-year expanse between old-est and youngest children in a large family could make, in their memories of the same parents. As a child, my grandmother remembered a twenty-five-year-old hotheaded and fun-loving father of two little girls, while her youngest sister, born twenty years later, only knew a late middle-aged father of ten. By then, his dancing days were obviously long over.

My Aunt Sheindl's disbelief in hearing this story from my grandmother epitomizes one of the difficulties in reconstructing history from the mem-ories of a large family, whose core-members ages spanned an entire gener-ation, or who scattered geographically. Every child has their own memories of their parents, siblings or hometown. But what of a family whose older and younger children never actually met? Who had never lived with their parents or in their hometown at the same time? Where the older children were born in one country, and the younger ones in another, although they were all born in the same house and bed?

In such cases, memories of people and places are often based on their personal chronology and geography; in other words, when and where some-thing took place, and how old they were at the time. As in every family, each Enzenberg child had his or her own memories of "the *Mameh-Tateh*", or of Mihowa, but they could also be categorized by age groups or geographical divisions. My grandmother and her next sister in line remembered people, places and incidents from their youth that none of the others could have known; the three siblings who came to America right before or soon after the First World War, had different memories of Mihowa than those who re-mained in Europe throughout the Second World War; the youngest children who were the last ones left at home never knew their grandparents, and had different memories of their parents, and so on.

And yet, even with these groupings, my grandmother was unique among the siblings. She was the only one to intimately know her own grandmother, the Baba Malka, and her uncles and aunts as a child; the only one who lived alone in America for close to ten years, until joined by the next two brothers in line, after the First World War; the oldest daughter who was expected to help raise her siblings and later to support them from afar; the only child who met her youngest brother and sister for the first time when they were already in their late thirties and she was nearing sixty. Her family memories were therefore different than those of any of her brothers or sisters, even those of the sister born two years after her, from whom she parted when they were fifteen and thirteen and never saw again. As the oldest daughter, she was the closest in age to her very young mother, who was still an adolescent when she was born. She was less than three years younger than her youngest aunt, her mother's baby sister. No wonder that her memories and perspectives of family members and matters were often different than those of her siblings.

My grandmother was extremely close to her mother Devorah, who was barely eighteen when her daughter was born; She was equally close, if not more so, to her mother's mother, her Baba Malka. It was from the Baba Malka that she heard stories about Devorah's youth, how Devorah and Nachman were introduced, and what happened afterwards. Sixteen-year-old Devorah was a fiery redhead with a temperament that matched her coloring, two traits that attracted her twenty-year-old neighbor, Nachman Enzenberg. Tall, handsome Nachman's piercing gaze and strong will were similarly attractive to young Devorah. Although they were technically "introduced" by the local *shadchan,* the matchmaker, it was indeed a love match. "Just wait, he will tuck her in under his chin", said Malka to her husband Avrum when they once talked about the engaged couple, referring not only to Nachman's height, but to his well-known stubbornness that even outdid that of their oldest daughter.

Nachman's unusual height was indeed a matter of discussion among the medium-size Scharfs and Hallers before he married Devorah. What type of marriage bed would Avrum and Malka have to prepare for the young couple? How would their future son-in-law be able to comfortably enter their home without having to duck his head each time he passed through the doorway? In a farming community surrounded by woodland, which boasted two steam-powered sawmills, the solution was obvious. As a wedding present, Avrum commissioned a special bed to be prepared for Nachman, half a meter longer than usual. He also had a special extra-tall doorway cut into their front room, similar to the one Nachman had built in the home he was about to share with Devorah.

Everything was almost in place for the wedding; the young couple's home was ready, the trousseau had been sewn, and the wedding date set for the middle of Tevet 5655, early January 1895. Both families were Vizhnitzer Hassidim, adherents of Rabbi Yisroel Hager, and followed similar Hassidic customs regarding prayer, dress, food, and wedding preparations. All that was left was to prepare the wedding feast, gather the relatives and set up the *chuppah*, the marriage canopy.

Suddenly, tragedy struck. Avrum became ill and passed away just before the wedding, leaving a young widow of thirty-five and ten orphans, the oldest of whom was the seventeen-year-old bride to be, and the youngest, her baby sister, two-year-old Sheina Sarah. Malka and her children sat *shiva* together, and on the late afternoon of the seventh day, Devorah got up, washed, and went directly to her *chuppah,* as one does not postpone a wedding, even after a tragedy.

Neither Baba Devorah nor Baba Malka ever told my grandmother stories about that wedding, but one can imagine that it was rife with mixed emotions. Who escorted my great-grandmother to her *chuppah*, her marriage canopy? What was it like for her, suddenly an orphan of seventeen, to leave her newly widowed mother and become a wife? How did twenty-year-old Nachman feel, knowing that from that day on, he would be stepping into his late father-in-law's shoes as male head of the family? We will never know. The numerous stories that my grandmother told me about her parents' lives, never included a description of their wedding, but only its chronological proximity to her grandfather's death. The rest is left to imagination, speculation, and everything in between.

The only story that came down to us regarding their first days of marriage is the one already noted, of my great-grandmother's refusal to cut her long red hair which Nachman adored, and her decision to pin it up under her short dark marriage wig, worn by all the older, pious Jewish women of Mihowa. I emphasize "older" as there were already winds of change regarding this matter that were reaching Mihowa and influencing the younger women. Just as in Lithuania it was becoming less and less customary for Orthodox Jewish married women to cover their hair after marriage, so there had already been talk in Mihowa among some of the young brides, about abandoning their kerchiefs and marriage wigs.

Devorah still kept the old customs, but as we have already seen, she scandalized her relatives and neighbors by her decision to keep her own hair intact. Nachman had pleaded with her not to cut her long beautiful hair after marriage, and to keep it for his pleasure, and she loved him enough to risk censure from her mother, aunts and neighbors on this matter. Winds of change aside, bearing in mind both families' Hassidic background, and the fact that both their mothers strictly covered their own shaven heads, the young couple obviously loved each other with great passion to be willing to fly in the face of convention regarding this matter. Or, possibly, Devorah was just very attached to her own long, red hair.

Devorah and Nachman began their married lives under the pall of Avrum's death, but soon fell into a routine. Devorah was in charge of the domestic arrangements and helped Nachman on their farm, located only minutes away from her mother's home down the road, where she visited daily. Like many of the Jewish men in Mihowa, Nachman also had a second profession, that of lumberman-overseer. In his book on western culture, *Landscape and Memory*, historian Simon Schama has written how common this profession was among Jews living in various wooded areas of Eastern Europe.[33] My Zeide Nachman was indeed a farmer, and quite attached to his land, but he was also one of many Jewish men who received contracts to chop down large tracts of local forests throughout Eastern Europe. There, the immense tree trunks would be floated for long distances down the local rivers, in order to reach the cities and become building planks, furniture and the like. Jews were rarely the lumberjacks. Instead they oversaw the work which was either carried out by locals or non-Jewish crews who traveled with the lumberman-overseer to the various forests, and worked under their supervision.

During his first months of marriage Nachman tried to stay close to home, all the more so when he found out that Devorah was expecting their first child in the autumn, barely nine months after their wedding. As the oldest of ten children Devorah was familiar with the basics of childcare, but realized that it would be different to have her own baby. Would it be a boy whom they would name after her father? Or a girl to be named after another family member, as "Avrum" was a purely male name with no female equivalent? As her mother, mother-in-law, and grandmothers on both sides were

---

33   Simon Schama, *Landscape and Memory,* New York: Alfred Knopf, 1995.

still alive, there was no one for whom it was urgent to name a baby. Under such circumstances, boys were often named after one of the late *Rebbes* or Sages, but with girls one had more leeway in terms of choice. What would they do if they had a girl?

As the holidays drew near, Devorah grew bigger, but was also filled with unusual strength and stamina. Women in Mihowa did not go to *shul* (synagogue) on a regular basis but only for the holidays, and especially the High Holidays. Devorah was not going to let a first pregnancy keep her from her prayers. That year, she went to hear the shofar blown on Rosh Hashanah, fasted without difficulty on Yom Kippur, and accompanied her younger brothers and sisters to *shul* on the night of Simchat Torah for what was the high point of the year for the Jewish children of Mihowa.

On Simchat Torah evening, after sundown, each child would be given a small flag, a hollowed out apple and a candle. The candle would be placed inside the apple which was then placed on the flagstaff and the *shamash* (beadle) would go from child to child with a lit candle, lighting fire from fire as was customary on a holiday, until the entire *shul* was ablaze with light. This was the one holiday in which no difference was made between boys and girls, and all the children would receive flags, apples and candles to dance with, symbolizing the light of the Torah. The children would march with their candles to the area directly in front of the *shul* where the men would be dancing with the Torah scrolls. There, the boys and very little girls would join the dancing, while the older girls would dance separately with the women towards the back.

Barely out of her own childhood, Devorah still considered Simchat To-rah as the high point of the year, and danced half that night with her young-er siblings holding apples and candles, taking advantage of the dispensation given to mourners on Sabbaths and Festivals that allowed them to sing and dance when it was part of a religious ceremony or *mitzvah*. Family lore states that Devorah went directly from *shul* to the labor bed, laboring all day Friday, and giving birth to her firstborn daughter late that Friday night. It was *Shab-bos Bereishis* (Genesis), the Shabbat of renewal, when the cycle of the Torah reading begins once again, and we read about creation of the world and of mankind. It was the day of my grandmother's birth, and the beginning of her story.

Freida Sima

In a world where one's legal identity is based on dates and numbers, it is hard to conceive of people living their entire lives without knowing their date of birth. That, however, was precisely my grandmother's situation. In spite of Mihowa being an administrative division of the Austro-Hungarian Empire, its residents were not required to register births, marriages, and deaths. Consequently, although she knew the Jewish significance of her birthday (*Shabbos Bereishis*, immediately following Simchas Torah), the day of her birth (Friday), and almost the very hour (late at night), no one ever bothered to note the actual date. Had she been a boy, the Hebrew date might have been more significant, as it would be used to calculate his thirteenth birthday, from which time on he would become *bar mitzvah*, be called to the Torah, counted for a *minyan* (religious quorum of ten men), and obligated to observe the commandments. True, at twelve, a girl was considered *bas mitzvah,* and obligated to keep commandments, but lacking any special public ceremony or performative action related to this birthday, her actual date of birth was not something worthy of note.

At first, the lacuna didn't bother her. Like many, if not most Jewish families in Eastern Europe at that time, her family never celebrated birthdays. After all, why give someone a *getoig,*[34] an "evil eye", and remind the spirits that they had survived another year? When my grandmother got older and had to fill out forms, such as for her *Arbeitsbuch,* her "work pamphlet" that she was issued in Europe at fourteen, she was never required to list a birthdate. The same held true when she immigrated to America, as Ellis Island officials only asked one's age, and not date of birth. It was only much later, when she had to fill out various American forms, that the matter of her date of birth became problematic. As a result, she invented a birthdate – October 21, 1894 – that had nothing to do with the real day, month, or even year she was born, and from that time on it appeared on all of her legal documents. The family, however, continued to celebrate her birthday on Shabbos Bereishis, regardless of the date on which it fell.

---

34   Different than the commonly used term *Ayin Horo* – literally, an "Evil Eye" (Hebrew), my grandmother would always use the term common in Mihowa, *getoig,* literally a "Good Eye" (German/Yiddish), following the Jewish custom of giving something negative the exact opposite meaning, in order to confuse the spirits. For the same reason, a cemetery is called *Beis HaHayim* – the House of Life.

Today, with internet tools at one's disposal, it is quite simple to calculate the precise date. My grandmother was born on Friday night, the 25th of Tishrei 5656, October 11, 1895, the only year between 1893 and 1902 when Simchat Torah fell on a Friday. The following morning, her father Nachman received an *aliyah* in *shul* to honor her birth, made the requisite blessings for the Torah, for the *kimpeturin*[35] (the term used for a woman after childbirth), and for the new baby, after which he named his daughter "Freida Sima". "Freida" meaning "joy", that would forever remind them of the Simchas Torah festivities heralding her birth; "Sima", in memory of a childless neighbor, possibly also relative, who has recently died, a special *mitzvah* towards the childless after their death, to ensure an *aliyah* (elevation) of the departed one's soul.

Already as a baby, one could see that Freida Sima's personality was like her name, cheerful and optimistic. It was this same optimism that would keep her going throughout her life, in order to fight for what she wanted. It was her never ending cheerfulness that allowed her to cope with and overcome the setbacks in her various plans. And it was her deep faith, learned at home in her youth, which enabled her to deal with what life had in store for her, most of which she never could have dreamed of as a girl in a small farming village called Mihowa.

A year after Freida Sima's birth, Devorah found herself pregnant once again. With a more difficult pregnancy than her first, an active young toddler in the house, and a husband who was often away on lumber business, she was beginning to find it harder to manage. She still visited her mother often, but now it wasn't so much that Devorah was helping her mother with her younger siblings, as Malka helping Devorah with Freida Sima. Besides, Malka was known for adoring small children, and most of her own younger ones were already in *cheder* (religious elementary school). There was also the psychological aspect. In spite of the two years that had passed since Avrum's death, Malka was still heavily feeling his loss. Playing with a small granddaughter a few times a week did wonders for her spirits.

When Devorah gave birth to a second girl, naming her Marium (the local pronunciation of Miriam) for a relative on Nachman's side, she also came up with an idea that could solve both the practical and psychological issues facing the family. Now that Freida Sima was completely weaned, why

---

35   The origin of the Yiddish term *kimperturin* is not clear, but appears to be based on the Hebrew term *patur* – exempt. It is used for a woman after childbirth who is exempt from many commandments during her convalescence.

not send her to live with her mother for a while? Devorah would be able to devote herself completely to her baby, Malka would have a new toddler to enjoy, and Freida Sima would have lots of older company to play with. Devorah would be able to visit daily, but go home with only one small baby, and not an active toddler who was even more exhausting in Nachman's absence. Besides, it was quite common in Eastern Europe to send children to live with young grandparents when new babies were born in the family, so no one would consider it strange.

My grandmother's first memories were therefore not of her parents' home, as the older sister of a new baby, but rather of her grandmothers' farm, and as the youngest of many children, her uncles and aunts. Her Baba Malka, then in her late thirties, was an excellent *balabusta* (housewife), patient, good looking and surprisingly independent. Having learned the importance of being able to cope on her own, she taught both her children and her grand-daughter, not only homesteading and farm skills (hence my grandmother's excellent milking ability) but also to speak their minds and follow their dreams.

This state of events lasted for close to three years, until Freida Sima was five. During her three years at the Scharf household, her closest friend and playmate was her eight-year-old aunt Sheine, who was like an older sister to her. Her other uncles and aunts, two girls and six boys, ranged in age from ten to twenty. Freida was treated as the pampered youngest child in a large family whose members doted on her, something that occasionally caused friction between her and Sheina who had been forced to relinquish the position of youngest child. In general, though, their relationship was warm and friendly, and she walked in Sheina's shadow, copying her in everything she said or did. In fact, family lore states that this copying was what got Freida Sima abruptly taken home, where overnight she turned from youngest to oldest.

In the interim, Devorah and Nachman had another baby, this time a boy whom they named for Zeide Avrum. Devorah found it harder to visit her mother daily with two small children, and must have taken a hiatus from regular visits while recovering from Avrum's birth. When she returned to her regular visiting routine, she noticed something disturbing. Just as her brothers and sisters called her by her first name, her daughter, copying them, was beginning to do the same thing. "No child of mine is going to call me *Devoraleh!*" she told Malka, at which moment the convenient arrangement of farming out her oldest daughter came to an abrupt end.

What was the genuine reason behind Devorah's decision to take Freida Sima home? Was it really a spontaneous decision made immediately after hearing her five-year-old call her by her first name? Did it have anything to do with Devorah's realizing that she needed an extra pair of hands to help with the younger children? We will never know. But as Freida Sima had neither her mother's red hair nor her father's fiery temperament, it appears that she cheerfully adapted to being the responsible oldest daughter instead of the pampered youngest child.

Although she missed her Baba Malka and her aunts and uncles, she soon understood that there was a great advantage to living at home: the opportunity to get to know her father better. Nachman, whose adoration for Devorah had once been the talk of the town, was equally enchanted by his firstborn, now the apple of his eye. With baby Avrum not yet old enough to help on the farm, as Freida Sima began to grow up, Nachman taught her to ride a pony and then a horse, both with a saddle and occasionally bareback, holding on to the pony's mane. Seeing that she had absolutely no fear of animals or heights, he taught her to rope cows and climb trees in order to bring him the finest apple from the topmost branch.

During the next year, at least when it came to the farm, he treated her as if she were not a daughter, but a son who would one day run the family farm. As soon as she was finished with the household chores, and milking the cows, she would follow him into the garden and then into the fields, learning how to plant, fertilize, plough and harvest. In Nachman's mind, however, what went on at the farm, stayed at the farm, and he was more conservative in his attitude towards his daughter's education. Reluctantly, he agreed to let Freida Sima attend *cheder* to learn the basics, as did many girls in Mihowa, although in Nachman's mind it would have been enough for Devorah to teach her what she needed to know.

This was the beginning of a clash between Freida Sima and her father which would change her life. From as far back as she could remember, Freida Sima wanted to learn new things. First to read and write, then to do sums and finally to study subjects like geography and history. She absorbed reading, writing, languages, numbers and Bible stories as a thirsty person gulps water. Luckily, the local Mihowa *cheder* followed Austro-Hungarian educational laws and taught secular studies along with Jewish ones. Reading, writing and arithmetic were taught in German while Jewish subjects were taught in Yiddish and *Loshon Kodesh*, the Holy Tongue. It also meant that for a fee, the local *melamed* allowed those girls whose parents sent them to *cheder*, to study along with the boys.

According to a survey of Jewish education in the Bukovina at the turn of the century, there were 8,866 Jewish children in the Bukovina studying in elementary schools at that time, in addition to another 4,531 who attended *cheder*. As there were approximately 80,000 Jews living in the Bukovina at the time, with a large population of children, it is obvious that there were still large numbers of girls who were not attending any type of official school. Freida Sima was therefore one of the lucky ones, staring *cheder* at five, two years after the traditional age of three when boys began their studies.[36] By the time she was seven, she was accompanied by Marium age five and Avrum, almost four. Having three children in *cheder* was no small financial burden for her father. Both farmer and lumberman, Nachman could provide his family with basic support from the farm, but knew that his real livelihood depended upon contracts to chop down local forests. By the time Freida Sima was ten and Marium eight, he also had three sons to educate, a fourth having died in an accident. He therefore decided that the girls had enough formal schooling and informed them that their *cheder* days were over.

Although he adored his wife and daughters, Nachman was not a staunch supporter of girls' education. His attitude at the time was not unique. American author and immigration rights activist Mary Antin wrote in her autobiography *The Promised Land*, about what Jewish girls' education often was at that time in Europe: "For a girl it was enough if she could read her prayers in Hebrew, and follow the meaning by the Yiddish translation at the bottom of the page. It did not take long to learn this much…a couple of terms with the *rebbetzin* (Rabbi's wife)…and after that she was done with books. A girl's real schoolroom was her mother's kitchen. There she learned to back and cook and manage, to knit, sew, and embroider…and while her hands were busy, her mother instructed her in the laws regulating a pious Jewish household and in the conduct proper for a Jewish wife."[37]

Nachman was particularly interested in having his daughters home as Devorah had a new baby every two years and needed help at home. True, there was the local non-Jewish girl who helped out around the house, but

---

36   A statistical analysis of Jewish education in the Bukovina in 1903 appears in: Dr. Herman Sternberg, "Geschichte des Schulwesens in der Bukowina" in: Hugo Gold (ed.), *Geschichte der Juden in der Bukowina,* vol. I, Tel-Aviv: Olameinu, 1958.

37   Mary Antin, *The Promised Land,* Boston: Houghton Mifflin, 1969: 34.

when Freida Sima was ten and Marium was eight, their father already expected them to stay home to help with the other children. Thus he could save on the *melamed's* fees for both girls.

Freida Sima's calm demeanor dissipated. She already heard that in the city there was a *gymnasium* where one could study after *cheder*, but for that one needed at least eight years of school. She knew they took boys, but there must be someplace in the Bukovina where girls could continue to study. How could she change Nachman's mind? How could she let her father's traditionalism and frugality thwart her dreams of getting an education?

"That wasn't going to happen", recalled my grandmother. "I was not going to give up *cheder* to stay home to rock a cradle, and I wouldn't let Marium do it either". Knowing her father's weakness for his daughters, his special love for her, and his enjoyment of a "negotiation", she combined all three for her benefit. Waiting until he came home and was sitting in his favorite chair, his young sons having vied with each other over who would get the honor of "taking off the Tateh's boots", she capitalized on his good mood, congratulated him on closing yet another lumber contract and offered him a deal.

At eight, Marium was still a schoolchild in everyone's eyes but Nachman's. If he removed her from *cheder*, people in Mihowa might gossip. Marium was, however, a reluctant student while Freida Sima thirsted for knowledge. She therefore proposed that she and Marium split child care and schooling, saving Nachman one set of *cheder* fees. One day she would go to school and Marium would stay home, and the next day they would switch off and Marium would take her place in *cheder*, while she would help with the babies and in the kitchen. Nachman could then save face by leaving Marium in *cheder* for another year or two, and Freida Sima could continue her education. How she got Nachman to agree is a mystery, but he acquiesced, reminding her that the arrangement could continue, only as long as her mother was satisfied with their help in child care and housework.

Freida Sima loved everything about *cheder* in Mihowa. She never had anything bad to say about her teachers, no stories about children being hit. In later years she only remembered the positive, unlike her brothers who told stories of old *melamdim* falling asleep while teaching, and their tying their shoelaces together to trip them when they awoke. Her favorite subjects were Bible, arithmetic and geography. While the boys studied Mishna and Talmud, the few girls were given Yiddish books about Biblical heroes to keep them busy. Numbers and counting she learned in German, and she could add up long sums in her head in German, a feat I remember her

doing even in her eighties. She was particularly fascinated by rivers, mem-
orizing the tributaries leading from the Mihowa River to the Danube, and
into the Black Sea which she recited to me sixty years later. A natural lin-
guist, she spoke Yiddish at home, picked up Ruthenian from neighborhood
children, and learned to read Hebrew for prayer and Bible studies.

Knowledge of several languages was not uncommon among Eastern
European Jewish immigrants coming to America during the Great Wave of
Immigration, although they were often only fluent in one language, while
having a rudimentary knowledge of others. Jewish men could usually pray in
Hebrew and often had an understanding of basic Biblical Hebrew vocabulary
from prayer and *cheder* study of Bible. Jewish men and women often understood a modicum of the local vernacular which they learned on a "need to
know" basis.[38]

Yiddish, however, was the most commonly spoken language among
Eastern European Jews, being a mixture of medieval German, Polish, Russian
and *Loshon Kodesh*, the "Holy Tongue", which was actually Talmudic Hebrew
with various proportions of Aramaic. Ultimately spoken in different forms by
Jews in many lands, at a later period this language acquired a quasi-sacred status, since it was the language that, for centuries, had kept European Ashkenazi
Jews separate from the general community.[39] And indeed it was Freida Sima's
mother tongue, the one she spoke at home, although she became fluent in
German during her school years.

The *Kresy*

Soon after Freida Sima reached *bas mitzvah* age, her idyllic educational life
was threatened. In 1908 her father's job of lumber-overseer uprooted the
entire family to Martnowy,[40] a small village located in the marshlands and

38   Bernard D. Weinryb, *The Jews of Poland: A Social and Economic History of the Jewish Com-
      munity in Poland from 1100 to 1800*, Philadelphia: JPA, 1972.

39   Miriam Isaacs, "Yiddish "Then and Now": Creativity in Contemporary Hasidic Yid-
      dish", in: Leonard Jay Greenspoon (ed.), *Yiddish Language and Culture Then and Now*,
      Omaha: Creighton UP, 1998: 165–188.

40   The name of the township, Martnowy, appears in Freida Sima's immigration papers,
      and from her descriptions was in Eastern Galicia, today the Ukraine. I have been

forests of East Galicia, known as the *Kresy*, so that he would not have to be apart from them for the duration of his five year contract. The *Kresy*, (Polish for "marsh"), which later became the eastern part of interwar Poland, boasted one major city, Lwow, a number of medium sized towns, and thousands of smaller hamlets of various kinds. Some 1.3 million Jews inhabited the *Kresy* in 1939, most of whom lived in small towns, townships and villages.[41]

This was the first time that Freida Sima came face to face with these small villages called *shtetlach* (sing: *shtetl*), where more than sixty percent of the *Kresy's* Jews, and a third of Eastern European Jewry lived. Used to a comfortable life in Mihowa where all the Jews she knew were literate, solvent, had owned land since the 1860s, and the only ones barefoot were children at play during the summer, Freida Sima was horrified by the poverty and illiteracy she saw among *Kresy* Jews, whom she termed "real country bumpkins".

Her description and evaluation of the early 20th century *shtetl* is borne out by the classical Yiddish literature of that time. Great Jewish writers such as Mendele Moicher Sforim (Shalom Y. Abramowicz), Sholem Aleichem (Shalom N. Rabinowicz), Yehuda Leib Peretz, Scholem Asch and others were harshly critical of the poverty and religious fanaticism that were rampant in many of these townships, noting the internal social conflicts, the corruption and anti-Semitism with which their inhabitants grappled. Daily life in the *shtetl* was a far cry from the romanticized and sanitized version presented to the public from the mid-1960s onwards, in the well-known musical and later screen film, *Fiddler on the Roof*, and in similar works and genre.[42]

Fiddler is based on a compilation of stories by Sholem Aleichem, many of the drama's major details had been changed to fit the nostalgic, post-Holocaust American attitude that tended to view Jewish life in pre-World War I Europe through a rose- tinted lens. In reality, the *shtetl*,

---

unable to locate it on any historical map. It is not connected to the town Martynovy, located in the Kirov district in a more northern area of Russia.

41   Ben-Cion Pinchuk, "The Eastern European Shtetl and Its Place in Jewish History," *Revue des Études Juives*, January-June 2005, 187–212; Ben-Cion Pinchuk, "How Jewish Was the Shtetl?", *Polin* 17 (2004), 109–119.

42   The musical *Fiddler on the Roof* was based on a complication of eight stories by Sholem Aleichem, entitled *Tevye der Michiker* (Tevye the Dairyman), originally written in Yiddish and first published in 1894. Prior to the 1964 Broadway adaptation of the series, other versions already had appeared on stage and screen, the first of which was an American silent film called *Broken Barriers*, released in 1919. Sholom Aleichem (Solomon N. Rabinovich), *Tevye the Dairyman and the Railroad Stories,* Library of Yiddish Classics, Hillel Halkin, tr., New York: Shocken, 1987.

including Martnowy, had little to do with the naïve, clever, religious description of goodness and ethical uprightness that was the mainstay of the musical and the later film of the same name. No wonder that both my grandmother and her younger brother Avrum, who were nine and twelve when they came to the *Kresy*, and the only surviving children in the family who really remembered life there, found the saccharine musical to be almost offensive to their harsh memories of the area.

Freida Sima's experiences in the *Kresy* during her early teenage years were the major factor in shaping her attitude towards Europe for the rest of her life. "After I got to America I used to have nightmares", she once told me. "Nightmares about missing your family?" I asked her. "Nightmares that something would happen and I would have to go back to Europe!" she responded. Although her daughter and son-in-law were travel agents and offered her almost yearly no-cost trips to Europe, she always refused, saying "I ran away from Europe! Why in the world would I ever want to go back?!" And indeed she did not, only once acquiescing to join them on a Greek Island boat cruise in her later years, and only because it took place on her way home from spending a month in Israel with her family. Continental Europe, however, was something else, and there was no way that she would step foot on its soil if she could help it. After all, as she told me only half in jest, someone might try to kidnap her, and bring her back to the *Kresy*.

The *cheder* in their new village was nowhere near Mihowa standards and it was almost unknown in the *Kresy* for older girls to study. However for a tiny sum the local *melamed* would let anyone sit in the back and listen. Freida Sima's thirst for education had intensified with age; Nachman was earning well and the sum could be found, but would he agree? Now she used a different ploy. True, another baby boy, Leibish, had just been born, but as they were not on their farm in Mihowa, there was less work to be done. In their new and somewhat dangerous surroundings, she told her father, it might be prudent if she or Marium could accompany their little brothers, Avrum, Ben-Zion (Tzeendl) and Srul, to *cheder* and back. If she was already there on alternate days, maybe Nachman could find the tiny sum to let her stay and learn a bit? Devorah probably intervened as she was the only one who could have convinced Nachman to agree, but agree he did, and Freida Sima spent alternate mornings sitting on the back bench in *cheder* absorbing everything she could.

As she passed her fourteenth birthday, however, Freida Sima began worrying how long this reality could continue, realizing that her father, a

48

firm believer in early marriage for girls, would soon try to marry her off to a local boy. For a girl who dreamed of getting an education, the idea of a match with an illiterate boy from the *Kresy* whose greatest ambition was to afford chicken for his Friday night soup, was horrifying. "Not only will I have to stop studying when I get married, I'll die a slow death if I end up like that" she told Marium, "better the *Tateh* should just kill me and be done with it." Marium understood her sister's fears but for her at twelve, the prospect of marriage was still far off. "I'm sure you'll find a way out of it Babaleh", she comforted her older sibling, using the family nickname of little grandmother, that Freida Sima had been given after a serious childhood illness. "Maybe if you tell him that you only want a boy from Mihowa, he will be willing to wait until we go back home."

Knowing her father well, Freida Sima didn't even try. She would have to solve this dilemma through a different type of bargain that would make it worthwhile for her father to let her leave the *Kresy* while still single, and continue her education. What were her choices? If she went back to Mihowa she could live with Baba Malka, but she was almost too old for the local *cheder* there. Big cities like Czernowicz or Lwow had a girls' *gymnasium*, but where could she live and how could she afford the school fees? Nachman certainly wouldn't pay! The harder she looked for a solution, the more she realized that only one option might solve both her problems, while offering her father something in return. To go to America. But it would have to happen soon, long before she turned sixteen, her mother's age when she had become betrothed to Nachman.

All this would require planning. Her first step was to convince her mother, a secret adventurer at heart, of her plan. One day, as if by chance, she began talking about her early years at Baba Malka's, how close she had grown to her aunt Sheine, and how much she missed her since they had left Mihowa. Devorah commiserated, talking about how much she missed her own family, and then returning to her baby sister Sheine, now seventeen. "Well, even when we go back to Mihowa, you won't see her anymore", Devorah remarked, "now that she has also left for America."

Devorah's offhand remark was a reminder of what was happening to the Scharf family, which was similar to the dynamics among myriads of Jewish families at that time in Eastern Europe. Either individually or as family groups, they were immigrating to America, in most cases, either for economic betterment or as an escape from persecution. The image of America as a country where people could earn more money than they could imagine was cultivated by a number of factors. Since the end of the nineteenth century, American companies had mounted a public relations effort aimed at recruiting young men and women of working age, by depicting life in America as an unending stream of money. This was done by distributing posters throughout southern and eastern Europe showing workers coming out of the factory, and walking into the bank with bags of money under their arms. Steamship companies also used advertising to attract immigrants, sending posters showing prices and sailing dates into the smallest villages throughout Europe. Local agents were recruited to work on commission and sell steerage tickets throughout the continent, and not only in the port cities of Hamburg, Antwerp, Amsterdam or Le Havre.

The public relations campaign could not have succeeded without the backup of letters from friends and family who had immigrated to the United States and wrote home about their experiences. Information about the immigration process, employment, the requirements of the American labor market, living conditions, salaries, and most of all, what one could do with that money in America, were great inducements to young men and women, both single and married, to consider travelling across the sea and making their lives in the "New World". In addition, many Jews saw immigration to America as a way to escape persecution in Eastern Europe, but Freida Sima was among the lucky Jews of the Bukovina who, at that time, had not experienced persecution firsthand. Her desire to move to America was fostered by one impetus: it was the only way she could think of to continue her education.

By the end of the first decade of the twentieth century, when this conversation took place, the Scharf-Enzenberg family already had quite a representation overseas. As the two familes were intertwined by marriage, together with a number of additional families from Mihowa such as the Hallers, Handels, and Steinbrechers, it was common for siblings, cousins or friends from the various families to travel to America together, or to bring each other over, eventually creating a "little Mihowa" on the other side of the Atlantic.

On the Scharf side, the first to move to America had been *Veter* (Uncle) Yossel Haller, Baba Malka's brother, who had immigrated to New York at the end of the 19th century where he worked as a winemaker, and later, according to another version of the story, as a bootlegger. Yossel had first brought over his son, Wolf, in 1902. Aware that Malka had been left a widow with a large family to support, he then offered to bring some of her children to America to help lessen the economic burden on the family. The first

Scharf sibling that he sponsored, sending money for her ticket to America, was Devorah's younger sister Marium-Rivka who came in 1904 when she was sixteen. At first Marium-Rivka helped Yossel in the winemaking business, and now there was talk of her marrying *Veter* Yossel's good friend, Srul Nachman Handel from Mihowa, who had just lost his wife. Srul Nachman had been Marium-Rivka's *melamed* in *cheder,* years earlier, and he was also related to the family through his cousin Leib Handel, who had married Nachman's sister, Marium Raisel.

When *Veter* Yossel had gone back to Mihowa for a family visit in 1906, he convinced Srul Nachman to come with him to America, where his family would have a better life than in Europe. Srul Nachman agreed, and travelled on the same boat to New York with *Veter* Yossel, arriving in January 1907. As was customary at the time, he immigrated alone, planning to send for his wife and two small children after earning the money for their tickets. In the interim, however, his wife Chana Yitta died in Mihowa, and his young son and daughter were now traveling with their uncle to New York, to be reunited with their father. Initially there had been talk of Marium-Rivka being their nanny, but it soon turned into talk of her marrying Srul Nachman, even though he was almost nineteen years older than she.

Marium-Rivka was not the only Scharf child that *Veter* Yossel had brought to America. After he returned from his trip to Mihowa, he sent money to bring over another Scharf child, this time his namesake, Devorah's seventeen-year-old brother Yossel. Yossel, who arrived in late 1907 and would soon became "Joe", later became a pivotal figure in the American branch of the Scharf-Eisenberg family. Immediately after arriving in New York, he went to work as a waiter, as the task of sending "home" money to bring over his younger siblings now fell on his young shoulders. In 1908, it was young Sheine's turn to join the growing family in New York. Initially, she, too, helped *Veter* Yossel make wine, and by the time Freida Sima had this conversation with her mother, Sheine had already gotten a job as a seamstress in a garment center sweatshop where by 1910, women made up over seventy percent of the workforce.[43] Finally, in early 1909 Joe brought over his brother-in-law Fischel Hirsch, husband of his sister Hudel. As was customary, Fischel went to work in New York until he

---

43   Elizabeth Ewen, *Immigrant Women in the Land of Dollars: Life and Culture on the Lower East Side 1890–1925,* New York: Monthly Review Press, 1985: 25.

had enough money to bring over his wife and five children, Rivka, Lena, Avrum, Chantche and Mantze.

Then there were the Enzenbergs, who by then also had established an overseas branch of the family. By the time Freida Sima broached the possibility of immigrating to America, Nachman already had siblings, nieces and nephews living in New York. His oldest brother, Meier Moshe, had accompanied his eleven-year-old daughter Feige to America in 1902, but at some point, he left her there with family, and returned to Mihowa. Feige was followed by additional sisters, Tziril, Ethel and finally Raisel in 1909, and in 1910 Meier Moshe travel to New York a second time, now bringing his eleven-year-old daughter Sime. At some point after that he left Sime with her sisters, and returned once again to Europe. Raisel would eventually return to Europe in order to care for her youngest sister, Lotte, after their mother Gittel died in childbirth, but three additional children of Meier Moshe, Malka, Nathan and Shmil, were also planning to come to America when they got older. Malka and her husband indeed came but returned to Europe before the war's outbreak.

The peripatetic Meier Moshe was indeed unique in the family, but another Enzenberg sibling, Nachman's sister Marium Raisel Enzenberg Handel, also immigrated to America in 1910, following her husband Leib who had moved there a year earlier. Leib and Marium Raisel had joined their children, Mendel and Lea, who had already immigrated in 1906. Aside from this group, additional Enzenberg cousins from Mihowa had immigrated to New York over the decade, and they all lived in the same two general areas near the Scharfs, Hallers, and Handels in New York. If following all these names sounds confusing, it shows the complexity of what happens when what looks like an entire town begins moving to America at the beginning of the twentieth century, something in which Mihowa was not alone. It gets even more difficult when they began to change their names to more American-sounding ones, at least the younger generation among them. But all this would be in the future, and meanwhile Freida Sima had a task ahead of her – to convince her mother to let her move to America on her own before she was sixteen.

Freida Sima now began to turn the conversation around to herself and her own future. "You know how much I love school *Mameh*", she continued. "What do you think will be with me? Do you really think I will be happy marrying someone that the *Tateh* will choose from around here, who wouldn't know from what side you open a book?! Who will get upset every time he realizes that at fourteen, I already knew more than he will at thirty? I'm not sure I want to get married at all if that's what's in store for me!" Another time she called her mother's attention to the difference between the Jewish men they saw in Martnowy and the ones they knew from Mihowa. "Look at the men here, *Mameh*, the ones here are ignorant *Hassidim*. You know what they say: an ignorant *Misnaged* beats his horse; an ignorant *Hassid* beats his wife! Better I should go to America like Aunt Sheina. Even if I go to work like she does, there no one gets upset when a girl wants to read a book. They even say that one can study at night in America, and it doesn't even cost anything!"

These were but the first of many conversations that Freida Sima initiated with her mother about this topic during the next few weeks. Ultimately, Devorah understood that her daughter would do anything to continue her education, even if it meant leaving her beloved parents and moving across the ocean. Now it was time for Freida Sima to try and convince Nachman of the wisdom of her plan. Turning to her father, however, required a very different set of tactics than turning to her mother. Nachman was quite familiar with the phenomenon of family members going abroad to better themselves economically. Knowing her father's well-developed economic common sense, to him Freida Sima stressed that if she joined the family in America she could do what myriads of Jewish immigrants were doing at that time – find work and send money back to Europe. After all, that was what his own brother Meier Moshe had been doing for close to a decade, bringing children to America and having them send back money to Mihowa so that he could buy more farmland!

Nachman loved his daughter greatly but was also aware that his eighth child, Elish had just been born. While each child brought his or her own *mazel,* their own fortune, children also had needs and expenses. Although he would miss his firstborn daughter tremendously, he was not blind to the benefits of Freida Sima's proposal. If she did go to America, there would be one less mouth to feed. And while he would never admit it outright, the thought of an additional income was tempting. There would also be one less dowry to provide, a fact that fathers of daughters always kept in mind.

But a dowry meant marriage, and if his Freida Sima went to America, what would be with her *shidduch*? If she got married in America, it would be bad enough that he and Devorah wouldn't be there for the wedding, but for a wedding one first one needs a husband. Who would take care of finding her a husband? At first, Nachman didn't dare voice that worry, but at some point he mentioned it to Devorah. "So how do you think my sister Marium-Rivka is getting married in America with the *Mameh* in Mihowa?"

she answered, "In America the family takes care of each other, the *Veter Yossel* is there, he watches out for us, and just look! My sister is marrying Reb Srul Nachman, her *melamed* from Mihowa!" Nachman realized that when the time came, the family in America would help find Freida Sima a suitable match, possibly a relative. Weighing up all the options, Nachman sighed and gave his oldest daughter his blessing. Thus the immigration of Freida Sima began.

Epilogue

It is difficult to reconstruct a person's history from family stories. It is even more difficult to do so, when it is not directly from the memories of the people involved, but through a filter: from stories that those people re-counted about themselves to their children or grandchildren, and which you hear only from that second party. The most difficult reconstructions are those which you hear from a third party: incidents which people were told, but in which they were not involved; incidents that they then recounted to their children or grandchildren, and which were then passed on to you. Similar to the game "telephone" when a message is passed from one person to another until a garbled version often ends up down the line, at times one wonders how much this "third party story", indeed resembles what actually occurred.

It is often possible to cross-reference a story with documents. At other times one can do so by comparing different versions that were passed down to different family members. I have tried to do so whenever documents or corroborative stories are available. But there are also stories for which there is only one version, whether because it was told to only one person, or because the other members of the first generation involved did not survive long enough to be able to corroborate the tale.

My grandmother was the oldest sibling in her family, and therefore, none of her brothers or sisters witnessed the incidents surrounding her birth and early years. The same holds true for her mother and grandmother as both Devorah and Malka were the oldest siblings of large families. What we are left with, are stories that Baba Malka told my grandmother – the only grandchild she actually raised – about herself and her early life, about her daughter Devorah's youth and marriage, and finally, about my grandmother's birth. I assume that throughout her childhood, my grandmother also heard her mother Devorah's version of the stories in which she had been directly involved, and the version my grandmother passed down to me is probably a combination of the two.

As for stories pertaining to my grandmother's early years, and particularly her deliberations about moving to America, the only persons who were privy to those deliberations were her mother Devorah and her sister Marium, neither of whom survived the Holocaust. The other children were too young to remember, and the youngest children in the family were born only after my grandmother left Europe.

One sibling, however, remembered her leaving Martnowy, as he was part of the story: her five-year-old brother Srul. It was both from her, and from him, that I heard the story of the final part of her life in Europe, and the story they told was identical.

In late 1910, my grandmother began preparing for her month-long journey to America, dreaming every night about how she would find part-time work and be able to continue her education and to start a new life. "Remember", she told me, "those were the days that most people leaving Europe thought they would never go back. Every night I would look at the *Tateh-Mameh*, wondering if I would ever see them again. Marium couldn't believe my courage in traveling all alone. I promised to write her and send her a picture of me in America." Little did she know that by the time she had enough money for a picture, a World War would break out, cutting off any correspondence with her family for more than four years. But that was still far in the future. Now all she could think of was the excitement of going to America, of being able to continue her education, of starting a new life.

The month-long trip from the *Kresy* to the new world took place in stages: horse-drawn cart, wagon, trains and finally a ten day boat trip in steerage. The entire family gathered in the yard to see her off. As she climbed into the cart, five-year-old Srul, who later dreamed of being a rabbi, ran after her, raising his fist and calling his farewell. "*Babaleh! Halt Yiddishkeit!!!*" ("Keep Judaism"), was his parting cry, as even five-year-olds knew that America was a *treife medineh,* an unkosher country where too many Jews gave up the religious customs of their forefathers. "I will Sruilinkeh, I promise", she called back, not dreaming what such a promise would eventually entail for her in America during the years to come. How did her very religious father agree to let her go under those circumstances? Like many, it appears that Nachman relied on the American-Jewish trinity – the *Ribono Shel Olam* (Master of the Universe), family, and that nebulous American dream – "Uncle Sam" – to keep his daughter safe.

When my grandmother waved at her family until they were no more than a speck in the distance, she could have no idea that very little would turn out as she planned, not work, not marriage and not even her education. But that is a very different story, one that we will begin in the next chapter.

Chapter 3 The Immigration of Freida Sima – New York (1911–1923)

Introduction

How many times can a teenage girl change her name, home, and language, without it altering her inner being? Where does she find strength to remain true to her beliefs and hopes when thrown into an environment so different than that which she had dreamed of when leaving her parents and siblings? What happens to her burning dreams, when 5000 miles away from home, she must first become self-supporting in a new language and culture? And what does she do when she has to choose between realizing these dreams and bringing the rest of her family to America? These are the dilemmas that my grandmother faced as a teenager when she immigrated to America to build a new life, a life that would include her becoming a teacher, her secret desire that she had shared only with one person, her younger sister Marium, while still in Europe.

When Freida Sima Ensenberg[44] left Europe in January 1911 she may not have known precisely what she was going to gain in America, but she had her eyes wide open regarding what she was leaving, and therefore had absolutely no intention of ever going back to Europe. She was among the first of the 879,000 immigrants who would reach the United States that year, 91,000 of

---

44 Although the family wrote their family name, Enzenberg, with a "z", all of Freida Sima's documents, including her *Arbeitsbuch,* her Austrian "Working Papers" that she received in Europe at age fourteen, spell her name with an "s". The Passenger Search of the Ellis Island Foundation, lists almost an equal number of Enzenbergs and Ensenbergs, originally from Mihowa: Ensenbergs – Hirsch Leile [Leib] (1905), Henora (1906), Lire (1906), Meier Moses (1910), Sure (1910), Sime (1910), Babe (1911), Smie (1912), Freide (1912) and Taube (1912), as opposed to Enzenbergs – Meier Moses (1902), Faige (1902), Brane (1906), Reisel (1909), Leib (1913), Nathan (1920), Abraam (1920), Benzieu (1923). <http://www.libertyellisfoundation.org/passenger-result>, retrieved December 6, 2015.

whom were Jewish.[45] This was the first wave of Jewish immigration where it was common to find girls and young women traveling on their own, without either friends or family.[46] Only among the Irish, where girls came to American to work "in service", was there a higher proportion of female immigrants, and particularly unaccompanied female immigrants, than among the Jews.[47] Also among the Jews, many underage girls travelled alone to the United States, presenting themselves as older than they were, and listing their profession as "domestic worker", or "servant". One of them was Freida Sima.

Jewish Immigration to America

My grandmother was neither a revolutionary, nor a pioneer. She was one of millions of Europeans, among them over two million Jews, who were then leaving their countries of origin and seeking a better life elsewhere. For most, "elsewhere" was the United States of America, a country whose population has traditionally been based on immigration of groups and individuals fleeing persecution, seeking economic betterment, or even just looking for adventure. Many, if not most of these groups of immigrants, left their mark on American life, and the Jews were no exception.

The few Jews who immigrated in the Colonial era days were primarily Sefaradi Jews from Holland and England, although they were joined by a handful of Ashkenazi Jews from Poland, one of whom, Haym Salomon, was responsible for bankrolling the American Revolution. Their numbers were small, and out of a total American population of 2.5 million when the country was established in 1776, the Jews numbered fewer than 2,500 souls.[48]

---

45   Hersch Liebmann, "International Migration of Jews" in: Walter Wilcox (ed.), *International Migrations v. II: Interpretations,* Cambridge: National Bureau of Economic Research, 1931: statistical table 200: 474.

46   Between 1899 and 1914, 44% of the Jewish immigrants were women, and every seventh female immigrant entering the United States during those years was Jewish. Liebmann, "International Migration of Jews", 482.

47   Liebmann, "International Migration of Jews", statistical table 206: 483.

48   <https://www.jewishvirtuallibrary.org/jsource/US-Israel/usjewpop1.html> retrieved Dec. 6, 2015; U.S. Bureau of the Census, *A century of population growth from the first census of the United States to the twelfth, 1790–1900* (1909), Ann Arbor: University of Michigan Library, 1909: 9.

Most Jews were farmers and merchants residing in and around colonial ports such as Boston, New Amsterdam (later New York), Newport, Rhode Island, Philadelphia, and Savannah, Georgia. Many intermarried, and as a result, the Jewish presence in the United States was rarely felt, and barely increased during the first decades of the country's existence.

All this changed during the mid-19th century when close to 150,000 Jews from Central Europe, fleeing persecution, restrictive laws, economic hardship and failed revolutionary movements advocating reform, came to the United States.[49] As with the Jews who had come in Colonial times, they, too, were part of a larger wave of immigration from Ireland, Germany, Britain and France, which began in the 1820s and peaked in mid-century.

The newly-arrived German-speaking Jews eventually changed the geographical spread, religious mode, economic structure, and organizational pattern of American Jewry. Unlike their Sefaradi co-religionists who had remained on the Eastern seaboard, many of these new immigrants from Central Europe began as peddlers, expanding American Jewish geography by traveling throughout the Midwest, eventually stopping at a town or crossroads and establishing a store there. Some of these stores were the forerunners of what later became major department stores throughout the country. They also brought the Reform Movement to the United States and a different form of communal Jewish life than had previously existed there. They and their children also established the first national Jewish organizations in America, some of which are still active today, such as Bnai Brith, the American Jewish Committee and the National Council of Jewish Women.[50] Belonging for the most part to a westernized secular culture, by the late 19th century the German-Jewish immigrants had slowly begun to assimilate into American life.

Just as they began to feel completely at home in America, they were faced with a new wave of Jewish immigration which they feared would threaten their hard-earned place in American society. These Jews were part of the largest wave of immigration to the United States which began around 1880, primarily from Eastern and Southern Europe and the Russian Empire. The development of the steam engine had shortened the transatlantic voyage from twelve to two weeks, reducing the fares and putting overseas travel within the reach of masses of immigrants. Over 22 million immigrants

---

49   Out of a total population of 31 million Americans in 1860.

50   Most of the documentation regarding the immigration waves is taken from: Jonathan D. Sarna, *American Judaism: A History,* New Haven: Yale UP, 2005.

from these areas entered the United States until the outbreak of the First World War, among them over 2,200,000 Jews from Russia, Rumania, and Austro-Hungary.[51]

The pogroms in the Russian Pale of Settlement, and the anti-Jewish legislation throughout the next decades, were a major impetus for the immigration of Russian Jews.[52] Rumanian Jews, as well, were beset with numerous economic restrictive regulations enacted against them from 1880 to 1889.[53] Jews in Austro-Hungary were not persecuted in the same way as their fellow Jews in Russia and Rumania; on the contrary, in many areas they were emancipated and in a few, such as the Bukovina, they were even permitted to own land. America, however, offered them countless opportunities which were unavailable at home, particularly for those beset with financial difficulty.[54]

The mass wave of Jewish immigration from Eastern Europe changed not only the demography and composition of American Jewry, but also its orientation. Most of the immigrants settled on the East Coast, and the majority – over 1,300,000 – in New York City.[55] The nominally Orthodox presence of Jews in America was strengthened by the immigration of large numbers of traditional Jews. Most of the immigrants found employment in factories, particularly the garment industry. Many labored in sweatshops and Jews stood at the forefront of the struggle for better working conditions. The socialist and labor movements grew, fed by Jewish activists from Eastern Europe. So did the Yiddish cultural movements, in the form of drama, journalism and prose. The Yiddish press flourished, and was an additional source

---

51   Immigration statistics by religion from the period are not precise, as only on July 1, 1898 did the United States begin to categorize immigrants using the category of "race or people". Liebmann, "International Migration of Jews": 471–520.

52   In 1850, only one Russian immigrant had entered the United States. By 1890, 35,600 immigrants arrived from Russia in one year. In 1907, 259,000 immigrants entered America from Russia, the majority of whom were Jews, and similar numbers began arriving every year until the First World War.

53   The first group of 261 Rumanian Jews, primarily single men, had arrived in the United States in 1860 as part of the Gold Rush, but by 1888 there were over 2000 Rumanian Jews in America. From then until 1914, 75,000 Rumanian Jewish reached America shores, more than three quarters of all the immigrants from Rumania to enter the United States during that period. Vladimir F. Wertzman, *Salute to Romanian Jewish in America and Canada 1850–2010,* Xlibris: Bloomington, 2010: 59.

54   Between 1898 and 1900 alone, more than 89,000 Jewish immigrants from Austro-Hungary entered the United States, reaching a total of 260,000 Jews from that area who arrived until 1924. Liebmann, "International Migration of Jews": 473; 479.

55   Liebmann, "International Migration of Jews": 519.

of describing the plight of the immigrant worker. These immigrants also brought unprecedented support for a Jewish national movement, augmenting the ranks of the Zionist movement which had already been founded by the Central European Jewish immigrants to the United States and their children.

Although the general feeling among many, if not most of the Jewish immigrants leaving Europe was that they would never return, there were definitely those who returned, some temporary, others permanently. Early studies like those of the Jewish demographer Hersch Liebmann had shown that shows that compared to other ethnic groups, the rate of Jewish return emigration was quite small, only a bit over 5% as compared to the 15% of German immigrants or 55% of Italian immigrants during the same period. If they did return, it was more likely that they would do so if they came from Austro-Hungary where the conditions were better for Jews, rather than from Russia or Rumania.[56]

In his examination of the "myth of no return", American Jewish historian Jonathan Sarna portrays a somewhat different picture. Particularly during the early years of the Great Wave of Immigration, it appears that larger numbers of Jews returned to Europe than originally thought.[57] Most of the immigrants returning were male and single, at times to care of elderly parents or to look for a bride. Often they waited for five years before buying a ticket back to Europe, so that they could first be naturalized and apply for an American passport, although the authorities could refuse to issue passports to Americans who were former immigrants, at will. These immigrants often considered their sojourn in Europe as a temporary step, and ultimately planned to return to the United States.

Inability to find work was another reason Jewish immigrants returned to Europe. In most of those cases, though, it was not the inability to find work, but to find meaningful work. Some wanted a more Orthodox Jewish life. Others were simply homesick. Reasons stemmed from an inability to adapt to indoor toilets, to an *agunah*'s (abandoned wife, grass widow) need to find her missing husband. Sarna concludes that return migration is basically a phenomenon through which we can view immigrant problems of the period. "Some Jewish immigrants of an earlier day, blessed neither with prophecy or historical hindsight, discovered that the life they remember

---

56   Liebmann, "International Migration of Jews", table 203: 477.
57   Jonathan D. Sarna, "The Myth of No Return: Jewish Return Migration to Eastern Europe, 1881–1914", *American Jewish History* 71:2 (Dec. 1981): 256–268.

having lost meant more to them than the American they had gained", he concludes.[58]

Many of these phenomena can be seen in the story of Freida Sima's life and in that of her family. After immigrating to America, several of them visited Europe, some more than once, all of them waiting the requisite five years until they received their Certificate of Naturalization and could apply for an American passport. Among them were her grandmother's brother, Yossel Haller, who appears to be the first family member to have immigrated to America in the mid-1890s, her uncle Joe Scharf, and her brothers, Abie and Benny Eisenberg. Moreover, on their visits to Europe, some of them managed to convince friends or other family members to accompany them back to America. Yossel Haller visited Mihowa in 1906 and returned with his good friend, who would later become a family member, Srul Nachman Handel. Abie visited Mihowa in 1928 and Benny in both 1929 and 1930, the second time returning to America with a bride. Joe Scharf visited Europe in 1933 and brought back family members who were then living in Germany.

Nachman Enzenberg's brother Meier Moshe travelled to America twice before the First World War, each time accompanying a daughter, and brought back money to buy more land in Mihowa. Another extended family member returned to Europe due to homesickness and the desire to find more meaningful work: Srul Nachman Handel's brother-in-law Shmiel (Samuel) Druckman. Druckman had accompanied Srul Nachman's minor children, Louis and Perla, to America as their guardian in 1910. Louis recalled: "Our Uncle Shmiel was not happy here. He missed his wife and children. He used to be a clerk in court in Unterviku, a German speaking town...Uncle Shmiel was the most educated of the Druckman brothers. He went back to Europe. It was no life for him here in New York."[59]

At a certain point, there were even those family members who visited America and did not intend to immigrate. Two of Freida Sima's close family came to America for extended visits during the 1930s – her mother Devorah Scharf Enzenberg and her mother's brother, Yankel Scharf, both had an opportunity to immigrate to America – and both nevertheless returned to Europe, each for their own reasons. There were those family members found it extremely difficult to maintain an Orthodox Jewish lifestyle, but nevertheless managed to find employment that allowed them to do so. Among them were

---

58   Sarna, "The Myth of No Return": 267.

59   Louis Handel, "My Life Story Continued", 1975, in the possession of his son, Bernard Handel.

Freida Sima's brothers and uncles. Her very religious father-in-law, however, who had immigrated to America in his early 50s at the turn of the century, found it more difficult to find a suitable job that would allow him to remain *Shomer Shabbos* (Sabbath observant). He ended up working part-time as a tailor and eventually being supported by his children.

Other than that, none of the family members appear to have had any problem adapting to the physical and social conditions of life in America. On the contrary; life in America was a step up for most of them, at least financially and in terms of physical conditions. Nor did I ever hear a word about their having been homesick, even those who came at the early stages of the family's immigration, before there was a large family in America which could cushion their arrival. The only criticism voiced of life in America that came down to us, were from the two family members who returned to Europe. In her letters home Devorah Enzenberg wondered how people could live in apartment houses without wide open spaces of farmland around them, enabling them "to breathe", echoing what many immigrants had thought during their initial encounter with urban America.[60] The second was Devorah's brother Yankel Scharf, who declined to move permanently to the United States, claiming that he could do better economically in Yugoslavia where he was then living. Of course, the fact that he was visiting New York at the height of the Depression might have had something to do with his claim, but that we will never know.

Freida Sima Arrives in New York

When the S.S. Rijndam docked in New York in the early morning hours of Friday February 3, 1911, Freida Sima was one of 1800 steerage (third class) passengers who peered out through the fog and rain at their new home, hoping the rest of their lives would be better than the events of the past two weeks. Since embarking at Rotterdam, choppy seas had kept her below deck, sick to her stomach. Boarding the ferry taking steerage passengers to

---

60   Elizabeth Ewen, *Immigrant Women in the Land of Dollars: Life and Culture on the Lower East Side 1890–1925*, New York: Monthly Review Press, 1985: 60–61.

Ellis Island for processing, she took her first breath of fresh air, concerned whether she would finish the immigration procedure before Shabbos.

Ellis Island was the nation's busiest immigration inspection station at the time, having succeeded the inspection station of Castle Gardens in lower Manhattan. By the time it closed in November 1954, over 12 million immigrants had been processed at Ellis Island. Like millions of immigrants before her, Freida Sima entered the Great Hall at Ellis Island and was immediately overwhelmed by its size. This was the Hall in which immigrants had their medical and legal examination to determine whether they would be permitted to enter the United States, or detained and possibly sent back to Europe.[61]

Immigration workers employed on Ellis Island were used to large groups of immigrants, but during the first decade of the 20th century, numbers grew to the unprecedented, and what had once been the unimaginable. On one day in April 1907, over 11,000 immigrants arrived at Ellis Island to be processed. Those thought liable to become public charges or contract laborers had their cases decided by special boards of enquiry and each board held fifty to one hundred hearings daily in the presence of an interpreter and stenographer.

Most of the immigrants, however, proceeded directly to the Great Hall where 2,000–4,000 passengers were processed daily, usually in under five hours – if they were healthy. Joining the lines of immigrants being examined in groups of thirty, Freida Sima inched forward, recalling her Aunt Sheine's instructions for answering immigration questions about who paid for her ticket and where she was staying. The girl ahead of her in line, Marium Strauss from Lomza, was around her age. Seeing Freida Sima's fearful look she nudged her in the ribs – "Remember, you are sixteen!" – reminding her of the cutoff for unaccompanied passengers wishing to work in America.

By the time Freida Sima reached the head of the line she was in a fog. Asked her name by the immigration officer, she automatically gave her childhood nickname of "Baba" or "Babaleh" and was listed phonetically on her immigration papers for all posterity as "Babe Ensenberg", passenger ID number 101067030197, age 16, single, from Mihova [thus in original], Austria, of Hebrew ethnicity, whose closest relative in Europe was her

61   Pamela Reeves, *Ellis Island: Gateway to the American Dream,* New York: Gramercy, 1991; David M. Brownstone, *Island of Hope, Island of Tears: The Story of Those who Entered the New World Through Ellis Island – in their Own Words,* New York: Barnes and Noble, 2000; Vincent J. Cannato, *American Passage: The History of Ellis Island,* New York: Harper Perennial, 2010.

father Nachman Ensenberg [thus in original] of Martnowy, Galicia, 5'1, with brown hair, grey eyes, in good physical and mental health, no identifying scars, neither polygamist nor anarchist, reading and writing German, domestic servant, possessing $20 and going to live with her Aunt Sheine Scharf, on E. 5th Street in New York City. Freida Sima may have left Europe, but Babe entered America to begin a new life.

Similar to many, but not all, of the Jewish immigrants of the time who reached Ellis Island, Freida Sima had no qualms about listing her ethnicity as "Hebrew", in other words, Jewish. As Barbara Shollar reminds us in her study of autobiographies of Jewish-American women of that generation, the word "Hebrew", literally means "one who comes from the other side – in other words, the immigrant…s/he who crosses borders".[62] Freida Sima was indeed an immigrant and a border crosser, but one who continued to see herself first and foremost as a Jew, unlike some of her socialist coreligionist immigrants, including her future husband and his revolutionary sister, who would list themselves as "Russian" when immigrating to America.

By mid-afternoon my grandmother had returned by ferry to Hudson Pier in Manhattan where was she was met by her dashing twenty-one-year-old uncle Yossel, her mother's brother who had come to America in 1906. Rushing to get home before Shabbos – home being her newly married aunt Marium-Rivka's apartment where the whole extended family in New York was living at the time – she got her first glimpses of the city. "How can you stand so much noise?!" she asked in dismay when passing under the elevated railway tracks. Little did she know that twenty years later she would live right next to the "L" as it was called, and would not be able to sleep during a train strike from lack of accustomed noise!

* * *

Freida Sima's reunion with her uncle and aunts was a tearful and joyous experience for all involved. She had not seen her aunt Marium-Rivka in over six years, as she had left Mihowa when Freida Sima was nine. Now she was a married woman of twenty-three with two step-children, Perla-Lena and Louis. Yossel she hadn't seen since he left for America when she was eleven, and Sheine, the aunt with whom she had been brought up as a sister, and whom she had loved, copied, and fought with as if she were a sister, had

---

62   Barbara Shollar, *Writing Ethnicity/Writing Modernity: Autobiographies by Jewish-American Women,* Ph.D dissertation submitted to the City University of New York, Ann Arbor: University Microfilms, International, 1992:1.

left Mihowa soon after Freida Sima's family had left for Martnowy in 1908. Now they would be Freida Sima's family in America, in place of the parents and siblings whom she had left behind.

"A main consideration in selecting a community is living among people who are somewhat like you", writes sociologist and New York City expert William Helmreich.[63] It was therefore not at all strange that Freida Sima's relatives in America were either living in the same apartment, such as her uncle and aunts, or were living within walking distance from each other, such as *Veter* Jossel Haller and his son Wolf, Srul Nachman and his brother Mendel, Marium Raisel (Enzenberg) and Leib Handel or uncle Fischel Hirsch. As opposed to previous waves of Jewish immigration to the United States, in which the immigrants had spread out in various geographical locales, this Eastern European wave of Jewish immigrants most commonly chose to live together, in major cities and in Jewish immigrant communities. These were often located in larger immigrant areas, such as the eastern areas of Lower Manhattan, in what was termed the Lower East Side, where one could find not only Jewish immigrants, but also Italians immigrants and which bordered another immigrant area populated by the Chinese. Two other Jewish areas in New York at the time were the area where Freida Sima's relatives were now living around 5th Street, somewhat further north in Manhattan, and Harlem where she and some of her relatives were soon to move. As many of the Jewish immigrants were traditional and required Jewish communal institutions such as synagogues, Kosher butcher shops, and ritual baths, it made sense for them to live both near each other and near their religious institutions.

It was also not at all unusual at the time to find several generations of immigrant families living together in one apartment, or for single brothers and sisters who had immigrated to live with married siblings for several years after they came to the United States. Every room was turned into a bedroom at night. Folding cots were regularly set up in kitchens, living rooms and dining rooms became bedrooms, and newly arrived uncles and aunts could sleep with the children of the family for several years before marrying and moving into their own apartments. It was not only a way to save on expenses; it was also a way of keeping the family together.

Even after moving out, it was very common for immigrants to remain in the same neighborhood as their relatives, even on the same block

---

63   William B. Helmreich, *The New York Nobody Knows: Walking 6000 Miles in the City*, Princeton NJ: Princeton University Press, 2013: 91.

and at times, in the same apartment building. Used to living near each other in Europe, these families attempted to recreate that feeling of closeness in America. For the most part, Freida Sima and her relatives would end up doing this for the better part of the 20th century. From the listings on ships' manifests it seems that when they first got to America during the early 1900s, the Haller, Handel, and Scharf descendents congregated around 155 Rivington street in the Lower East Side. By the beginning of the second decade of the century some in the group had moved to E. 5th street, and soon after they began moving to Harlem where they all lived between 111th to 112th street. After the First World War, most of the group ended up in the East Bronx, in the triangle between Beck Street, Trinity Avenue and 158th streets. Many of Nachman's brother Meier Moshe's children went through the same process, beginning their American stay on the Lower East side, and some then moving together to the same street and even building in Newark, New Jersey.[64]

During the next two weeks Freida Sima acclimatized to her new surroundings. She explored the streets of Manhattan, attempted to eat an unknown fruit called a "banana" with peel intact, and practiced crossing streets, avoiding the unfamiliar, never-ending traffic. Wanting to sound "American", she carefully pronounced her first English phrases exactly like her aunt, unaware that even after over six years in America, *Tante* Marium-Rivka still spoke like a "greener" and that "coss de stid" and "wayfa monyee" were actually "cross the street" and "wait for Monday".

And then there were the names. Marium-Rivka and Sheine had become "Mollie" and "Sadie", Yossle was "Joe", Yehuda Leib was "Louis", Wolf was "Willie". Only her new uncle, Srul Nachman Handel, married to her aunt Mollie, kept his old name. Like many religious functionaries from the "old world", the middle-aged Srul Nachman could not find full-time work as a *melamed*, and therefore supported his family by becoming a "presser" in the rapidly expanding New York garment industry, moonlighting as a part-time *melamed* in Brooklyn.[65] Middle-aged and overtly religious with a head covering at all times (unlike some of his more Americanized brothers-in-law), he was not expected to be too modern, but Freida Sima was definitely expected to Americanize her name. "Why not call yourself Bertha?" suggested Aunt

---

64 Author's correspondence with Irving Levine, February 18, 2016.
65 Joel Seidman, *The Needle Trades,* New York: Farrar and Reinhard, 1942; Roger D. Waldinger, *Through the Eye of the Needle: Immigrants and Enterprise in New York's Garment Trades,* New York: NYU Press, 1986.

Sadie, a popular name sounding like "Babaleh". "I'll think about it", replied Freida Sima tactfully, still unwilling to completely relinquish her European identity.

Freida Sima's explorations of her new city took her to various areas populated by immigrants, first and foremost to the Lower East Side, one of the oldest immigrant neighborhoods of the city. Born of James Delancy's pre-Revolutionary farm east of Post Road, the area eventually became a lower-class working area which, during the Great Wave of Immigration, was also a primarily Jewish neighborhood. In 1910, well over 2.3 million people lived in Manhattan, half a million of whom were packed into the dumbbell-shaped tenement housing blocks on the lower East Side. Before the First World War, a quarter of New York City's Jewish population of somewhat over a million persons lived in that area.[66]

Used to more spacious living conditions even in the hovels of the *Kresy*, she was shocked to discover packed apartment blocks with "railroad flats" and windowless inner rooms where over 70 people would share less than 5,000 square feet. True, she learned, there had been a reform ten years earlier requiring running water and a water closet in each "new" tenement apartment, but it had not yet been instituted in the older five and six floor walk-up buildings that still relied on air and light shafts to provide ventilation.[67] Describing the Jewish area of the Lower East Side years before, Danish-American social reformer, journalist and social documentary photographer Jacob Riis wrote: "It is said that nowhere in the world are so many people crowded together on a square mile as here…In Essex Street two small rooms in a six-story tenement were made to hold a "family" of father and mother, twelve children and six boarders…the homes were also workshops and it is not unusual to find a dozen persons – men, women, and children – at work in a single small room."[68]

Although he would later become a champion for the rights of Jewish immigrants, Riis's initial descriptions of the Jews of the Lower East Side were

---

66   Lawrence J. Epstein, *At the Edge of a Dream: The Story of Jewish Immigrants on New York's Lower East Side 1880–1920*, San Francisco: Jossey-Bass, 2007. Reliable estimations of the Jewish population of New York in 1910 ranged between 1,050,000 to 1,265,000. See Paul Ritterband, "Counting the Jews of New York 1900–1991: An Essay in Substance and Method", *Jewish Population Studies (Papers in Jewish Demography)* 29 (1997): 199–228.

67   Hasia R. Diner, *Lower East Side Memories: A Jewish Place in America*, Princeton: Princeton UP, 2002.

68   Jacob Riis, *How the Other Half Lives*, edited by Hasia Diner, New York and London: W. W. Norton and Co., 2010: 63–65.

somewhat tinged with prejudice. Stating that money is the God of the Jews, he claimed that life in "Jewtown", as he called it, was of little value compared to even the leanest bank account. However even in his earliest accounts, his factual descriptions of life in the area were unfortunately quite precise. "Thank heavens *Tante* Mollie doesn't live in a building like that", thought Freida Sima, returning from visiting other relatives from Mihowa who were now living on the Lower East Side. No wonder that the "Board of Health", which was supposed to inspect the area and insure decent living conditions, was called the "Board of Hell" by many of the immigrants at that time, my grandmother included.

Another expedition took her northwards to Central Park, a breath of fresh air for a country girl who was still overwhelmed by the masses of people she was seeing every day in the city that was now her new home. As she walked through the snow-covered rolling hills leading to Sheep Meadow, home to a flock of purebred sheep that were housed in winter in the Victorian building that was later to become "Tavern on the Green", she thought about where she had been just a month ago. "Who would believe that I, Freida Sima Ensenberg, am in America! That I am walking around in the middle of New York City! I wish Marium were here, we would be throwing snow at each other, away from all the little ones."

She indeed missed her little brothers and her parents, but it was her thirteen-year-old sister, with whom she had been closest, who was never far from her mind. How was Marium now coping as the oldest child in the family? The only girl among five boys? One day she would bring them all to America, but for that she would have to begin work and send money back home. To get a decent job, she needed to continue her education, complete *Gymnasium* and teacher's training, and become a teacher. But meanwhile, no one mentioned work, and she was going to try to see as much as she could of her new city, snow and all!

Finding Work

During her second week in America, Uncle Joe explained to Freida Sima that she would soon have to support herself. Adolescence was a foreign concept among the immigrants, as it was in the society that they had left back in Europe. It was a time of work, responsibility and cooperation, with special responsibility often falling on the shoulders of older daughters.[69] As her childhood accomplishments of bareback horse-riding, milking cows and climbing trees were of little help in finding a job, her best option was to find employment as a domestic, just as many girls had done during their first years in America. A second possibility would have been to work in a factory, but without a working knowledge of English that was a big more difficult. Furthermore, factory work in those days was a six-day-a-week job, and she would have had to work on Saturday, making it impossible for her to remain *Shomer Shabbos*. Finally, work as a domestic provided her with a place to live, and it was already somewhat crowded at her *Tante* Mollie's home, with *Tante* Mollie, Uncle Srul Nachman, his two children, her Aunt Sadie and her Uncle Joe all living in the small apartment.

Within days, her family found her a place as a live-in nanny for a traditional Eastern European Jewish family with several children, living in Harlem, whose father was a pocketbook manufacturer. For the princely sum of three dollars a week she would sleep on a folding cot in the kitchen, take her meals with the family, be responsible for the children, clean the house, and be given off Sunday afternoons to see her family.

At the time that Freida Sima came to America, Harlem, which would later become an African-American residential, cultural and business center and neighborhood, was still very Jewish. In spite of its tenements and pre-1900 brownstone flats, Harlem had become a safety valve for the over-crowded Lower East Side, attractive to immigrants seeking to improve their living conditions. The development of mass transit was making it more accessible, and Jewish families with means had been moving there since the turn of the century. When Freida Sima moved to Harlem, it was the second major center of Jewish life in Manhattan after the Lower East Side, and by the end of the First World War, it would boast a Jewish population of over 178,000. In 1911, when she began work for the manufacturer's family, Harlem was already a center of Jewish religious organizations, educational institutions, and *landsmanschaften,* the social, mutual aid or burial societies created by Jews from the same European town or region.[70]

---

69   Elizabeth Ewen, *Immigrant Women in the Land of Dollars: Life and Culture on the Lower East Side 1890–1925,* New York: Monthly Review Press, 1985: 99–101.

70   Jeffrey S. Gurock, *When Harlem was Jewish, 1870–1930,* New York: Columbia, 1979: 137–156. That population would decline rapidly in the postwar years when Jews would begin moving out to the suburbs, and the Harlem Jewish population would drop to

But what about Freida Sima's education? After all, that was what had brought her to America in the first place! For years in Europe she managed to continue learning through negotiations with her father, and had been allowed to attend *cheder* long beyond what was customary for girls in her hometown. And now she was in America! The country, where by 1910, women comprised over forty percent of the undergraduate student body.[71] For the first time, she found herself in a non-negotiable situation. Daytime school was out of the question and now even "night school" was impossible, as she had to care for the family toddler around the clock.

"Night School" was indeed the solution for many immigrants of that period who wished to learn English properly and further their education. Having begun as classes for farm or industry workers in various places in the United States in the 19th century, during the Great Wave of Immigration, "Night School" became the main educational framework for immigrant adolescents and adults. Utilizing existing school buildings, the classes given in the evening by the Board of Education, were often taught be teachers who knew the immigrants' native languages. In cities such as Baltimore there were night classes for immigrants that were offered within the Jewish community and not only in the public sector.

Not all immigrants took well to "Night School". There were those who were upset that instructors wasted time, and in the words of budding labor activist Rose Schneiderman, "seemed more interested in getting one-hundred-percent attendance than in giving one-hundred-percent instruction."[72] Other immigrants were offended by the assumption of idiocy that they felt had guided those preparing their textbooks, offering pictures of cats, tables, chairs and chickens with sentences like "the pretty black cat likes white milk", particularly as quite a number of young immigrants already spoke more than one language. Nevertheless, even those who disliked the format of the classes continued to attend them, as they were determined to learn as much English as possible, despite their criticism of the process.

123,000 by 1925, to 88,000 by 1927 and to 5,000 by 1930. On *landsmanschaften* see: Daniel Soyer, *Jewish Immigrant Associations and American Identity in New York 1880–1939*, Detroit: Wayne State University Press, 2002.

71 Gerda Lerner, *The Creation of Feminist Consciousness from the Middle Ages to Eighteen-seventy*, New York and Oxford: Oxford UP, 1993: 44.

72 Quoted in: Melissa R. Klapper, *Jewish Girls Coming of Age in America 1860–1920*, New York: NYU Press, 2005: 126–127.

"Night Schools" were also frameworks for indoctrinating immigrants with American values. In Leo Rosten's fictional account of Eastern European Jewish immigrant Hyman Kaplan trying to learn English in such a school, there are many examples of his chafing at the rules while his teacher, Mr. Parkhill, attempts to correct not only his English but his behavior.[73]

Freida Sima did not give up easily. Realizing that as a nanny her educational options were limited, she made a tactical decision. "First, I'll learn to speak English from the children", she told herself, especially from the older ones who already attended school. Once she had a decent command of the language she could reevaluate her employment options and begin to fulfill her dream.

The first part of her plan was easy to implement. She developed a natural rapport with her young charges who were happy to speak English with her and not Yiddish, as they did with their parents. Within a few weeks she spoke a halting but unaccented English and within a few months, other than a slight inflection, she could pass as a native speaker. She learned to read English from the children's schoolbooks and within a year understood newspaper headlines. She was a natural autodidact. On her visits to her aunts and uncles, she realized that she spoke English better than they did, even though some had been in America for years. Luckier than some of the women who Sydney Stahl Weinberg describes in her book about the lives of Jewish immigrant women, her long working day had not been detrimental to her learning English but just the opposite.[74] Caring full-time for schoolage children enabled her to be immersed in the language almost naturally.

She also decided to adopt the American name "Bertha", which her family subsequently pronounced "Boytee", as did their children. Freida Sima, Babaleh, and Babe were gone, and her citizenship papers would eventually mark her officially as Bertha. This was one of the first steps in her Americanization, which Elizabeth Ewen, in her book about immigrant women on the Lower East Side reminds us, is a deceptive term if taken literally, implying exchanging one nationality for another. In truth, it was both a political and cultural term, and one that described initiating people into an emerging industrial

73   Leonard Q. Ross (Leo Rosten), *The Education of H*Y*M*A*N K*A*P*L*A*N*, New York: Harcourt Brace, 1937.

74   Sydney Stahl Weinberg, *The World of Our Mothers: The Lives of Jewish Immigrant Women*, Chapel Hill and London: The University of North Carolina Press, 1988: 170.

and consumer society.[75] It was that society in which Freida Sima would ultimately function, to which she would contribute, and through which she would make a living.

Freida Sima was always curious to learn more about what was happening both in her closer surroundings and in the world at large. Long before she could understand the headlines in the paper, she would ask her employers about the news. Some things she heard about, even before she had to ask. Seven weeks after she reached New York, everyone was talking about the deadliest industrial disaster in the history of the city, the Triangle Shirwaist Factory Fire. On Saturday, March 25, 1911, 123 women and 23 men, mostly recent Jewish and Italian immigrants, lost their lives when a fire broke out in the three-floor factory in which they worked. The fire began in a scrap bin under one of the cutter's tables, spreading rapidly to the eighth, ninth and tenth floors of the building which housed the factory. Although each factory floor had several exits, few could be used to flee. Flames prevented a number of them from being used; most of the rest had been locked by the owners to prevent workers from taking breaks during the workday. As a result, the young men and women trapped in the building began jumping to their death from the windows of the burning floors.

The most poignant story being told was that of the young man who had appeared at one of the windows which the fire truck ladders, reaching only to the sixth floor, could not reach. Next to him on the window sill stood a young woman to whom he had offered a hand in assistance, as if he were helping her alight a high step. Turning to the young woman, the man kissed her and the two linked hands, jumping to their death.

The next day scores of victims were laid out at a makeshift morgue at Charities Pier off E. 26th street to be identified. Newspaper accounts said that over 100,000 people lined up to examine the bodies. The tragedy was so deeply felt, as was the trial of the factory's owners who had escaped by fleeing to the roof of the building, that it galvanized unions and officials to pass path-breaking laws protecting worker's rights and ensuring building safely.[76] "Some of those girls were only here as long as I am", thought Freida Sima when she heard about the tragedy, grateful for the fact that she was living with a Jewish family and not having to earn her living in a sweatshop or factory.

---

75   Elizabeth Ewen, *Immigrant Women in the Land of Dollars: Life and Culture on the Lower East Side 1890–1925*, New York: Monthly Review Press, 1985:1 6.

76   Joseph Berger, "City Room: Long Lost, Little Known", *The New York Times,* March 27, 2011.

As the year progressed, she continued to feel that way even more. Although the first part of her plan – to learn English – was going well, the second turned out to be much harder to implement than she could have imagined. Within a few months she was being treated as a member of the family where she worked, more like an older daughter than a nanny. She took all meals with them, was introduced to their friends, went on vacation with them, and became very attached to the children who reminded her of her younger brothers and sister. She didn't yet have enough skills to look for anything but the most menial job in the garment district where Aunt Sadie worked, that would leave evenings free for study.[77] Besides, if she worked in a factory she would have to pay for a furnished room and who knows whether she would earn enough to afford it. Now she had free room and board and of the three dollars a week she earned, one went for personal expenses or savings, one to pay Uncle Joe for her ticket and one was sent back to Europe. "Better I should let things stay as they are for a while longer", she thought, continuing to working on her reading skills.

And indeed she did. One of the first things she remembered reading about in an English language newspaper was the sinking of the luxury liner the RMS Titanic in April 1912, a year and two months after she had reached America. In one of the most deadly commercial maritime disasters in modern history, 1500 passengers and crew lost their lives when the British passenger liner collided with an iceberg during its maiden voyage from Southampton to New York. Apart from its first and second class passengers, the Titanic also had a steerage section that was being used for immigrant and lower class travel.

Like other ships of their line, the route the Titanic had taken began at Southampton, continued via Cherbourg, France, where it picked up additional passengers, mostly steerage class immigrants, then to southern Ireland for more passengers, and finally, from there to New York. Passengers from all travel classes lost their lives in the terrible accident but the highest percentage had been in steerage in which 54% of the women, 66% of the children, and 84% of the men had drowned. "I could have been one of them", thought Freida Sima, recalling her own voyage from Europe fourteen months earlier.

Only one ship, the RMS Carpathia, responded to the Titanic's distress signals and stopped to pick up 710 of its survivors from the lifeboats floating

---

77   Barbara A. Schreier, *Becoming American Women: Clothing and the Jewish Immigrant Experience, 1880–1920*, Chicago: Chicago Historical Society, 1994.

in the freezing water and bring them to New York. From the survivors' stories, the public also learned about those who did not survive, such as the sixty-seven-year-old Jewish businessman and Macy's co-owner Isidor Strauss and his wife, Ida. Ida Strauss had refused to leave her husband saying "As we have lived, so we will die, together". Although offered a place in a lifeboat with his wife, Isidor refused, saying that while there were still women and children aboard the ship, he, as a man, would not enter a lifeboat. Ida insisted that her personal maid save herself, giving her the fur coat she was wearing, and telling her "take this, you will need it, and I will have no need for it anymore". The couple held hands on deck as the ship went down. While Isidor's body was recovered, Ida's was not, and he was buried, first in Beth-El Cemetery in Brooklyn and later in the Strauss family mausoleum at Woodlawn Cemetery in the Bronx.

When the story of the Strauss family was known, Rabbis spoke to their congregations about Ida Strauss' sacrifice and articles in the Yiddish press extolled her courage. Like many of the Jewish women at that time, on the High Holidays that year when saying Yizkor for her little brother Mendel, who had died when Freida Sima was six, she also recited the special memorial prayer written in Yiddish for the souls of "Isidor ben Rabbi Eliezer and Ida bas Rabbi Natan, the loving couple who died hand in hand…the noble couple who lost their lives in the Titanic ship disaster".[78]

By the holiday season of 1912 Freida Sima already felt herself a veteran immigrant, and was slowly separating her life in America from what her family was going through in Europe. Long before the end of Nachman's five-year contract in the *Kresy,* his crew had completed chopping down the forest he had contracted for, and the family had returned to Mihowa ahead of schedule. The letter telling her that they were back in Mihowa also announced that a new baby had also been born that year – Tuleh (Naftali), the seventh boy in a row if one included little Mendel who had died. How was her mother coping with a new little one? And how was Marium at almost fifteen?

This Shabbos Bereishis would be Freida Sima's second birthday in America; she was already seventeen, quite a young lady. Last year, right before Shabbos Bereishis, her family, and especially Uncle Joe who already had an eye for her, had introduced her to the American custom of "sweet sixteen". For the first time in her life she received a birthday present, a

78   "*A Hazkoro fir Isidor und Ida Strauss*" ("A Memorial Prayer for Isidor and Ida Strauss"), *Shas Techina Rav Pninim,* New York: Hebrew Publishing Company, 1916: 257–258.

beautiful miniature manicure set in a turquoise fabric-covered case which her aunts and uncles had bought her for the occasion. From then on, turquoise became her favorite color and she always insisted on doing her nails to perfection. Sixty-four years later, she would bequeath that same manicure set to me on my sixteenth birthday, and long before that, the same love of anything turquoise.

Freida Sima realized that she was lucky that she was working for employers who became part of her extended family, and that she had so much family in New York in the first place. More than one teenage immigrant girl coming to the United States alone at that time, and without family to envelop her, or a domestic working environment that acted as a quasi-family ballast, found herself facing poverty or even ended up "on the street", either literally and figuratively. Jewish women's organizations in New York City, Sisterhoods of Personal Service, and other Jewish organizations of the time, were aware of the problem, and devoted their charitable work to ameliorating the plight of Jewish immigrant women and children, creating social clubs and culture classes for young women employed during the day, in order to "keep them out of trouble" at night.[79] Luckily, Freida Sima was not in need of their services, having uncles, aunts, and cousins nearby, and most of all, by working in domestic service for a family that became "her family". Not all immigrant girls of her age were as fortunate.

Soon it was 1914. By this time Freida Sima had been in America for three years and could read a book in English. As time passed she became a voracious reader, frequenting the public library several times a week. Deep in her heart she was certain that she would go back to school to become a teacher, and for that reason, even at eighteen she refused to consider marriage. "There was a time everyone wanted me to marry Uncle Joe", she recalled. "After all, we were close in age and so many of our family had married relatives". But she announced that marriage was not yet on her agenda, and Joe went back to Europe, married his sister-in-law's niece, Rivka, and brought her back to America in late 1913. Instead of coming back to New York, though, Joe and

---

79   Felicia Herman, "From Priestess to Hostess: Sisterhoods of Personal Service in New York City, 1887–1936" in: Pamela S. Nadell and Jonathan D. Sarna, eds. *Women and American Judaism: Historical Perspectives,* Hanover and London: Brandeis University Press, 2001: 148–181. See also: Mary Odem, *Delinquent Daughters: Protecting and Policing Adolescent Female Sexuality in the United States 1885–1920,* Chapel Hill: University of North Carolina Press, 1995; Ruth M. Alexander, *The "Girl Problem": Female Sexual Delinquency in New York, 1900–1930,* Ithaca: Cornell University Press, 1995.

Rivka went to live in Philadelphia where he thought he could better himself economically, the first of the Scharfs to leave the greater metropolitan area. Freida Sima had been very close to her uncle and missed him greatly, and she prayed daily that one day the couple would return to New York.

By mid-1914 Freida Sima felt it was time to implement part B of her plan and try to continue her education. She spoke English pretty fluently, although she still read much slower than she would have liked. She was still young enough at eighteen to want to go to school and figured she could make up her high school education within two or three years at night school. Most of all, she already began to look American, having used a dollar here and there from her salary to buy herself American-made clothing in order not to be branded as a "greenhorn".

But just as she began thinking of looking for another job, Archduke Ferdinand was assassinated in Sarajevo. Six weeks later, in August 1914, war broke out and all contact with Eastern Europe was severed. What was happening to the family in Mihowa? Like everyone, Freida Sima followed the news and her nights were sleepless with worry about her parents and siblings. "I got so thin with worry that a doctor even prescribed a special tonic to give me appetite", she recalled. A picture taken of her at that time shows a pale young girl with long hair and a tiny waist, leaning against a tree, so different than her usual ample figure.

Freida Sima's fears for her family in Europe during the war were typical of what was happening to an entire generation of young Jewish immigrants from Eastern Europe in the United States during those years. This was the first time that they were cut off from contact with their parents, siblings, uncles and aunts for any period of time, other than when they were enroute to America. It was also a maturation process for these immigrants who would experience their first period of independence, not only from their Eastern European families, but from Eastern European norms and criticisms that they heard in correspondence with their families. It was a harbinger of what all of American Jewry would go through during the Second World War, when the American Jewish community realized that it would have to take up the reins of world Jewish leadership which in various spheres, such as religion or Zionism, had been held by its European brethren until the war.

Apart from Freida Sima, Mollie, Joe, Sadie, Fischel Hirsch, Marium Raisel and Leib Handel, there was an additional family member in America frantically worrying about the family in Europe. Three months after Freida Sima had come to America, another one of Devorah's younger brothers –

Moshe Leib – had joined the Scharf-Enzenberg clan in New York, working first as a waiter and later as a tailor. Unlike Devorah's other siblings who had immigrated as singles, Moshe Leib was already married and had left his wife Hudel, and their three small children, Meir, Avrum and Minna, back in Europe, planning to send for them as soon as he had the necessary funds. The war, however, intervened before he could do so. Now he was stuck on one side of the Atlantic while they were only heaven knows where in Europe.

That was also Freida Sima's greatest worry at the time, not knowing where her parents and siblings were. She had read the news reports about the Bukovina becoming a battlefield between Austrian and Russian troops, and the Russian occupation of the area. She knew that her family had returned from the *Kresy* long before the war's outbreak, but had no idea whether they had to flee Mihowa because of the battles and if so, to where. She had heard stories of Jews from Galicia escaping the advancing Russian forces by fleeing to Austria and even to Germany, but could not guess what direction her family would take if they had to leave their home. Only at the war's end would she find out that the entire family had fled for several years to Poland via Slovakia, their train tickets having been paid for by the Austrian government.

It was from this story that Freida Sima would also learn that the winds of change had reached Mihowa long before the war. Although they were still quite devout, by that time, none of the younger married women in Mihowa were covering their hair, Devorah being an exception to the rule. When they passed through Slovakia, the very devout local Jewish women, seeing the bareheaded Mihowa women, declared that the community must have had to flee from disaster because the religious husbands had allowed their womenfolk to go around with uncovered hair.[80]

Freida Sima's aunts in America also appeared to have adopted the same custom. Despite her deep devotion to her religious beliefs, and the fact that her husband was a *melamed*, a teacher of religious studies who not only always wore a yarmulkeh but also a hat above it, *Tante* Mollie did not cover her hair after she married. Neither did *Tante* Rivka, Uncle Joe's wife. And when Sadie would marry Sam (Solomon) Korn in 1917, she, too would not cover her hair. Devorah, as the oldest sibling, still belonged to a different generation, and would continue covering her hair with a marriage wig. But none of the younger generation would follow this tradition, which would

---

80   Author's telephone interview with Muriel Arens, 12 November 2015.

only be revived a generation later among some of Devorah's grandchildren and great-grandchildren.

These winds of change had long been the norm among American Jews, including devout women. In the 1975 film "Hester Street", based on Yiddish author and newspaper editor Abraham Cahan's novel, *Yekl: A Tale of the New York Ghetto,*[81] there is a poignant scene where Gitl, a young devout married Jewish immigrant from Eastern Europe, is told by her American Jewish immigrant neighbor that she should take off her head covering, as Jewish women in America don't wear them anymore. "When you get older there will be enough time for the *petsch*", she tells her, and the young immigrant then learns to style her hair in a sweeping updo with a knot, covered by an elegant hat, the most common hairstyle among young women in New York at the turn of the century.[82]

At that time, marriage was the last thing on Freida Sima's mind. She was still working round-the-clock most days as a nanny, but the children were already getting older, needing less care during the school day, and allowing her a free morning here and there, which her employers encouraged her to spend with her *Tante* Mollie who lived nearby and ran a chicken market. Coming from Europe, the mother of the family where she was employed fully understood her worries, and encouraged her to spend time with her family for her own peace of mind.

As 1916 dawned, Freida Sima realized that she was soon celebrating her fifth anniversary of reaching the United States. "Incredible how much my life has changed!" she mused, only realizing a moment later that she was already thinking half in Yiddish and half in English. The major memory she would retain of that spring would not be the stories she read of the German zeppelins bombing Paris or the American hunt for Mexican Revolutionary general Pancho Villa, but of the funeral of the famous Jewish author Sholem Aleichem, who died of tuberculosis and diabetes at age 57. During his funeral in May 1916, over 100,000 mourners lined the streets of Second Avenue, East Houston, Eldridge and Canal Streets on New York's Lower East Side, paying their respects to the world-renowned figure. One of them was Freida Sima. Her future husband was also in the crowd lining the streets, but it would be more than a decade before the two would meet, exchanging at their first encounter memories of that momentous day.

81   Abraham Cahan, *Yekl: A Tale of the New York Ghetto,* New York: D. Appleton and Company, 1896.

82   Hester Street, directed by Joan Micklin Silver, 1975.

As the High Holidays of 1916 approached, Freida Sima was about to turn twenty-one, had been in America for over five years, and could now apply for citizenship. Although going to America had been one of her greatest desires, the situation in Europe was constantly on her mind. In view of her concerns, she decided to postpone the great moment of naturalization until the war was over and she could fully appreciate it. After all, she wasn't about to travel to Europe, didn't need a passport, and wasn't afraid of being deported. Becoming an American citizen could wait.

In spite of birthday celebrations not being an Eastern European Jewish tradition, her family in America nevertheless decided to mark her birthday that year in a special way that would emphasize the seriousness of the age she had reached. Right before Rosh Hashanah, in anticipation of her twenty-first birthday, her *Tante* Mollie gave her a woman's *Techina,* a woman's book of Yiddish prayers, written in the first person, just published before the holidays in New York, the *Shas Techina Rav Pninim.*[83]

The *Techina,* along with the *Tzena-u're'ena* (colloquially called the *Tzena-rena* by most), were the two educational and devotional works in the vernacular that had pervaded the lives of Ashkenazi Jewish women since the seventeenth century.[84] The Yiddish versions of the *Techina,* first as pamphlets and later as books, were printed in Eastern Europe from the seventeenth century onward, and when Freida Sima received hers, were being printed as books throughout Eastern Europe, in Krakow, Vilna, Lemberg, Budapest and other places. Although a number of Jewish women's devotional books had been printed in the United States from the mid 19th century onward, usually in German or English, the book that Freida Sima's aunt presented her with in honor of her birthday, appears to have been the one of the first two Yiddish *Techinas* printed in the United States, both in 1916. Based on the original *Shas Techina* (*Shas* bearing the numerical value of 360), published by Lewin-Epstein publishers in Warasaw in 1905, the title meant "360 Supplications, Many Pearls". While most of the prayers in the book had been composed by men, a number of them had ostensibly been authored by women.[85]

---

83   *Shas Techina Rav Pninim,* New York: Hebrew Publishing Company, 1916.

84   Chava Weissler, *Voices of the Matriarchs: Listening to the Prayers of Early Modern Jewish Women,* Boston: Beacon Press, 1998; Rivka Zacutinsky, *Techinas: A Voice from the Heart,* New York: Aura Press, 1992.

85   Macy Nullman, "Prayer and Education in the Life of Jewish Women", *Journal of Jewish Music and Liturgy* 19 (1997): 31–41.

The prayers in Freida Sima's *Techina* reflected the time and place where it had been published. In addition to the traditional prayers found in a *Techina,* it contained a number of newly authored prayers that were indicative of the Jewish geographic shift to America and its consequences, of major world events of that period, and of the Great War's impact. Among them: "A new *Techina* before candle lighting written especially for Jewish women in America", whose husband and children, working to support the family, were unable to keep Shabbos; "A memorial prayer for those killed by fire" in memory of the immigrants killed in the Triangle Shirtwaist Fire in 1911; "A memorial prayer for those (immigrants) drowned at sea" in memory of those killed on the Titanic; "A special memorial prayer for Isidor and Ida Strauss", who had drowned on the Titanic, as we saw above; "A new *Techina* for those who have children or relatives in the war"; and "A new *Techina* for those in America who heard bad tidings from the *Alter Heim",* ("Old Country"). Other prayers, common in the European versions of the *Techina* were either missing in Freida Sima's American edition, or marginalized to a single short devotion, particularly those having to do with marital laws, childbirth, or events in children's lives such as their beginning their religious studies or marriage. That, too, was an indication of the differences between European and American-Jewish life during the first decades of the twentieth century.[86]

During the next twelve months, Freida Sima shed many a tear over her new dark-blue bound *Techina,* particularly on the pages of the prayer for those with relatives in the war. The hostilities were deep into their third year, and she had not heard a word from her parents or siblings for close to thirty-six months. Hopes of a swift end to the war grew in the spring of 1917 with America's entry into the conflict, and again at the end of the year when Russia withdrew from the hostilities. However the war continued.

Like many immigrants from Austro-Hungary, Freida Sima was in a dilemma. Other than for the safely of her family, of course, which side was she supposed to pray for? Doing a swift calculation, she realized that there was a chance that her brother Avrum who was now eighteen, was fighting for Austro-Hungary. She, however, was living in America and should obviously pray for the soldiers of her new homeland. She solved the dilemma by directing her prayers towards the Almighty, beseeching him to end the

---

86 This topic is further developed in a separate study which I have undertaken: "My Grandmother's *Techina*: Immigrant Jewish Women's Lives, Identities, and Prayers in Early Twentieth Century America".

war as soon as possible and keep her family safe. As for who would win the war? That she left up to him.

Freida Sima's relationship with the Almighty was undergoing somewhat of a transition during the war years. Her belief remained strong, as it would until the end of her life, but after more than five years in New York, she was first beinning to sense the influence of the secularization that was pervading much of Jewish life in America. One night, for the first time in her life, she fell asleep without saying *Kriyas Shma*, the nighttime *Shma* prayer one says before going to sleep. "When I woke up in the morning and I wasn't dead, I realized that a lot of what I had been taught in Europe might not be exactly as I had been taught", she recalled years later. The incident made a great impression on her, causing her to reexamine her beliefs and actions. "At the end I decided to keep on doing just what I had been doing until then, but it made me realize that many of the explanations I had been given were either superstition or *narishkeit* (nonsense)."

Narishkeit or not, early teachings run deep. Years later, when it came to childraising, she would suddenly find herself giving her daughter, and later her granddaughter, those same explanations for religious actions: "If you go to sleep without saying *Krishma* (the Yiddish pronunciation of *Kriyas Shma*) you won't wake up; if you go into the water on Tisha Be'av (the Fast of the ninth of Av) you will drown." "Do you really believe that Baba?" I once asked her, to which she responded without missing a beat: "Do you really want to risk it?!"

Freida Sima was also at a professional crossroads. By the middle of the war, the children she cared for had grown up, and their father suggested she come and work in his pocketbook factory, thus staying in the family, so to speak. Freida Sima agreed, and for the first time since coming to America found herself working on a "sweatshop" factory floor with other young Jewish immigrant men and women, manufacturing handbags for seven dollars a week. Unlike small-scale manufacturing immigrants who had set up a "shop" in their tenement apartment, and employed a few even "greener" immigrants in addition to their family members, this was a real factory, employing dozens of men and women in a larger space and with better conditions.

Working in the factory was very different than living and working with a family, and Freida Sima soon made friends among the young women with whom she would spend her lunchtime break. Many of them were in the same situation as she was, alone in America with families in Europe from whom they hadn't heard in years. They understood her situation and could commiserate with her. Although they all had spoken Yiddish at home, by now many of them were speaking English to one another at work, a sign of how long they had already been in their adopted country. She was also very lucky that in a generation whose employment experiences were often characterized by corruption and exploitation, she rarely came across those phenomena, possibly because she was considered by the shop owner as being almost "family".

Now she finally had free evenings to study "but I was so worried about the family in Europe that I had no head for night school", she recalled sadly. Fearing they would be her only family left, she spent almost every evening with her aunts, uncles and young cousins before returning to the furnished room she was now renting on 112th street in Harlem right near her *Tante* Mollie, Uncle Srul Nachman and their family. Uncle Joe and *Tante* Rivka had finally moved back from Philadelphia and they, too, rented an apartment on 112th street in Harlem, in order to be down the block from the rest of the family. Freida Sima was not only lucky to have family around at this time, but during all the years that she rented a furnished room, she never experienced the hardships of other immigrants who grappled with exploiting landlords, refusing to provided their tenants with decent living conditions. Immigrant writer Anzia Yezierska's stories that describe landlords who were "worse than pawnbrokers", continuously raised the rent, or evicted tenants, were a far cry from Freida Sima's personal experiences, and she was grateful for not having to deal with such issues, particularly as a young woman living alone.[87]

In November 1918, the war finally came to an end. For over four years Freida Sima had heard nothing from her family Europe. She had already been self-supporting before the war, but during those years she became an adult, making decisions without consulting with her parents, even by letter. True, she had her aunts and uncles with whom she was very close, especially *Tante* Mollie and Uncle Srul Nachman who were much older than she and acted as substitute parents, but she had indeed become independent.

Not only had Freida Sima become independent, but so had the entire last wave of Jewish immigrants who had become part of American Jewry. For close to three and a half decades before the outbreak of the First World War, the American Jewish community had absorbed a continuous stream of immigrants from Eastern Europe. As each group of new immigrants began

---

87   Anzia Yezierska, *Breadgivers,* Garden City, N.Y.: Doubleday, Page, and Co., 1925.

to internalize the American way of life, it was replaced by a newer group of immigrants, still tied to European traditions, who had to be taught what it meant to live in America. Consequently, there was an unbroken link of immigrants from Europe which continued to impact on its members living in the United States.

In early 1919 the American-Jewish community as a whole had not been diluted by immigration for almost half a decade. The total halt of immigration from Europe for close to four and a half years meant that by the end of the war, the last group of immigrants had long become Americanized. The total severance of communication with Europe began a maturation process within the American-Jewish community in general and the Eastern European immigrants in particular, who now had to look inward and not outward for answers, and in various matters would no longer take its cues from "home". It was therefore not surprising that during and after this period, the Eastern European Jewish immigrant community began to produce its own leaders and initiate or participate in the creation of various national organizations such as the American Union of Roumanian Jews (1916) or the Red Mogen David of America (1918).

Because there had been no communication with Europe during the war, Freida Sima had also been unable to send money back to her family for several years, and instead, she had amassed her first savings of close to $200, a significant sum for a young immigrant woman. Her ticket to America in 1911 had cost $30.[88] With part of those savings she would now be able to send money for Marium's and maybe even for Avrum's tickets. First, however, she had yet to hear from her family.

In early 1919 she received her first letter from "home" saying that the family was alive and well and that she had a new sister, Sheindl, who had been born in late 1915, a girl after seven boys. The letter also told what her family had been through during the war, running away to Poland and living *"auf der flucht"* ("in flight"), in her mother's words, for months at a time. They had also suffered a loss during the war: Baba Malka, the grandmother who had raised her, had passed away in 1916 while the family had been in Poland.

Her uncles and aunts in America – Mollie, Sadie, Joe and Moshe Leib – received the same news and now sat *shiva* together for the requisite hour that one sits when learning of a first-degree relative's death more than thirty days

---

88   Brandon DuPont, Drew Keeling, Thomas Weiss, Passengers Fare for Overseas Travel in the 19th and 20th Century, Paper presented for the Annual Meeting of the Economic History Association, Vancouver BC Canada, Sept. 21–23, 2012.

after it occurred. Freida Sima shed tears with them over her beloved grand-mother, but was incredibly relieved that her parents, brothers and sisters were alive and well. Towards the end of the war, Avrum had indeed served for a short time in the Austrian army, as she had feared, but his only wound was from a kick in the head by a horse, whose shoe he was trying to change. As Marium did not want to leave the family in Mihowa, a decision that would have dire consequences for her later, Avrum would be the next of her sib-lings that she would now bring to America. As soon as she could, she sent the family the cost of his ticket so that he could make the trip.

In August 1919 Avrum, his cousin Nathan Enzenberg, son of Nach-man's brother Meier Moshe, and a friend, Nathan Rosenberg, left Mihowa on their way to America. Being adventurous unattached young men in their early twenties, they figured this was their last opportunity to see the Continent before they left Europe forever, and decided to travel for several months to "take in the sights", ending up in Paris towards the end of the year. The three arrived in New York City on January 6, 1920, and passed through Ellis Island, just as Freida Sima had done nine years earlier. This time, though, the short stay at Ellis Island would have a long-term impact on the entire American family. Having noted Avrum's name, the Ellis Island immigration official suggested that Eisenberg would be easier to spell in English than Enzenberg. Avrum agreed, and from then on, all members of the American branch of the family adopted the new name.

This, at least, was the story that "our" branch of the Scharf-Eisenberg family always told about the name change. However historical documents tell a slightly different story. In December 1916, a bit more than three years before Avrum came to America, his first cousin Ethel, one of Meier Moshe's daughters, married Joe Samet. The beautifully calligraphed bi-lingual (English-Yiddish) wedding invitation states that "M.M. Eisenberg and Mr. A. Samet request the honor of your presence at the marriage ceremony of their children Ethel to Mr. Joe Samet".[89] It appears that the peripatetic Meier Moshe was not actually in America at the time, but ob-viously some of the Enzenbergs in America were already using the name Eisenberg by the end of 1916.

The joy that Freida Sima felt seeing her brother after close to a decade was indescribable. She had last seen him as a boy of eleven, and now he was

---

89   From the collection of Bob Friedman. Author's correspondence with Bob Friedman, Feb. 9, 2016.

a grown up man of twenty! From him she got first-hand news about the family in Europe, stories about her parents, and descriptions of the little brother and sister whom she had never met. He also told her a tale that left her speechless. Shortly after the war's end, Avrum had found work and saved up enough money to give his father a present before he had left for America: a deed to a parcel of land in the Wiznitz district of the Bukovina, not far from Mihowa. To his surprise, Nachman vehemently refused the present, seemingly upset that he son was trying to provide him with a livelihood.

"So why did the *Tateh* have no problem taking money from me?" she mused. Could it have been because he didn't have to take the money directly, as it came in an envelope from overseas? Would he have reacted like he did to Avrum's gift, had she presented it to him face-to-face? Yet throughout Eastern Europe, the continuing survival of many Jewish communities, small or large, often depending on receiving assistance from the United States. That constant flow of assistance caused the Jewish immigrants to be depicted in the popular American press as being miserly hoarders, refusing to part with their hard-earned wages for any reason other than rent, and the most basic of foodstuffs, something that was anathema in a consumer society based on spending money on consumer goods.[90] But in truth, that image was the result of their saving their money to send back to Europe to their familes, and to pay for membership in lodges and mutual benefit societies which would take care of the sick and also function as burial societies.

In the long run, however, she realized that her father's reaction was of no matter. The money she would be sending in the near future would not be used for the family's income, but rather to bring the rest of her siblings to America. The story did, however, bring home to her how much the roles in their family had reversed since she moved to America. She was the one sending home money for Marium's *nadan*, her dowry, while at the same time being expected to raise money for her own dowry and future. Bearing that in mind, she realized that the time had finally come to achieve the dream she had when she left Europe. Her mind was at ease regarding her role in bringing over her European family, but was she too old at twenty-three to finally begin her formal American education?

Ultimately, age was less of a problem than mindset. During the war, family issues had supplanted education as my grandmother's main concern.

---

90   This echoed descriptions of the Jews in Jacob Riis's study, *How the Other Half Lives*, previously cited.

As much as she had wanted an education, she first wanted to bring her siblings and possibly even her parents, to America. "Who could think about studying? At night I would bring home piecework from the factory to make extra money to save up and to eventually send to Europe for tickets". Even after Avrum, now called Abie, came to America, she continued with her plan, and in 1923, the two of them brought over the next brother in line – nineteen-year-old Benzion. The Scharf-Eisenberg family was growing by leaps and bounds. Shortly before Benzion's arrival, their uncle Moshe Leib had also finally brought over his family from whom he had been separated throughout the war. In early 1922, his wife Hudel and their three children arrived in New York.

Both Abie and Benny rapidly settled into American life, Abie becoming a salesman on the Lower East Side, Benny a dental mechanic making false teeth and later a butcher, jobs where one could remain *shomer Shabbos*. Freida Sima, specializing in popular beaded handbags, was appointed factory forelady and now earned eleven dollars a week. Thrilled to be reunited, she and her brothers formed a close family unit, and together they began sending money back to Europe to bring over additional family members. Freida Sima realized her dreams of an American education had slipped away. "Abie managed to go to night school", my grandmother sighed, "but for me it was already too late". But not too late to continue learning outside of the classroom, any way she could, something she continued to do for the rest of her life.

Abie had indeed managed to attend night school, as would two more of Freida Sima's brothers who would come to America after the Second World War. In light of that fact, was her decision to abandon the dream of a formal education actually a result of the war, or was it, in truth, a product of class and gender? Did she somewhere internalize the fact that after marriage she would not be working in any case, and therefore, as she got older, it became less important for her to complete formal schooling and get a degree?

Education, as Susan Tananbaum reminds us, provides cultural capital and is a crucial marker of class. Middle class Jewish families in America took girls' education for granted long before it became possible for the working class.[91] Among young Jewish immigrants in America, education had two goals: acculturation, and a greater opportunity to earn a livelihood,

---

91 Susan Tananbaum, review of *Jewish Girls Coming of Age in America, 1860–1920*, (review no. 612) <http://www.history.ac.uk/reviews/review/612>, retrieved Jan. 4, 2016.

as education was the key to numerous professions. Although working class girls and young women often found it harder to acculturate than those of the middle class, Freida Sima had succeeded by learning from her broader surroundings, reading voraciously, and absorbing American culture by alternative and non-traditional means. She was not afraid that education would estrange her from her American family as she was not looking to become "American", but rather "American-Jewish", something that they could understand and appreciate.

As for earning a livelihood, immigrant girls and women of that time had increasingly internalized a middle class gendered ideology separating "work" and "home". Although they had to support themselves while single, that was hopefully considered to be a temporary state. After marriage, most of them fully expected to remain at home to care for their husband and children, and Freida Sima was no exception. At fifteen she could dream of becoming a teacher, but by the time the war was over, she was twenty-three, and she knew it could only be a temporary profession as the "marriage bars", which would remain in place until 1941, prohibited women in America to teach after marrying. By the time her two brothers had come to America she was twenty-eight, fluent in English, no longer in need of an acculturating framework, and quite ready to marry and stop working. In addition to postponing her education in order to reunite her family, it appears that class and gender expectations also played a role in Freida Sima's never completing her formal education.

They did not, however, prevent her from taking other steps to strengthen her position in America. One was to finally apply for American citizenship. She had brought her brother Benny to New York earlier that year, was already twenty-seven years old and wanted an official document that would tie her to her adopted country. On Thursday July 12, 1923 she proudly received a Certificate of Naturalization, number 1944241, from the New York Southern District Court, listing her as the new American citizen Bertha Eisenberg, formerly a citizen of Austria-Rumania, five foot four, with white skin, dark complexion, brown eyes, brown hair, and not married. At the time she spoke English with an American accent, read fluently and could certainly pass as American born. The only remaining vestige of her lack of formal English language education that would remain with her for the rest of her life would be her spelling which was mostly phonetical, as she never had the opportunity to write at length in English.

Now it was time for the three Eisenberg siblings to build their lives in America. Benny was still too young for a match, but Abie had already set eyes on his teenage cousin Minnie, declaring she would one day be his bride. Traditionally, however, he knew he would have to wait for his older sister to marry first, and he began urging her to choose a husband from among the many suitors who had expressed an interest in her throughout the years. Thus, the courtship of Freida Sima began.

Chapter 4 The Courtship of Freida Sima – New York (1923–1928)

Introduction

There is an old custom dating from Biblical times, which later became an accepted Jewish norm that parents do not marry off a younger sister before the older one. In many families, both brothers and sisters had to wait for an older sister to marry before becoming betrothed. But what happens when the oldest sister, the first of ten children in a very traditional family, is still single at thirty-two? How long do you wait if you are next in line and have been unofficially engaged to your first cousin for almost six years? Or if you are the brother after that, afraid to be introduced to a young lady because even if she is "the one", you can't marry her yet? What do you tell your brothers if you are the sister in question? This was the situation Freida Sima found herself in at the beginning of 1928, seventeen years after immigrating to America.

Looking back, it was hard for Freida Sima to imagine how fast the previous decade had gone. As soon as the war was over, she had begun to bring her family over from Europe, first Abie, then Benny, and before long, all three were sending money to their parents in Mihowa to pay for tickets for the next two brothers, Srul, and Leibish. The money kept being sent, but surprisingly neither Srul nor Leibish arrived. Only then did Freida Sima find out that her father had been so devastated by his two oldest sons leaving for America, that he could not bear to think of losing any more children to the *Goldeneh Medineh,* the "Golden Country". Instead, he used that money to buy land and livestock, claiming that the boys were still too young to leave and meanwhile, the extra income would help the entire family.

Like many of the pre-war immigrants who had left family in Europe that they wanted to bring to America, Freida Sima's desire to bring the rest of her brothers to America as soon as possible took on a new urgency after 1924, in view of the Johnson-Reed Act introducing immigration restrictions that would some come into effect over the next four years. Since the end of the Great War the United States Congress had passed several immigration acts, each of which limited immigration in a different way. In 1917 the Literacy Act implemented a literacy test for immigrants over the age of sixteen who had to prove an ability to demonstrate basic reading comprehension in any language. In 1921 a first quota act was passed, and in 1922 it was renewed for another two years. Based on a three percent quota of foreign born Americans living in the United States in 1910, this initial act allowed in some 350,000 immigrants per year.

But all these were temporary measures. The Immigration act of 1924 limited the number of immigrants allowed into the United States through a national origins quota of all American inhabitants, not only those who were foreign born, providing immigration visas to only two percent of each nationality in the United States, living in America in 1890. Through the new act, immigration fell to a bit under 165,000 immigrants per year. Preference was given to certain relatives of US residents including parents and unmarried children under twenty-one, spouses aged twenty-one and over, and immigrants skilled in agriculture. Non quota status was given to wives and unmarried children under eighteen of US citizens, natives of Western Hemisphere countries, non-immigrants, and certain others.

In view of the new act that was about to be passed, Freida Sima, Abie and Benny realized that it was imperative to send money to bring over as many siblings as soon as possible. Knowing that if they sent any more money, their father would just use it for other purposes, they purchased a pre-paid ticket and sent it to Mihowa. But Nachman Enzenberg was adamant. No more children of his would be going to America. This time he cashed in the ticket, and once again used the money to buy more land for the family. His love of Mihowa farmland seems to have been an Enzenberg family trait. Each time his older brother Meier Moshe had accompanied yet another immigrating daughter to New York, he spent his time there trying to earn enough money to buy more farmland, which was, in his opinion, a major goal of the entire immigration enterprise.

Nachman may have loved his farm, but he loved his children more, and would do anything not to part from them, and certainly not to have them living across the ocean where he wouldn't be able to see them anymore. At that time, his decision was certainly made from his heart, based on what he, as patriarch, thought was best at the time for everyone involved. In his worst nightmares, he could not have dreamed that this decision would one day have more than economic consequences for his sons who remained in

Europe. In the mid-1920s, Adolph Hitler was almost unknown in the Bukovina. For those who followed European news in detail, he was a minor, ridiculous, and almost comic figure, who had staged an unsuccessful *putsch* in Munich earlier in the decade, and published a strange and not particularly popular book of anti-Semitic rants entitled "My Struggle", *Mein Kampf.*[92] Who could take him seriously?

Daily Life in the 1920s

Meanwhile, everyday life continued for Freida Sima and her American family, similar to the lives of hundreds of thousands of young Jewish immigrants who had come to America before the Great War. She continued to work and send money back to Europe, but as time went on she began to feel more and more Americanized, or at least "American-Jewish" in terms of her social and cultural frames of reference. So did her brothers. Each time another male family member came to America from Europe, *Tante* Mollie would ask her handsome young stepson Louis to show them around New York. His idea of giving them "a night on the town" was probably slightly different than hers, but his family and friends from Europe had no complaints whatsoever. While no one would ever give full details, years later some of them recalled their first nights out in America as being filled with "wine, women and song", maybe not what usually comes to mind when thinking about acclimatizing Jewish immigrants, but in truth, quite appropriate for young single men coming to a new country. As Louis was not a great drinker of alcohol it was more likely that he took them to a burlesque or Yiddish theater event. In current terms the evening was surely fairly tame, but it was certainly memorable for the newcomers.[93]

The Europe that these young Eastern European immigrants had left was changing during the 1920s, but so was the America that they had come to a decade or two earlier. By the mid-1920s immigrant girls and women, including those who had remained traditional like Freida Sima, had already

---

92   After a first-year run of almost 10,000 copies in 1925, sales of *Mein Kampf* remained low throughout the rest of the decade. Recently (2016) it has been re-issued in Germany with high sales.

93   Author's correspondence with Bernard Handel, Jan. 21, 2016.

adopted an American mode of dress. They still tended to borrow beautiful clothing in order to take pictures to send back to Europe, giving the mistaken impression of being more well-to-do than they actually were. But by that time, their daily mode of dress no longer shouted "immigrant", something which was detrimental to them in finding and maintaining employment and being considered a "success" among their peers.

Having come to America on her own, Freida Sima also did not face the dichotomy between traditional life, which immigrant parents often unsuccessfully demanded of their children, and the promises and demands of modernity. And coming to a big family in America, she also did not experience the sense of lack of community and support that the first immigrants felt being truly alone. Unlike what Elizabth Ewen describes in her study of women immigrants during the first decades of the twentieth century, Freida Sima's daily life was not a "theater of cultural conflict"[94] as she had no daily clashes with parents at home. On the contrary, most of her relatives were as Americanized as she was, in dress, in attitude, and in daily life.

Organized sports, which had been almost unknown among traditional Jews in late 19th and early 20th century Eastern Europe, were part of the American way of life, and immigrants and their children were rapidly swept up in the sports culture. Soon after Benny came to America, "the Yankee stadium", as it was commonly called, opened in the Bronx.[95] Never a sports fan, the event meant about as much to Freida Sima as Wembley Stadium opening a month later in England. But her young, American-born cousins couldn't stop talking about it, and she soon resigned herself to hearing long stories about the Yankees, the Red Sox, and Babe Ruth every time she came to visit, ultimately making her more familiar with American baseball practice and history that she ever thought she would be. "So tell me about the latest ball game", was her opening line to some of the boys in the family, at which point they would tell her stories of what would later be called "the house that Ruth built", and would once again lead her into the world of innings, fouls and home runs.

More important to her was that for the first time since coming to America thirteen years earlier, she was able to vote. Although women in New York State had gotten the right to vote in 1917, the 19th Amendment

---

94   Ewen, *Immigrant Women in the Land of Dollars*: 266.

95   Harvey Frommer, Bob Sheppard, *Remembering Yankee Stadium: An Oral and Narrative History of "The House that Babe Ruth Built"*, New York: Stewart, Tabori and Chang, 2008.

permitting all women in the United States to vote had only been passed four years earlier, and this was the second Presidential election in which all women who were American citizens could vote.[96] For an entire generation of immigrant women who had come to the United States before the First World War and were now citizens, these elections were a watershed event in their lives. Like hundreds of thousands of immigrant Jewish women, now that she was a citizen, Freida Sima participated in the 1924 American presidential elections, in which the incumbent President, Calvin Coolidge was voted in for a complete term after having succeeded the late president Warren G. Harding a year earlier.

At the end of November that year, she stood on the streets of New York with 250,000 people to watch the first Macy's Day Parade. Hundreds of the store's employees, many Eastern European immigrants like herself, marched to the flagship store on thirty-forth street in brilliant costumes, with floats, professional bands, and live animals borrowed from the Central Park Zoo. It was, indeed, a sight to see. Years later, when the parade was broadcast on television, she would watch it again with nostalgia, telling stories about how she had stood in the crowds that year, watching "the first parade ever", as she called it, which took place on Thanksgiving day in 1924.[97]

Like many of the immigrant relatives of the time, Freida Sima may have preferred to imbibe her culture from the Yiddish theater district on Second Avenue, but she also followed the films, performances, events and publications of a more general nature. The most popular activity of those years were the movies where the industry had found its first audience in the poor tenement districts of America's larger cities. By 1909 New York City already had over 340 movie houses with 250,000 people attending every week day and 500,000 on Sundays at five cents a ticket.[98]

During the mid-1920s Freida Sima noted the appearance of two new publications, Time Magazine and The New Yorker, mourned the deaths, three months apart, of the Italian-born screen heartthrob Rudolph Valentino,[99]

96 Corrine M. McConnaughy, *The Women's Suffrage Movement in America,* Cambridge: Cambridge University Press, 2013.

97 Stephen Madden, Robert Sullivan, Willard Scott, *America's Parade: A Celebration of Macy's Thanksgiving Parade,* Springfield MO: Life, 2001.

98 Ewen, *Immigrant Women in the Land of Dollars*: 216.

99 Emily W. Leider, *Dark Lover, the Life and Death of Rudolph Valentino,* New York: Farrar, Strauss, Giroux, 2003.

and Hungarian-Jewish stunt performer and escape artist Harry Houdini,[100] both from complications of appendicitis. A lifelong movie enthusiast, she applauded the first talking film, The Jazz Singer with Al Jolson, about the son of a cantor who defies his devout Jewish family to become an entertainer, but ultimately returns home to his traditions.[101]

Freida Sima also followed the political developments of those years. One was Vladimir Lenin's death and Josef Stalin's ultimate takeover as Secretary General of the Central Committee of the Communist Party of the Soviet Union. Another involved Benito Mussolini, the youngest Prime Minister in Italy's history, who was turning that country into a Fascist dictatorship. Then there were the German elections that made the Great War Hero Paul von Hindenburg's into the second President of the Weimar Republic, and the coronation of Hirohito Showa as Emperor of Japan.

Always interested in current affairs, she would avidly read the English and Yiddish papers to keep abreast of anything of interest. Since her steamship voyage to America in 1911, she was intrigued by everything having to do with transportation, and she avidly followed the rapidly developing automobile and airline industries: the Chrysler corporation founded in 1925, the first Pontiacs introduced by General Motors in 1926, and the new Model A Fords released in late 1927 and priced at $460. "That's almost a year's salary!" thought Freida Sima in amazement. "I guess I'll never own a car." Then there was the development of air travel, beginning with the two US army planes that completed the first round-the-world flight in 1924 that took 175 days, Charles Lindburg's 1927 Atlantic crossing,[102] and the creation of the first American airlines, such as Florida Airways, Western Air Express and Pan American World Airways. She was fascinated to hear about the first trans-Atlantic telephone call from New York to London in 1926. "If only I could call Mihowa and hear my mother's voice", she thought, while reading the news report of that momentous event.

Culture aside, the majority of the immigrant's waking hours were taken up by work. Many of the Eastern European immigrants arriving before the war had already been part of socialist movements in Europe and were naturally drawn to support the unions. Even those immigrants like Freida Sima, who had not been part of such movements while in Europe, found

100 William Kalush and Larry Sloman, The Secret Life of Houdini: The Making of America's First Superhero, New York: Atria Books, 2007.
101 Michael Freedland, Jolson: The Story of Al Jolson, New York: Virgin, 1995.
102 A. Scott Berg, Lindburgh, New York: Berkeley, 1999.

themselves working in sweatshops and factories when they arrived, and had become staunch supporters of the unions which promised them supervision of working conditions and limited working hours. But the 1920s were a period of prosperity and thus, they were also a period of decline for the American labor movement. The lack of leadership in the movement and anti-union sentiments among both employees and the government made it more difficult to organize strikes. On the local level however, factory employees, had already made great progress since the beginning of the century, and there was less of a necessity to fight for changes in conditions and working hours. The prosperity of the postwar decade had even made it possible for some of them to even move up the ranks in their place of work. One of them was Freida Sima.

By the mid-1920s, Freida Sima had thrown herself wholeheartedly into her work where she was an anomaly, an older self-supporting single woman who was interested in both the technical and the financial side of the business. Having previously worked for the factory's owner as his children's nanny, she was almost the equivalent of a family member and thus, felt a proprietorial interest in the business's success. But they both knew that it was a small factory, with no room for advancement. With her employer's blessings, she left to work for a friend of his who ran a larger handbag factory where she could develop her skills.

With the development of the "flapper costume" in the early 1920s[103], she was the one who suggested to her new employer that it would be profitable to begin manufacturing beaded bags on frames that women could use as both day and evening wear. Taking upon herself to develop an assembly line for those bags, she succeeded not only in finding a special niche for her factory, but also in creating an efficient and cost-effective method for their manufacture.

Soon after, she was promoted to factory forelady with a raise in salary that allowed her to save more for her future, even while sending more money back home. As forelady, however, she no longer worked on the assembly line, but kept her hand in the manufacturing side by specializing in sewing top of the line bags to their special frames. By now, she was also somewhat removed from the "girls" with whom she had been working on the factory floor, as it was harder to be friends with the workers that one was supposed to supervise.

---

103 Joshua Zeitz, *Flapper: A Madcap Story of Sex, Style, Celebrity and the Women Who Made America Modern*, New York: Broadway Books, 2007.

There were fewer opportunities to go out with them for entertainment after work, and even during the workday, she often ate her lunch alone or with the boss, instead of with the other girls.

The days when she and the other girls working on the factory floor would divide up the leftover fabric at the end of the day to take home for their own personal use were long gone, she thought, remembering a memorable summer years ago when she was new to the business. At the time, the factory had received a large shipment of what appeared to be very absorbent fabric, and with the foreman's blessing the girls took home the scraps for their own personal use. "This soft material will be great for 'those days'," she said to her girlfriends when the foreman had left the factory floor and the girls were on their own, as that was a topic that one never referred to in front of a man. Her workmates all nodded in agreement, filling bags of it to roll into absorbent pads to use for that purpose. What they didn't realize was that the dye in the fabric would cause them to break out in hives. Within weeks, most girls in the factory spent most of their time trying not to scratch their red, itching extremities. "Oh how we all laughed afterwards", Freida Sima remembered, "but it wasn't too funny while it was going on!"

With her promotion to forelady, and the changes in her social life, it was time for Freida Sima to concentrate on her future. Finally, after putting off suggestions for years, she now agreed to meet potential suitors. True, she had dated in the past, but her dates had just been casual acquaintances who, like her, had looked for companionship during the war, as they were alone in America. Now it was time for the "real thing". Having exhausted the list of eligible young men in the family, her uncles and aunts in New York did what was customary and turned to the local *shadchan*, the matchmaker, to find a suitable candidates for their niece. Thus, the courtship of Freida Sima began.

The *Shadchan*

"So what does she look like and what is she looking for?" asked the elderly *shadchan*, sitting across the kitchen table from my grandmother's married aunts. *Tante* Mollie, the older of the two, pulled out pictures of her niece, one by herself and another with her brothers. The *shadchan* took out his glasses, peering at the portrait of a serious looking young woman wearing wire-rimmed glasses, her brown hair pinned up behind her head, wearing an elegant black dress to her ankles, cinched by a beaded belt around her ample waist. "She has meat on her bones", remarked the *shadchan*, "our men like that". Moving to the next picture he saw a smiling figure in a flowing dress with a modern bobbed haircut, her brother Abie's hand resting on her shoulder. "Look at the beaded handbag she's carrying!" interjected Aunt Sadie, "she's a factory forelady and made that bag herself!" "Forget the bag", stated *Tante* Mollie. "Look at the necklace! The earrings! See how *fapitzt* (fancy) she is. That's what my Boytee always looks like; she takes such good care of herself."

Peering closer at the picture of "Boytee" – her American relatives' and friends' pronunciation of "Bertha", the *shadchan* nodded in agreement. "*A sheine maidel*" – a pretty girl – "so how old is she? Twenty? Twenty-two?" The aunts looked at each other and sighed. "Twenty-nine, but such a good catch! A forelady with a good salary…and she has savings too…" Looking at them quizzically as if to ask how such a good catch is still available, *Tante* Mollie jumped to her niece's defense. "She wouldn't consider marrying until she brought her brothers over. Now they are here and working so she can look. And she needs a traditional young man" she added in an aside, "not *chas veshulem* (Heaven forbid) a *freier*, (a freethinker)."

The *shadchan* placed the pictures face up on the kitchen table and took out his notebook. "This isn't going to be so easy", he began. "She isn't young and she needs a traditional man who makes a decent living. I assume she won't want to work after marriage." The aunts nodded vigorously in agreement. After all, what woman in their circle would want to keep working in a factory? Women were supposed to raise the children, take care of the housework and have supper on the table when their husbands came home. Packing up his notebook the *shadchan* put on his coat, promising to return soon with names of suitable young men for Freida Sima.

And indeed he did. The first on the list was a heavy-set immigrant from the Bukovina who worked as a *shochet*, a ritual slaughterer. "Oy the chicken-killer!" recalled my grandmother with mirth. "All he did was talk about chickens! How loud they were, how they hopped around without a head, how you had to be careful or the blood would get everywhere. Chicken parts, chicken feathers, chickens, chickens, chickens! At least make it interesting and tell me about a cow! But he only knew to talk about chickens!" After several dates, when the "chicken-killer" was about to propose, my grandmother beat a hasty retreat, remarking to her aunts that one day longer with him and she would have become a vegetarian.

The next candidate was an immigrant from Poland who worked in the garment district but dreamed of being an entrepreneur. "He was a nice young man, very ambitious", Freida Sima recalled. "We went out a few times and all of a sudden he started saying that after we get married I will continue to work for another seven years and that will give him enough money to open his own business." She shook her head in dismay. "To work another seven years in the factory, I didn't have to get married. So I gave him a polite 'no thank you' and that was that."

Then there was the young man who was wonderful, told her that he loved her and wanted to take her home to meet his mother. The problem, he said, was that his mother hated girls in glasses so he asked her to take off her glasses when they meet his mother. "So I told him that I really felt for him and maybe he should find another girlfriend as I wouldn't be able to find him in a room if I would take off my glasses," she replied.

The list of candidates went on and on but many were not what they presented themselves as being, particularly when it came to religious tradition. "Eventually I figured out a system", Freida Sima recalled. "On the second or third date we would walk by a silver store and I would point to a set of *lachter,* silver candlesticks in the window, saying we should have something like that when we get married. If the young man would say 'what for?' I knew he wasn't for me. What good Jewish boy wouldn't think his wife deserved nice *lachter* to *bench lecht* (light candles) on for Shabbos?!"

Other dates were just boring. Freida Sima was full of life and adventure and in her younger days had a wicked sense of humor. "There was one young man who was sweet but boring. Sweet like sugar and sticky like honey. You couldn't get rid of him. And much too proper. He wouldn't even call me by my first name. Miss Eisenberg this, Miss Eisenberg that. My girlfriend from the factory had the same problem with her young man. So we went on a double date and at the train station, we told them that we needed to use the ladies room for a minute. As soon as the front door closed we climbed out the back window and took the first train in another direction!" For years after hearing that story I imagined an earnest young man standing outside the subway station's ladies room door for hours, asking each woman entering if she could check if a Miss Eisenberg inside was all right.

The list of suitors for Freida Sima went on and on, but the months passed with no progress in sight. Some candidates were unsuitable but others were handsome, traditional, hard-working young men who for one reason or another she rejected as marriage partners. When pressed by her aunts for an explanation, all she could say was that they "weren't right" and that when her *bashert*, her destined one, would come along, she would know it straight off. "By the time this one finds her *bashert Moshiach* (the Messiah) will have come and gone", sighed *Tante* Mollie in despair.

Why indeed did my grandmother remain single for so long? Why did she reject all her potential suitors? When I asked, she would answer with stories about the dating world of the 1920s. How she and her girlfriends would go to the *shvitz*, the public baths, and the sauna, in order to sweat off a few pounds. How they would then take Epsom salts before dates to lose weight and fit into their fancy dresses, bought years earlier when they were slimmer. How they wouldn't even drink even a glass of water during the date so as not to burst their seams. How she preferred adventures with her brothers and cousins to those with her suitors, as with family she could be herself, rather than always being on her best behavior. The more things change, the more they remain the same, I thought, comparing it to the world I knew decades later. But even so, there was always a part of the story that was missing, one I discovered only after meeting Lilly.

Coming home from school one day I found a middle aged brunette with apple cheeks and a beaming smile sitting at our dining table. "Come and meet Lilly", said my grandmother, who by then was living with us. Staring at a pile of chocolate yeast cakes heaped on the table, which I would later learn were Lilly's trademark, I discovered the full story of my grandmother's "lost years" from the woman who had disappeared from her life for decades and suddenly returned after she had learned of my grandfather's recent death, realizing that it would now be acceptable for her to re-enter my grandmother's world.

When Freida Sima was in her mid-twenties, seven-year-old Lilly and her father became her neighbors in the boarding house on 112th street where she rented a furnished room. Lilly's mother had refused to immigrate to America, staying behind with the other children while sending her husband and youngest daughter to the New World. She also refused to accept a *Get*, a religious divorce, from her husband, preventing him from remarrying in America.

The situation that Freida Sima found herself in was not unique. More than one Jewish immigrant from Eastern Europe had left a wife and children behind in Europe, and at some point, had decided to make a new life for himself in America, leaving their European "baggage" behind. Some men had "disappeared" deliberately. Others did not disappear but just refused to send for their families, or pretended to their new surroundings that they were single. Many immigrants in such situations married illegally and began life anew, and Jewish newspapers like the *Forverts* had entire sections in their famous advice column, *A Bintel Brief*, devoted to the issue for years. There, editor Abraham Cahan gave advice to women writing about their husbands having deserted them and starting life anew in America with a new wife and new children.[104]

However, Lilly's father was a religious man and doing so was unthinkable. He therefore accepted the situation, and travelled to America with his youngest daughter in order to give her a better life. At the same time, like so many immigrants including Freida Sima, he would set aside some of the money he earned every week to send back money to Europe for the rest of his family.

Meanwhile, his wife took her other children and went to live with her parents, while keeping up minimal postal contact with her husband and daughter in America. Lilly, however, desperately wanted a mother and "adopted" Freida Sima as such, spending her free time in my grandmother's furnished room, doing her homework under her supervision, learning from her how to run the kitchen and keep house. Baking was never my grandmother's strong point, which might explain the consistency of the yeast cakes we began receiving from Lilly three times a week. In all other aspects, however, Freida Sima was Lilly's role model to the point where she even called her "Mama". My grandmother often invited Lilly and her father for Friday night dinner, offered to do their washing, and Lilly's father took to consulting her about how to raise a daughter alone. In time, young Lilly got to know the rest of Freida Sima's family, accompanying her to her aunts and meeting her young cousins. She became particularly fond of Freida Sima's brothers who reminded her of her own older brothers back in Europe, and more than once she told Benny, then in his early twenties, that he should wait for her to grow up so that she could marry him!

Although undoubtedly no overt lines of propriety were crossed, over the years Freida Sima developed a fondness for Lilly's father, looking at him as the type of man that she would have wanted to marry. Consequently, she also began comparing most of her potential suitors to him, and continuously found them wanting. That was the real explanation behind her advanced

---

104 Isaac Metzker, *A Bintel Brief: Sixty Years of Letters from the Lower East Side to the Jewish Daily Forward,* New York: Schoken, 1990.

spinsterhood, and the secret hope she nursed, that one day Lilly's mother would agree to accept a *Get* from Lilly's father, and the three of them could finally become a real family. But Lilly's father was a devout man, and one would never find his picture in the "Gallery of Missing Husbands" that the *Forward* column wrote about, together with the "National Desertion Bureau".

This situation continued until mid-1927 when Freida Sima came home from work one day to find Lilly sitting in front of her door in tears. That afternoon her father had received a letter from Lilly's mother, the first letter in over two years. Lilly's mother's parents had both passed away, she wrote, leaving her and her children with no one in Europe. She was therefore writing her husband in order to tell him to send money for tickets for her and the children to come to America. Lilly was distraught, claiming that she didn't even remember her mother, that Freida Sima was her real mother, and why did this have to happen and ruin everything?! But happen it did.

Freida Sima always faced reality head on, and realized that her reality was about to change abruptly. She was about to celebrate her thirty-second birthday, and for the first time in her life she admitted to herself that she was on the verge of becoming an old maid. Looking at her future with a critical eye, she realized that her chances of marrying at that point were slim, particularly as she couldn't even bring herself to think about going out to meet eligible young men. But she knew that her brothers in America, and her sister in Europe, were all waiting for her to marry before they could settle their own future.

The one she was most concerned about was her brother Abie, who had been unofficially engaged to their cousin Minnie for years and had longed to get married. Before the holidays that year, she therefore informed him of her decision that he should break custom and marry, regardless of what would happen to her. Taking him aside, she turned to him and said: "Avrum, if I don't get married by a year from now, you don't have to wait for me anymore, not you, not Marium, and not Tzeendl", referring to her younger brother Benzion by his family nickname. "You and Minnie should officially get engaged and plan to get married within the year, no matter what happens to me."

Another decision had to do with her relationship with Lilly and her father. Although she comforted Lilly and continued their usual closeness during the following weeks, as soon as Lilly's mother arrived, she deliberately cut off all contact with the family. While it pained her greatly, she realized that this was the only way to deal with the new reality of her life and boardinghouse neighbors. Knowing how this would change her life, she made plans to be away from her furnished room as much as possible, and even considered moving so that she would not have to live near Lilly's newly reunited family. Decades later, when Lilly came back into our lives after my grandfather's death, my grandmother was careful never to mention her father by name, always referring to him as "Lilly's father". Even half a century later, it was obvious that the memories of that period were still somewhat painful.

At the time, though, it was more than painful for Freida Sima; it was devastating. The emotional upheaval took its toll and soon after Lilly's mother arrived, she came down with a serious head cold that lingered for weeks. Aware of the situation, her closest friends, Fanny and Morris Carlin, tried to get her out of the house and invited her to a party at their home on Saturday night. It would be a small gathering, Fanny Carlin said, just a few friends and people that Freida Sima already knew. "It will do you good", Fanny said, "much better than sitting home on a Saturday night, all alone".

My grandmother begged off, citing her stuffed nose and red eyes. "I look like a witch!" she said. But Fanny didn't relent. "No one cares, there will be good food and you know almost everyone there". Morris was also a pocketbook manufacturer; in fact he and Fanny were young friends of her employer who had introduced them to Freida Sima close to a decade ago, saying "you and Fanny will have a lot in common". Over the years, Fanny Carlin had become Freida Sima's closest friend and confidant, taking the place of the sister that she had left behind in Europe. Now, as forelady at her pocketbook factory, Freida Sima and Morris could also talk business, and enjoyed discussing the latest trends in bag manufacturing and sales.

Unable to withstand Fanny's urging, and knowing that it would probably do her good to get out of the house, even for a short while, Freida Sima reluctantly agreed to come over to them, which is how she found herself trudging up five flights of stairs on a cold Saturday night in early February 1928. Opening the Carlin's front door, she found herself facing another guest whom she had never met. Dressed in a dapper striped suit and tie, he looked a bit older than she was and very good looking, with brown wavy hair, deep brown eyes, and a sunburned complexion, quite unusual in the frigid New York winter.

"Come in and meet Mordche", said Fanny, gesturing towards the gentleman standing at the entrance, holding an unlit cigarette in a long metal holder. "He's a family friend who recently came back to New York." Freida

Sima looked at the slightly built man in front of her and found herself mesmerized by his dark brown eyes, unable to remove her gaze from him. From that moment on she would always tell the story the same way. "We shook hands and forgot to let go". Freida Sima had no idea yet how much her life would change from that moment on, and that the jolt of electricity that she felt while shaking this unknown man's hand, would be the power behind her happiness for the next forty-two and a half years to come.

The Engagement of Freida Sima

In a perfect world everything always happens at the right time. One marries one's childhood sweetheart, raises a family, and lives happily ever after. In a perfect world there are no worries about finances, age gaps, ideological differences or background. Like often marries like, or if not, at least as close to it as possible, to avoid serious clashes. In a perfect world one's family is happily supportive of one's choice. At times, they are even among those who engineered that choice in the first place. But what happens when at a chance meeting you fall in love at first sight, at the most unforeseen time and in the most unexpected place? When you are traditional and believing and find out that that the man you have just fallen in love with is an atheist and a communist to boot? When you, a single young woman with no "baggage", find out that your love has a past life that isn't about to go away? And what do you do when he expects you to give up your entire life less than twenty-four hours after you met, and marry him the next day?

This is what happened to Freida Sima that evening, when all she had been looking for on a rainy Saturday night was to keep her mind off a miserable head cold, and ended up meeting the love of her life. Of all evenings, she had decided not to dress up, and was wearing a plain sweater and skirt that had seen better days, although she wore her long string of yellow jade beads which she always claimed brought her luck. Taking a step forward she smiled at the interesting looking stranger and held out her hand. From that moment on, everything changed. Taking her arm, Mordche led her to a chair at the dining room table and sat down next to her, saying "here they call me Max". "But I will call you Mordche", she answered, unable to tear her eyes away from his.

The next few hours passed in a blur. As always, people came and went at the Carlin household, passing in and out of the kitchen and dining room. But the two sat at the table, talking in Yiddish, oblivious to everything and everyone around them. She told him she was from a Vizhnitzer Hassidic family from the Bukovina; he said that his family was a Misnagdic one from Kiev. She told him how she had brought two of her brothers over after the war; he related how he and two sisters had escaped Russia after the unsuccessful revolution in 1905 in which one sister had even been involved, and that his parents, two brothers and three sisters were all living in America. They compared name changes – how her "Enzenberg", which she had been writing with an "s" and not a "z" like most of her family in Europe, had become Eisenberg because of her brother Abie's Ellis Island experience, while "Karasik" had turned into Kraus because of his older brother Morris's decision to have a more American sounding name. She told him about her work as a forelady at a pocketbook factory run by close friends of their host, Morris Carlin. He told her how he and his brothers had all learned trades in America and even his sisters had studied practical nursing.

"I'm a housepainter and I make a good living, but most important I'm a union man!" he announced, spending the next hour extolling the virtues of a socialist and preferably a Communist society in which the working man is valued above the businessman. Listening with raised eyebrows, Freida Sima had no problem countering his arguments, although she was also grateful to the unions for having regulated working hours in the factories. But she was unwilling to hear someone speak about Marx and Lenin as if they were God. "If communism is so wonderful then why don't you go back to Russia?!" she countered and the two began a vocal ideological battle that only ended when they began to argue about religion. "Religion is the opiate of the masses, how can a beautiful, intelligent woman like you be taken in by such *narishkeit!*" bellowed Mordche, having left the stage of calling her "Miss Eisenberg" long behind. "One day when you find out there really is a God it will be too late. Only idiots have to wait until they are dead to get proof!" she countered. And so they continued for hours.

The two continued to battle over what appeared to the onlookers to be every subject possible. "You are here for how long and you aren't a citizen?! I got my citizenship papers in 1923!" Freida Sima said proudly. Mordche looked at her in surprise. "Why in the world would I want to be a citizen before we bring the revolution to America? I've done fine like this for the past twenty-two years." And so it continued. In between sparring over politics and religion they found that they did indeed have a few things in common – among them, a love of *hazonnes* (liturgical music), *schmaltz* herring, and the ocean. But within moments they returned to ideological battles, each in turn citing classical Yiddish writers such as Sholem Aleichem or Y.L. Peretz to support their position.

As vehement as each of them were, the debates could stop in mid-sentence when one of them said something that set the other off on a tangent. As soon as Freida Sima mentioned Sholem Aleichem, Mordche stopped arguing, and looked at her, cutting her off and saying "do you remember his *levaya?* I was there!" "So was I!" responded Freida Sima with excitement, and the two began reminiscing about the great writer's funeral in 1916, and how the famous Cantor Yossele Rosenblatt invoked the *El Mole Rachamin* memorial prayer that had thousands in tears. "I really love listening to *hazonnes*", Mordche told her "it does something to me that I can't describe". "What can *hazonnes* do to a *freier,* a freethinker?!", Freida Sima retorted with unveiled sarcasm, realizing how much she was enjoying arguing with this man about everything and anything. "I may be a Freethinker, *aber ich bin a Yid*! (but I am a Jew!)", he countered.

It was close to eleven PM when Fanny Carlin came to the table, putting her arm around Freida Sima's shoulders. "Mordche, I have to take your debate partner away for a few minutes, I need her help in the kitchen to prepare the hot drinks." "Feel free, Fanny, he answered, as long as you bring her back to me as soon as possible, we still have a lot left to argue about tonight!" "And this time maybe you shouldn't bring out anything stronger than tea, Fanny, it's *lebedig* (lively) enough tonight without it", called out Morris Carlin as he saw his wife enter the kitchen. Although these were the years of the Prohibition, when it was forbidden to manufacture, transport, or sell alcoholic beverages in the United States, Jews were permitted to purchase sacramental wine for "religious purposes". Along with the wine, it was often possible for them to surreptitiously purchase hard liquor, which made its way into many a Jewish kitchen during the 1920s and early 1930s.[105]

Leading her girlfriend into the kitchen, Fanny began to not-so-gently question her about Mordche. "Nu, so what do you think of him?" she asked, as soon as the kitchen door had closed behind them. "He's fascinating!" answered Freida Sima. "Even if I don't agree with him about much, he has experience and intelligence". "Well he is definitely intelligent enough to be

---

105 Daniel Okrent, *Last Call: The Rise and Fall of Prohibition,* New York: Scribner, 2011.

interested in you", Fanny retorted, "but there is one think that you had better be aware of." Freida Sima stood with her arms folded in front of her chest, looking at her friend. "Nu, Fanny, don't keep it to yourself", she said, "what are you talking about?"

Fanny took a deep breath and look back at Freida Sima as she loaded the tea samovar onto a tray to bring into the dining room. "You know he isn't a *bochur*", she began. "So what is he? A *katchke* (duck)?" countered my grandmother, raising her eyebrows. "Don't be silly", chucked Fanny. "Didn't he tell you that he is a widower with four grown sons?!" Hiding her surprise Freida Sima put a hand on Fanny's arm. "Of course he did", she answered. "He told me all about it!" "Good", countered Fanny. "I wouldn't want you to get involved with him before you knew the whole story." "*Zorgt Nisht* Fanny, don't worry, he told me everything", my grandmother responded, before leaving the kitchen and going back to sit with Mordche at the dining room table.

Late evening turned to night and by three o'clock in the morning Fanny and Morris were rubbing their eyes in the hope that their guests would get the message and leave. But Freida Sima and Mordche were in the middle of yet another argument, this time about the upcoming Presidential elections that would take place later that year. "Talk all you want, but you aren't even a citizen, and thank God you can't vote!" shouted Freida Sima at Mordche after he made a comment about how the American Communist leader William Foster would make a better President than any of the other potential candidates.

By that time Morris Carlin had lost his patience with the couple and handed them their coats and hats, shooing them out the front door, begging exhaustion and claiming it was time for them to go home so that he and Fanny could finally go to sleep. At the top of the stairwell Mordche turned to my grandmother and took her hand once again. "This has been such a wonderful evening", he said to her with a smile, "So tomorrow we get married, right?" Freida Sima pulled her hand back in shock. "Married?!" she shouted, "This is how you are asking me to marry you?!" "I thought that it was settled already", Mordche replied, "but if you want time to think, you can give me your answer by the time we get down to the street".

How long does it take to descend five flights of stairs? How many thoughts go through a person's mind during the time it takes to walk down one hundred steps? How fast can someone who thought she would remain a spinster forever, decide to marry a man who is the opposite of everything she had ever dreamed about: a communist, a freethinker, an atheist, a widower with four sons? How could she dare to even consider such a match, when he hadn't yet told her about his family and expected her to fall seamlessly into his plans, whatever they might be? And how could she dare refuse, when this was the first time in months, maybe in years, that she had felt totally alive, infused with spirit, and wanted this evening to go on forever and ever?

The trip down the stairs took less than five minutes, but for Freida Sima it seemed an eon. Mordche remained silent as they descended the stairs, holding her hand to make sure that she wouldn't slip in the dimly lit stairwell. At each landing Freida Sima changed her mind about what she would answer when they reached the ground floor. Just as some girls pluck off flower petals saying "he loves me", "he loves me not" alternately, until no petals are left on the stem, so Freida Sima was saying to herself alternately, "Of course I'll marry him", "What? Am I crazy?!" over and over, at each landing, until they reached the bottom of the stairwell.

As they stepped out of the apartment house's front door, Mordche turned to Freida Sima with a gleam in his eyes. "So, Bertie, do you have an answer for me?" he asked, for the first time using the nickname that he would call her by for the rest of his life. "They tell me that you are a widower with four grown sons, is it true?" she asked him quietly, standing in the glow of the streetlight on the wet pavement and looking up at his face. "Does it make a difference?" he countered, looking back at her with an intense gaze. "No, it doesn't", she answered truthfully. "So now will you marry me?!" he asked softly, in a voice so different than the booming bass she had heard for the past few hours as they argued every subject possible from "A" to "Z". "Yes I will", she answered, "but not tomorrow. In two weeks", recalling the requirements of Jewish marriage law. Mordche let out a long sigh, as if he had been holding his breath for the entire five flights of stairs. "Good. In the morning tell your boss that you are quitting, and come and meet my parents. Oh and yes, I'm a widower with four sons; tomorrow you meet the boys as well."

The Marriage of Freida Sima

Until this point in Freida Sima's odyssey her life had indeed been similar to that of many young Jewish immigrant girls and women who had come to the United States during the Great Wave of Immigration in search of a better future. She had travelled alone but come to friends and family. She had worked as a domestic and later in a factory. She had sent money home to her family and assisted other family members to immigrate to America. She attempted to remain traditional, but had adopted many American customs. She was, indeed, somewhat out of the ordinary in the fact that she was a traditional young woman, but had reached her early thirties before she had found her match.

She was not a socialist but as a factory worker, was sympathetic to the Labor movement and much of what it represented. She was willing to work hard, but did not want to remain working in a factory after she married. Like many young Jewish women immigrants of her generation, she wanted a husband who would be "a good provider", and whose wages would help her rise out of the working class and escape the factory. In her study of immigrant Jewish women, Syndney Stahl Weinberg describes Rose Cohen, who after seeing how hard her father worked in America asked him if everyone in America lived as he did, going to work early, coming home late, eating and going to sleep day after day. When she added: "Will I have to do that too? Always?" her father thought a while and then replied, smiling, "No, you will get married."[106] That had been Freida Sima's hope as well, to ultimately find a man who would get her out of the factory, even if she were already a forelady. But she wanted love as well, and had not been willing to relinquish that dream.

The fact that her match was another Jewish immigrant, a man who came from a similar Eastern European background, but was far from her political orientation and lifestyle, was not that uncommon. Had the two stayed in Europe, it would have been difficult for them to have met. No shadchan would have introduced them, and also it would be difficult to imagine them having mutual friends. But the Great Wave of immigration had been a great equalizer in certain senses, making it possible for immigrant men and women who would never have met each other in Europe to meet and match up. Mordche may have been older than Freida Sima, a freethinker and even anti-religious, but his family background in Europe had not been that different than hers, and their social and cultural worlds were similar or at least familiar to each other. Although on the political and religious scale they might be considered an extreme example of a match,

---

106 Rose Cohen, *Out of the Shadow*, New York: George H. Doran Co., 1918:74.

on the linguistic, social and cultural scale they had much in common that would act as ballast for their marriage for many decades.

"Did it really happen or was it a dream?" Freida Sima asked herself when she got up a few hours later. But looking at the piece of paper next to her bed with Mordche's parents' address, she realized that it was not only real but that she was expected to be ready within an hour in order to meet her new future in-laws. Dressing in a respectable black dress with long sleeves and a round collar, she remembered how before he left her at her furnished room, Mordche asked her if she wanted an engagement ring or whether it would be enough to get her a beautiful wedding band. "Engagement ring?" she answered. "Who has money for an engagement ring?!" "Don't worry about money", he answered, "I earn enough to be able to support a family and to buy you an engagement ring as well". Freida Sima looked at him quizzically, and when he told her that he was earning seventy dollars a week as a painter, her mouth hung open in shock. "That's a fortune!" "It better be, because in two weeks you are about to stop working and become the mother of a family with four children." he answered.

The next few hours passed in a blur as Freida Sima met her future in-laws and stepsons. Abraham and Chana Kraus were religious Jews in their late seventies, spoke a Russian Yiddish which took Freida Sima a while to get used to, were thrilled to hear that she came from a traditional home, and that Mordche had agreed that their new home would be run along the same lines. "Finally we will have a child with a kosher home where we can eat!" said Chana to Freida Sima with a broad smile, taking her future daughter-in-law's hands in her own. Abraham sat there in his square black Russian skullcap, stroking his white beard and looking at Freida Sima thoughtfully. "Tell me about yourself, *mein tochter* (my daughter)", he said, and she did, explaining that she was the oldest daughter of a large family of Vizhnitzer *Hassidim* from the Bukovina, and talked about her parents and siblings.

Now it was time to meet the boys who filed into the room to be introduced. "This is Hymie", said Mordche, pointing to his oldest son, a tall young man with the first hint of a moustache. "And this is Sammy", he said, gesturing to the second young man in the room, who already looked just like his father. Two younger boys now entered the room, glancing at Freida Sima expectantly. "This is Ben", said Mordche, pointing to the older of the two, a handsome young teen with a shock of wavy dark black hair, "and this is Herschel, my youngest", he said, gesturing to his fourth son, a young boy with an impish face. Looking at his boys, Mordche now took Freida Sima by the hand. "And this is Bertie", he said to the four boys who were now standing next to each other in a row. "She is going to be your new Mama."

One by one the boys came and shook her hand formally, greeting her properly as if they had been rehearsing all morning and at the same time telling her their English names – Herbert, Stewart, Ben and Harry. They then all sat around the dining room table and Mordche explained that he and Freida Sima would be getting married in two weeks, and they would all be leaving the grandparents' home and moving into their own apartment. "You should just know, things are going to be a bit different than they were at home", Mordche concluded, referring to their previous lives. "First of all, our kitchen is going to be kosher", he continued, "Just like it is here at Baba Chana and Zeide Avrum". The two older boys looked at him with raised eyebrows, well aware of their father's atheism and his views on anything having to do with Jewish religious practice. Shifting his gaze to his younger boys, Mordche continued. "And second of all…" he trailed off, looking back at his older sons and deciding it might be prudent to leave things as they were, at least for the time being. "We will talk about second of all another time", he concluded.

If Abraham and Chana Kraus, had been thrilled with Freida Sima's insistence on a traditional home, Mordche's older sons were less so. At eighteen and seventeen they were staunch "freethinkers" like their father. It had been hard enough for them to remember the rules of a kosher home since living at their grandparents for the past few months. At ten and fourteen, the younger ones appeared to be less bothered by the matter and they cared more about what it would be like to have a mother again. Their mother Sadie had died six months earlier of a bad heart, but had been ill for almost a decade. That was the reason the family had moved to California years earlier. Promising beneficial weather for invalids, it was also a place where Jews found it easier to carve out a new, less traditional identity for themselves.

After Sadie's death, Mordche moved the boys back to his parents' home in New York where after four months of caring for her grandsons, his mother had told him unequivocally: "I'm too old for this, you need a wife!" Protesting that he was not interested in remarrying, he was shocked at the intensity of his feelings when introduced to Freida Sima, an attraction so powerful that he even acceded to her religious conditions. Later that day, after buying her the *Shabbos lachter* she would light every week for the rest of her life, Mordche agreed once again to her keeping a kosher home, holiday traditions and marital laws, while she promised to turn a blind eye to what he did and ate outside the house. They both agreed to argue politics and religion no more than once a day. If possible.

That same evening Freida Sima introduced Mordche to her family. Like a great deal of the Jewish population of Harlem, by the late 1920s, most of the family had moved elsewhere, in their case, to the South Bronx where they all lived either on or around Trinity Avenue and 158th street. From the first decade of the twentieth century, rapid transit had been pivotal to rapid growth of the Bronx, especially the subway that reached the Bronx in 1905. The new accessibility of the borough initiated a tremendous building boom that would cause a spurt in the Bronx population, leading to 153,000 residents by 1920 and one million plus residents by 1930. Ninety percent of them were foreign born, primarily Italians and Eastern European Jews who had left the Lower East side and East Harlem, like Freida Sima's family, and who flocked to the newly-build multistory apartment buildings.[107]

Freida Sima and Mordche's first stop was at her *Tante* Mollie's apartment at 744 Trinity Avenue, a few floors away from her Uncle Moshe Leib who lived in the same building and two buildings away from her Aunt Sadie and her family. Her brothers lived there as well. "Your *chossen* (bridegroom)?!" said Mollie in shock when Freida Sima made the introduction, recalling how two days ago her niece had mentioned that she wasn't going out with anyone at the time. Quickly she called her brother and sister-in-law in the building, and sister and brother-in-law from next door to come and drink a *lechayim* (toast) to the newly engaged couple. When your niece was over thirty-two, you didn't ask too many questions, and were just grateful that he looked like a decent man. The next stop was at her Uncle Joe around the corner on 158th street, in order to get his approval. He and *Tante* Rivka were also thrilled that their niece had finally found herself a husband, and a good looking one as well. It was time for another *lechayim*.

During the next two weeks Freida Sima prepared to get married. She gave in her notice at work, informing her boss that he would need a new forelady within a week. She also sat down and wrote a long letter to her parents, telling them that she had finally found her *bashert* and was about to marry Mordche Kraus, originally from Kiev, a painter, and a widower with four sons. She convenient omitted several details, such as the fact that he was

107   Evelyn Gonzales, *The Bronx,* New York: Columbia University Press, 2003.

a communist and an atheist, and that they were planning to get married in less than two weeks. As a letter took a month to six weeks to reach the Bukovina from New York, and the same amount of time to send a response, by the time she received her father's answer in which he expressed his definite lack of enthusiasm for the match, in view of beginning life with four stepchildren, she was long married and already expecting a child of her own.

Spending a bit of time with her future in-laws, Freida Sima learned more about the family into which she was marrying. Avraham Kraus had been a tailor in Russia and Chana a housewife. The family had four daughters and three sons, and in addition, they had raised a fourth son who was actually Chana's nephew and had lost his parents when he was a young boy. That, Chana explained, is how they had two sons with the same name, both named after her father. Isaac, her nephew, and Mordche, whose second name was also Yitzchok-Isaac.

The first of the family to leave Kiev for the United States was her oldest son Morris who emigrated at the turn of the century in order to escape being inducted into the Czar's army. He was followed by his brother Adolph and then his father Avraham, who came to prepare the way for the rest of the family. Isaac, meanwhile, had married and moved to Lodz, leaving her with Mordche and four daughters, Mata, Rose, Rivka and Chaya Dvora, ranging in age from twenty-eight to seven. Mata also was getting married, and she and Isaac were the only two of the family who were not being swept up in the socialist and revolutionary movements of the time.

Mordche had been a rebel since before he entered his teens, having asked one *Shabbos* when he was eleven why he wasn't allowed to comb his hair, and not receiving what he considered a logical response. As a result of that, and possibly of listening to the communist speeches of his older sister Rose, he decided that just like her, he, too, believed that there was no God and that religion had been made up as a means of controlling the working man. As time passed, Mordche began to be involved with revolutionary circles, and his father thought it prudent to send him to live for a while with his older and very religious brother-cousin Isaac in Lodz, who might be able to put him on the straight and narrow. Abraham was mistaken. Not only was Isaac even more of a disciplinarian than Abraham had been, but Mordche had gotten older and was less willing to be disciplined. Falling in with a bad crowd in Lodz, he was sentenced to six months on a chain gang, yet another story in his life that Mordche had conveniently omitted when telling Freida Sima about his past history.

114

As soon as he could, the sixteen-year-old Mordche returned to Kiev to his family, and was once again drawn in to his sister Rose's revolutionary crowd. In fact, it was the mass political and social unrest of 1905 which was known as the unsuccessful Russian revolution, that was the impetus for his immigration and that of two of his sisters, Rose and Rivka. Rose had been involved in something concerning a gun that no one wanted to talk about, an act that left her name on a list and a price on her head, making it prudent for her to leave the country immediately. In view of the fact that Morris, Adolph and Abraham were already in America, the three joined them in early April 1906. Looking at the way they were listed at Ellis Island one could already see their future attitude towards religion and ethnicity. While Rose and Mordche declared their ethnicity as "Russian", Rivka, the more traditional sister who travelled with them, had listed herself as "Hebrew".

Only in 1912, almost a decade after her husband Abraham has left to build them a new home in America, did Chana arrive in New York with their youngest daughter, seventeen-year-old Chaya Devorah, who now called herself Vera. The family settled in New York where Abraham had attempted to find work as a tailor in the garment district, but was fired week after week when Friday afternoon came around and he packed up his things, stating that he was a strict Sabbath observer and he would not work on Friday after sundown. Not only that, but in a world where most factories ascribed to the saying "If you don't come in on Sunday (meaning for Jews, Saturday, the Sabbath), don't come in on Monday", there was little work for Sabbath-observing Jews. The phenomenon had even earned itself a Yiddish term, *minhag America,* the "American Tradition", leading to a series of new Jewish traditions, such as men who would go to early-morning prayer services on *Shabbes* morning and then would have to leave for work. In fact, one of the new women's prayers in Freida Sima's *Techina* had been a candle lighting prayer for Jewish women in America whose husband and children "were forced to make their Sabbath into a weekday in order to support their families".

After more than a year of Abraham changing jobs every week, there were few sweatshops or factories that he had not been to, and his sons turned to him with a proposition. He could be a tailor who mended garments for people at home, and they would provide him with the rest of his living, so that he would not have to worry any more about finding a job that would allow him to properly observe the Sabbath. Understanding more than he had a year earlier about what working in America entailed,

Abraham accepted their proposal, trying to turn a blind eye to the fact that he was being supported by his children's Sabbath desecration.

By the time Chana arrived in America with Vera, he had amassed a small clientele of people who would come to him for tailoring repairs, and they settled down to a simple existence in the New World. The only people who were missing were Isaac, who had written them from Lodz that he and his wife had become Zionists and would soon be moving to *Eretz Yisrael*, to the Land of Israel, which was still part of the Ottoman Empire, and Mata, who remained in Kiev with her husband, saying that she would not move to a country where she heard that it was impossible to keep Shabbos properly.

In March 1908, almost two years after coming to New York, twenty-year-old Mordche, already a painter, married his first wife, Sadie Oberund, at a civil ceremony held at city hall. Eighteen months later their first son, Hymie was born, followed a year and three months later by a second son, Sammy, two years later by a third, Ben, and a bit over four years later, by their last child, Herschel. "So they were never married 'in Jewish'?" asked Freida Sima? Her future mother-in-law gave a sigh, "no, they were both *freier*, Freethinkers", she said, once again grateful that she was now going to have a traditional daughter-in-law.

As her wedding day drew near, Freida Sima prepared the last of her trousseau which she had been putting aside for years. To her new linens, underwear and night clothing she now added more bath and kitchen towels, in view of the fact that she was about to begin married life as a homemaker in a family of six. Used to living very frugally, she had decided not to spend money on a dress that she would wear only once in her life, and instead put on a new two piece outfit which she would later use for the holidays. The morning of her wedding she dressed in that outfit, to which she added a veil that her *Tante* Mollie had prepared for her. Her possessions were all packed up and had been moved to their new apartment on Beck Street in the Bronx, only minutes away from her aunts, uncles and brothers.

Leaving her furnished room for the last time, she made her way to her *Tante* Mollie's apartment where the living room and been cleared of furniture, and her wedding would take place. As she sat in the bedroom, before the *badeken* when Mordche would lift her veil over her face, her soon-to-be mother in law came in to sit with her for a moment before the ceremony. Taking Freida Sima's hands in hers, just as she had at their first meeting, Chana now looked closely at her future daughter-in-laws fingers, smiling when she found what she was looking for. Seeing the blunt cut short fingernails, she understood that the evening before Freida Sima had been to the *mikva,* the ritual bath in which a bride immerses before her wedding, and every month afterwards during her fertile years to purify herself before resuming marital relations. Freida Sima had indeed done everything according to Jewish tradition, but with her oldest aunt accompanying her instead of her mother who was half a world away.

On a beautiful Sunday afternoon in February, fourteen days after they met, Mordche and Freida Sima were married in her uncle and aunt's apartment, surrounded by their families. In a rented tuxedo and wearing bowtie, Mordche was escorted to the *chuppah* by his elderly parents, joined by a radiant Freida Sima, led by *Tante* Mollie and Uncle Srul Nachman. As she stood next to Mordche under the wedding canopy held by her brothers and uncles, she thought of her parents who did not yet know of her marriage, and of the fact that just a few weeks ago she had despaired of ever finding the man of her dreams. Now, within a fortnight, her world had turned upside down, but for the good. Not only her world, she thought, but also that of her brothers in America and sister in the Bukovina who could finally get married.

"It was a simple wedding and a short one", recalled my grandmother years later when I asked her about her wedding day. "We had some sponge cake that my aunts had made, and drank a *lechaim*, and that was that." Mordche had drawn the line at having a week's worth of festivities in the form of *sheva brochos* and Freida Sima let the matter slide, settling for a festive family meal later that day as she knew that by Jewish law her marriage had been over and above board with the blessings under the *chuppah* and already recognized when it was better not to press her husband beyond a certain point.

Although a year later her brother Abie would already get married in a hall, Freida Sima's marriage in her aunt's living room was not at all unique among the less well-to-do Jewish immigrants of that period. Those immigrants who had family in America often held their ceremonies at home, whether weddings, *brisses*, engagements or bar mitzvah parties. Life for these immigrants was a frugal affair. Close relatives were expected to bring cake, the bride and groom, or their parents if they were in America, supplied drinks, and that was that. The closing scene in the 1975 film "Hester Street", in which immigrant bride and groom are walking in the street in their wedding finery, instead of spending money on a ride, was not all that uncommon.

That evening at the dinner table, looking at her new family with love, Freida Sima was also filled with caution. How would the boys treat her? What would happen if she and Mordche had a child of their own? Basking in wedding bliss she couldn't imagine that childbirth, the Great Depression, and life-threatening illness would turn their lives upside down within two short years.

Chapter 5 Marriage, Motherhood, and Money: Freida Sima and the Great Depression – New York (1929–1939)

Introduction

How does a thirty-two year old spinster cope when two weeks after meeting the love of her life, she marries him and finds herself the stepmother of four orphan boys ages ten to eighteen? What if she wants to keep a traditional home but the boys and their father have been used to living for years as free-thinkers? How do they respond when less than a year later a new baby – this time a girl – enters into the existing family equation? Where does this young mother turn when weeks after her daughter's birth, her husband is stricken with a life-threatening illness? And how does she cope when several months after that, she finds herself with an unemployed husband and a household of people to feed?

When Freida Sima and Mordche (Max) Kraus were married in February 1928, they had reached a compromise: he would not interfere in household matters of religion, while she would turn a blind eye to whatever he would do outside the home. Things were less simple when it came to her four step-sons. At eighteen and seventeen, Herb and Stewart had been used to a very different way of life for years. Although they always treated Freida Sima with respect, soon after they realized that she would not compromise on running a strictly kosher home, they made plans to return to California where they had been raised and where their late mother Sadie had family. Hitting the road, they eventually reached Los Angeles where they began working in the jewelry business.

The two younger boys, Ben and Harry managed the transition with less difficulty. At fifteen Ben was more withdrawn than his brothers and adapted to the changes with little comment. Harry on the other hand, seemed quite amenable to have a stepmother, as his own mother had been incapacitated with heart disease for much of his young life. The feeling was mutual and he soon became "my Harry" for Freida Sima, who became "Mom" to Harry. That closeness grew through an interesting twist when Max reluctantly informed his new bride that he couldn't take her on their planned and paid for honeymoon due to an unexpected painting job that he had accepted. "Just because you can't go, Mordche, I'm not giving up on that honeymoon. I'll take Harry!" she retorted. Stepmother and stepson then spent a week together in the mountains, taking a picture to mark the occasion, and forging a bond that lasted throughout their lives. The picture shows a smiling Freida Sima with her arm around an equally smiling young Harry's shoulders, standing in front of the mountain hotel in early spring vacation clothes, wearing long sleeves and a sweater against the morning chill.

Freida Sima recalled how on her first Yom Kippur eve as a married woman, when she prepared to go to *shul* alone, eleven-year-old Harry suddenly stood next to her. Recalling the previous Yom Kippur when he and his newly orphaned brothers, living with their very religious grandparents, were told to accompany their *Zeide* to *shul* to say *Kaddish* and *Yizkor* (memorial prayers) for their mother, he suddenly blurted out: "I don't have to say *Yizkor* anymore because I have a mother again". Taking his hand, Freida Sima explained that if he didn't want to go, he didn't have to, and promised to say *Yizkor* for his mother for the rest of her life. And so she did.

Married Life

As immigrants from Eastern Europe with similar backgrounds, the Kraus and Eisenberg families had much in common. The first was language. Although the Kraus family was from Russia and the Eisenbergs were from the Bukovina, similar to most of the Jewish immigrants who had come to America from Eastern Europe before the First World War, both families spoke Yiddish at home. The second was tradition. Although the Eisenbergs had come from Chassidic stock and the Krauses had no connection to the Chassidic tradition, both families had been fully observant in Europe and the older generation, although more modernized in America, was still fully traditional. The third was culture. Not only did both families live in the Yiddish speaking world of American-Jewish Eastern European immigrants, they also lived in the Yiddish cultural world, reading the Yiddish language newspapers, going to the Yiddish theater, and reading the same famous Yiddish authors. It was therefore easy enough for the two families to understand each other, even if certain members held very different political and religious viewpoints.

During her first year of marriage Freida Sima found herself growing close to her in-laws, as her own parents were five thousand miles away in the Bukovina. They, in turn, were delighted to finally have a child with a kosher home in which they could eat. Her mother-in-law enjoyed telling her stories about Mordche's childhood in Kiev and about their own lives in America. As baking was never Freida Sima's strong point, Chana Kraus enjoyed helping her with the baking, spending hours whipping up "snows" of egg whites and sugar in Freida Sima's kitchen, from which she would then bake feather-light cakes for the family, that her grandsons particularly enjoyed.

Freida Sima's marriage strengthened the bonds within the Eisenberg family as well. Now that she had married, it was possible for her younger siblings, who had waited for years, to finally do the same. The first to take a step in that direction was the next brother in line, Abie. After almost six years of courting his first cousin Minnie Scharf, Abie and Minnie finally became officially engaged and planned to get married in February 1929. Why the long wait? Because before they would get married, Abie wanted to take a trip back to Mihowa and see his family.

Abie had wanted to do so for years, but couldn't consider it before he had obtained his American citizenship and applied for an American passport, ensuring that he would have no trouble leaving Europe and returning to the United States. A year earlier, in March 1927, he had finally received his Certificate of Naturalization and had saved up enough money to make the trip. Now in 1928 he applied for an American passport and once he received it, made plans to go back "home" to see the family one last time before he married.

Abie had long carried a picture of himself and his mother that had been taken before he left for America in early 1919. Now, almost ten years later, he had another picture taken with his family during his visit, in order to have a souvenir of his trip. The difference between the two pictures exemplifies not only the changes that had taken place in the Enzenberg family in Mihowa between his emigration and return trip, but also those manifesting themselves in large parts of the traditional European Jewish world over that almost ten year period.

Eric Hobsbawm, the British Marxist-Jewish historian, has written about the long 19th century, lasting between 1789 and 1914, characterized by a particular essence, nature and set of attributes, and the short 20th century, beginning with the First World War in 1914, marked by very a different and distinct set of characteristics.[108] Although according to his view, the 19th century ended with the outbreak of the First World War, for large parts of traditional European Jewry, the war years were still a transition period, characterized by many vestiges of 19th century social, cultural and religious norms. Much of this can be seen in the first picture, taken right after the war's end, while the second, taken almost ten years later, emphasizes that its subjects were now living deep in the 20th century, with all that it entailed.

The first picture shows a twenty-year-old Abie in a high collared white shirt, dark vest, loose jacket, bowtie and hat, standing stiffly next to a forty-two-year-old dark-wigged Devorah, sitting upright in a chair next to him, in an old-fashioned black dress with satin trim on bodice and cuffs. Both were quite thin, a legacy of the World War that had ended only a few months earlier. In the picture, Abie's left hand is griping the back of Devorah's chair and his right hand is resting on a high table on which the photographer had placed a book. Like most pictures taken then, a rarity in itself, it was a posed studio picture, with both mother and son looking serious and even extremely solemn. This was understandable, not only because it was a posed picture, but in view of the fact that it was being taken right before Abie left for America, when neither he nor his mother knew if they would see each other again. The picture was also taken just around the time the family in Europe had received their first letter from Freida Sima since the war began almost half a decade earlier, reminding them of what could happen when a family member moved overseas and how all communication could abruptly cease at times of crisis.

The second picture, taken in the Enzenberg garden in Mihowa during the summer of 1928, shows a twenty-nine-year-old, well-fed Abie, once again in a three piece suit, white shirt and bowtie, but this time hatless and sporting a small mustache. Next to him is his thirty-year-old sister Marium, wearing a stylish, light colored open V-necked blouse with a dangling necklace. Abie's his hand is resting on Marium's shoulder, and to her right stands their twenty-year-old brother Leibish, also hatless and wearing a white shirt, suit and tie. All three look jovial. Seated in front of them are their parents,

---

108   Eric Hobsbawm, *The Age of Revolution; 1789–1848,* New York: Vintage Books, 1972; *The Age of Capital 1848–1875,* London: Weidenfeld and Nicholson, 1975; *The Age of Empires 1875–1914,* London: Weidenfeld and Nicholson, 1987; *The Age of Extremes: The Short Twentieth Century 1914–1991,* New York: Vintage, 1994.

the bewigged Devorah in a fashionable two-piece dress with a plaid bodice insert, and a bearded Nachman wearing a high black yarmulkeh, a white shirt, three piece suit and elegant striped tie. All but Marium, who seems to be squinting in the sun, are smiling broadly at the camera. All look well-fed and relaxed, their hands in a comfortable pose, either on their hips, in their laps, or on each other's shoulders.

In this picture one could see that the wartime famine was long over, the Enzenbergs were more comfortable having their picture taken, the occasion was a joyous one of greeting a visiting son from overseas, and their dress more modern and fashionable. The Enzenbergs may have been living in a tiny farming community, Mihowa, but their mode of dress, especially Marium's, had modern flair that appears light years away from the way Abie and Devorah were dressed in the previous picture.

This difference in dress and bearing between the Enzenbergs of 1919 and those of 1928 is even more striking in a second picture taken that day, one of Devorah and Nachman standing in their garden. In a posed picture of the two taken immediately after the war, they were dressed in dark old-fashioned clothing, Nachman in a large black hat, and Devorah in a floor length black dress, both thin, unsmiling and not touching while standing in a rigid studio pose The second picture, taken the same day as the family portrait in mid-1928, has them standing next to their garden fence, smiling, with Devorah's hand resting familiarly on Nachman's shoulder, and one of Nachman's hands resting on the wooden fence while his other arm leaned into his wife's ample side and hip. With a bit of imagination, in this picture one can actually see the fun-loving and adventurous parents that Freida Sima had once described from her very young childhood, when Nachman would come home from work to dance his Devorah around the room to the delight of his two little girls.

There was one more reminder of the changes that had taken place in the family that can be found in the 1928 pictures. In the background of both pictures one sees horses on the Enzenberg property, a legacy of the money that the three children in America had sent, originally for their siblings' tickets to America. Nachman, however, had been extremely attached to his children and decided that no more of his sons would leave for overseas. He was going to keep them as close as possible. One way of doing so would be to expand the farm and buy land and horses to be used for the family's benefit, and so he did.

During his trip to Mihowa, not only did Abie delight his parents with the news of his engagement to their niece Minnie and their upcoming marriage. He also had the opportunity of meeting the young man with whom his sister Marium had begun to "step out" with, Feivel Rosenberg. They too eventually decided to get married and planned their wedding for June 1929. Undecided about finding a bride in America, Benny, Freida Sima's second brother in America, said that after Abie's wedding he might take a trip back to Mihowa just like Abie did, possibly for Marium's wedding, and who knows, maybe he would find a wife there as well.

Meanwhile, the family's needs in America were changing. Seeing the family get older and aware that after Freida Sima's marriage there would be a rush of marriages among the siblings, Joe and Moshe Leib realized that it was time for them to found their own *landsmanschaft*, a Scharf-Eisenberg benevolent society. Since the 19th century, Jewish immigrants in America had founded benevolent societies, usually based around a synagogue. With the start of the great wave of immigration in the 1880s, secular *landsmanschaften*, organizations based on place of origin, began to take the place of these synagogue societies. These organizations provided interest-free loans, sick benefits, aid and burial rights to families of their members, and by the outbreak of the First World War there were over 500 such *landsmanschaften* throughout the United States. For many of the early immigrants who had come to America without family, the *landsmanschaften* took the place of family, not only in time of need, but also as a social group. For others who had come with family but missed community, the *landsmanschaft* served as their community, their *shtetl* or their town. Finally, the *landsmanschaft* ensured that they would be buried according to Jewish tradition, in a Jewish cemetery, with all the necessary rites and ceremonies.[109]

For years, Abie had been secretary-treasurer of the First Mihowa Berhometh Bucowiner Society K.U.V.[110], founded in 1910 to provide sick and death benefits for members and function as a burial society. The Society's constitution, written in 1925, contained an "Oath of Membership", requiring that secrets of the Society not be divulged, and even specifying a password to be used for admittance to meetings. Now he, Joe and Moshe Leib decided

---

109   The Yiddish Writers Group of the Federal Writers Project, *The Jewish Landsmanschaften of New York,* New York: I.L. Peretz Yiddish Writers Union, 1938. A "Master List of New York *Landsmanschaften* 1970–1980" had 2,445 such societies listed. See: <https://archive.org/stream/Landsmenshaftn/Landsmenshaftn_djvu.txt> retreived on Jan. 14, 2016.

110   KUV – *Kranken Unterschitzungs Verein,* which was usually translated as Sick Benevolent Society. See archives of the First Mihowa Berhometh Bucowiner Society K.U.V. 1925–1988. RG 1801, YIVO Archives, Center for Jewish History, New York City, N.Y.

to establish their own organization, with a constitution, but without an oath or password, laying the groundwork for the family to be together both in life and death. The death of Joe and Moshe Leib's sister Hudel Hirsch in 1928, only three years after she came to America, reminded them that the new organization should also function as a burial society. Hudel had been buried in Montifiore cemetery through the First Mihowa Berhometh Bucowiner Society, but it was a reminded that their new organization should also function as a burial society for the Scharfs and Eisenbergs in America. At first, they did not speak of buying a family burial plot, that could wait; right now the Scharf-Eisenberg Family Circle, as they called it, would begin as an official social and mutual aid organization focusing on life: to help the family in America and to remain in touch with and, if necessary, to provide aid to its members overseas. Hudel had been the first of the Scharf or Eisenberg siblings in America to pass away and hopefully, no additional family members would need a burial society before the Family Circle would be able to organize itself as such in the future.

Motherhood

Indeed there was a new life to look forward to. Thrilled to be expecting just weeks after marriage, Freida Sima informed her husband, whose income as a house painter well supported the family, that they needed to move to a bigger apartment and not a fifth floor walk-up whose stairs were torture for her growing girth. She also stated that contrary to common practice, although his boys had been born at home, those stairs were the reason that his next child was going to be born in a hospital. "It's a woman's decision", his mother told him, and he reluctantly agreed to the move, beginning to look for a new apartment for his family.

On January 14, 1929, eleven months after their marriage, Freida Sima gave birth to her firstborn at Prospect Hospital, a private Bronx hospital boasting a new maternity ward. The ward may have been state of the art at that time, but the communications in the South Bronx were less so. Having left her at the hospital the previous night when her labor began, Max telephoned the hospital from the local candy store that morning, as the Krauses had no telephone at home like most South Bronx residents, and was told that early that morning his wife had given birth to a baby boy. "Another boy", he said, thinking of the *bris* that would take place the following week. "What a mistake", recalled my grandmother. "And what *mazel* (luck) that he got to the hospital before I really had the baby, otherwise after four boys he would have always believed that the hospital had switched babies on him when he saw I had a girl!"

Unexpectedly allowed to remain for the un-medicated birth which took place only at 1 P.M., Max had tears in his eyes as he held his first and only daughter, whom he and Freida Sima decided to name "Shirley Rosalyn". As her husband would never step foot in a *shul* other than to hear *hazzonus*, Freida Sima asked her Uncle Joe to make the *misheberach* (blessing) for the *kimpeturin* (new mother) the following Shabbos and give her daughter the Hebrew name Sarah Raizel. Just as *Tante* Mollie and Uncle Srul Nachman had named their first daughter Chana Yitta (Anne) in memory of Srul Nachman's first wife, Freida Sima had wished to commemorate Max's late wife and assumed Sarah to be Sadie's Hebrew name. Raizel was for a great aunt. Informing Max only after the deed was done, the surprise was on Freida Sima. "Actually, Sadie's name was Sima, just like yours", he told her. She now understood why he had never asked to name the baby for his late wife, as contrary to the Gentile custom, Jews do not give a child their own first name.

Shirley's birth cemented them as a family. The two brothers still at home were thrilled with their little red-headed green-eyed sister. Harry held her constantly, propping her up for the professional photographs they took when she was six weeks old and reluctantly relinquishing her to their father's arms for the formal family portrait to be sent to Europe. The photograph shows Max elegantly attired in his striped wedding suit. Seated in an ornate chair, he is proudly holding his daughter. A smiling Freida Sima stands at his side wearing a formal three-quarter length black dress, a pendant, and the yellow jade beads that she had worn the night they met. Behind them stands a young smiling Harry, and on the other side, a more reserved Ben, both in suits and ties.

Soon after having given birth, Freida Sima made a decision about Shirley's upbringing: that she would speak to her only in English. Like many of the younger Eastern European immigrants of that generation, Freida Sima lived much of her life in a Yiddish-speaking environment. She spoke Yiddish to her husband and to her relatives, just as Max had always spoken Yiddish to his first wife, his parents and sons. She had spoken Yiddish to many of her co-workers and to her boss, and even in some of the neighbor-hood stores where Jews worked, she spoke to them in Yiddish. In her world there was no stigma attached to speaking Yiddish. It was not a repressed language, and in the late 1920s the Yiddish speaking community in New York was alive and well. Nevertheless, her decision to speak only English to Shirley was prompted by two factors: her own fluency in the language, and her observations of what had happened to her American-born cousins.

As a young girl in America Freida Sima had made great efforts to speak fluent and unaccented English, realizing that fluency in the language would be the first step towards her being able to continue her education in America. Her aunts and uncles in America all spoke to their children in Yiddish, and as a result, when the children began school, many of them spoke no English. It was a family joke that when a first-grade teacher held up a spoon and asked the children what it was called, one of the cousins raised his hand and answered "I know teacher, it is a *leffel!*" using the Yid-dish word for a spoon, and causing great mirth in the classroom. "No child of mine is going to make that mistake and get laughed at", thought Freida Sima. Even though she and Max spoke to each other in Yiddish, she insisted that they both speak to Shirley in English so that she would be fluent in the language when she reached first grade. As a result, Shirley became a "fluent comprehender" in Yiddish, but only spoke it to the much older relatives in the family, for whom it was still easier to understand Yiddish than English.

For the first time since coming to America eighteen years earlier, Frei-da Sima began to relax. Less than a year ago she had been an "old maid" and now she was a young mother with a handsome, attentive husband who made a good living, with whom she argued daily about politics and reli-gion, "to spice things up when they get boring", she would say. Her two stepsons at home adored their baby sister while the two in California cele-brated her birth by mail. Shirley was an easy baby whose coloring reminded Freida Sima of her redheaded mother Devorah whom she missed so much at these moments. Having raised enough siblings in the past, Freida Sima knew how to care for a baby. But there were times a new mother wished to speak to her own mother for advice.

All in all, however, life was good, in fact, better than she had ever im-agined. The family moved into a larger and more expensive apartment on Beck Street in the Bronx with separate bedrooms for each child, including one for Shirley when she would be weaned. For the first time in her life, there was almost money to spare, and Freida Sima joined her brothers in setting aside money to send to Europe to bring over some of their other siblings. Nachman, however, was in no hurry to let his sons leave for overseas and once again, he used the money to buy horses and land, instead of tickets. The children in America sighed but were not adamant about the matter. The situation in the Bukovina under Rumanian rule between the wars was indeed not as beneficial for Jews as the Austro-Hungarian rule had been, but it was still quite bearable. Certainly none of them, neither in Europe nor in America, could dream that within a few short years the Jews there would face annihilation.

"If things are too good, be careful", my grandmother used to say, "because you never know what's coming around the corner". Within months of her daughter's birth, Freida Sima's idyllic existence changed. Noticing that Max was constantly thirsty, she pressed him to go to a doctor where he was diagnosed with juvenile diabetes at age forty. Had it been five years earlier, he would almost certainly have been dead within the year, the fate of most diabetics until that time who were put on starvation diets of 500 calories a day in an attempt to lower their blood sugar and buy them another month or two of life, as no other treatment existed.

Although today science thinks differently, during the first decades of the 20th century, diabetes was considered a "Jewish disease", as it was thought of as being transmitted within a specific group, in this case, Jews. Diabetes was conceptualized as a Jewish disease not necessarily because its prevalence was high among this population, but because medicine, science, and culture reinforced each other, helping to construct narratives that made sense at the time. At the time when diabetes was so closely associated with Jews, Jews were considered a race, and race was viewed as a combination of biological, linguistic, and cultural traits that distinguished particular groups of people, including in matters of illness, from other groups. It is not at all clear if Jews suffered from diabetes disproportionately at the time. However the pseudo-scientific literature referred to the Jews as disease carriers, similar to the medieval attitude towards Jews as being those who had brought about the plague. Science, medicine, and culture fed each other during those years, creating a narrative which placed all forms of diabetes firmly within the Jewish racial framework.[111]

---

111 Arlene Marcia Tuchman, "Diabetes and Race: A Historical Perspective", in: *American Journal of Public Health* 101(1) (2011): 23–33.

The world in which diabetes was a death sentence had changed abruptly in 1921 when synthetic insulin was discovered and made commercially available by the Eli Lilly pharmaceutical firm a few years later. Unfortunately, many doctors at the time were still unversed in how to treat diabetics correctly, and until patients found a specialist who could guide them, they lost valuable time and some became too sick to survive. Max may have not been a believer, but Freida Sima's prayers and tears upon hearing her husband's diagnosis must have made some kind of impression in heaven. Sent from one specialist to another, the couple ended up at a hospital where they met a knowledgeable doctor who had been part of an insulin trial and gave them the guidance they needed. This was particularly important in view of the fact that until slow-acting insulin was produced in 1936, diabetics walked an hourly tightrope in terms of insulin dosage.

Max began a lifetime regimen of checking his urine sugar several times a day and injecting himself with insulin, adjusting the dose to meals and physical activity, and always carrying a candy in his pocket in case of diabetic shock. Freida Sima removed sugar from the menu, eschewed baked goods, and watched his diet like a hawk from that day onward, checking his feet on a daily basis for the sores to which diabetics were prone. Having finally found the love of her life at thirty-two, she was not about to lose him a year and half later. Forty years afterwards, on his eightieth birthday, Max announced to all that it was mainly "his Bertie's care", as he called my grandmother, that had kept him alive and healthy so long, augmented possibly by their daily arguments over politics and religion which had kept his wits and nerves sharpened, sometimes more than he would have liked.

Freida Sima and Max settled into a new routine of work, family, food, sugar-dipsticks and insulin injections, hoping that they might even be able to one day expand their family and have another baby. The news from the family in Europe was hopeful. Marium had sent them a beautiful wedding picture inscribed in German, the language in which she and Freida Sima had studied in *cheder*. Benny had met the love of his life – Bruche (Betty) Lobel – on a trip to Europe that he took during the summer of 1929, and was about to return there and bring her to America as a non-quota immigrant. Abie and Minnie were about to become parents in another month. No one could dream that only days later everyone's world would turn upside down when the Great Depression would begin on "Black Tuesday" in late October 1929.

The Great Depression

Tuesday October 29th, 1929 began for Freida Sima like every other day. She got up early to nurse nine-month-old Shirley, set out breakfast for her husband and stepsons Ben and Harry, and made plans to visit her cousin and sister-in-law Minnie who was heavily pregnant with her first child. It was a cloudy day, chillier than usual, and she bundled up the baby for the eight block walk from Beck Street to 158th street in the Bronx. Walking by the newsstand, she glanced at the papers which had been writing about panic stock selling since Thursday, but did not see anything different than on previous days. "Lucky we never invested in the stock market", she thought on her way to Minnie, her mind on the small savings account they had in a nearby bank.

Soon after reaching Minnie, their *Tante* Rivka, who lived in the same building, came to spend the morning with her nieces. Talking about family, babies, and husbands, the women compared notes. Uncle Joe worked at the Astor hotel, Minnie's Abie had a good job at Eckstein Brothers dry goods on Orchard Street on the Lower East Side, "and *Keneine Hora,* may the evil eye stay away from us, my Mordche has plenty of work as a house painter," Freida Sima added. Little did she know that during the length of her visit, close to ten billion dollars of stocks were being wiped out at the New York Stock Exchange, on a day that would forever be known as "Black Tuesday". Nor could she have imagined that within a few days their bank would close and they would lose every hard earned dollar that they had put aside for years.

The Wall Street Crash of 1929 was an event that would change not only Freida Sima's life and that of her family, but the lives of millions of people in dozens of countries throughout the world. In spite of the dangers of speculation, until late autumn 1929 there were many who acted and believed that the American Stock Market would continue to rise forever. Although it had been heralded by a crash of the London Stock Market in September that year, when top British investors were jailed for fraud and forgery, it took another two months until the process would begin in the United States.[112]

It was only in late October 1929 that the economic bubble, on which the continuous stock price rises had been based, actually burst. The reasons

---

112 William E. Leuchtenberg, *The Perils of Prosperity 1914–1932,* Chicago: University of Chicago Press, 1993.

were numerous, beginning with a falling commodity and industrial production market, continuing with the rapidly destabilizing wheat prices worldwide, and ended with the wild economic speculations that had characterized the previous years. But burst it did, leading to panic selling, bank closures and ultimately mass unemployment. The "Roaring Twenties" had come to a shuddering halt, leading to a decade that would be known as the "Lean Thirties" and remembered worldwide as the years of "The Great Depression".[113]

"At least Mordche has his job", Freida Sima thought gratefully, aware that there were more important things in life than one's life savings. Such as one's life. Only weeks earlier, a doctor had informed her husband that he had diabetes, but that it was no longer a death sentence, as insulin had recently become commercially available. Careful with his diet, he now measured his sugar levels every few hours, and injected himself several times a day with the life-saving drug. Finally getting back the energy he had lost during months of illness, he had lined up back-to-back house-painting jobs through the painters' union in which he was active.

One by one the jobs faded away. "No one is moving," he told his wife, "so no one is painting." Trying his luck at selling vegetables, he rented a horse and wagon and walked the streets of the Bronx, but was unsuccessful, claiming that the competition was fierce. Night after night Freida Sima took the wilting vegetables home to cook until she put a stop to the enterprise that was costing them money they no longer had. "That's how I found out that my Mordche was no businessman", she recalled, better understanding the story she had heard of his having run a Chinese laundry when he and his late wife lived in California with their boys, but losing it overnight in a card game.

What do you do when you find out that your husband has lost his job and it doesn't look like he will find another in the near future because millions have lost their jobs along with him? When unemployment insurance and welfare do not yet exist? How do you cope when at the same time you have just signed a lease on a big apartment because you had a new baby? And when soon after, the bank in which you kept your life savings suddenly collapses and closes, taking with it every hard earned dollar that you put aside week after week for the nineteen years since you immigrated to America?

This is the situation that many Eastern European Jewish immigrants found themselves in during the last weeks of 1929 and the first weeks of

---

113   Robert S. McElvaine, *The Great Depression: America 1929–1941,* New York: Time, 1993.

1930. Unlike those who had been born in America and were surrounded by generations of family, who had a home town or farm to fall back on, or who had put their savings into housing, most Eastern European Jewish immigrants in the 1920s had either kept their meager savings at home or put them in a bank, as Freida Sima had done. Few had bought property, few were surrounded by large rural families, few were living off the land and would therefore have what to eat. They were by and large urban, still part of the working class, and thus subject to the employment or rather unemployment issues that would now plague the American public for the next decade.

This is the situation that Freida Sima faced during the winter of 1929. It was twenty months after marrying Max and becoming a stepmother to his boys, and less than ten months after Shirley's birth. Now she had five mouths to feed and suddenly found herself with zero income. There had been no warning, no chance to prepare for the disaster they now faced. But nothing would daunt Freida Sima, who for years had fought to shape her own fate. "With God's help we will get through this", she told her communist husband who had agreed to let her run a traditional home. "Let's see your God help us this time", he muttered in response. "When one door closes another one opens", she answered, her mind already a whirlwind of plans that would change their lives for the next two decades. Once again she would take fate in her hands, this time not only hers but that of the entire family.

Freida Sima was thirty-four years old, but practically a new bride. She realized that with the financial crisis, the family had moved overnight from lower middle class to poor. She was aware of the fact that she was dealing with a newly ill and newly unemployed husband during a worldwide economic disaster and that all their savings had been wiped out overnight. She knew that she had to put food on the table day after day for him, two stepsons and a new baby, at a time that one out of five children in New York City was suffering from malnutrition. She fervently hoped that she would never lose both her faith in God and the belief that she could keep a roof over their heads while two million Americans were becoming homeless. But how exactly would she go about doing this?

Freida Sima understood that until people would need housepainters it would be up to her to support the family. "With a nursing baby and a sick husband I couldn't go back to the factory", she recalled. Looking around at the apartment where they had moved when Shirley was born, she calculated, transposed furniture in her head and recognized the possibilities at hand. The next morning a sign went up in her ground floor window – "rooms for rent, inquire within".

Taking in boarders had always been a way for immigrants to add to their meager salaries. In spite of the fact that reformers in the housing movement saw boarding as a factor in breaking down the family and encouraging immorality, it was a common way of life at a certain period for for natives and immigrants alike.[114] During the first decade of the twentieth century at least one out of four new immigrants would fill their small apartments with roomers in order to send more money home.[115] It was usually described as a stage in an immigrant family's life cycle, and when children got older and could bring in money, it was no longer necessary to have boarders. But Freida Sima was no longer an immigrant, and everyone was having difficulty finding work, including her older stepsons. She also had a small baby and her options were limited.

The response to her sign was almost immediate. Singles and widowers were always looking for an inexpensive place to live. Freida Sima could supply them with an airy room, clean linens, bathroom privileges and a feeling of home. Harry and Ben moved into the smallest bedroom, Shirley would continue to sleep in her parents' bedroom until she was eight, the living room became another bedroom, and the dining room turned into the living room which would eventually become Shirley's bedroom at night and remain a living room during the day. Except on special occasions, the family would now eat in the kitchen as none of the roomers received kitchen privileges. As Evelyn Vogelman, a Lithuanian immigrant who came to America in 1905 recalled "When you have roomers in your home, it's not your home. They take it over."[116]

Losing her privacy, having to always be fully and modestly dressed at home, and sharing a bathroom with strangers were small prices to pay for having a steady income, Freida Sima thought. Only once a week did she allow herself the luxury of dreaming what life would have been like, had things gone on as they were during her first year of marriage. Every Friday afternoon she would draw a hot bath in preparation for Shabbos, sinking

---

114 Lawrence Veiller, "Room Overcrowding and the Lodger Evil," in: *Housing in America: Proceedings of the Second Annual National Conference on Housing,* Philadelphia, 1912: 60–63, quted in Ewen, *Immigrant Women in the Land of Dollars*: 119.

115 E. A. Goldenweisser, "Immigrants in Cities", *Survey* 19 (1908):1050 quoted in Ewen, *Immigrant Women in the Land of Dollars*: 119.

116 Quoted in Ewen, *Immigrant Women in the Land of Dollars*: 120.

into the large tub used during the week for everything from washing clothes to keeping live carp before cooking. Closing her eyes and floating in the water, she would remember how she agreed to marry Mordche after knowing him for less than five hours, even before he told her he was a widower with four sons, the older two now in California with his sisters. "I'm a successful painter", he told her before they got married, "You will never want for anything!" Shaking the water from her short hair which was already going white in her mid-thirties, she shook the thoughts of what could have been from her mind, and prepared to dress for Shabbos.

In a clean blouse and skirt with a pink kerchief covering her hair, she would turn towards the candles placed in two tall silver candlesticks that her atheist husband had bought for her out of love before they married. Slowly circling her face with her palms three times, she covered her eyes and *benched lecht,* praying for her husband's health and livelihood, for her stepsons, for her daughter Shirley, for her parents on the farm in Mihowa in far-away Bukovina, and finally for herself, thanking God for having lived another week and asking for strength to get through the week to come. Turning to her husband, a communist who in those days still believed that the truth would ultimately come from "The Sun of Nations" in the East, Comrade Stalin, she wished him a good Sabbath. "*A Gut Shabbos, mein* Mordche", to which he would always reply respectfully, "*A Gut Shabbos, mein* Bertie". In spite of their daily political and religious arguments on the theoretical level, he never mocked her candle lighting, *shul* going, or insistence on a strictly kosher home.

The years of the Great Depression continued with Mordche working less than six months out of every year, and Freida Sima expanding her boarding house. She even agreed to take on a boarder with kitchen privileges, Mr. Rosenthal, whom everyone called "Rosie". A widower and traditional Jew who soon became a member of the family, "Rosie's" weekly payments enabled them to breathe financially, to become "the less poor among the poor" as Freida Sima once said. The tall, kind widower lived in the Kraus home until his death twenty years later, and was mourned by all as if he were indeed a relative. Leaving his *tallis* (prayer shawl) and *tefillin* (phylacteries) to his landlady as his own freethinker son had no use for them, they sat in her drawer for another three decades until there was finally a religious man in the family who was tall enough to wear "Rosie's" oversized prayer shawl.

Poverty and ill-health were the fears of every former immigrant at that time, and during the Depression Freida Sima's family were, like many, only one step away from taking "home relief", as welfare was then called. "It was a great shame to anyone who took it, if someone would know", she once said to me, alluding to the unsubstantiated rumors among some in the Sharf-Eisenberg family that the Krauses had received such assistance during the 1930s. "Never!", she told me adamantly. For that she was willing to give up her privacy and that of her family, to "stretch the dollar until the eagle looked like an ostrich", as per the saying of that time, and to rely on the Almightly and the boarders.

In spite of the Depression, Freida Sima's family continued to expand on both sides of the Atlantic. Three weeks after "Black Friday", Abie and Minnie had a girl, naming her Muriel in memory of their mutual grand-mother, Baba Malka. Several months later, in Mihowa, her sister Marium gave birth to a daughter, Tzili. A year later, her younger brother in America, Benny and his wife Betty had a daughter, Bernice, and two and a half years after that Muriel was joined by a baby sister, Sheila.

Despite the fact that she would have wanted to have another baby, Freida Sima realized that her family's economic tribulations of the time made that an impossible dream. Only once did she talk to me about what the Depression had done to the reproduction of women of her generation. "Lucky that your mother had been born just before it started", she said "because afterwards it would have been very difficult, maybe even impossible, for us to have a baby. After all, we already had four big boys." More than one married former-immigrant who found herself pregnant during the Depression, ended up going to a back-street abortionist to rid herself of a situation that could have devastating economic consequences. Even in a culture stressing procreation, the medical practice of midwives had often included abortion, and it was already estimated that at the beginning of the century over 100,000 (illegal) abortions were performed every year in New York City alone.[117] The price of abortions was high, women often paid over weekly installments, and from their stories of attempts at "family planning" during the 1930s, it appears that little had changed between the beginning of the century in this matter, and the years of the Great Depression, two decades later.

"So we will have one daughter and four sons", Freida Sima once said to Max, who reminded her how grateful he was to even have one more child than he had previously. "Besides, we have your whole big family, they are always here anyhow", he added. And it was true. One of the things

---

117 F. Elizabeth Crosswell, "The Midwives of New York", *Charities and the Commons* 17 (1907): 668; "Large Immigrant Population Conference on Infant Morality", *Survey* 27 (1911): 671, both quoted in Ewen, *Immigrant Women in the Land of Dollars*: 133.

that helped Freida Sima's family get through the Depression years was her physical closeness with her aunts, uncles, and cousins. Much of the extended Scharf-Eisenberg-Kraus family lived within in walking distance from each other, as did many families in those days, and they would constantly be going back and forth to each other's homes, giving the younger cousins the feeling of belonging to a clan that stretched throughout the Longwood section of the South Bronx. They not only lived in each other's homes, but they frequented the same schools, *shuls*, and Family Circle.

A large portion of the family *davened* (prayed) at the storefront *shul* on Intervale Avenue, across from the Minsker *shul*, "which was only for the Russians", Muriel recalled.[118] She also recalled how her older cousin Shirley developed a sense of adventure that matched her red hair. "One Yom Kippur eve when we were quite small she found a baby kitten that she decided to take into *Kol Nidre*. Hiding it in her sweater, the kitten was quiet until it decided to start meowing right in the middle of *davening*. Her mother and my grandmother looked straight at me, as Shirley with her white skin and big green eyes put on this innocent look so no one suspected her. But I just shook my head and shrugged my shoulders."

"*Dor Holech Vedor Ba*"- one generation goes and another comes. In early 1932 Max's father Abraham became ill, passing away in May at the age of 83. "Atheist or not you will say *Kaddish* for your father!" whispered Freida Sima to Max as the funeral procession reached the "Minsker Old Men's Benevolent Association" section, in the Old Montefiore Cemetery in Queens, the *landsmanschaft* Abraham Kraus had joined when immigrating to America decades earlier. For the first time in their life together Max gave her a stony look. "As if I would do anything else", he responded, gesturing towards his very religious mother, a long black lace kerchief covering her *sheitl*, walking with the women.

Less than a year later they were back at the cemetery to bury Max's mother Chana who had passed away on the seventh day of Pesach 1933, two days after her sons had finished eleven months of saying *Kaddish* for their father. Earlier that afternoon she had been fine, standing in Freida Sima's kitchen and vigorously beating up a snow of egg whites by hand for a holiday

---

118 Author's interview with Muriel Arens, Nov. 6, 2015. There were several synagogues on Intervale Avenue at the time, most of which closed when the South Bronx changed its ethnic composition. A book has been devoted to the history and continuous survival of one of them, Jack Kugelmass, *The Miracle of Intervale Avenue: The Story of a Jewish Congregation in the South Bronx*, New York: Columbia University Press, 1996.

dish. Bidding her family a *gut yuntif* (happy holiday) and a good night, the eighty-year-old grandmother went to sleep and did not wake up. Because of it being a three day holiday, she could only be buried two days later.

It was not an easy time for the Kraus family. Since Max was out of work, he had spent a lot of time helping his elderly parents. Now that they were gone, when he was not on an occasional paint job, he spent most of his time with his friends, either downtown at the Workman's Circle or the Painter's Union, talking about world news or how they hoped the new president, Franklin Delano Roosevelt, would change things to the better.

In 1932, Roosevelt had run as the Democratic candidate, winning 57% of the vote and carrying all but six states. When he came to power, a quarter of the American workforce was unemployed, two million people were homeless, and industrial production had fallen by more than half since 1929. When he was inaugurated on January 4, 1933, the New York Federal Reserve Bank was unable to open the next morning because panicky customers had withdrawn huge sums on the previous days. Roosevelt had campaigned on a platform of promising the reduction of public expenditures, abolishing useless commissions and offices, consolidating departments and eliminating extravagances. Now it would be time to see if he could carry out his promises.

Roosevelt's "New Deal" would barely affect Max's employment status, which would only change with the outbreak of the Second World War. However his Social Security Act of 1935, introducing universal retirement pensions, would ensure Freida Sima and Max's old age.[119] Changing the future of the Eastern European Jewish immigrants in the United States, it would enable them to retire, and not work until they dropped as their parents had to. But that would be long in the future and now the challenge was still finding and keeping a job. Although Freida Sima and Max would never have considered accepting public aid during this period, it was a time that the Jewish communities of New York reexamined their attitude towards the much debated subject, realizing it would be impossible during the Great Depression, for the Jews to continue to care for their own without outside assistance.[120]

---

119   Alonzo L. Hamby, *Man of Destiny: FDR and the Making of the American Century,* New York: Basic, 2015; Roger Daniels, *Franklin D. Roosevelt: Road to the New Deal 1882–1939,* Champaign: University of Illinois Press, 2015; Andrew Dobelstein, *Understanding the Social Security Act: the Foundation For Social Welfare in America in the Twenty-First Century,* Oxford and New York: Oxford University Press, 2009.

120   Beth Wegner, *New York Jews and the Great Depression: Uncertain Promise,* New Haven: Yale, 1996.

Freida Sima, however, was busier than ever running her boardinghouse. In spite of her in-law's deaths and the family's economic pressures, she was more content than she had been in years. After much pleading by her three children in America, their mother Devorah had agreed to come on an extended visit to New York. Not having seen her mother since she was fifteen, Freida Sima would finally be able to hug, kiss, and talk to her face to face.

Baba Devorah Comes to America

What is it like to be reunited with your mother for the first time in twenty-one years? How does a young woman of thirty-six suddenly juggle the responsibilities of being a wife, mother and daughter after not having lived in the same country as her parents since she was a teenager? How does she explain to her very religious mother that she, her beloved firstborn, is actually married to a freethinking communist who is both unemployed and diabetic; facts that she had conveniently glossed over in her letters "home"? That she, too, was more "modern" than her devout parents, although quite traditional, compared to many Eastern European Jewish immigrants in America?

These were the issues that Freida Sima faced when her mother Devorah Scharf Enzenberg came to America for an extended visit beginning in early 1932. Not only did Devorah have three children in America whom she hadn't seen in years; she also had brothers and sisters who had immigrated from Mihowa long before the war. As the Scharf and Enzenberg – now Eisenberg – men either came to America married, married family members there, or returned to Europe to find a bride, she already knew most of her sisters-in-law, daughters-in-law and brothers-in-law from Mihowa. But she had never met her sister Sadie's or Freida Sima's husbands. There were also three small granddaughters whom she had only seen in photographs which her children diligently sent "home" after each birth.

Now that her six remaining children in Europe were older, it had been possible to consider taking the trip she had dreamed of for years. Both Abie and Benny had come back to Mihowa to see her during the 1920s after becoming American citizens, but she longed to hold her oldest, her "Babaleh", Freida Sima's childhood nickname, in her arms. "After all", she told her husband Nachman, "it won't cost us anything". The family in America had sent money for tickets and she would stay with her son Avrum and his wife Minnie, her niece and now daughter-in-law. Her children in Europe encouraged her to go; even her youngest, Sheindl, who went by the Rumanian name "Jenny", assured her that at sixteen she could handle the farm kitchen on her own. Putting aside her qualms about leaving Nachman for the first time in their thirty-seven year marriage, Devorah packed her bags for the two-week journey that began by wagon, continued by train and ended with a six day steamship voyage across the Atlantic. She had left Mihowa before because of Nachman's lumber contracts, and when the family ran away to Poland during the Great War, but this was different. This was the first time she would board a ship and see the ocean. Life was wonderful! Devorah was going to America!

* * *

As wonderful as it was to see her family, nothing was as she had imagined, thought Devorah towards the end of her stay in New York. Not the city, not her family, and not even her longing for those she had left in Mihowa. Even though they had all described their lives in the letters that they sent home throughout the years, it was nothing like seeing and experiencing it herself.

First there was New York. None of her visits to Czernowitz, the "big city" closest to Mihowa, could prepare her for where she was now living. Imagine a city with close to seven million people, a quarter of whom were *yidden* (Jews)! Czernowitz only had 112,000 people, but at least more than a third of them were *unzer* (ours), she recalled from her son Elish's stories, her *talmid chochom* (scholar), who studied there at the *Gymnasium*. She had visited Elish in the city and seen what it was like, with buildings and people everywhere. Still, it was nothing like the number of people she saw in New York.[121]

And the buildings. Just last week Avrum, now "Abie", had taken her to see a tremendous building, the Empire State Building, which he had called "The Empty State Building" because most of it floors were empty as no one had money to rent the offices. Looking down at the city from the observation deck she couldn't believe how high up they were. This is what birds see, she thought, smiling, and if it were only a bit higher and she stood on tiptoe, she might even be able to see Mihowa beyond the ocean.[122]

---

121 See figures in: *Recensamantul General al Populatiei Romaniei*, 1930, vol. 2, Bucuresti, 1938. Census of Romania for the year 1930, Province of Bukovina by Departments and Districts.

122 John Tauranac, *The Empire State Building: The Making of a Landmark,* Ithaca: Cornell, 2014.

Her children also took her to see a motion picture, something about a Tarzan man, and had translated the dialogue for her. What a strange story, about a pretty girl who goes to Africa and falls in love with a handsome man who lived with the monkeys and protected the jungle. Johnny Weiss-muller, he was called. Oh how her children loved adventures, and this was an adventure film, they told her.[123]

Her family was indeed adventurous and special. From the minute she got off the boat they had treated her like a queen. When she took a bath, her Avrum would sit outside the door, talking to her the whole time to make sure she didn't drown! He was always giving her American candy he carried around, something called "charms".[124] It meant *chayn* in Yiddish, he said, *mazeldik chayn.* And indeed he was *mazeldik,* lucky, with a good job on Orchard Street. A few times Devorah visited him there on the Lower East Side. What a neighborhood, full of Jewish stores! But a few streets away they were gone and all you saw were Chinese people. Chinatown they called it, with beautiful signs in pictures that they told her were letters. The Chinese liked to live together, like the Jews, which was why so many of her family in New York lived near each other.

Her sisters and brothers in New York — Mollie, Sadie, Joe and Moshe Leib, and their families — either lived near each other or came to visit all the time, as did their children. Mollie and her husband Srul Nachman now had three children of their own — Anne, Milton, and Dorothy — in addition to Srul Nachman's children from his late wife, Louis, and Perla, who had trag-ically passed away at a young age. Sadie and Sam had three as well — Lenny, Bummie (Avrum) and Molly. Joe and Rivka had two — Abe (Avrum) and Mitzi, while Moshe Leib and Hudel had three — Max, Al (Avrum), and their youngest, Minnie, who was now Devorah's daughter-in-law.

Finally, there were the children of her late sister Hudel who had mar-ried Fischel Hirsch. Fischel had come to America before the war, like Freida Sima, but Hudel and the children had only come years later, in 1925. Poor Hudel, so sick and dying only three years after she came to America. Fischel wasn't so close to the rest of the family in America. But his five children,

---

123 The 1932 film, Tarzan of the Apes, was based on the 1914 classic by Edgar Rice Burroughs by the same name. See the Penguin classic reissue edition from 1990.

124 The Charms Candy Co. was founded in 1912 by Walter Reid Jr., as "Tropical Charms" which were the square-shaped, fruit-flavored, hard candy he manufactured, among the first candies to be individually wrapped in cellophane. <http://www.nj.com/news/local/index.ssf/2012/08/glimpse_of_history_sweet_treat.html> (retrieved Dec. 17, 2015).

Anna, Rebecca, Lena, Minnie, and Avrum, were. How comforting it was that her father Avrum, who died so young, had so many handsome grandsons named after him.

The next generation had no boys yet. Benzion and Betty had Bernice, a sweet baby girl who reminded Devorah of her granddaughter Zilly in Mihova. Tzeendl, as she called Benzion, was a butcher but had been a dental mechanic and he still made tiny false teeth as a present for every new baby born in the family. How the mothers would laugh when they saw those teeth! Benzion had made a set for Zilly but by the time Devorah brought them home Zilly would already have real teeth! Freida Sima and Mordche had their Shirley with her big green eyes and Devorah's fiery red hair, and Abie and Minnie had beautiful Muriel with her long black curls. Like the man in the film they saw, little Muriel was crazy about monkeys. During Devorah's first year in America, every day she would take Muriel to the nearby Bronx zoo to see the monkeys. What a place that zoo was! All these buildings filled with animals and in the middle the big round pool with seals and their long whiskers. They reminded her of some of her neighbors in Mihowa, with their long mustaches sticking out in all directions.[125]

As for Mihowa, even in America there was no getting away from that village! Before she had left Europe, some non-Jewish neighbors had asked Devorah if she would be willing to speak to their *landsleit* (fellow town members) in America who had immigrated years ago, and were now living in a community near New York. "Why not?!" she answered, which is how she found herself, traveling with Mina and little Muriel to Newark, New Jersey where these former Mihowians lived.[126] The address where she was supposed to speak turned out to be an Orthodox church! Imagine me, Devorah Scharf Enzenberg, standing at a church lectern and talking for an hour in Ruthenian about Mihowa to a bunch of *goyim*! They obviously enjoyed it as they invited her back three more times to speak. In another life I could have been a lecturer in a *Gymnasium,* Devorah thought with a smile, recalling how her audience drank up every word that she had spoken.

---

125 William Bridges, *The Bronx Zoo Book of Wild Animals,* New York: New York Zoological Society, 1968.

126 There were several enclaves of Bukovinian Ruthenians who had moved to America during the Great Wave of Immigration. Apart from those in New Jersey, there were enclaves in Ellis, Kansas; Yuma Country, Colorado; Naperville, Illinois; Lewis County, Washington. See: Bukovina Society of the Americas, <http://www.bukovinasociety. org/> retrieved, Dec. 17, 2015.

Only her Babaleh, her Freida Sima, her oldest daughter whom she hadn't seen in twenty years, still remembered the kind of things Devorah had been capable of when she was younger. Now Freida Sima was so busy running her boardinghouse, and taking care of little Shirley, that she only got to visit her mother once or twice during the week. "Maybe I should spend Shabbos with you?" asked Devorah at the beginning. But Freida Sima explained that even though she and her freethinking husband had an agreement where she would run a traditional home and he could do what he wanted outside, it probably would still not be to her mother's liking. Well at least Freida Sima had taught her daughter Yiddish so that she could speak to her Baba Devorah, and maybe she would still turn out to be a *gut yiddisheh tochter,* a good Jewish daughter.

It had been Mordche's newly widowed mother Chana, who told Devorah how sick he was with diabetes and how lucky Freida Sima was for him to be alive. At eighty, Chana was old enough to be Devorah's mother, but Devorah could talk to her about things the others didn't understand. Like Devorah, Chana wore a *sheitl* (wig), hers covered with a Russian-style lace *tichel* (kerchief). When Devorah mentioned that her children in America were so modern, Chana told her to be grateful that they kept kosher, as two of Chana's daughters were "revolutionaries" and she couldn't even eat at their homes.

Chana was right, Devorah thought. At least her family was alive and well, and except for her struggling Freida Sima, the others even seemed prosperous. Joe's son Avrum was talking about becoming a lawyer: an immigration lawyer to help the family come to America! He kept saying one has to keep "proof" of things, a piece of paper or picture, proof that something really happened.

Well now he would have "proof" of her visit. Joe had arranged a farewell party for her this past week and had a photographer come to take pictures of the whole family. In addition to the different family groupings, one of which even included a picture of Nachman which the photographer had inserted to complete the portrait, they had taken a group picture of the whole family, all thirty of them. Little Bernice was sitting on her lap, the younger children at her feet, her children, brothers, sisters and their families surrounding her. How was it, she thought, that I'm the only adult smiling in the picture? Maybe it's because I'm the only one who can really appreciate what it is like to be here and not in Rumania. My sisters, brothers, and children all look so serious, some as if the world was coming to an end. Do they know something I don't? Mollie's very *frum* (religious) husband, Srul Nachman, who kept his hat on in the picture, looks a bit happier, maybe because he is older than anyone else in the family and knows one should enjoy every moment of happiness, but otherwise? They should know how lucky they are to be in America!

Bringing the Family Over from Germany

Devorah stayed in New York for a year and a half, and in the summer of 1933 returned to Mihowa. At first, she told the children that the Rumanian authorities hadn't let Nachman come because he was a landowner, but later she let slip that in truth, he was simply afraid to leave the farm for too long. For the same reason he hadn't been willing to immigrate with Devorah to America in the past, although she begged him to consider it. Nachman was indeed a multifaceted man whose frugality could be counterbalanced by his generosity. He was tremendously attached to his farm and possessive of his land, and therefore willing to sue anyone – even relatives! – whom he thought were harming his farmland. Yet he was at the same time known to give hospitality to any Jewish visitor passing through Mihowa, and was in need of a place to stay for Shabbos.

The only thing he was more attached to than his land, was his children. He had let Freida Sima immigrate to America when he was living in the *Kresy*, far away from the Bukovina, when he realized that it would be a solution to a number of problems at that time, not the least of which was her reluctance to marry a local boy. He was also not unhappy when he considered the advantages of having an added dollar income that would be sent regularly to the family from America. But when it came to his sons emigrating years later, particularly when he was back on his farm in Mihowa after the Great War, he was less enthusiastic, both about Abie leaving and later about Benny following. After having lost his two oldest sons to the New World, he was not about to let any more of his children leave for overseas and his greatest wish was to have them continue living in Mihova along with him. But that was not to be.

Already in the late 1920s, the next son in line, Srul, had left for Czernowitz where he began working in a saw mill, utilizing the knowledge and training he had gotten from Nachman during their years of cutting down forests. Srul had once dreamed of being a rabbi, but he knew that he had to be practical as he had to be able to earn a living. As time went on, he decided that life was definitely more enjoyable if one was not a rabbi. Srul must have inherited his father's early love of dancing, for he frequented dances in Czernowitz and at one of them, he met the woman he decided to marry, Anna (Chana) Rosensweig. Family lore has it that he was first interested in her older sister, but as soon as he met Anna, he made up his mind and the two spoke seriously about marriage. Srul's Rumanian army service intervened, and only three years later, in late 1932, did the couple begin to make concrete wedding plans.

Nachman was not particularly happy with the match. Chana's father Nute had immigrated to New York before the war, planning to bring over his entire family. However the war had intervened before he could carry out his plans, and Nute died in the flu epidemic of 1918. Money was tight and his widow Zipporah, supporting the family in the Bukovina on her own, sent her children out to work as early as possible. As the years passed, and times were hard, the family had become less careful about religious practice. Although Chana was a proficient seamstress and could earn a good living, the extremely devout Nachman was quite upset at the thought that his oldest son in Europe would be marrying into a not particularly religious family. As Devorah was in America at the time, and not around to mediate, as she often did when Nachman's temper flared, Srul and Anna married in early 1933 without Nachman having attended the wedding. "Oy my Nachman", sighed Devorah when she received a letter about the wedding that she, too, had missed, "and oy my Srulik," she thought. It is time for me to go home and make peace between them.

With a heavy heart and bitter tears, Devorah parted from her children in New York, fearing she would never see them again. Before leaving, she blessed her children and grandchildren one by one, wishing them good health, a long life, and plentiful *parnosseh* (livelihood) for all their days. She hoped that she would be able to make another trip to see them in the future, and that if things would get better financially, maybe they or their children would be able to visit the family in Mihowa in a few years. She then parted from her brothers and sisters and their children, wondering if she would ever see them again. Now she understood them so much better, and why they loved living in America, although it still bothered her that people lived in such crowded conditions apartments, with no land around them where they could walk around and just breathe the garden smells, as she would do every day at home.

Devorah was in for a surprise. Her brother Joe, who felt very responsible for the family in America, was not about to part from his big sister so fast. Not wanting Devorah to travel alone, Joe accompanied her on the ship to Hamburg giving them an extra week together and insuring that he would put her on a train to the Bukovina to make sure she got home safely. But Joe also had another mission, one that would be the beginning of a task that he and Abie would take on themselves for years to come: to help bring over the relatives now living in Germany. Joe's in-laws, Schlome and Rachel Weiner, who were also Abie's mother-in-law's brother and sister-in-law, were living in Germany at the time, and having followed the news from Europe from the beginning of the year regarding Nazi Germany, he knew that he had to now help them immigrate to America. For that reason, he remained in Germany until August, insuring that they had the necessary documents and money for tickets and waiting with them until they had passed the various bureaucratic hurdles.

Joe's short stay in Germany brought home to him what it was like for Jews to live under the Nazi regime. Realizing what their daily life was like and understanding some of the potential dangers ahead, he understood that it was imperative to get all of his wife's relatives in Germany out as soon as possible. Some of these relatives were actually his blood relatives as well, and not only related by marriage, as one generation back, one of the Weiner grandmothers had been a Scharf.

As a result, he made plans to help his Weiner relatives, and during the next years he sponsored his brothers-in-laws' immigration. From then on, Joe and his nephew Abie constantly filled out affidavits for other family members in Germany wanting to leave Europe: Joe's sister-in-law's brother and his family; Abie's mother-in-law's niece and her family; and various additional relatives. Joe had the advantage of working at the Astor Hotel and under the guise of the hotel needing experienced culinary and hotel employees, he listed some the immigrants from Germany and Austria as coming for that purpose, giving them preference within the quota system. Abie had a steady well-paying job during the Depression, and was able to put up the fifty dollar bond necessary as a guarantee for each immigrant. As a child, Muriel remembered going with her father on his lunch break to the Immigration and Naturalization offices at Rockerfeller Center, waiting with him while he filled out the necessary affidavits to help sponsor these relatives coming to the United States. The Scharfs and Eisenbergs in America were now joined by the Weiners, Rennerts and Gottfrieds who had come over from Germany. All joined the Family Circle and eventually became one big family.

Eventually, but not immediately. The introduction of the new family members from Germany into the Scharf Eisenberg Family Circle was not a simple process. Although some of the older ones came from an Eastern European background and had an easier time fitting in culturally with the original Scharfs and Eisenbergs, the younger ones had been brought up in Germany and were already part of the Central European cultural milieu. Language was less of a problem, as those coming from Mihowa spoke fluent German, but for years, some of the newcomers were referred to as "the Germans", not in a derogatory sense, but to mark the difference between them and the original Family Circle members.

The absorption of "the Germans" within the Family Circle, mirrored a process that was occurring among American Jews of the time, a reversal of the roles from that which had existed at the turn of the century, when the Jewish immigrants from Eastern Europe had arrived in America. At that time, the American-Jewish community that absorbed them was composed primarily of German-speaking Jews originating in Central Europe, who considering themselves "westernized" and refined. These were the Jews who had brought the Reform Movement to the United States and who viewed themselves as part of a culture that included liberal values.

Initially, the German Jews in America did not look kindly upon their Eastern European brethren who were arriving. In their eyes, the Eastern European and often traditional newcomers were part of a less enlightened culture and had to be educated towards more western values. In addition, most of the Jewish immigrants arriving were poor, and were creating what appeared to the German Jews as a "ghetto" in downtown New York. Not only did these Jews offend the sensibilities of many German Jews; they also raised fears of a rise in anti-Semitism that might increase in the face of massive Jewish immigration.

The German Jews in America and their descendants realized that they could not ignore the indigent Jewish immigrants reaching America's shores. As early as 1881 they had founded the first organizations to help these new immigrants such as HIAS (Hebrew Immigrant Aid Society) or the "New Hebrew Technical Institute" in New York to provide industrial training to immigrants that would make them independent of the various Jewish charity organizations.[127] As time passed, two group of German Jews in particular forged a bond to offer great assistance to their Eastern European brethren: the radical idealists such as Emma Lazarus, Henrietta Szold, and enlightened members of the Reform Rabbinate, who reacted warmly and sympathetically to the newcomers, and the rich, high placed Jews such as the Jacob Schiff who became leaders during the immigration crisis. Nevertheless, the Eastern European Immigrants often referred to what they considered a cultural and class of German Jews who, they claimed, treated them with condescension and "cold philanthropy".[128]

Forty years later the wheel had turned and the Eastern European immigrants were now absorbing the Jewish refugees from Germany. Although many leaders of the major Jewish refugee organization at the time such as the American Jewish Joint Distribution Committee were descendants of the 19th century Central European wave of immigration, the American Jewish community absorbing them was overwhelmingly Eastern European. As for the masses of Eastern European Jews in America, although no one could have anticipated the horrors of the Holocaust, there was nevertheless an acknowledgement of what anti-Semitism could lead to, and an understanding of the fact that American Jews must do their utmost to help their persecuted brothers escape Germany.

As soon as it became known that the German-Jewish Children's Aid organization, established in New York in 1934 to rescue Jewish children from Germany, was looking for foster families in America, Freida Sima offered to take a refugee child into her home and provide for his or her needs. In spite of the Depression, and the fact that her own family was living only slightly above the poverty line, she understood the importance of rescuing Jewish children from Nazi Germany, and was willing to make the necessary sacrifices in order to help. Nevertheless, her offer was turned down by the organization as she could not meet a central requirement that the United States Children's Bureau in Washington had set for potential foster parents: providing the refugee children with a separate bedroom. In view of the fact that her daughter was sleeping in the corner of the living room at the

127 Irving Aaron Mandel, "Attitude of the American Jewish Community Towards East-European Immigration As Reflected in the Anglo-Jewish Press (1880–1890)", *American Jewish Archives* (June 1950): 11–36.

128 Gerald Sorin, "Mutual Contempt, Mutual Benefit: The Strained Encounter Between German and Eastern European Jews in America, 1880–1920", *American Jewish History* 81:1 (Autumn 1993): 34–59.

time, in order to free bedrooms for the boarding house, it was an impossible demand.

In 1938 Joe's son Abe became an immigration lawyer and was of tremendous help to the family in bringing over relatives from Germany. For his graduation, Joe organized a banquet – "reception dinner and dance" – at the Paramount Mansion, inviting the entire family to celebrate. Knowing how to organize a party from his experience working at the Astor Hotel, he arranged for a dais where he put the family, including his boss and his wife. The rest of the friends and family were seated at round tables placed around the dance floor, each with long tapered candles, flowers and drinks at their center. The picture taken at the banquet, which hung on Freida Sima's wall for the rest of her life, along with the large family portrait taken at her mother's farewell party, showed tables filled with dozens of smiling friends and family.

This was the Family Circle's last big celebration before the war that would devastate the Scharfs and Enzenbergs in Europe, killing young and old. But none of that was in anyone's mind in late 1938 during this party. At the time they were just happy that another of their children had made them proud. Each child in the family was his or her parents' child, but the family circle was a unit, and at the same time, they were collective children of "the family". Each of the brothers and sisters attending that party was as proud of Abe Scharf as if he were their own child. Each cousin, including those who had "married in", saw him as if he were a blood relative, which for many of the in-laws, he actually was, as so many of them had Scharf ancestors. His success was his and his parents', but it was also theirs, testimony to what "one of their own" could do in America. He was the first of the Scharf-Eisenberg children to be born in America, the first to finish college, the first to finish law school. As time went on he would be joined by other children in the family who would also get degrees, some of whom would eventually become lawyers, doctors and professors. But on that day he was the first, and the only, and that deserved a party.

Chapter 6 Freida Sima and the Holocaust – New York, Rumania, and Transnistria (1939–1945)

Part I The Scharfs-Eisenbergs and the War

Introduction

Friday September 1, 1939 began for Freida Sima like every other Friday that year. Getting up early, she opened the kitchen window, put on her apron, and started preparing for Shabbos. Rosh Hashanah was less than two weeks away, she noted, and next week she should go over to *Tante* Hudel to decide how they would be dividing up the holiday food preparations. As she worked in the kitchen, she thought about the news they had been hearing from the relatives whom Uncle Joe and Abie had brought over from Germany. Everyone there was desperately trying to leave, as it was just a matter of time until war would break out. True, the Bukovina where her family lived was a long distance from Germany, but who knows how far a war could spread?

For the thousandth time she berated herself about not pressing her father to leave Mihowa, something he refused to consider, even though his children had sent him money for tickets year after year. Why did I let Mama go back after she came to visit us here? What will happen to them if war breaks out? And what of her six brothers and sisters still in the Bukovina? The family in Europe had their recent share of tragedy when Marium had lost a newborn baby and her little Tzili had died of appendicitis. But they had also had *simchas* (festivities) when Srul's Anna gave birth to Yulbert (Yehuda), the first boy of the next generation, and when Sheindl, Leibish and Elish had married.

In early 1938, Sheindl, born after Freida Sima had left Europe, had married Schaje Steinbrecher, and had moved to nearby Behromet. Schaje's mother was a Haller cousin whose sister, Gittel, was married to Nachman's brother Meier Moshe. At the end of the year Sheindl and Schaje had a little girl, Marta. Leibish and Elish, both of whom had been living in

Czernowitz, had married their brides in the spring of 1939. Leibish had been introduced to Frieda Sheitel-Reiss, a seamstress, and they were married in March. Elish had met his "Lola", Charlotte Wagner, on the train when they were both on their way home from studying in Czernowitz, and they were married in June. This time, both Devorah and Nachman had attended all three weddings, unlike when Srul had gotten married a few years earlier without either parent being present. Devorah had been in America and Nachman, upset with the *shidduch* (match), had refused to attend the wedding. Nachman was indeed a stubborn man at times, and it often took Devorah's gentle presence to make him come around. But Devorah hadn't been there and thus, Srul had gotten married with only his brothers and sisters attending.

The family in America was also expanding. After Baba Devorah had gone back to Mihowa, Abie and Minnie had another little girl, Sheila, bringing the total of female granddaughters in America to four. Family had always been important for Freida Sima, even more so since losing her best friend in America, Fanny Carlin, to illness, several years ago. Morris and Fanny had introduced her to Mordche, and the successful match had cemented their friendship even more. But suddenly Fanny was gone and Morris was left with children of all ages, some married but others still small and at home. No wonder he remarried within a short time, just as Mordche had done, and hopefully Morris and his wife would be as happy as she and Mordche were. At least all of Morris's family was in America and he wasn't worried about brothers and sisters left in Europe.

What *mazel* (luck) that most of her Mordche's family had immigrated to America as well, except for his sister Mata and her family in Kiev, and his brother-cousin Isaac, who had moved to Palestine. Almost twenty-five years after they had first intended to move, the Zionist Isaac and his wife, had finally moved to Palestine in 1935, and tried to convince Freida Sima and Max to join them in *Eretz Yisrael*. It was the Depression, Max was out of work, and Isaac promised them that "There is more than enough work here for painters". Initially, Max had considered it, but in view of Roosevelt's economic plans he decided to delay the decision by a year. Had it not been for the "New Deal", thought Freida Sima more than once, Shirley could have grown up in Tel-Aviv.

Isaac and his wife Helena-Genia lived in a building with marble steps, so he had written them, describing their nice house on Cremieux Street, in central Tel Aviv. As he and Helena had no children, and they felt very close to

Mordche who had lived with them in Lodz as a teenager, Isaac asked whether they would eventually like to inherit the house. The only problem would be the yearly property tax which Mordche and Freida Sima would have to pay after inheriting. Although it was a lovely gesture, Mordche knew it was an impossible sum for him to consider. After all, there was a Depression going on, he was out of work half of every year, and Freida Sima was keeping them fed with her boarding house income.

Mordche thanked Isaac, but was forced to refuse the offer. Isaac wrote back that he understood, and that they would then leave the apartment to the *Keren Kayemeth,* the Jewish National Fund, which would also take care of their burial arrangements and tombstone when the time would come. When Isaac died in 1938, the *Keren Kayemeth* had arranged his funeral, and constructed a beautiful tombstone for him at the Nachlat Yitzchak cemetery in Tel-Aviv, noting on it that Yitzchak-Isaac Karasikov, as he was known in *Eretz Yisrael*, had willed his home to the *Keren Kayemeth* "for the redemption of the Land of Israel".[129] Helena, had sent them a picture of the tombstone, and kept in touch with Freida Sima. Well, at least Helena wasn't in Europe and they wouldn't have to worry about her if there would be a war.

Busy with Shabbos preparations, Freida Sima didn't think of turning on the radio early that morning. Only when her boarder "Rosie" came in from his morning walk did she hear the news. Less than twelve hours earlier German forces had attacked Poland, bombing Warsaw and seizing the "free city" of Danzig. Giving a sudden shiver, Freida Sima thought that no one could guess how things would develop, but one thing was certain. War had begun.

The Outbreak of War in Europe

When the war in Europe broke out, the young Jewish immigrants from Eastern Europe in the United States who had come right before or after the

---

129 For a history of the *Keren Kayemeth,* see: Yossi Katz, *The Battle for the Land*, Jerusalem: The Magnes Press, 2006.

First World War were no longer young, no longer immigrants and were no longer acquainted with what daily life was like for Jews in Eastern Europe. Many, if not most, had continued to live in a Yiddish-speaking environment in America, but by now the younger ones were completely fluent in English, either from night school or having picked up the language at work. Culturally they were "American-Jewish", a mixture of Eastern European Jewish and American cultural elements.

Many of those who had come from a *shtetl* were already far removed from the small-town way of life they had lived as children, but then again, during the first decades of the twentieth century, Eastern European Jewry had also undergone a certain degree of change in both the demographic and cultural spheres. Much of Eastern European Jewry has become urbanized to some degree, and the geographical transition from *shtetl* to larger town had its cultural impact as well. But even if the Eastern Europe of 1939 was not what the former immigrants who had left three decades earlier remembered, many still had relatives there, and were distraught about what was happening.

The German invasion of Poland was the first step in a war that had been long in the making, and seemed like a continuation of the Great War and its aftermath. Since Hitler's rise to power in 1933, Germany had slowly been retreating from the agreements reached at the end of the Great War, leaving the League of Nations, stopping reparation payments, taking over Austria and the Sudetenland in the spring and summer of 1938, and finally the rest of Czechoslovakia in March 1939. The invasion of Poland was the first military step where Nazi Germany's army clashed on a battlefield, as previous takeovers had been preceded by either local or foreign agreement, but the Polish military resistance did not last long.

Within days of the invasion, France and Britain declared war on Germany. In mid-September the Soviet Union invaded Poland from the East, and when Poland surrendered, it was divided up between Germany and the Soviet Union. Years later the reason was revealed, a secret non-aggression pact that the foreign ministers of both countries, Joachim von Ribbentrop and Vyacheslav Molotov, had signed shortly before the war's outbreak. Meanwhile, Rumania's King Carol II officially adopted a position of neutrality. At the same time, the Fascist Iron Guard in Rumania was rising in popularity and strength, and calling for an alliance with Nazi Germany. Everyone knew that Rumania's main guarantors of territorial integrity were Britain and France, and its survival as a sovereign country depended on their strength. Meanwhile, as Nazi Germany had not turned its armies against the West, Britain and France still held strong.[130]

Ten weeks after the war's outbreak, the Scharf-Eisenberg Family Circle gathered for its monthly meeting, just as its members had been doing for over a decade. Held in turn at the various family members' homes, there was little of the usual chatter or card playing. Instead, Abie, the circle's secretary and treasurer, called the group to order, and they commemorated Srul Nachman Handel, *Tante* Mollie's husband, who had died in mid-October 1939. The seventy-year-old Srul Nachman had a heart condition for years, but worked both as a *melamed* and as a part-time tailor. Although he hadn't felt well in the autumn, he insisted on going to work, as he wanted to buy a *tallis* for his grandson Bernard, son of his son Louis from his first marriage, who would soon become bar-mitzvah. One morning, four days before Bernard's bar-mitzva, Srul Nachman suffered a fatal heart attack while *davening* at the storefront *shul* near the tailor shop where he worked.[131] The family was devastated. Not only had Srul Nachman's gentle nature made him beloved by all, but long before he married *Tante* Mollie, he had been both friend and family to the Hallers, Scharfs, and Enzenbergs in Mihowa. He would be sorely missed. At fifty-one *Tante* Mollie found herself a widow, and although she would live for another thirty-six years, she would never remarry.

"Ay, Uncle Srul Nachman", thought Freida Sima. "You were the closest thing to a father that I had here in America". But much more soft spoken than Nachman was, she recalled, and with a quiet but pointed sense of humor. She remembered how at a family gathering, Mordche and Abie were trying to show Srul Nachman how little Shirley and Muriel could already read Yiddish. Trying to show off, Mordche gave Shirley a page of the *Freiheit*, the Yiddish Communist newspaper, to read to Srul Nachman, which she did without mistakes. The bearded Srul Nachman smiled at the little girl and then turned to Mordche and raised his eyebrows. "Now let's give her a real newspaper to read…" he said, handing Shirley a page of the Orthodox, and politically conservative *Morgen Journal* in place of the Communist daily.

Srul Nachman's death also reminded the members that their Family Circle had to think about fulfilling its second purpose. Similar to other *landsmanschaften,* the Scharf-Eisenberg family circle had been created in 1928 as a benevolent society for the family, but also as a burial society.

---

130 For a history of the war see: John Keegan, *The Second World War*, New York: Penguin, 2005.
131 Author's correspondence with Bernard Handel, Dec. 29, 2015.

However, it had not yet purchased cemetery plots for its members, and Srul Nachman had been buried in Riverside, a Jewish cemetery in Saddle Brook, New Jersey. Srul Nachman had been older than most in the immediate family and had already thought about the need to buy *karka* (land), as cemetery plots were called, years earlier, long before the First Mihowa Behrometh Bucowiner K.U.V, established in 1910, had begun functioning as a burial society. He had therefore bought his final resting place through his *shul,* Congregation Shaare Tfiloh, as soon as the family had moved to Harlem in 1911. True, Riverside was located only a short distance over the George Washington Bridge from where most of the family lived in New York, but it was not in a family plot. Srul Nachman's death was a timely reminder that the Circle was getting older and should think about buying a large cemetery section in order to be buried together.

After that, all talk turned to "the situation". Despite the fact that Abie and Uncle Joe had brought out twenty-two families related to the "Circle" before the war, others, from *Tante* Rivka's side, were still living in Germany, and had not made it out on time. What would happen to them now?

Even when discussing fears and worries one has to eat, announced *Tante* Hudel, as she and the other aunts brought out the "Circle's" traditional lunch: delicatessen platters of corned beef, pastrami, salami and tongue that Benny, the family butcher, always brought, supplemented by Freida Sima's mouth-watering potato salad and coleslaw. As the family filled their plates, talk turned to Mihowa. Nachman and Devorah were now alone at the farm, and most of the Enzenberg children were living in Czernowitz, called Cernauti by the Rumanians. Rumania had declared its neutrality, said one of the uncles, but who knows how long that could last. France and Britain were now at war with Germany, and since Poland's defeat, Hitler had made no more military moves, added another cousin, but what would be later? Only time would tell.

After lunch came the traditional hour of letter writing. For years, once a month, the Eisenberg siblings would sit together at the family circle meeting and write a joint letter to their parents, brothers and sisters in Europe, relating the family news of the past few weeks. The paper would then be passed to the uncles and aunts – Devorah's brothers and sisters – for their own greetings and news. "Hopefully this war will be over before it can spread any further", said one of the aunts, while a more recent arrival from Europe, shook her head at the naïve statement.

How long will it take before we stop getting letters from "home"?, thought Freida Sima, recalling how she had been cut off from her family for over four years during the Great War. This time, her parents were twenty-five years older and not surrounded by seven young children. How would they cope? Her heart went out to her mother who had wanted to stay in America, and who had cried her heart out to her oldest daughter the night before she returned to Mihowa, six years ago. "You know the *Tateh*", she had sighed. "I can't leave him for any longer". Now it was too late and Freida Sima could only pray that Rumania would indeed remain neutral for as long as possible.

Her prayers were not answered. In June 1940 the Rumanian government evacuated northern Bukovina, surrendering it to the Red Army. The Fascist Iron Guard then staged a takeover, Marshall Ion Antonescu came to power, and Rumania soon became a Fascist dictatorship. As the Iron Guard stiffened the already existing anti-Semitic legislation, German troops entered Rumania, which officially joined the Axis powers in November 1940. Meanwhile, the area of the Bukovina that the Enzenbergs lived in had been taken over by the Soviets.[132] Letters from the Bukovina stopped arriving just as Freida Sima had feared, and she was once again cut off from her parents, bringing back memories of isolation and dread that she hadn't felt for over twenty years. This time, at least, she had a husband, children and brothers surrounding her, unlike the last war when she had only uncles and aunts. But this time her parents were no longer surrounded by their children as they had been during the last war. The situation was now reversed.

The same war that made her fear for her family in Europe was having a very different effect on her family in America. Even before America entered the war, it was changing the American economy. For the first time in a decade Max Kraus was working full-time, with union-backed painting jobs lined up weeks in advance. Just like before the Depression, he would hand his weekly pay envelope to Freida Sima, keeping only enough for cigarettes and carfare.[133] "Now I can put aside a dollar a week again to

---

132 Randolph L. Braham (ed.), *The Destruction of Romanian and Ukranian Jews during the Antonescu Era*, New York: East European Monographs (Columbia UP), 1997.

133 This was the most common system adoped by many men of the immigrant generation, who would automatically turn over their wages to their wives and would receive from them, in turn, a fixed sum for their needs. In this way, immigrant women, who no longer worked outside the home after marriage, acted as family cashier, and maintained an important economic position in the household. Mary Kingsbury Simkhovitch, *The City Worker's World*, New York: The Macmillan Company, 1917: 102.

send back 'home' for tickets", she automatically thought, the first time her husband brought in a full week's salary. Only after a moment did she realize that even if she could find a way to get the money to Europe, her family could no longer leave.

During these months Freida Sima felt herself in limbo. On the one hand, America was not officially at war, and the American economy was finally returning to a state of greater prosperity. Daily life was much less of a struggle than it had been a year or two earlier. The boarding house was still functioning full-time, keeping Freida Sima busy with cleaning and laundry on a daily basis, but with Mordche working, things were a bit easier. Harry and Benny were both working, and even little Shirley was growing up and beginning junior high school. At twelve she was finally starting to dress like a girl, having preferred until now to wear Mordche's old workpants when she wasn't in school.

A few times this summer they had even been able to afford to rent a car and visit Mordche's family outside of New York, especially his brother Morris in New Jersey, and his sister Becky and her children in Shenendoah, Pennsylvania. Mordche knew how to drive from years ago when he still lived in California, but Freida Sima had never driven with him until now. It was an experience! At other times during the summer they took the train to Brighton Beach and Coney Island, watching the people on the rides at Steeplechase Amusement Park which they still couldn't afford, but mainly for Mordche to teach Shirley how to swim. As a boy in Kiev, he had learned to swim in the Dnieper River and had fallen in love with the water. "Just imagine Bertie", he once said when they were walking on the Boardwalk in Coney Island, "If we lived near the beach I would be able to go swimming every single day after work!" Gevalt!, thought Freida Sima wryly, that's all she would need, to live two hours away by train from her family in the Bronx and have him bring all that sand into her kitchen every single evening. But let him dream. After all, he worked so hard these days to support their family and everyone deserved their dreams, didn't they?

The growing economic prosperity in America in the early 1940s actually did allow people to dream, and for some of them, to move into more spacious apartments in newer buildings and in better areas. Some of Freida Sima's family was also on the move. After having lived for years in the same neighborhood in the South Bronx, parts of the family were now moving south, to Washington Heights in upper Manhattan, where large numbers of German-Jewish immigrants had settled after coming to America during the 1930s. The first of the family to move were Abie and Minnie and their girls in early 1941, and along with them went Minnie's parents, *Tante* Hudel and Uncle Moshe Leib, and Minnie's brother, Max. The family had indeed moved up in the world in all senses, and they all moved into the same building on W. 196th Street, the first building with an elevator that anyone in the family had ever lived in. Uncle Joe and *Tante* Rivka then rented an apartment a few blocks away from them, and finally, *Tante* Mollie moved in with her daughter Anne and her husband Joe, also in Washington Heights. The Family Circle continued to get together every month, and it now had a new "home", the Inwood Jewish Center in Washington Heights, where Abie and Uncle Moshe Leib *davened* every morning.

Everyone's life was progressing as usual in America, but Freida Sima's heart was elsewhere, in Mihowa with her family. She had heard stories from Abie and Benny, who had been children during most of the First World War, about what it had been like in Europe at that time: running away to Poland with Baba Malka dying there, coming back to Mihowa to find things in shambles after the Russians had occupied the Bukovina, Abie being taken to the army during the last months of the war. The last time the war only ended after America had finally gone in to fight in 1917. What would happen this time? Would America under Roosevelt eventually join the war? On the one hand she feared for her stepsons who would surely be taken to the army. On the other hand, she feared for her family in Europe and especially for her elderly parents, worrying about how they were surviving under Soviet rule. With all of Mordche's talk about Communism, no one really knew what was happening to the Jews under Stalin.

No one, that is, except Mordche, the self-appointed expert on the Jews under Communist rule, thought Freida Sima, making a face. At almost every Family Circle meeting, once everyone had eaten their fill of the delicatessen Benny brought and the salads she had made, Abie would read out the minutes, the women would go off to talk, and the men would sit around at the tables to discuss "the situation". At that point, her bare-headed Mordche would stand up, and for close to an hour would expound in his elegant Russian-style Yiddish, on the joys of Communism and the wonderful life that Jews had under Communist rule, compared to the persecution they had endured under the Czar. Sitting and looking at him with rapt attention were most of the older men in the family, almost all strictly traditional, wearing hats or high black *yarmulkehs* (skullcaps), some with both, almost none of whom understood a word of what he was saying in his Russian Yiddish. But they would always look attentive and made sure to give him a rousing hand of applause when he finished, which would just encourage him to repeat that performance at the next meeting. "Oy Mordche", thought Freida Sima. "If only you knew that they were sleeping with their eyes open!" But they loved him as he never refused their request to help paint their house, their *shul*, or anything else they needed. Athiest he may be, but he was an intelligent, loving, and good-hearted man, even if he had a blind spot or two when it came to Marx, Engels and the rest of that crowd.

There was another change in the Family Circle's business at that time. Whether it was the result of Srul Nachman's death soon after the war began, the news from Europe, or the lack of it during wartime, it was natural that death was on everyone's mind. The Scharf-Eisenberg Family Circle had functioned mainly as a social and mutual assistance group since its inception in 1928, and Abie now decided that it was time for it to take on its second purpose, to become a Burial Society. At a meeting held in late March 1941, he announced that the Circle had bought cemetery plots at Wellwood Cemetery on Long Island where the First Mihowa Berhometh Bukoviner Society, for which he also served as secretary-treasurer, already had plots. From now on the family would not only live together and celebrate together, but when the time would come, they would also be buried together for all eternity.[134]

For the next few months the Family Circle's meetings revolved around the question of how the family plot would be laid out. Should they have a gate made with the Family Circle's name? Should they have a bench to rest on at the entrance to the Family plot? Maybe two benches would be better? As the deliberations were going on, the first death in the family, a Rennert baby, who died in September 1941, made it imperative to make some basic decisions. One was that babies would be buried at the end of the long, narrow plot and thus, "Baby Rennert", the first family circle member to be laid to rest, was buried on the far left side of the Family plot. Less than a year later, in June 1942, "Baby Scharf" was laid to rest next to "Baby Rennert". The deliberations regarding the rest of the plot's layout continued, and would be temporarily settled in 1945 when the first adult in the family was buried in the plot, Anna Hirsch Pacht, *Tante* Hudel and Uncle Fischel Hirsch's daughter.

---

134 Agreement between Abe Eisenberg, representing the Scharf Eisenberg Family Circle and Moses Jaffe, President of the Wellwood Cemetery Association, Inc., March 12, 1941, Wellwood Cemetery Archives, Farmington, New York.

Another change in the Family Circle's mood took place during the summer of 1941 when Germany invaded the Soviet Union.[135] On June 22 Nazi forces crossed the Soviet border as part of "Operation Barbarossa", the largest German military operation of the Second World War. Hitler had long wanted to destroy the Soviet Union by military force, eliminate the perceived Communist threat to Germany, and seize prime lands within the Soviet Union. Both Stalin and Hitler understood that any agreement reached between their countries was temporary, and each country was suspicious of the others' intentions. In late June 1941, the state of understanding between Nazi Germany and the Soviet Union rapidly turned into an ideological and military battle for which both sides had long prepared, and would eventually be a major factor in determining the war's outcome.[136]

As a member of the Axis powers, Rumania joined the Soviet invasion, providing equipment and oil to Nazi Germany and committing troops to the Eastern Front. The Rumanian Third and Fourth Armies fought side by side with German troops, sending more soldiers to fight in Russia than all the other Axis allies combined. Like everyone else in America, the Scharfs and Eisenbergs only knew what was being written in the press about the war, and had no idea what was happening to their families in the Bukovina, which had once again become Rumanian territory. They were, however, becoming extremely worried, as there were rumors of massacres of Jews in Moldavia and the Ukraine, and of a pogrom that had taken place in June 1941 against the Jews of Iasi.[137]

---

135 David Stahel, *Operation Barbarossa and Germany's Defeat in the East,* Cambridge: Cambridge University Press, 2011.

136 Christian Hartmann, *Operation Barbarossa: Nazi Germany's War in the East, 1941–1945,* Oxford: Oxford University Press, 2013.

137 In the Iasi Pogrom, between 13,000–15,000 Jews were murdered by Rumanian and German soldiers, some were murdered in their homes or on the streets while others were herded into death trains and moved from station to station until they died. Radu Ioanid, "The Holocaust in Romania: The Iasi Pogrom of June 1941", *Contemporary European History* 2:2 (July 1993): 119–148.

America Goes to War

Throughout the summer and autumn of 1941, the Scharfs, Eisenbergs and Krauses continued their lives as usual, in spite of the war news and their fears for their family. All this changed on December 7, 1941, when 353 Japanese fighter planes, bombers and torpedo planes attacked the American naval base at Pearl Harbor in the United States territory of Hawaii, killing over 2400 Americans. The day after the attack, American President Franklin Delano Roosevelt addressed a joint session of Congress, calling for a formal declaration of war on the Empire of Japan. Within an hour, Congress obliged his request. Although Congress had only agreed to declare war against Japan, within days Germany and Italy, Japan's allies, declared war on the United States, opening the door to its involvement in the European theater. America was now officially at war.[138] "Thank God", thought Freida Sima. "Maybe now with America in the war, the Allies will be able to win faster against the Germans."

The outbreak of war changed numerous aspects of daily life in America. In the early days of the war, panic gripped the country as people feared a Japanese attack of the American mainland, particularly on the Pacific coast. As a result of this fear of attack, most Americans accepted the need to sacrifice in order to achieve victory. During the spring of 1942, the government established a rationing program that would last for the next four years, and included meat, sugar, fat, butter, vegetables, fruit, gasoline, tires, clothing and fuel oils. At the same time, children and adults participated in scrap drives to collect metals, aluminum cans and rubber, which were recycled and used to produce armaments. Freida Sima got used to shopping with her ration booklet, allowed to exchange her sugar ration, unused because of Max's diabetes, for other items which were more important for her family's diet.

A two-front war in both the European and the Pacific theaters meant that American industries were literally fueling two wars simultaneously. This had a tremendous impact not only on the war's economic consequences, but also on its social ones, which were also profound. Along with the great migration of Americans, and particularly Afro-Americans, from the rural south to the industrial north, new opportunities opened for women in

---

138   Gordon W. Prange, *At Dawn We Slept: The Untold Story of Pearl Harbor v. 1*, Norwalk: The Easton Press, 1981.

industry as workers producing the vitally needed war-related materials. As a result, most Americans now enjoyed a standard of living far above that to which they had been accustomed during the Depression years.

Freida Sima had already felt this change since the war's outbreak in 1939, and she could now allow the family a number of luxuries they could never have afforded before. The first was in the area in which she felt most comfortable – the kitchen. Even with rationing, Freida Sima allowed herself to buy larger quantities and better qualities of food for the family than she had during the lean years of the Great Depression. Nothing ever went to waste, and she would stand in the kitchen for hours, singing to herself, and creating delicacies out of the wartime fare for everyone to enjoy. That was one of the things that Mordche had loved about her from the first moment they married, how she would sing to herself all day long as she worked around the house, Yiddish songs, English songs, anything she heard on the radio. "You get up smiling and singing like the birds every morning" he used to say to her when they were first married, bringing back early childhood memories of her parents and how her father would sing as he danced her young mother around the house. But lately she sang less, her mind on the events in Europe and at home. At least now when cooking she could afford to made more than necessary, and she occasionally took delicacies over to her aunts and uncles, for the younger cousins to enjoy and to keep the older generation's mind off what everyone was constantly asking themselves, even if they didn't always voice it: what was happening to the family in Europe?

Another luxury that the Kraus family could now afford was money for everyone to go to the movies. Almost a year after America had entered the war, the family went to the movies right before Thanksgiving and won the daily raffle among the ticket holders – a live turkey! Years later, Shirley recalled with a shudder how her mother had kept the live turkey in the bathroom, its leg tied to the sink with a thin long string, until she could take it to the local *shochet* (ritual slaughterer) and prepare it for the holiday. "It was a battle between the turkey and me every time I had to go in to the bathroom for anything. There I would be, trying to brush my teeth with this giant bird hopping around my legs. I would try to take a bath and it would stand at the side of the tub, staring at me with its little beady eyes. What a horror! And then to have it served at the table on Thanksgiving? How could I eat that bird after sharing a bathroom with it for close to a week? It was almost family!"

Indeed daily life was changing. The question of what "daily life" should entail during wartime arose as early as January 1942 when the national commissioner of baseball wrote a letter to the American president, asking whether professional baseball should shut down for the war's duration. Roosevelt responded that professional baseball should continue as it was good for the country's collective morale, and would serve as an important social diversion during this time of collective stress. Nevertheless, many professional baseball players were directly involved in the conflict. Future stars such as Hank Greenberg, Joe DiMaggio, and Ted Williams exchanged their baseball jerseys for army fatigues. They were but a small number of the hundreds of able-bodied athletes who served in the United States Armed Forces during the war, and they all also served as an example to the nation.

As a result of expanding the 1940 "Selective Service Act", over sixteen million American men and women would eventually serve in the military during the next five years. Within months, Freida Sima proudly pasted three blue stars on her first floor window, one for each of her three stepsons, Stewart, Ben and Harry, serving in the United States Armed Forces. Only Herb, almost thirty-five and married with a daughter, received a deferment due to age. Now, when she *benched lecht* on Friday night, Freida Sima *davened,* not just for her family in America and Europe, but also for the stars. "*Ribono shel Olam* – Master of the Universe, please let them stay blue", she would murmur week after week, "Let them never turn gold", as a gold star meant a family member who had lost his or her life in the military.

Many of Freida Sima's younger cousins also served overseas in the Armed Forces, and their wives and children often moved back to live with their parents, the "uncles and aunts", for the war's duration. Feeling a need to do even more to strengthen everyone's morale, Freida Sima began to cook large batches of food on a regular basis and bring them over to her extended family throughout the Bronx. Her young cousin Jeffrey Sanders recalled meeting her on a cold snowy day pulling a sled through the snow and slush: "What was so important that it had to be delivered in that horrible weather? She had a freshly made batch of chicken schmaltz that she had put up in Nescafe' jars and was delivering them to family and friends. I'll always remember Nescafe' jars!"[139] If her boys were fighting their war at the front, Freida Sima would fight her war in the kitchen, doing what she could to keep the family together and well fed.

The war in Europe was taking its toll on the Scharfs and Eisenbergs in America in more ways than one. There was no news from the family

---

139 Author's correspondence with Jeffrey Sanders, Oct. 11, 2015.

overseas, but reports spoke of the Rumanians re-occupying northern Bukovina and deporting the Jews to an area between the Dniester and the Bug rivers, known as Transnistria. Rumors of the ill-treatment, starvation and death of Rumanian Jews deported to that area began reaching the West during 1942, although it would take until February 1943 for the New York Times to carry a report from London of a Rumanian government offer to transfer 70,000 Jews from Transnistria to some place of refuge. The Rumanian proposal called for transporting these refugees to Palestine via Rumanian ships, and requested payment of 20,000 Rumanian lei (approximately $50) for each refugee who exited its borders.[140] In the final analysis, the plan was not implemented, and it was never determined whether the entire proposal was realistic or fraudulent.

"What can I do in order to keep my family safe?" was a question that Freida Sima constantly asked herself during those years. From her traditional background she knew that *tefilah* (prayer) and *zedakah* (charity) were two very important spiritual components which would hopefully have practical applications in this case. She was therefore very careful every Friday night before candle lighting to put aside a few coins for charity, "for the merit of my boys in the war and my family in Europe". For the same reason she was careful to recite prayers from her *Techina* every week, especially the one written for "A women who has children or relatives in the war".

But from her Chassidic upbringing she knew that it was even more beneficial to take upon oneself some pious act connected to the issue of concern, and perform it for the merit of the person or people involved. It is customary that when Jews return from a cemetery they wash their hands to dispel the spirits of uncleanliness which might cling to one's person, these being the demons which follow people home. In the psychological sense, it is a metaphoric cleansing from a place of death to a place of life. As Freida Sima lived on the ground floor, with her living room window facing the sidewalk used by many friends, neighbors or family members returning from funerals, she took upon herself to be the "water provider", both assisting in a *mitzvah,* and hoping that it would protect her own family from the Angel of Death. If she saw Jews from the neighborhood going to a funeral, she would make sure to be at the living room window upon their

---

140 The New York Times, February 16, 1943. See also: Hava W. Eshkoli, "The Transdnistrian Plan: An Opportunity for Rescue or a Deception", in *American Jewry during the Holocaust: A Report for the American Jewish Commission on the Holocaust,* ed. Seymour M. Finger, New York: Holmes and Meier, 1984: 237–260.

return, passing them cups of water so that they could wash their hands as one traditionally does when returning from a cemetery, spilling the water on the ground and not wiping one's hands until the water dries naturally.

As the war progressed, additional family members reached military age and were sent overseas, including some of Max's nieces who had trained as nurses. His sister Becky's daughter Dinah Schoor, a military nurse, even met Harry in Italy and brought back pictures of him in uniform for the family. Hitching her way from there to Palestine on a joint Anglo-American military medical transport, she then spent a week with Helena, Isaac's widow, hearing about life in *Eretz Yisrael*.

During these years, the family in America got used to a routine of living a double life. To the outside world it projected "business as usual". On the administrative level the Family Circle was incorporated in July 1943, enabling it to be listed as an official organization for business purposes.[141] On the personal level, the adults continued working while the younger children graduated from elementary and junior high school. Most of the family was doing well financially, but Freida Sima and Max, who had it hardest in the family during the Depression, were still unable to afford many of the things that her brothers or cousins' families could. When Shirley had been younger, Freida Sima had not been able to give her music lessons or send her regularly to Hebrew school like her cousins. Running a full-time boarding house also meant that she could not take her away to the Catskills for vacation in a *Koch-alein*, literally a "cook alone", as self-catering establishments were called. Now in 1943, when Shirley graduated from junior high school and needed a special sailor top and white skirt for graduation pictures, Freida Sima borrowed them from friends as she could not afford to buy her daughter such an expensive outfit for a one time occasion. "She did, however, make me a beautiful corsage that she pinned to my blouse that morning, so that I would look like all the other girls celebrating that day", Shirley later recalled.

Like many Jewish women of her generation who did not work outside their homes, Freida Sima would have scoffed at the thought of an identity crisis, feeling secure in defining herself as a Jewish daughter, wife and mother. Although her parents were overseas, she was a dutiful daughter who had sent money "home" to support her family and whose thoughts were with them

---

141 Scharf-Eisenberg Family Circle Certificate of Incorporation, Department of State in Albany, July 2, 1943. Scharf-Eisenberg Family Circle Archives, New York.

daily, even during that time. In practice, she transferred that love and care to her brothers and their families, and her mother's brothers and sisters and their families in America. She was a devoted wife who watched over her diabetic husband like a hawk to keep him alive, their arguments making sure he would never become complacent, "because making up afterwards is so good", she would say. But it was her role as mother which now worried her the most, with the boys fighting overseas and with Shirley beginning to grow up.

Throughout her junior high school years Shirley had begun to mature, taking Mordche's socialist talk seriously and beginning to become interested in politics. "*Oy gevalt*, another Communist in this house is all I need", Freida Sima sighed to herself, thinking of the political arguments with which she had lived at home for the past fifteen years. But now Shirley was becoming a true intellectual, having decided to switch high schools less than six weeks after her first term began. "Ma, I want to go to Walton", she said one day, referring to the prestigious all-girls high school in the Bronx, one of the largest girls' high schools in the world and which prepared its students for college, unlike the commercial high school that she had begun to attend in 1943. Freida Sima was still thirsting for her own formal education which had propelled her to move to America in 1911 and which, despite her dreams, she had never been able to fulfill. Hearing Shirley's decision, she had acted wary, but was secretly thrilled. "You know that this means no more games", she told her daughter who, as usual, put on her most innocent face, widening her big green eyes as if to say "who me?!" and trying hard not to smile.

Shirley had indeed "raised hell" during her younger years, although Mordche never disciplined her like he had the boys, being more lenient to his youngest child and only daughter. He was only strict with her over one issue, respect. If Mordche ever heard Shirley referring to Freida Sima as "she", he would bellow "'SHE' has a name, and it is Mother!" In all other issues the discipline had been left to Freida Sima who had no problems with a *potch* (slap) on the backside here and there. But Shirley's kind of mischief was different, and she often used her innocent "blank look", as she later called it, to her benefit. Freida Sima had even been called once to Shirley's school to see if she had any suggestions on how the teachers might deal with her not-so-innocent daughter. Egged on by her closest girlfriend in junior high school, Rose Grossman, who practically lived in Freida Sima's kitchen and called her and Mordche "Mom" and "Pop", Shirley had often been chosen by her classmates to "waste" the time before exams in order to make sure that the test would not be given that lesson.

The highlight that had preceded the note Freida Sima had received requesting her presence at school, was a science lesson during which Shirley had spent the entire period intended for an exam, repeatedly asking her teacher whether fish slept. Each time the teacher answered, Shirley asked her to please elucidate once again, as she did not yet fully understand the answer. At one point during this unending dialogue Shirley even had tears in her eyes, ostensibly crying for the poor fish which she thought had never slept. Poor Miss Martin, Freida Sima recalled with a mirth that she would never show her daughter, had fallen for it "hook, line and sinker", as Rose later told "Mom", explaining to a weeping Shirley over and over that while fish do not sleep as mammals do, she shouldn't worry, they do rest, but we can't perceive it as sleep as they don't have eyelids to close. The class ended up with an extra day to study for the exam, Shirley came out of it with a name as a lover of animals, and only later in the day did the elderly Miss Martin realize that she had been "had", precipitating the note to Freida Sima. "Oy Shirley, you are going to get yourself in deep *tzurris* (trouble) one day", her mother thought at the time, but now with her daughter's new intellectual ambitions, maybe something good would come of her. Good also that her beautiful friend Rosie who wanted to be an opera singer, had no intentions of following Shirley to Walton High School. Better she should spend time with her more studious cousins Muriel, Sheila and Bernice who might be a more positive influence on her.

Rosie Grossman would eventually become artist and singer Lisa Lawrence, but Muriel and Sheila no longer lived in the Bronx, as Abie had been the first of the family to move to Washington Heights. The first, but certainly not the last. Throughout the early 1940s, more of the family moved to Washington Heights which became the new locale for family gatherings. But the Kraus family was also expanding, joined by another Shirley, Harry's fiancée, Shirley Goldberg, who spent time with them while Harry was overseas. The two Shirley's became very close, and would often sit in Freida Sima's kitchen as she cooked, talking about Harry, now fighting in Europe, and singing the song that he loved and had taught them before the war, Billy Mayhew's "It's a Sin to Tell a Lie".[142] "Millions of hearts have been broken, just because these words were spoken", went the lyrics, and Freida Sima prayed that no one's heart in the room would be broken because of anything that might happen during this war.

---

142   Billy Mayhew, *It's a Sin to Tell a Lie,* Sheet Music, WB Music Corp., 1936.

The older Shirley often took the younger one to the movies, introducing her to different types of American culture. At the time, a trip to the movies was not always an escape from the war but often a learning experience. The movies usually began with a ten minute newsreel, showing images of recent battles. And although there were many non-war-related dramas, comedies, and western that were shown during those years, a great number of films were nevertheless devoted to the war or to war-related themes.[143]

Like the other American children and teenagers of those years, the younger members of the Scharf and Eisenberg clan became well versed about what was going on in the war, not only from the newsreels but from the radios which were always on in many of their homes. Shirley and her cousins Sheila and Muriel remembered how the Yiddish radio station WEVD, named in honor of the late union leader and Socialist party activist Eugene V. Debs, played constantly in their homes, giving them a continuous stream of war news. Facetiously know by the children as "WBVD" for the well-known men's underwear brand of that name which later became "Fruit of the Loom", news programs or commentaries broadcast on that station regarding the war's development often set the barometer of their families' moods for the rest of the day.[144]

Freida Sima's one escape from the fears exacerbated by the war was her kitchen, the place where she felt best about herself, and where she could express her creativity at the same time as nurturing her family and friends. These were the years when her cooking became legendary among all those who knew her, and many of her younger relatives' memories of her were connected in one way or another to a culinary-related experience of that time. Her neice Sheila remembered how she stood in awe in Freida Sima's kitchen, watching her stuff *kishke* (derma), one of her tastiest

143   Such as „Wake Island" (1942), „Guadalcanal Diary" (1943), „Bataan" (1943) „Back to Bataan" (1945) focusing on specific battles; „Nazi Agent" (1942), „Saboteur" (1942) and „They Came to Blow Up America" (1943) which portrayed America's enemies as spies and terrorists. „So Proudly We Hail!" (1943) and „Cry 'Havoc'" (1943) about women nurses and volunteers; „Tender Comrade" (1943), „The Human Comedy" (1943) and „Since You Went Away" (1944) exploring the fear that a loved one who went off to war might never return. The struggles of citizens in occupied countries were portrayed in such films as „Hangmen Also Die!" (1943) and „The Seventh Cross" (1944).

144   Ari Y. Kelman, *Station Identification: A Cultural History of Yiddish Radio in the United States,* Berkeley: University of California Press, 2009. Seymour Zimilover, "Radio Days: A Life Heard", *The Forward,* March 4, 2005, <http://forward.com/culture/3049/radio-days-a-life-heard/> retrieved on Dec. 22, 2015.

delicacies. Various cousins would talk about how they would lick their lips just hearing that she was going to bring them potato salad or any other of her specialties to a family gathering. Her kitchen was open to all friends and relatives who passed through the Bronx, and not a visitor left without enjoying an apple latke or at least a piece of rye bread, a pickle and a slice of the long salami which she always had hanging behind the kitchen door.

It was during this period that the kitchen became Freida Sima's undeclared throne room, so to speak, even though she stood at the stove and rarely sat at the kitchen table to prepare food. In her study of the religious significance of food to medieval women, Caroline Walker Bynum reminds us of the special connection between women and food, and between food and power. The traditional association of women with food preparation is to paraphrase Bynum, a traditional sense of women's power. "To prepare food is to control food"[145], with food not being merely a resource that women control, but *the* resource that women traditionally control for themselves and others, the means by which they regulate their world. While it was true that throughout history "women cooked and men ate"[146], Freida Sima never saw herself as providing a service to others through her kitchen, but as using it as a lynchpin for the nuclear and extended family, friends and neighbors, "keeping things together". As long as she had control of her kitchen, she was happy. What would happen when she would get old and not be able to run the household? That was still a long way off.

As much as they were trying to live in the present in America, at the same time, the older family members were also living with their head in another place – Europe. Not a day went by that Freida Sima, Abie and Benny didn't think of their parents, brothers and sisters. Where were they? Had they managed to stay together? What of the little children? How did they all survive? Did they all survive? Had anyone new been born? The questions multiplied, but there were no answers, only worries, speculations and hopes that everyone in the family would get through the war alive.

By the spring of 1944 the Red army had advanced towards Transnistria, liberating it from the Rumanians. By the end of the summer, Rumania proclaimed its loyalty to the Allies, announced its acceptance of an armistice, and declared war on Germany. As part of its armistice, it then announced its unconditional surrender to the USSR, the representative of the Allied

---

145   Caroline Walker Bynum, *Holy Feast and Holy Fast: The Religious Significance of Food to Medieval Women,* Berkeley, Los Angeles, London, University of California Press, 1987: 191.

146   Bynum, *Holy Feast and Holy Fast: 277.*

forces which now occupied Rumania. Yet no one had received any word from Europe.

One morning in early autumn 1944 Freida Sima heard a knock at the door. Abie stood there with a grief-stricken look in his eyes. "He walked in and 'took me around'", my grandmother recalled, using her expression for giving a hug, "and then said one sentence: 'Take off your apron and come with me'. Then we both went to Tzeendl and Abie told him to close the butcher store. Turning to us with tears in his eyes, he gave us the news that he had learned that morning: 'The parents are gone. So is Marium'. Then the three of us cut *kriya* (the mourning custom of rending one's garments) for each other and sat *shiva* for an hour for the family, and that was that."

Early that morning Abie had received an airmail letter from one of the Transnistrian orphans who had been allowed to leave for Palestine in late 1943. Little Mendel was a Scharf cousin who had been deported with the family to Transnistria. Following his parents' death, he and his little sister ended up in a Jewish orphanage there, and after his sister's death, he had been chosen to join a children's group of orphans, permitted to leave for Palestine. Before departing, he had been given a list of the family *yahrzeitzs* and Abie's address in America, to which he was told to send them when he reached Palestine. And so he did. When Abie had opened the letter that morning, he found a list that spoke for itself. Devorah Enzenberg, 27 Adar 1942, Nachman Enzenberg, 28 Adar 1942, Marium Enzenberg Rosenberg 9, Nissan, 1942. They were yet to find out about Sheindl's Schaje who had disappeared at the beginning of the war, and Leibish and Frieda's little girls, Rivka and Malka, who were also gone.

It was now time to concentrate on those who survived. First, to find them. Then, to hear what happened to everyone during the war. And finally, to figure out how to get them to America. In truth, however, it would take years before they would know what their family in Europe had really gone through during the war, and some of the things they would never know, as Sheindl would only record the full story for posterity in March 1998 when she was eighty-three, by which time the older generation of the family who had spent the war in America, was long gone. What they did learn, they eventually put together piece by piece, as each of their brothers and sisters in Europe had undergone different wartime experiences in different places. It was a story of tragedy and loss, but for some, it was also the story of the *mazel* which had kept them alive throughout the disaster.

Part II The Enzenbergs and the War

Introduction

Over fifty years after the end of the Second World War, Sheindl, the young-est of the Enzenbergs, recalled the day that the family was deported from Mihowa. "There was a very religious man in Mihowa who we used to go to for *paskening shailos* (determining religious matters), Berel Surkis. On the day we left Mihowa every transport was accompanied by thunder and lightning like the heaven was crying. Berel Surkis went with us. I said to him, 'Reb Berel, what are they doing to us?' And he answered: 'Sheindeleh, this way will take us to *Eretz Yisroel*, but it will take a very, very long time, and a very sad time.' I said "Where is G-d", and he answered again, "This way will bring us to *Eretz Yisroel*, but it will be very *shver* (difficult). How could he know already then? But he did."[147]

Only years after the war's end did Freida Sima learn the details of what the family in Europe had endured during the Holocaust. Initially, she and her brothers read the bare facts in letters which the family sent from Rumania when postal service resumed. The detailed stories were shared in face to face meetings years later. Sheindl, the youngest sister, eventually left a recorded testimony of her experiences which filled in some of the gaps left in what had previously been imparted to the family. The other stories were pieced together over periods of time, recalling the horrors that the family experienced in various locales throughout the war.

The experiences of the Enzenberg family during the war were, of course, unique to the family, but were similar to those which much of Bu-kovinian Jewry experienced during that period. The Soviet occupation of 1939, the Rumanian re-takeover of the Bukovina in 1941, wartime life in the Czernowitz ghetto, the deportation of Bukovinian Jewry to Transnis-tria, life and death in the forced labor camps, illness, starvation, hiding – all

---

147 All of Sheindl's quotes in this section are taken from her testimony given to the USC Shoa Foundation: Jenny Bernthal, USC Shoa Foundation, The Institute for Visual History and Education (Spielberg) – March 30, 1998.

were the fate of various segments of Bukovinian Jewry during the Second World War.

Before the war there were approximately 108,000 Jews living in the Bukovina, who were a bit less than 11% of the region's population. Over 90,000 Jews were deported from the Bukovina to Transnistria: some 58,000 from the rural areas in July and August 1941, approximately 28,000 from Czernowitz in October that year, and another 4,000 from Czernowitz in the summer of 1942. In Transnistria the Jews were herded into several dozen ghettos, the largest of which was Moghilev with 15,000 Jews, or were sent to labor camps. More than half of the deportees were murdered in Transnistria, or died there of illness and starvation. Close to 2,500 Jewish children who lost their parents in Transnistria were placed in hastily organized orphanages where they suffered from hunger, overcrowding, and Siberian-like cold during the winter. In Moghilev alone, there were 900 orphans in buildings with broken windows and with four to six shivering children sharing a single bed. The various members of the Scharf and Enzenberg families in the Bukovina underwent different Holocaust experiences, depending on where they were during the war. But by the war's end, the family's "sum total" included all of the above experiences, without exception.[148]

The Soviet Occupation

At the end of the summer of 1939, Nachman and Devorah lived alone on the farm while the rest of the family was scattered throughout the Bukovina. Marium and Feivel lived elsewhere in Mihowa. Sheindl, Schaje and their daughter Marta lived in Behromet, an hour away. The two newlywed couples, Leibish and Frieda and Elish and Lola, lived in Czernowitz, as did Srul, Anna and their four-year-old son Yulbert. So did Tuleh, the last unmarried Enzenberg, who spent a lot of time with Srul and Anna's family, as they had been his "home away from home" for the years that he lived alone in Czernowitz. All the Enzenberg men, other than Elish who was an accountant,

148 Radu Ionid, *The Holocaust in Romania: The Destruction of Jews and Gypsies Under the Antonescu Regime 1940–1944,* Chicago: Ivan R. Dee, 2000; Jean Ancel, *The History of the Holocaust in Romania (Comprehensive History of the Holocaust),* Lincoln and Jerusalem: University Press of Nebraska and Yad Vashem, 2012.

worked in wood-related professions that they had learned from Nachman during his years in the lumber business.

Even before the war, the Rumanian nationalists had shown their colors, forbidding any language but Rumanian to be spoken in public. Sheindl recalled how she had given birth in Czernowitz, and her mother Devorah came to bring her back home to Mihowa to recuperate with the baby. Not daring to say a word to her mother in Yiddish while in Czernowitz, the two walked in silence to the train. They then sat for an hour across from each other on the journey, still not saying a word, and just looked at each other with longing until they had almost reached Mihowa and knew that they wouldn't be reported. Only then did they fall into each other's arms, laughing and crying together over the birth of the family's youngest granddaughter at the time.

During the first few months of the war, Rumanian officers entered the villages, billeting themselves where they wished. While the women continued their lives, men were taken to forced labor but eventually returned. "You didn't know which world it was, you didn't know what to think", recalled Sheindl. "And then all of a sudden, the *yeshia* (salvation) came – the Russians".

In June 1940 northern Bukovina was ceded to the Soviet Union. Considered "productive", Nachman was allowed to continue working his farm. He hoped that his good relations with the local peasants who had worked with him on the farm, and had used his well – the only one in the area – all those years, would hold him in good stead. Meanwhile, he was correct, but he would soon be in for an unfortunate surprise.

None of this was to last. In 1941, just as some of the Eisenbergs in New York were moving by choice from the Bronx to Washington Heights, the Enzenbergs of the Bukovina were also moving, not by choice, but due to forced conscription or deportation. In June 1941 the Rumanians, now firmly on the Axis side, had reoccupied the Bukovina. In the villages, the army and the local Ukranians went into the Jews' homes, helping themselves to anything they wanted, "and you couldn't say a thing". Tuleh had married Toni (Tauba) Cumpana a few weeks earlier and they were visiting Sheindl and little Marta. Schaje was away on business and the three adults decided that under the circumstances, it would be best to take Marta and go to the farm for a few days where it might be safer, and where they could check on the parents. After all, Schaje was a cousin and his family lived on the outskirts of Mihowa. He would therefore know where to find them when he returned. "We took nothing, as we thought we would come home in a few days, but we never came home", Sheindl recalled. She never saw Schaje again.

When the four of them reached the farm, Nachman and Devorah were already standing outside their house, holding bundles. Nachman had left the house coatless, and as he walked out the door he had seized with a floor rug and thrown it around his shoulders to remain warm. Eventually, Nachman, Devorah, Marium, Feivel, Sheindl, Marta, Tuleh and Toni were deported on foot to Bessarabia, along with other Jews from the area. Tuleh eventually secured a place for Devorah on one of the wagons, while Nachman, in his late sixties, walked the entire trip. Sheindl recalled: "the people in the wagon kept throwing Mama off and Tuleh would then throw her back on again and this went on over and over until they let her stay and ride."

It was then that Sheindl, too young to remember the family's escape from Mihowa during the Great War, got her first lesson about wartime. Watching her trying to figure out how to heat up water for her little girl on Shabbos, Devorah told her: "*Töchter* (daughter), when we are *auf der flucht* (in flight) you can do everything. When we come home you can be religious again."

The group was taken first to Strojinet, Wiznitz, Yedenitz (Edinet) and in the autumn of 1941, after three months of wandering, finally reached Ataki in northern Moldavia on the Dniester River. Known as one of the "gates of Hell" by some of those deported through there, Ataki was the last waystop before crossing into Transnistria, or being drowned in the Dniester. As one of the deportees from the Czernowitz ghetto wrote about what happened to his group when they reached Ataki, "Hell that Dante described is only a pale reflection of what is happening around us".[149] Unlike the thousands of Bukovinian and Bessarabian Jews who had been murdered there and thrown into the river, their group was permitted to cross the bridge to Moghilev into what was being called Transnistria – the area between the Dniester and the Bug Rivers, which under German and Rumanian control became an area of mass ghettos and concentration camps.[150] In Moghilev, eighteen people from the family shared two rooms including Toni's parents, cousins from Mihowa, Leibish and Frieda, who had been deported from the Czernowitz

149 Florence Heyman, "Bottles in the Sea: Letters of Deported Jews in Moghilev (Transnystria) November-December 1941", in: Valentina Glajar and Jeanine Teodorescu (eds.), *Local History, Transnational Memory in the Romanian Holocaust,* New York: Palgrave Macmillan, 2011: 81.

150 Dalia Ofer, "The Holocaust in Transnistria: A Special Case of Genocide", in Lucjan Dobroszycki and Jeffrey S. Gurock (eds.), *The Holocaust in the Soviet Union: Studies and Sources on the Destruction of the Jews in the Nazi-occupied Territories of the USSR 1941–1945,* Armonk, N.Y.: M.E. Sharpe, 1993:133–154.

ghetto. Like most of the Moghilev Jews, the extended Enzenberg family that had been deported to Transnistria subsisted primarily from a soup kitchen, augmented by the few things they could buy through barter.[151]

Luckily for them, the other Enzenberg brothers and their families had remained in the Czernowitz ghetto, primarily because of the next genera-tion. In the autumn of 1941 both Srul's Anna and Elish's Lola were expect-ing, and their families escaped the transports to Transnistria as both women insisted they wished to give birth in the ghetto. Born seven weeks apart in late 1941, the two baby boys, Srul and Anna's Freddie (Efraim) and Elish and Lola's Max (Meshulam Yehuda) saved their parents from their deported rel-atives' fate. While the women remained with the babies, Srul and Elish were taken by the Rumanians to labor camps where they spent most of the war.

In March 1942, as Harry was busy sending Freida Sima pictures of army life before being sent overseas, and Freida Sima was busy cooking away in her kitchen to feed her extended family in New York, keeping away the specter and fears of the war, her family in Moghilev was literally starving to death. It was an extremely cold winter, they had no heating in the small house, and more than once Nachman's hair had frozen to the wall next to his bed while he slept. One time he was actually unable to get out of bed, whether from weakness, or because of the hold that his frozen hair had on the wall, until Tuleh had cut that part of his hair loose in order to release him.

Weakness, age and starvation ultimately took their toll on the older generation in Transnistria, even among those who were not sent to labor camps.[152] Devorah and Nachman died of hunger one day after the other. Sheindl recalled: "When Mama died, Tuleh and I were so close, but we didn't want to tell each other. So he looked at me, and I looked at him, and we both knew but no one wanted to tell the other she had died." That day Tuleh went with his mother's body to the cemetery to make sure that she would not be buried in a mass grave but given an individual burial in the Moghilev cem-etery, set aside for deported Jews, the "mad dog's cemetery" on what Sheindl referred to as Sharagrader Hill.

Nachman was already dying, and did not know of Devorah's death, but spent the last hours of his life calling for her, wanting to see his beloved wife

---

151   Dalia Ofer, "Life in the Ghettos of Transnistria", *Yad Vashem Studies* 25 (1996): 229–274.
      Julius S. Fisher, *Transnystria; The Forgotten Cemetery*, New York: South Brunswick, London: Yoseloff, 1969.

152   Avigdor Schachan, *Burning Ice: The Ghettos of Transnystria,* Boulder: East European Monographs, 1996.

before he died. The next day, already ill with typhus, Tuleh returned to the cemetery, this time with Nachman's body, ensuring that he receive a Jewish burial and saying *Kaddish* at the grave. Risking his life, Tuleh later traded his portions of bread to put tombstones on his parents' graves to mark them for the future. Sheindl was left with three mementos which she would one day pass on to the next generation: her mother's *sheitl* (wig) and *siddur* (prayer book) and the floor-rug that her father had worn over his shoulders for warmth since leaving Mihowa.

During the days after her parents' death, Marium laid deathly ill with typhus. Sheindl recalled how religious and good natured Marium was, even in Moghilev. "Feivel her husband used to bring her candies he got from somewhere in Moghilev to eat to have strength. She was a *Zadekes* (saint). He watched to see that she would take it, so she would put it in her mouth, but the minute he would turn around she would take it out of her mouth and give it to Marta to have something sweet."

On the tenth day after her parents passing Marium appeared to be close to death. "Her husband Feivel covered her with the blanket, and I took off the cover and screamed. You heard my screams to the heavens. Marium opened her eyes, looked at me, and said 'I'm dying *shvester* (sister)'". Later that day, Marium died of typhus. As everyone in the house was too ill to go out with her body to the cemetery, no one could ensure that she had an individual burial, and thus she was buried in a mass grave.

Sheindl recalled how ill they all were at the time: "Everyone had typhus. First Tuleh and Toni and then Leibish and Frieda and their baby, and then me. My sister-in-law's father died of typhus too, on the same day as my mother. The doctor refused to come into the house as he said we would die anyway, but we didn't." Two other cousins who had been with them perished of starvation and their children, Rosa and Mendel, were taken to a Moghilev orphanage. Rosa eventually died there and Mendel was sent to Palestine with a group of Transnistrian orphans. Before he died in Palestine of war-related illnesses, he managed to send Abie the letter listing Devorah, Nachman, and Marium's *yahrzeit* dates, the first letter that the American relatives received from Europe since the war's outbreak.[153]

During the summer of 1942, the family in Moghilev split up. Leibish, Frieda and their daughter Rivka, who had been born in Moghilev, were sent

---

153 For a first-person account of the plight of orphans in Transnistria see: Joil Alpern, *No One Awaiting Me: Two Brothers Defy Death During the Holocaust in Romania,* Calgary: University of Calgary Press, 2001.

to the labor camps of Skazenitz and Derechin (Dziarcecyn), where another daughter, Malka was born. Rivka and Malka both died in Derechin, three-year-old Rivka of tonsillitis, and four-month-old Malka of starvation. At the time Leibish and his family were deported, Tuleh had been working for a local engineer, Viktor Nikolaiwitz, outside the ghetto. Hearing that the Jews were being deported to labor camps, Tuleh managed to secure permission for himself, then for Toni, and later for his remaining family in Moghilev, to live with him in the little room he had been given in the engineer's home, thus escaping deportation. Tuleh continued working for the engineer throughout the war, while the women hid there, sewing, and tending the engineer's home, garden and cows.

Even there, starvation was fierce. At the same time as Freida Sima was fighting her war in the kitchen to keep the American family's morale up while their children fought overseas, Sheindl's daughter Marta was too weak from hunger to walk. Toni was so hungry that she had a recurring dream: "when the war is over I'm going to cook a whole pot of potatoes and eat them all by myself". As cousins still living in the Moghilev ghetto had more food than the Enzenbergs had in hiding, Sheindl would occasionally risk her life to go there to get food for her daughter. The months passed, and Sheindl began to grow potatoes in the engineer's garden so that they would all have what to eat.

In early 1944, a Soviet offensive began in the area, and by the end of March 1944, no more German troops remained east of the Dniester River, other than those in the encircled capital Odessa. By the middle of April the Red Army took Odessa, and within days, all of Transnistria finally fell into Soviet hands. Soon after, the Jews were released from the labor camps, and Leibish and Frieda returned to Moghilev where they were reunited with the family.

But not for long. Soon after, he and Tuleh were taken by the Russians along with the other Jewish men in town, to aid the war effort and work at the front. The women and children were free to return home. Before leaving Moghilev, the women for the Bukovina and the men for the Russian front, the entire family went together to the Jewish cemetery for a last look at their parents' graves. Sheindl then traveled with Marta to Behromet with the thought of returning to her home, and in the hope that she might find family there. When she reached Behromet, she stood on the street outside her old house, looking at it from the outside before she entered.

As she stood gazing at her old home, a non-Jewish former neighbor came up to her, asking whether she was planning to move in, and telling her about the unfortunate fate of another Jew who had tried to move back to his Behromet home a few days earlier. It was only then that she fully realized the dangers of being alone in Behromet with her young daughter, and at that moment she decided to abandon her plan and continue on to Mihowa where she hoped to be safer. After spending one night at the Mihowa farm, she parted from her childhood home in the morning and never looked back. Continuing on to Czernowitz, she joined her sisters-in-law already there and waited for her brothers' return. By that time, Srul and Elish had returned from their labor camps, and they were soon joined by Tuleh and Leibish. Eventually, the various family members made their way out of Soviet occupied Czernowitz to Bucharest where they remained for the next few years before continuing on their journey to Israel and the United States.

After the War

Similar to what had happened to them during the first World War, most Eastern European immigrants in the United States had once again been cut off from their relatives for more than half a decade. It was almost impossible to receive mail from Europe during the war, and newspaper reports of war events were a poor substitute for direct information about what was happening to their families. Now that the war had ended, these immigrants awaited word of their loved ones' fate with trepidation. Freida Sima and her brothers having learned of their parents' and sisters' death while the war was still going on, was indeed unique. In most cases, correspondence from surviving European relatives only reached the United States after the war was over.

Holding a first letter from her siblings in her hands after the war, Freida Sima thought how greatly the Scharf and Enzenberg families in Europe had suffered during the past years. They had lost Nachman and Devorah, Marium, Leibish's daughters, cousins, and Sheindl's Schaje was still missing. Most of Nachman and Devorah's siblings who had remained in Europe were now gone. Nachman's brothers Leib, Chaim, Meier Moshe, and some of their family, Devorah's brothers Ya'akov and Gedalia, and their families, and Velvel and his wife. Velvel's children had made it to America before the war, along with her mother's brother Shmilitzie (Shmuel Yitzchak)'s son, Abe. Shmilitzie and Feige had survived the war in the Czernowitz ghetto and it was hoped that they could bring them to America.

"Oy *Veter* Ya'akov", thought Freida Sima. "Why did you go back to Yugoslavia when you had been visiting America when Mama was here? Why did I let my Mama go back, and why didn't I insist that the Tateh come here as well? You could all be alive today!" she agonized. But it was no use thinking that, what was done was done and now the family had to think about the future.

The Krauses had also been touched by tragedy. The same week that the Enzenbergs were being herded across the bridge from Ataki to Moghilev, Mordche oldest sister Mata and her family, the only Karasik who had refused to come to America because she had heard that "there Jews can't keep Shabbos", were being been murdered by the Nazis at Babi Yar, along with the 34,000 Jews of Kiev.

Still, they were luckier than those families where only one out of ten had remained alive. Four grandchildren were ultimately named for Nachman and Devorah. Benny and Betty's son, David Nachman was born in America towards the end of the war, soon after the family had received word of the deaths in Europe, and was named for both grandparents. Elish and Lola's younger son, Nachman David (Norman), born years later in America, was given the same name in reverse. Devorah had two granddaughters named after her: Leibish and Frieda's daughter Dora (Devorah), born in Czernowitz, and Tuleh and Toni's daughter Dora, born later in Bucharest.

As much as the Eisenbergs wanted to bring all of their European family to the United States immediately after the war, it was impossible to do so because of American immigration regulations. Only special categories could receive immigration visas at that time, such as parents with minor children in the United States, or clergy. All others had to wait their turn. The Enzenbergs were therefore listed for America but at the same time, planned to immigrate to Palestine which they hoped would soon become an independent State.

Elish, Lola and their older son Max, born during the war, were the first of the European family to come to the United States, even before the others left Bucharest for Israel. Aware of his younger brother's scholarly background, Abie, together with a rabbinical friend of the family, had dreamed up a scheme to bring Elish to America on a rabbinical visa. With a letter from Rabbi Lewis Kaplan, head of Baltimore Hebrew College, guaranteeing Elish a job as Hebrew teacher and Rabbi, it was possible to set the bureaucratic wheels in motion. Informed of the move, Elish, whose family had already been listed for immigration to Palestine, rapidly grew a beard. In March 1948 the family flew to Italy, and within weeks they sailed to New York. As they stayed with Abie's family for their first few weeks, Sheila remembers being told: "If anyone asks you about Elish and ask what he does, just tell them he's a Rabbi."

Elish gave the family in America a more detailed description of what he and the others had undergone during the war. He also gave them one piece of good news. There had recently been a family *simcha* in Bucharest, Sheindl's marriage to Naftula (Naftali) Bernthal. Sheindl had known Naftula, a baker, in Mihowa before the war, but they had never courted and both had married other people. Soon after the war's end, Sheindl learned that her husband Schaje was dead, but she refused to think about remarrying. Elish had nevertheless re-introduced Sheindl to Naftula, who had been with him in the labor camp, had lost his wife during the war, and was left with a daughter, Yehudit. Besides being a family friend, Naftula had, in fact, been part of the Scharf family, at least by marriage. In her latter years, Baba Malka had remarried, and her second husband has been Naftula's grandfather, making Naftula Sheind's (step) second cousin. More than two years after the war's end Sheindl and Naftula had married, creating a new family unit with the two girls.

At the end, Berel Surkis had been correct, thought Sheindl in the autumn of 1950. They way had been very *shver* (difficult), but she, Tuleh, Leibish, Srul and their families had finally come to Israel with the first wave of immigrants from Rumania. Now it was time to begin a new life in a new country.

As letters began arriving on a regular basis, Freida Sima turned to Mordche: "How can I have a brother and sister whom I have never seen?" she asked. Knowing that she could now do what she could not have afforded before the war, she informing him that despite the cost, she planned to visit Israel within the next few months to see her siblings and to see about reuniting them permanently. After a devastating war, a new chapter of her life was about to begin.

Chapter 7 New Beginnings: Freida Sima and her Reunited Family – New York and Israel (1945–1953)

Introduction

On May 8, 1945, millions throughout the world celebrated "V-E Day", marking Nazi Germany's unconditional surrender to the Allied Forces. As droves of rejoicing New Yorkers filled the streets, Freida Sima stood at the window with the three blue stars, symbolizing her three stepsons in the American Army, and blessed the Almighty for letting them remain alive and well throughout the war. Soon the boys will be coming home, she thought, and life will begin anew. Soon we will hear from the family in Europe, and can bring those who survived to America. Untying her apron and hanging it behind the kitchen door, she decided to make her way over to her brothers, uncles and aunts to celebrate with them.

Maybe Shirley wants to come along, she thought, walking towards the living room where her daughter had been earlier. Instead of rejoicing, the sixteen-year-old was now sitting in a corner, silently weeping. "The war is over, Mama, but who knows what's going to happen in the world!" she responded to Freida Sima's quizzical look. "Nothing will ever be the same again!" Taking her daughter's hand, she once again rued Mordche's communist polemics and political pessimism that Shirley had grown up with. "No, my Shirlinkeh, nothing will be the same", she answered quietly. "Some circles will close but others, maybe better ones, will open".

Similar to other European Jewish immigrants of her generation, Freida Sima found herself closing many doors in her life after the Holocaust. The Europe that they remembered no longer existed. In many cases, their European families' homes were gone, either destroyed or taken over by local non-Jewish inhabitants. Most had lost family members in the war, and those family members who had survived, often no longer lived in the town, city or even country where they had resided when the war had begun. Their European families often had to begin life again from scratch as their pre-war belongings and savings were gone. In some cases, their physical and mental health had been affected by the horrors that they had experienced. Now that the war was over and the survivors began reconstructing their lives, it would be up to their American families to help them in whatever way possible to complete this process.

The First Postwar Years in America

Over the next months, a number of circles indeed closed, but there were also new beginnings. One by one the Kraus boys came home from the war and began building their postwar lives. After being engaged for years, Harry finally married Shirley Goldberg and the two moved to California where the other brothers were living. It was a wrench for both Freida Sima and her daughter Shirley, as they had both grown accustomed to having Harry's Shirley around on an almost daily basis. Not long after, the last two Kraus brothers settled down and established their own homes in California. Stewart married Reba, Ben married Anne, and the next generation of Krauses began to grow in the west. In fact, the largest enclave of Kraus descendants living together in close proximity was Los Angeles, as Max's sisters Rose and Vera had also moved there with their families in the 1930s. "I miss them Bertie", Mordche would say to Freida Sima every once in a while, and she would reassure him "Don't worry, we will go to California and visit them as soon as you retire".

The Kraus families who had moved to Los Angeles were part of a growing number of Jews moving westward in those years. During the postwar years California was indeed becoming a more Jewish State. After the end of the Second World War large numbers of Jews began immigrating to California and in 1946, over 2,000 Jews a month were settling in Los Angeles alone. By 1950 almost 300,000 Jews lived in Los Angeles, and by the end of the decade, that number had risen to 400,000, around 18% of the city's population.

In New York, as well, the Scharf-Eisenberg family went through changes as cousins came back from the army. For many of the older generation, to which Freida Sima, at fifty, now belonged, it felt as if they were living in two dimensions at once, mourning their relatives lost in Europe while celebrating their soldiers' safe return. This interplay of sorrow and joy was strongly felt, and it played a major role in the gala celebration which the Scharf-Eisenberg family circle held to mark the war's end and the safe return of the cousins who had served in the military.

The America that they returned to after the Second World War was a very different country than they had left when they had gone into war in 1941. In the aftermath of war, the United States began what was to be an economic boom, called the "Golden Age of Expansion" which would last until the 1970s. As the Cold War unfolded, the United States entered into a period of sustained economic growth. Industry, which had ceased to produce war equipment, now began to produce goods that made peacetime life more pleasant. New products, services and even industries such as commercial aviation, were either created or began to expand. Manufacturing was soon aided by automated technologies, and fewer workers produced goods while more were providing services.[154] Neither the veterans in the Scharf-Eisenberg family returning from war, nor the high school age teens in the family looking for after-school or summer jobs, had any difficulty finding employment in those years, as the economy blossomed and the last vestiges of the Depression years were finally left behind.

Even Shirley, Freida Sima's little revolutionary who had no training in anything, had no trouble finding summer jobs, and spent each summer since she was fourteen working full time, once serving sodas behind a counter in a branch of the chain restaurant Needicks, another summer packing cosmetics in a factory. "Ma, I knew it! The capitalists are busy scamming all the ladies!" she said one day when she came home from that job. "Do you know that they put the exact same powder into the compacts from the cheap companies as they do in those from the 'luxury' ones? We should picket them for false packaging!" What will become of that one? Freida Sima asked herself, thinking of how her daughter had started smoking already, just like Mordche, in order to look older for her job. If she would have grown up on a farm like I did, she would maybe have a different outlook on life, but who knows. Even farming wasn't what it used to be a few years back.

During the post-war years, American agriculture was being revolutionized. New chemical fertilizers were developed, tractors became the norm in farming, and a wide range of pesticides were introduced, all of which

154 Samuel Rosenberg, *American Economy Development Since 1945: Growth, Decline, Rejuvenation*, Basingstoke: Palgrave Macmillan, 2003.

changed American farming beyond recognition. Yet farmers faced tough times as farming became a big business and family farms found it difficult to compete. Consequently, more farmers began leaving the land, looking for their future in industry and services. At the same time, however, the food rationing of the war years came to an end, and the production of food, including items considered a luxury during the war years, such as tea bags, paper napkins, and instant cooked cereals, became more commonplace.[155] As a result, Freida Sima blossomed even more in her kitchen, enjoying the wide variety of raw materials now at her disposal.

The rapid demobilization of the United States Armed Forces after the war also changed the social, economic and demographic composition American society. Within two years of the war's end, active duty military personnel had been reduced from 12 million to a bit over 1.5 million soldiers, sailors, marines and air personnel. The Servicemen's Readjustment Act of 1944, known more popularly as the "G.I. Bill" provided a wide range of benefits for the returning veterans who had served on active duty during the war for at least 120 days, and had not been dishonorably discharged. These included low-cost mortgages, low-interest loans to start a business, cash payments of tuition and living expenses for those veterans interested in finishing high school, attending college, or getting vocational training, as well as a full year of unemployment compensation.[156] When the Kraus boys came back from the war, they felt themselves too old to return to school, and preferred to enjoy the low-interest loans that would enable them to take advantage of the peacetime prosperity, start a business, and make a good living. Other members of the extended Scharf-Eisenberg family who had served in the armed forces decided to take advantage of the G.I. Bill, and completed their schooling after the war's end.

But where would they live? Within months after the war ended, tens of thousands of service personnel had returned home, and housing was in short supply. As the veterans came home, married or returned to their families who were often living with parents during the war, they looked for available and affordable housing. Surplus pre-fabricated Quonset huts, over 150,000 of which were produced for the military during the war, were sold

155 Bruce E. Field, *Harvest of Dissent: The National Farmers Union and the Early Cold War,* Lawrence, KS: University Press of Kansas, 1998.

156 Suzanne Mettler, *Soldiers to Citizens: The G.I. Bill and the Making of the Greatest Generation,* Cambridge: Oxford University Press, 2007.

to the public as temporary housing.[157] Aunt Sadie's daughter and son-in-law, Molly and Joe Sanders, were among those who lived in a Quonset hut in New York after the war, in an area of such huts that had been set up to meet the immediate needs of demobilized soldiers and their families.

Another post-war phenomenon was the post-war baby boom which began in 1946 and changed America's demographics.[158] As single veterans returned home, many, such as the Kraus brothers, married and began their families. Others, such as Joe Sanders, or Fred Hecht, married to Uncle Joe's daughter Mitzi, had gone to war leaving wives, and even children. Now they they returned home, and started or expanded their families. By the end of the 1940s around 32 million babies had been born in the United States compared with 24 million in the 1930s. This baby boom, combined with the fact that many G.I.'s could now complete their education and get better jobs, was a major factor in the growth of suburbia.

With the growing post-war use of private transportation, more and more young families began moving out of the crowded cities to areas where they hoped to find affordable housing. Developers like William J. Levitt build new communities of homes that all looked alike, using mass production techniques and pre-fabricated sections that cut costs and allowed the veterans to become part of the American Dream.[159] During the 1940s most of the Scharf-Eisenberg clan still lived in the city, but within years, some of the younger members would begin to move out of greater metropolitan area, following the lead of hundreds of thousands of their contemporaries throughout the United States.

Meanwhile, the next generation, composed of the small children who had sat on the floor in the family portrait taken when Baba Devorah had visited America, was also growing up. Max had been working full-time since the war began, and there was enough money for Shirley to finish high school, instead of going to work at sixteen as had her older brothers. Shirley had been totally unaware that there was any question of her completing high school, and from the day she entered Walton, the prestigious all-girls high

157   Chris Chiel and Julie Decker, *Quonset Huts: Metal Living for the Modern Age,* Princeton: Princeton Architectural Press, 2005.

158   Rusty Monhollon (ed.), *Baby Boom: People and Perspectives*, Santa Barbara: ABC-Clio, 2010.

159   Susan Kirsch Duncan, *Levittown: The Way We Were,* Huntington: Maple Hill Press, 1999; Margaret Lundringan Ferrer and Tova Navarra, *Levittown: The First Fifty Years,* Mount Pheasant, S.C.: Arcadia Press, 1997.

school in the Bronx, she knew that she wanted a higher education, and not a commercial course as she had been offered in her previous school. During her high school years Shirley became more and more politicized, talking to her father about Socialism and Communism, reading pamphlets from the various movements, joining politically minded groups and even learning the rudiments of Russian in order to be able to read some of the literature in the original.

Freida Sima was thrilled when her daughter announced her decision to attend Brooklyn College and become a language teacher, compensation for her not having been able to complete her own formal education. Knowing her daughter's socialist tendencies, she had feared that Shirley intended to join her aunt Rose, Max's older sister, on an extended visit to the Soviet Union that the older woman was planning. "That's all I would have needed", she thought with a sign, "to have her disappear somewhere in Russia, joining the Communists!" After all, this was the daughter whose high school yearbook opened with her homeroom teacher's parting note: "Come the revolution, Shirley, don't forget to take care of me".

In fact, Eastern European immigrants in the United States had always been overwhelmingly Zionist. As members of Zionist women's organizations such as Hadassah, American Mizrachi Women or Emunah, women from the immigrant generation played an important role in Zionist fund raising and political support. While never defining herself as a "Zionist", Freida Sima belonged to a generation of Eastern European Jewish immigrants who considered the establishment of a Jewish State a natural and necessary culmination of traditional Jewish beliefs, particularly after the Holocaust, and fully supported any "pro-Israel" endeavor.

As she entered her fifties, Freida Sima's life was changing. Max was making a living and she no longer needed to run a boardinghouse to support the family. One by one her boarders left until only "Rosie", the elderly Mr. Rosenthal who had no family in New York, and was like family to the Krauses, remained. At eighteen, Shirley could finally have her own bedroom, instead of sleeping in the corner of the living room as she had done since she was a child. Catering to his beloved youngest child's fantasies, Max painted the ceiling black and pasted tin stars on it, which at night reflected the streetlights coming through the window. One evening, having fallen asleep on her daughter's bed while waiting for her to return from college, Freida Sima opened her eyes in shock. "I thought I had died and gone to heaven!" she recalled, laughing about it years later. "I remember sleeping there once and being scared to death of it", recalled Muriel.[160] But Shirley loved her room, the first private place she ever had in her life. More than that, it was a tangible sign of her family moving out of the "poor" and into the "lower middle class", and the Kraus family coming closer to the living style of the rest of the Scharfs and Eisenbergs in America.

It was also the beginning of a new era for Freida Sima. Now that the boarding house had closed, Freida Sima had not just free bedrooms, but free time. For the first time in her adult life she could allow herself the luxury of sitting and reading to her heart's content. But years of caring for others had taught her that life was more than self-indulgence. The war, and especially the fact that she hadn't been able to save her family, still weighed heavily on her mind. She and her brothers had been instrumental in participating in the Bukoviner relief committee that sent packages to survivors, including her own family, now in Bucharest, but she wanted to do more.

The kitchen had always been Freida Sima's kingdom and she was known as one of the best cooks in the family. She therefore decided to put these skills to use and volunteered to cook and serve lunch at a local yeshiva in the Bronx, Salanter Yeshiva, whose student body and faculty included Holocaust orphans and survivors. For several years, Freida Sima spent three mornings and early afternoons each week cooking and serving "good Jewish food" to the students and staff, often sitting with the youngest children to tell them stories while they ate. Described by Jewish communal leader, author and activist Victor Geller, who had studied there during the 1930s as having three guaranteed features, the "three S's – sound, speed and starches",[161] in the late 1940s and early 1950s these lunches became more homey as Freida Sima dished up wholesome food and often acted as a mother figure to those small children in need of one.

Freida Sima was also busy with her own daughter, Shirley. As a talented student of Russian, Shirley had been offered a scholarship to attend the language school at Middlebury College in Vermont. Max was happy that she was studying Russian and he may have been a "revolutionary", but he was quite a reactionary when it came to his own daughter. Aghast at the thought that twenty-year-old Shirley wanted to study away from home, he sent Freida Sima up to Vermont with Shirley in the spring of 1949 to examine the College and the area. After she found a few Jewish families in town,

160 Author's telephone interview with Muriel Eisenberg Arens, Sept. 22, 2015.
161 Victor B. Geller, *Take It like a Soldier: A Memoir,* Jerusalem: Self-published, 2007: 69–70.

and met the director of the Russian Summer School, she and Max agreed that Shirley could attend the school for two months during the summer, but would return to Brooklyn College to complete her degree.

A year later Shirley was offered a scholarship to complete a graduate degree in Middlebury, but that was already too much for Max. Shirley returned to Middlebury for a final summer session in 1950, studying advanced Russian and working as the aide-to-the-director of the Russian summer school, but Max let her know that this would be the end of her Vermont adventures. Shirley returned from her second summer in Middlebury with graduate credits but never finished her Masters' degree in Russian. Years later, she would say that the most important thing that she earned in Middlebury was a drivers license that the elderly man testing her agreed to give her, only after she promised him that she would never use the license, and would let her future husband do the family driving. "Otherwise you will put all the drivers around you in the cemetery, and possibly yourself as well", he said to her when he signed her final forms.

And indeed the Scharfs and Eisenbergs had spent a lot of time dealing with cemetery issues that year. During this period the Family Circle finalized the layout of the Family Circle plot that had been bought in 1941 in Wellwood Cemetery on Long Island. How should the plot be set out? Should there be a gate at the entrance? And what about a bench to sit on? Or possibly two, one on each side of the gate? Numerous Family Circle meetings were devoted to the topic, because as one member had said "We will probably be there longer than we will be here". Finally, in 1951, the matter was settled. Members would be buried in two long rows on each side of the extended narrow plot, with a walkway separating the two sides. The plot was entered through a stone and chain gate on which the words "Scharf-Eisenberg Family Circle" were engraved, and which stated that the Circle was organized in 1928 and the gate erected in 1951. Two stone benches with inscriptions were placed at either side of the entrance, one presented by Kraus and Eisenberg Families, and the other in memory of Israel Nachman Handel, who had died before the plot had been purchased, and was buried in Riverside cemetery in New Jersey.

During the next few years, the newly laid out cemetery plot became the final resting place for five Family Circle members who joined the two babies and one adult already buried there since the 1940s. Among them were two of Freida Sima's aunts, sisters-in-law of her mother Devorah. The first was *Tante* Feige (Fanny) Scharf, Devorah's brother Shmilitzie's

(Shmuel-Yitzchak), wife, who had moved to America after the war. The second was *Tante* Hudel, Devorah's brother Moshe Leib's wife, who was also her brother Abie's mother-in-law.

During the same years the Family Circle also began to expand once again through both births and immigration. The Enzenberg family from Europe was on the move. Elish, Lola, and Max had come to America in 1948, shortly before Muriel left for Israel, and changed their name to Eisenberg to match the rest of the family. After several months of living in Abie's home, Elish and his family moved to their own apartment in Washington Heights and a year later to an apartment in the Bronx. Even though he lived in a different neighborhood than Freida Sima, she was thrilled to finally have another brother in the Bronx again in addition to Benny, something she had missed since Abie had moved to Washington Heights in the early 1940s. Slowly she began getting to know the brother whom she had last seen in his cradle when he was eleven months old as she prepared to leave for America. Elish had a warm and friendly personality and in spite of being a newcomer from Europe, within a short time he, Lola and Max fit seamlessly into the American branch of the family. Behind his kind and generous nature was also a wicked sense of humor which he was careful to show only to those who would not take it the wrong way. His "thank you for coming, and thank God you're leaving!" was reserved for the few who would appreciate the jest, and would not take offense. Freida Sima was one of them.

Elish had been as an accountant before the war in Czernowitz and after the war in Bucharest. When he came to the United States he began working at his brother Benny's butcher shop, but soon realized that he was not suited for that line of work. His son Max recalled: "My father once told me that there were a few times he thought he was going to pass out on the train coming home from the butcher store, from what he had seen during the day".[162] Elish thanked his brother profusely for teaching him the profession, but soon moved into the tie business, eventually opening his own store on Allen Street on the Lower East Side. Fulfilling Freida Sima's dream from childhood, he had been the first in the European family to continue on to *Gymnasium* in Czernowitz and get a degree. Now he decided it was time to further his education in America and registered for night school in order to learn proper English, and to also study Spanish which he would need for his work. Always a good student, Elish eventually graduated as valedictorian of his night school class.

---

162 Author's telephone interview with Dr. Max Eisenberg, Nov. 18, 2015.

Elish and Lola also decided to expand their family after they came to America. In early 1951 Lola gave birth to their son Norman (David Nachman), named after both grandparents. Norman was the youngest of Nachman and Devorah's grandchildren, and he came into the world not long before their first great-grandchild, Muriel oldest son Yigal, was born. The family had every intention of continuing to grow and next generation of Scharf-Enzenberg-Eisenberg's was now beginning.

The Enzenbergs Move to Israel

A year and a half after Elish moved to New York, the rest of the European Enzenbergs joined the first wave of Rumanian immigrants to Israel. These included not only Freida Sima's brothers and sister, but also those of her cousins – Nachman's siblings' children – who had survived the war. Since its establishment in May 1948, over 400,000 Jews, mostly from Europe, had immigrated to the State of Israel, joining the 650,000 or so Jews already living there at the time. The first immigrants to reach the new State were Holocaust Survivors. Some came from the Displaced Persons Camps in Germany and Italy, others from the British Detention Camps in Cyprus. The remnants of certain communities immigrated almost in their entirety, such as the Jews of Bulgaria or Yugoslavia. Large parts of other communities, such as the Jews of Poland and Rumania, also came to Israel during the first years of the State. At the same time, a number of special operations brought Jewish communities perceived as being in serious danger, such as the Jews of Yemen, Aden and Iraq, to Israel. Vast numbers of Libyan Jews immigrated to Israel in those years, as did considerable numbers of Jews from other Oriental and North African countries such as Turkey, Iran, Morocco, Tunisia and Algeria.[163]

The immigration of Jews from Rumania to the newly established State of Israel was not a simple matter. Although the Rumanian government had not stopped Jews leaving for Palestine during early post-war years, after the establishment of the State, Zionism came under new scrutiny and the

---

163 Dov Friedlander, "Mass Immigration and Population Dynamics in Israel", *Demography* 12:4 (Nov. 1975): 581–599.

government began liquidating Zionist training farms. At first, only a handful of Jews, mostly the sick and elderly, were permitted to leave. Eventually, however, an agreement was arranged with the Rumanian government, encouraged by a Jewish Agency financial enticement, enabling approximately 100,000 Jews to exit the country. By December 1951, close to 115,000 Jews had left Rumania for Israel including Srul, Leibish, Tuleh, Sheindl and their families.

They were, indeed, among the lucky ones who got out, as emigration from Rumania to Israel would shortly come to a standstill that would last until almost the end of the decade. Soon after the first wave of immigration from Rumania began, the Jewish Agency in Israel was faced with the embarrassing realization that it could not cope with processing the large numbers of immigrants who were arriving. Consequently, they, together with the Israeli government, began deliberating how to achieve more manageable numbers, even discussing the possibility of manipulating the Rumanian authorities in order to achieve this end. Because of the "head price" they were receiving from the Israeli government for each immigrant's ticket, the Rumanians were initially interested in having as many Jews leave the country as fast as possible. For that reason, at a certain point, they separated the Jews from their baggage in order to put as many Jews as possible on each transport ship, while sending the baggage separately at lower cost to themselves. While the Israeli government continued to deliberate how to deal with the situation, the Rumanians basically took the initiative out of Israeli hands and continued to raise the "head price" for each Rumanian Jew being let out of the country until it was impossible to meet those costs. In response, Rumania abruptly halted the flow of immigrants to Israel for close to eight years, until it began once again in 1959.[164]

The first order of priority for the Israeli government was to find the masses of immigrants a place to live. At the time the State was established, the Jewish Agency ran only a small number of hostels which could offer immigrants overnight lodgings. Initially, new immigrants settled in formerly Arab towns and cities such as Jaffa, Ramle and Lydda, and formerly Arab neighborhoods of major cities which were now empty of their inhabitants, who had either fled, or had been encouraged to leave by military or civilian means. When these areas were full, tent camps were established

---

164 Dvorah Hacohen, *Immigrants in Turmoil: Mass Immigration to Israel and Its Repercussions in the 1950s and After*, Syracuse: Syrcuse University Press, 2003, 75–78.

to meet the needs of the growing numbers of immigrants. Thus, the date of immigration was a crucial issue that often determined where the immigrant would be living. Those who came earliest were sent to the more desirable areas, near places of employment. Those who came later were often sent to the periphery, or to live in tent camps. By the end of 1949, some 90,000 immigrants lived in tent camps, and there was great concern about their condition.[165]

The need for temporary housing, coupled with the problems in the tent camps, led to the establishment of immigrant transit camps called *ma'abarot* (singular: *ma'abara*). From the spring of 1950 onward, these transit camps were supposed to supply housing and employment for the new immigrants until they would be absorbed in Israeli society. By the end of 1950, sixty-two transit camps (as opposed to tent camps) throughout the country housed over 93,000 immigrants, especially those from Rumania and Iraq who had arrived during the year. Families lived in small shacks of cloth, tin or wood and the services, such as kindergartens, schools, infirmaries, and synagogues, were housed in similar shacks throughout the camp. Central faucets, providing the inhabitants with running water, were placed in strategic areas. Drinking water, however, required boiling before it could be used.

Like most of the Rumanian immigrants, the Enzenbergs were initially sent to various immigrant tent camps around the country. Leibish and his family were dispatched to the north, to the Sha'ar Ha'aliyah immigrant camp near Haifa. He, Frieda and little Dora were among the unlucky immigrants from Rumania who were separated from their meager baggage, with which they were united only after immigration. Srul, Tuleh and their families were sent to the center of the country, Srul and family to the immigrant camp and later *ma'abara* of Shechunat Ezra in southeast Tel-Aviv where they were among the few European immigrants in the area, and Tuleh and family to the Pardes Katz *ma'abara* north of Bnai Brak, about half an hour distance from where Srul's family was living. Sheindl, Naftula and their daughters were dispatched further south to the Ramah *ma'abara* in Rehovot.

Within three years, all members of the family had managed to coalesce in the central region and moved into *tzrifim* (shacks) before obtaining more permanent housing. But until then, at least one of them experienced first-hand the Israeli government's policy of sending new immigrants to settle the border areas. Soon after making *aliyah*, Leibish, Frieda and Dora were

---

165 Hacohen, *Immigrants in Turmoil*: 45–46.

loaded onto a truck with a group of immigrants from Sha'ar Ha'aliyah, and taken to Kiriyat Shmona, a newly established *ma'abara* on Israel's northern border. The group was told that as soon as they got off the truck, they would be given weapons in order to protect themselves. Having gone through so much during the war, and because of her trauma from weapons-carrying soldiers who had threatened to shoot them at any moment in the various camps in Transnistria through which they had passed, Frieda made a split second decision, and refused to get off the truck. "We are in our forties", she declared, "and not youngsters like the rest of these immigrants. We are too old to carry guns around all the time."[166] After long debates with the truck driver, he agreed to drive the family back to Sha'ar Ha'aliyah. Eventually, the family was transferred to the Tel Litvinsky *ma'abara* near Tel- Hashomer (Sheba) Hospital in Ramat-Gan, a short distance from both Srul and Tuleh.

Daily life in the *ma'abarot* was a constant struggle. Like many institutions and establishments in the new State, the *ma'abarot* were highly politicized, as the various political parties saw the new immigrants primarily as potential voters. Work was not always available, and to receive work, immigrants often had to list themselves as belonging to a particular party. Thus, for the first two years while they lived at Tel Litvinsky, Leibish could only work at various temporary jobs one after another, because he was not yet listed as belonging to a political party. Ultimately, the family moved to the Neve Amal *ma'abara* in Herzliya where he was given a job paving roads. Eventually, he began working at the Tnuva Dairy Cooperative and the family moved to Ramat-Gan when the Dairy moved to that area. Srul continued working in the lumber business, just as he had done in Europe, finding a job in a lumberyard while Anna worked as a seamstress. Naftula also continued his work as a baker while Sheindl picked oranges in the Rechovot orchards. Tuleh worked and raised pigeons next to the family's shack in Pardes Katz, while Toni was a seamstress.

In addition to politization and unemployment issues, the *ma'abarot* suffered from a lack of teachers and educational resources. As a result, the educational system often had to employ new immigrant teachers who were barely familiar with the norms of their new country. Veteran teachers became the agents of change for their pupils, but in many cases, the attempt to inculcate the young immigrants with Israeli social norms clashed with

---

166 Author's correspondence with Techiya Hildenbrand, Leibish and Frieda's granddaughter, Nov. 21, 2015.

the children's own cultural background and family ties. As was common among immigrants, the children lived in two worlds simultaneously: the local Israeli culture in school, and their own immigrant culture at home. This immigrant subculture continued to exist for years as an accompaniment to everything that the agents of Zionist culture and institutional representatives were trying to impart to them.[167]

Srul and Sheindl had come to Israel with children of school age, while Leibish and Tuleh had younger daughters who began to attend kindergartens. Soon after arrival, all four families were exposed to various facets of the school system and everything that it entailed. Yulbert, who at fifteen was the oldest of the children, had suffered from a hearing impediment since being ill with scarlet fever in the Czernowitz ghetto as a child, and being hit on the head by a soldier during the war. He was first sent to the Helen Keller Institute in Tel Aviv where he learned British sign language, and later studied vocational training where he was taught to sew handbags. Freddie at nine, went to elementary school in Tel Aviv, and was later sent with other children from the Rumanian *aliyah* to Kfar Batya, the religious Mizrachi Women's school in Ra'anana. Marta and Yehudit went to school and later took a secretarial course, Leibish's Dora began primary school in Herzliya, and Tuleh's Dora attended kindergarten in Pardes Katz.

For both the older and younger children in the family, the school system was the first framework in which they were immersed in their new language, Hebrew. Later it was also a framework for their socialization into the culture of their new country. While kindergartens were established inside the *ma'abarot,* the same was not always true for elementary schools which were often in the nearby town or rural settlements. Leibish's daughter Dora remembered having to walk and hour and a half each way to school when they lived in Neve Amal as there was no school nearby, and her family didn't have money to pay her carfare.[168]

Apart from housing, language, culture and employment issues, the new immigrants had to face growing economic challenges characterizing Israel

---

167 Judith Tydor Baumel (Schwartz), "In Everlasting Memory: Individual and Communal Holocaust Commemoration in Israel", *Israel Affairs* 3:1 (1995): 146–170; Tali Tadmor Shimony, Nurit Raichel, "The Hebrew Teachers as Creators of the Zionist Community in (the Land of) Israel", *Israel Studies Review* 28:1 (Summer 2013): 120–141.

168 Author's correspondence with Techiya Hildenbrand, Leibish and Frieda's granddaughter, Nov. 21, 2015.

at that time. Needing to rapidly absorb large numbers of new immigrants, and lacking the financial reserves of a veteran State, in 1949 the Israeli government declared an austerity program (*Tzena)* of price control and rationing. Citizens received ration booklets and were limited in what they could buy in terms of foodstuffs, clothing and other daily necessities. Eggs, sugar, chocolate, fish, soap, milk powder were only available in limited quantities. Meat was rationed to 75 grams (2.65 ounces) a month per person. As a result, a black market flourished among new immigrants and veteran Israelis alike, ultimately leading to public protest. Although the policy began collapsing by the end of 1951, various facets of the *Tzena* remained in force throughout the 1950s, ending officially only at the end of the decade.[169]

Of all the problems that immigrants faced, the *Tzena* was one of the first things that the Enzenbergs wrote about in their letters to America. As soon as they could, the American family began to think of creative ways in which they could make life easier for their brothers and sister in Israel, even before they could actually help them immigrate to the United States. The first to make a trip to Israel was Abie, who in late 1950 brought them what he could in his suitcases. Upon his return, he reported back to the family in America about the conditions under which Srul, Leibish, Tuleh, Sheindl and their families were living. Hearing her brother describe what it was like to be reunited with the brothers and sisters he hadn't seen in over two decades, Freida Sima announced to Max that more than anything else, she wanted to visit her family in Israel, to meet the brother and sister whom she had never seen, and to become reacquainted with the two brothers who had been small children when she left for America.

Freida Sima didn't want to make the trip alone, but Max was working and Shirley had just finished college and couldn't leave her first full-time job. She therefore turned to a cousin and the two agreed to travel there together during the early summer of 1951 and visit the family. Freida Sima prepared for the trip by filling two suitcases with food and presents for everyone she was to meet. Unlike her journey to America by boat forty years earlier, this time she made the trip by plane. The flight to Israel took almost three days, with refueling stops in Greenland, Ireland, France, Switzerland, Italy and Greece. Although when they left New York the only person she knew on the trip was her cousin, Freida Sima would always say "by the time we got

---

169   Orit Rosin, "The Struggle for the Tzena: Housewives and the Government" (in Hebrew), *Israel* 1 (2002): 81–118.

off the plane in Lod airport, seventy-two hours later, everyone on the flight had become good friends."

Sheindl and Tuleh had never met Freida Sima, Elish has been eleven months old when she last saw him, and Srul had been five and the only one who had a faint memory of how she used to look as a girl. Sheindl remembered her excitement when she greeted the sister who was older than she was by over twenty years. "All along I used to say 'I have a sister on paper whom I have never seen', and now I finally met her!" Unlike her American brothers, who for years had called her "Boytee", their pronunciation of "Bertha", these siblings knew of her as Freida Sima, the name Nachman and Devorah had used for their oldest daughter. Only years later, after Tuleh and Sheindl moved to America, did they begin calling their sister "Boytee", like their older brothers in New York. In the European fashion of treating much older siblings with deference, Srul and Leibish rarely called her by her first name, usually referring to her as *Shvester* (sister), just as one would refer to a parent as "Mother" or "Father".

As much as Freida Sima's arrival caused excitement, the contents of her suitcases were what caused a major sensation. When she arrived in the summer of 1951, the newly founded State of Israel was still deep into rationing and deprivations. Trying to think of what the family might need and enjoy, she had packed her bags with food, clothing and small luxuries. Each of her brothers in America had given her their contribution to bring to the family in Israel. Abie from the dry goods store, Elish from the tie business, and Benny from the butcher shop had each done her proud. Out of one suitcase came shirts, pants, ties, socks and underwear for the men and boys; out of the other, skirts and blouses for the girls, and dresses and cologne for the women. From her hand luggage she pulled out numerous salamis, which had given the plane a distinctive and unforgettable odor, familiar to anyone taking the long flights to Israel in those days, along with chewing gum and candy for the children, something that they remembered over sixty-five years later.

The Enzenbergs were always a very emotional family and easily shed tears at both sad and happy occasions. No one's eyes were dry when they got together for a festive gathering at Sheindl's *ma'abara* at Ramah. After eating, the entire family went outside to take pictures to send to America, just as Freida Sima and her brothers had done in New York before the war, when they sent pictures "home" to Europe. Initially posing in different family groupings, the picture session ended with a full family portrait, similar to the one which the American family had taken when Baba Devorah had come to visit. But unlike that picture, for which everyone had put on their best dress or suit, this one was more informal, being taken outdoors in the summer heat. Nevertheless, Srul, Tuleh and Leibish dutifully wore the ties they had been sent from New York with crisp new white shirts, to thank their American family.

Freida Sima also used the six weeks that she spent in Israel to tour the country. She travelled north, visiting Haifa and the town of Zichron Ya'akov, and later travelled to the south, visiting Rehovot, the town next to which her sister Sheindl lived, and even went to see the rapidly expanding Beersheba to which new immigrants were being sent. "And then I went to Jerusalem to see the real sights", she recalled. In those days the trip from Tel Aviv to Jerusalem was a half day adventure in itself, using the road that had been cut only three years earlier to bring provisions to the beleaguered city under siege. Freida Sima visited Mt. Herzl, which had already become the resting place for the Zionist visionary Theodor Herzl, and ascended the YMCA tower from which one could see the walls of the Old City, then under Jordanian rule.

Finally, she got to spend time with Helena, Mordche's late cousin's wife, in Tel Aviv, visiting her at the apartment on Cremieux Street, the one with marble steps that Isaac had offered to leave them in his will, but Mordche had turned down as they didn't have money to pay the land taxes. "Oy Mordche, I wonder if we will regret that decision one day", she now thought, surprised to see the beautiful building in the well-developed neighborhood of central Tel-Aviv. In her wildest dreams she would not have believed that less than twenty-five years later, she would be living in Israel in an apartment only fifteen minutes away.

Israel was indeed a surprise to Freida Sima who had until then thought of it either in terms of the Holy Land about which one prayed, or a country filled with marauding Arabs, orange trees and sand. "Well I was right on two counts", she later told Mordche after her return. "There are lots of orange trees and even more sand". Coming from America, Israel of the early 1950s seemed totally primitive to Freida Sima, almost as bad as the Europe she had left forty years earlier. The outdoor privy at Ramah was definitely not the indoor plumbing that she had become used to. Her family cooked on pres-surized-burner kerosene stoves, called Primus Stoves, which were actually gas containers with a cooking ring above, a far cry from the stove she used in the Bronx. "This is not for me", she thought, each time she visited one of her siblings and saw their living conditions.

Looking at how her brothers and sister were living in Israel made Freida Sima even more grateful for the life she was living in America. Before she began her three-day flight home, she reiterated what Abie had already told his siblings when he came to visit a few months earlier: "Life in Israel is very hard, and the family will be very happy to help any of you who want to come to America to do so." At the time, however, that was easier said than done, as none of the family in Israel had been eligible for the Displaced Persons Act of 1948, enabling DPs residing in Germany, Austria and Italy to immigrate to the United States. But there was talk of new legislation being prepared that would change the immigration restrictions and possibly make it easier for the Enzenbergs in Israel to move to America if they so wished. Meanwhile, the American family would continue sending packages and money to make daily life easier for everyone.

In the autumn of 1952 another family representative visited Israel, Shirley, who came with two large suitcases, heavily loaded with food, clothing, and small luxuries which she, together with Freida Sima, had hoped the family would enjoy. By that time, some of the family had moved into more permanent housing. Srul was talking about moving into an apartment in a new neighborhood being built near Shechunat Ezra, Yad Eliyahu, where he, Anna, Freddie and Yulbert would live. Leibish, Frieda and Dora had moved to the *ma'abara* in Herzliya, Tuleh, Toni and little Dora were still in Pardes Katz but had moved into a *tzrif,* a wooden shack, and Sheindl, Naftula, Marta and Yehudit were soon to move to a small house in Ramat Chen. On her next trip to Israel in 1955, Shirley would spend a night in the house with them in Ramat Chen "in the middle of the dark and in the middle of nowhere", as she recalled, hearing strange sounds at night. "Don't worry, it's only the jackals", Sheindl told her, already used to the sounds of the area.

Shirley could allow herself to make the trip because by then, she had finished college and after a short stint as a language teacher, and secretary in the import-export business, had begun working for Patra, the New York branch of an Israeli travel agency, and was eligible for an agent's travel discount. Patra's manager was a middle-aged religious widower and Holocaust survivor who had lived in Israel for a few years after the war, and Shirley had become his secretary and assistant. Used to being everyone's "mother", Freida Sima "adopted" Shirley's boss, Chaskel Tydor, who was only seven years her junior, treating him to homemade kosher delicacies that she brought for the staff of the midtown Manhattan office, and buying him his first short-sleeved American shirts. Learning of Freida Sima's desire to see her siblings a second time, Chaskel helped arrange her second trip in 1953, giving her the address of his late wife's family in Israel, who were also Patra's owners, and even asking her to represent him at the wedding of his unofficially adopted daughter in Haifa that summer.

By that time Freida Sima knew the drill well, what to pack, what to bring, what the family's sizes were, and what to expect both in transit and when she arrived in Israel. Not only did she bring things for her own family, but this time she brought half a suitcase for Chaskel's family as well. The trip was once again spent with her brothers and sister, although she did visit Haifa for the wedding. This time, when she spoke with her family about the possibility of coming to America, it was more feasible than it had been two years earlier. At the end of the previous year, the "Immigration and Nationality Act of 1952", known as the McCarran-Walter Act, had finally gone into effect, simplifying the immigration procedure for relatives of American citizens.

In addition, by now, some of her siblings were more amenable to the thought of moving to America. After three years in Israel, the Enzenbergs better understood what life in the new State was all about. The sense of being a pioneer and creating a Jewish country was an omnipresent ideal and a positive challenge for those living in Israel during the 1950s. Daily life, however, was another story. Not only was it difficult, particularly for new immigrants, but for some it often resembled a step backwards in time, attitudes, and options. Like many Holocaust survivors who had come from Europe and had lost everything during the war, the Enzenbergs had begun life from scratch in 1945 when they moved to Bucharest. But unlike the survivors living in the DP camps after the war, they had already been rebuilding their lives for five years by the time they came to Israel. They were used to living in permanent structures and not in tents or makeshift shacks. They had hoped to be able to find work without having to endure endless political questioning. They had also had little preparation for what they would find in Israel. During the postwar years they had not been subject to the politization rampant throughout the DP camps, which prepared the survivors living there for the all-pervasive role that politics played in the new State. They had hoped and dreamed that their children would be able to receive an education similar to that which the younger ones among them had already received before the war, or the older ones had not merited, but had dreamed of for their children.

What they were going through was not unique. Many of the newcomers from Europe had grown weary of the hardships and the sacrifices that the country demanded of its citizens in their daily lives. Some wanted a higher standard of living when it came to hygiene, nutrition, health care and privacy, something that the country could not provide during the years of austerity. Others could not cope with the collectivist ideal in which daily life was conducted in the first person plural, a phenomenon which would already begin changing during that decade, but not fast enough for some. The immigrants were actually one of the main factors in creating that change, but the feeling of being "faceless" within a bureaucratic tangle that focused on the system and not the individual, and the paternalism of the ruling Mapai party, were enough to make some of them question their future in the State of Israel.[170] Asking themselves whether it would not be better for them to live out the rest of their lives elsewhere, they felt it was not so much for their sake, but for that of their children, for whom they wanted to give the best chance in life.

Throughout the early 1950s a significant number of Israelis, mostly new immigrants, were leaving the country, and in 1953, the number of emigrants from the country actually exceeded the number of immigrants. When immigration to Israel grew once again during the mid and late 1950s this trend was reversed, but by the end of the decade, approximately 10% of the immigrants had left the country. Some attempted to return to their countries of origin, others sought their future in Europe, Australia, South America, or the United States.[171] By 1955 what Israel was calling "negative immigration" (emigration) had become widespread enough for the Jewish Agency to set up a special committee of inquiry to examine the phenomenon. The committee concluded that "the economic element is not the main reason for this migration".[172] Other reasons the committee listed included older age, unemployment, social isolation, and the fact that from the outset, Israel was often considered by some immigrants to be no more than a stopover point. They did not mention two other reasons, both of which played a role in the Enzenbergs' future: the desire to join their families who had emigrated to other countries, and the hope of giving their children what they considered to be a better future than the one they envisaged for them if they would remain in Israel.

---

170 Orit Rosin, *The Rise of the Individual in 1950s Israel: A challenge to Collectivism*, Brandeis: Brandeis University Press, 1911: 189.

171 Marcos Silber, "'Immigrants from Poland Want to Go Back': The Politics of Return Migration and National Building in 1950s Israel", *The Journal of Israeli History* 27:2 (2008): 201–219.

172 Hanna Yablonka, *Survivors of the Holocaust: Israel After the War*, New York: NYU Press, 1999:16.

The Family Comes to America

Tuleh was the first of the Enzenbergs to express an interest in coming to America. Among his considerations, it appears, was a hope of giving his daughter a better chance at a full education, as in Israel of those years, 90% of the children in the country, both immigrant and native born, were leaving school at fourteen and not continuing on for high school.[173] Tuleh agreed to go on his own and leave Toni and Dora in Israel until he was settled and had a job. In November 1954 Tuleh reached New York, began writing his first name as Tuly, changed his last name to Eisenberg, and went to live with Benny and his family in the Bronx, where he learned from him how to be a butcher. Nine months later he was reunited with his wife and daughter, accompanied on the boat from Israel by Lola and four-year-old Norman who had visited family there. Tuleh and his family soon moved to their own apartment in the Bronx. Toni found work as a seamstress, and Tuleh eventually opened up his own butcher store. Freida Sima was thrilled to have three brothers living in the Bronx, in addition to Abie who lived in Washington Heights.

The next of the family to come to America was Sheindl, who first came for a visit towards the end of the decade to see what it was life was like in New York. Sheindl recalled: "When we came to Israel I had said this was my *tachana sofit,* my final destination, that I would never leave there, but life was so hard. There was rationing, and then I was working, but I wanted it to be better for my daughters." Her rationale for remaining in America appears to have been the same as Tuleh's: a desire to give Marta and Yehudit a better life than she thought she would have in Israel. Once again, cousin Al Scharf, the immigration lawyer, entered the picture. This time he helped Sheindl fill out immigration forms for herself and her family so that she would not have to leave the country to return as an immigrant. Marta and Naftula eventually came to America but Yehudit, who had married an Israeli in the interim, decided to remain in Israel. Like Toni, Sheindl found work as a seamstress and Naftula began working as a baker.

What made Srul and Leibish decide to remain in Israel while their brother and sister moved to America? There appears to be no single answer

---

173 See: Tali Tadmor Shimony, *Shiur Moledet: Chinuch Leumi Vekinun Medina 1954–1966 (National Education and Formation of State in Israel),* Sde Boqer: Ben Gurion University Press, 2010.

to this question. Could it have been family ties? Unlikely as both Anna and Frieda had siblings in Israel, but so did Toni and Naftula. Another possibility was economic status. Although all four families had arrived from Rumania in the same year, with few possessions, within a few years of living in Israel, there were already differences between them. Srul and Anna were an example of successful immigration *klita* (absorption) and adaption in Israel of the 1950s. Within five years of arrival they purchased an apartment in a developing area of Tel-Aviv, Yad Eliyahu. Both Srul and Anna had good jobs, Srul in a lumberyard, just as he had before and after the war in Europe, and Anna as a seamstress. In addition, Yulbert was already twenty, and there was the worry that his hearing disability might make immigration more difficult. They therefore didn't feel that they could do better in America and decided to stay in Israel. In that, however, they were unique among the siblings who had immigrated from Rumania to Israel.

Why then did only Tuleh and Sheindl come to America, while Leibish remained in Israel? Apart from the economic aspect, a decisive factor appears to have been the willingness to initially come to America alone without one's family. If a brother or sister from Israel wished to just visit America to see the extended family, the family in America was willing to pay for their ticket, but could not afford to bring over an entire family just for a visit. And if they decided to emigrate, the same system held true. The family would pay for them to come so that they could work for a year or so in order to earn enough money to bring over the rest of their family. This was the system the family had used forty years earlier, before the First World War, in order to use their limited resources to bring over as many people as possible from Europe. It was now the system that they put into effect in order to use their limited resources to bring over the family from Israel in the most cost-efficient way. The only exception had been Elish, who had come on a different type of visa at a different time, a Rabbinical visa with a promise of immediate employment, which required him to immigrate together with his family who otherwise would not have been able to enter America separately because of existing immigration regulations.

Unlike Srul and Anna, Tuleh and his family had been living in a wooden shack in a *ma'abara* that was becoming a low-class immigrant neighborhood. Tuleh was not working in a profession that he loved, and his only daughter was still very young. Thus, he and Toni agreed to the idea of his going to America alone, first to work and later to bring over the rest of the family. Sheindl had come to America as a visitor, not yet sure if she was willing to stay. But she, too, had been willing to travel on her own, leaving Naftula and their daughters in Israel while she made up her mind. It was only after experiencing life in New York that she made her final decision that it would be better for them to move to America, at which point she found a job and began working in order to bring everyone to New York. Leibish had also been offered the possibility of visiting the family in America on his own to see whether he wanted to immigrate, but he declined the offer, not wanting to even visit America without his wife and daughter, and certainly not to work there alone for a year as Tuleh had done, while leaving his family Israel.

Srul and Leibish and their families remained in Israel, but within a few years Srul's family already had a representative in the New York. In March 1962, Yulbert married Hedy Pahmer, an American girl who had been studying in Israel, and the two moved to New York where they would later raise their family. Like the rest of the Enzenbergs who had moved to America, Yulbert, too, changed his last name to Eisenberg. By the early 1960s, six of the eight Eisenberg siblings lived in New York, five in the Bronx, not far from one another, and one in Washington Heights. Srul and Anna would now begin visiting New York for various family *simchas,* getting to know the family in America.

Fifteen years after the war's end, Freida Sima's dream from the end of the First World War had come true. She, together with Abie and Benny, had finally managed to reunite most of the family in America. For that it had been worth sacrificing her dreams of a formal education and becoming a teacher.

The hope of reuniting her family after the war was not only Freida Sima's dream but one common to many of her immigrant generation who had relatives that had survived the war in Europe. Those who had gone through the war in America often felt a sense of guilt for not having been able to get their relatives out before the war or for having passed the war years in relative safety and comfort. For some, like Freida Sima, it had been their intention to reunite their family in America since their own immigration decades earlier, and only now was it possible to bring it to fruition.

Like many of the 140,000 Holocaust survivors who had immigrated to the United States after the war, Freida Sima's three siblings who came to America soon managed to build themselves a new life. In his book about Holocaust survivors and the successful lives they made in America, William B. Helmreich describes the stages that the survivors went through during this rebuilding process.[174] Like the majority of survivors, they remained in the New York metropolitan area, secured employment, and learned the language, either in night school or by picking it up at work. They were successful in their occupations, and ended up living a middle-class life. They exemplified the personality traits and characteristics that Helmreich lists as being the key to the survivors' success in America: they were willing to work hard, had determination, skill and intelligence, good fortune and were willing to take risks. They were tremendously concerned with their children's welfare, were very protective of them, and provided their offspring with the best education they could afford.

But in other ways they were different than the majority of Holocaust survivors who had come to the United States. They had come to America ten years or more after the war's end, after having spent several years in the State of Israel. They may have come to America under less than ideal conditions, but these conditions were different than those which most survivors experienced. Unlike the majority of survivors who came to America from the DP camps with the assistance of refugee organizations, the Enzenbergs came to a large family in America who not only helped them immigrate, but also provided them with a place to live for their first weeks or months in America, and assisted them in finding employment. They did not have to found their own *landsmanschaft* as did other groups of survivors, for they came to a ready-made Family Circle which automatically became their first social framework, although each of them also formed their own social relationships, unconnected to the family. All in all they were satisfied with their post-war lives.

Looking at her brothers and sister in America, Freida Sima could indeed say that she had fulfilled her dream of reuniting her family. Looking at her daughter Shirley, who had finished college, she realized she had also fulfilled her earlier dream, that of getting an education, through her daughter. Similar to the vast majority of immigrant Jewish young women who came to the United States during the Great Wave of Immigration, Freida Sima had to wait another generation to see her educational ambitions fulfilled. Just as former immigrant seamstress Sarah Reznikoff had written about her own educational ambitions: "We are a lost generation, it is for our children to do what they can",[175] Freida Sima had encouraged and enabled her

---

174   William B. Helmreich, *Against All Odds: Holocaust Survivors and the Successful Lives they Made in America,* New York: Simon and Schuster, 1992.

175   Sarah Reznikoff, "Early History of a Seamstress", in: *Family Chronicle,* by Charles, Nathan and Sarah Reznikoff, New York: Universe Books, 1971: 99.

daughter to fulfill her own dream, that of studying to be a language teacher in college. A college education may have been beyond Freida Sima's reach when she was still young enough to have that aspiration, but she made sure it would become the natural conclusion of her only daughter's school years.

And there were always new dreams. Soon after Freida Sima had returned from Israel, Max turned sixty-five and could retire from painting. "Don't get too comfortable Mordche", she told him, when he sat down the first morning of his retirement in a comfortable living room chair with a cigarette. "I have a list of things I've been waiting for us to do for years!" Their adventures in the years that followed were more than even she had dreamed of, and thus they begin a new chapter of their life together.

Chapter 8 Brighton Beach Memoirs: Freida Sima, Max and the Golden Years (1954–1974)

Introduction

1953 was a watershed year for Freida Sima, marking the end of an era in her life, but also the beginning of a new one. In February, she and Max celebrated their 25th wedding anniversary with family and friends, at a gala party that Shirley had arranged. "Who would have believed that we would both still be here, alive and well, after all we went through", she thought, as Max gave a speech in Yiddish, thanking everyone for coming. This time, at least it wasn't a political speech like the ones he used to deliver regularly at Family Circle meetings, while all the older men politely nodded and didn't understand a word! Now everyone listened, understood, and was happy for them. Neither she nor Max had been young when they got married, and after that came Max's diabetes diagnosis, the Depression, the war, and an operation she had gone through a year earlier. "Thank you *Ribono Shel Olam,* Master of the Universe", she thought, "for having given us life and allowing us to reach this day. *Shehechiyanu Vekimanu Vehigiyanu Lazeman Hazeh*".

In the spring of 1953, her boardinghouse days ended forever with the death of her last boarder, "Rosie", whom she nursed through his final illness. Her second trip to Israel that summer strengthened her ties with her European brothers and sister, and was another step towards bringing more of the family to America. In August she lost an aunt in America, *Tante* Fanny (Feige) married to Uncle Shimlitzie, her mother's brother. Their son Abe had immigrated to America long before the war, and even appeared in the big family picture taken during Devorah's visit. But Shmilitzie and Fanny had only come to America after having gone through the war in the Czernowitz ghetto. Now that Fanny was gone, Uncle Shmilitzie was talking about moving to Israel in order to live with his daughter Rio (Rivka) and her family, and spend the last years of his life in the Holy Land. In 1957 he indeed travelled to Israel by boat, living with his children until he passed away a year later.

In September Max had a short hospital stay when his diabetes had worsened and he needed treatment. Thank heavens he had gotten through it without any serious repercussions, said Freida Sima to herself over and over. In October Max turned sixty-five, and began to collect Social Security – "Roosevelt's Miracle", they called it – and could finally retire from house-painting. Although physical labor had been beneficial to his diabetes, it was becoming increasingly harder for him to carry his ladder, heavy paint cans, and drop cloths around the city by public transportation. In November, Freida Sima and Max reached a long-awaited stage and began making plans about what they wanted to do with the rest of their lives. Their "Golden Years", as retirement was now being called, had finally arrived!

Brighton Beach Adventures

Freida and Max were part of the first generation of Americans for whom "retirement" was even possible, and not necessarily synonymous with "poverty". In 1900, when many of that generation began working, life expectancy in the United States was approximately forty-nine years at birth. Individuals who reached sixty could expect to live, on the average, another twelve years, and almost all workers continued to work for as long as they were able. If for any reason people were unable to work, they were forced to live on their usually meager savings until they were gone, or they were supported by their children. Consequently, for financial reasons alone, old age was not necessarily seen as a blessing, and the customary Jewish expression of "May you live until 120" often merited the response "why do you curse me?"

When the Social Security Act of 1935 was enacted, sixty-five had been set as the normal retirement age.[176] At the time, life expectancy was

---

176 Age sixty-five was chosen as the age at which Social Security benefits would begin because the few private pension plans that existed at that time used age sixty-five. Furthermore, half of the thirty state pension systems used age sixty-five as the retirement age. At the time, the Committee on Economic Security (the committee in charge of drafting the Social Security legislation), had an actuarial study commissioned which showed that using age sixty-five produced a manageable system that could easily be made self-sustaining with only modest levels of payroll taxation. Another scholar argues that age sixty-five was chosen because policy makers believed that age sixty-five

approximately sixty years at birth, with individuals reaching sixty-five being expected to live on the average another twelve years, thus receiving Social Security benefits for a limited amount of time.[177] By the time Max retired in late 1953, life expectancy at birth was already almost sixty-seven, yet individuals reaching sixty-five were still expected to live on the average another twelve years, similar to what had been calculated when creating the Social Security Act almost twenty years earlier. Freida Sima and Max began making plans for their future, and how they would begin to enjoy their "golden years". "Let's plan for at least ten good years ahead, maybe fifteen", said Max, in view of the fact that his parents had lived until their eighties.

For the first time since their marriage a quarter of a century earlier, Freida Sima and Max were alone at home. Shirley had moved out when she married shortly after finishing school. The marriage soon ended, but Shirley preferred to remain in her apartment in Queens, and not move back to the Bronx. Concerned that her parents might be lonely, she surprised them one day with a small dog to keep them company. Watching the puppy's wobbling walk, she named him *Umbriago*, similar to the word "drunk" in Italian and Spanish (*embriagado*). As the neighborhood was rapidly becoming Hispanic, the name was a cause of confusion and mirth. Freida Sima would let the dog wander the neighborhood alone, and when she called from the ground floor window "Umbriago, you dog, come home already!" half the men on the block would turn around, thinking someone was referring to them.

The changing neighborhood was one reason behind Freida Sima and Max's decision to move. During the post-war period, the Bronx had begun to suffer from the results of urbanization and suburbanization without a viable plan. As a result, the borough's racial and ethnic profile began to rapidly change. In 1950 the South Bronx was two-thirds white. A decade later, it was two-thirds black and Hispanic.[178] True, there was still the famous Bronx zoo and the beautiful parks, but the population of the cooperative houses

---

marked a decrease in mental and physical abilities. Dora Costa, *The Evolution of Retirement: An American Economic History 1880–1980,* Chicago: University of Chicago Press, 1998: 11–12.

177 A Timeline of Evolution Retirement in the United States, Workplace Flexibility 2010, Georgetown University Law Center, <http://scholarship.law.georgetown.edu/legal/50>, retrieved on Jan. 1, 2016.

178 Gonzales, *The Bronx*: 144.

was changing, the progressive politics were at a standstill, and what has once been a safety valve for Italian and Jewish immigrants seeking refuge from overcrowded Manhattan, was now serving the same purpose for other ethnic groups. These new residents brought a new culture with them, but many also brought the culture of poverty from which the Jews of the South and East Bronx had escaped, causing the Jewish minority of these areas to think of making their home elsewhere.[179]

The other reason for their decision to move was their mutual love of the ocean, Max for swimming, and Freida Sima for the salt smell and sea breeze. Now that Max was a man of leisure, they decided to finally indulge in a dream. Looking at affordable possibilities in New York City, in early spring 1954 they moved to a one-bedroom rental in Brighton Beach, half a block from the Boardwalk, and less than three minutes from the water's edge.

Already in 1868 Brighton Beach had been carved out of Gravesend, Brooklyn, as a resort community. Developed by William A. Engeman who had made his fortune during the Civil War, and named for the English town of Brighton, the oceanfront community grew in size as soon as it could be accessed. Crowds began to arrive by stagecoach, steamboat, and finally by the Brooklyn, Bath and Coney Island Railroad. Initially, a pier was built to accommodate arriving steamboats, and several hotels were opened in the area to house resort guests. Towards the end of the 19th century, Brighton Beach began offering entertainment that would compete with events in nearby Coney Island. William "Buffalo Bill" Cody rode into town with a re-creation of cowboy life, vaudeville theaters presented different kinds of shows, the Brighton Beach Music Hall offered concerts with famous performers such as Sophie Tucker, and the Metropolitan Orchestra played at the Brighton Beach Pavilion. These were accompanied by a "Dime Museum" and a horse racing track opened for the enjoyment and entertainment of the resort's guests.

In 1905 a mile-long boardwalk opened along the beach boasting an open midway with various attractions including a wild animal arena, a scenic railway, a carousel, an Irish fairground, a bathhouse and a steel roller coaster, which was later destroyed in the 1919 fire. The Brighton Beach Baths

---

179   Oscar Lewis, *Five Families: Mexican Case Studies in the Culture of Poverty*, New York: Basic Books, 1959; Oscar Lewis, *La Vida: A Puerto Rican Family in the Culture of Poverty – San Juan and New York*, New York: Random House, 1966.

opened in 1907 as a private club, which at its zenith would boast 12,000 members. It offered swimming in one of its three pools, tennis, handball, miniature golf, card games and entertainment.

Jews began moving to Brighton Beach at the beginning of the 20th century, leaving the Lower East Side, Brownsville and East New York. Over the years they developed a rich cultural life and religious presence, and as early as 1918 the Brighton Beach Music Hall was turned into a Yiddish theater. By the early 1920s a developer began building bungalows along the oceanfront and on the former racetrack site, but as soon as the Coney Island Boardwalk was extended to Brighton Beach, land became too valuable for single family housing, and apartment buildings were built instead. By then, Brighton Beach was no longer a resort community, but had become a year-round neighborhood for families living in apartments being built throughout the area.

During the 1930s and 1940s Brighton Beach began to be inhabited by an influx of Jewish refugees from Europe, and later, from other areas. To make it easier for the immigrants to navigate the neighborhood, street names leading to the beach area were changed to numbers added to the word Brighton: Brighton 1st Street to Brighton 15th Street. In addition to the year-round inhabitants, the extension of the boardwalk and development of inexpensive rapid transit once again made Brighton Beach into a desired destination for overwhelming numbers of summer visitors. Despite efforts by homeowners and community groups, infrastructure problems caused a gradual deterioration of the neighborhood and beach. During the 1950s, Brighton Beach received an influx of retirees and became a more elderly neighborhood. Within the next few years it would also become a somewhat impoverished neighborhood as well. But at the time that Freida Sima and Max moved to 101 Brightwater Court, it was still a popular summer destination with a large expanse of beach and beautiful boardwalk and three covered pavilions beckoning to young and old.

Max took to swimming almost every morning, while Freida Sima would wait for him in one of the boardwalk pavilions, enjoying the sea air. For the next twenty years, their apartment would become a summer haven for family and friends visiting the beach, who would stop off there to change, and often ended up staying for dinner. Among them were the married daughters of Fanny and Morris Carlin, and their husbands, the couple who had introduced Freida Sima and Max more than a quarter of a century earlier. Another circle had closed.

California Adventures

Summer turned to autumn, and winter was around the corner. One evening after dinner, Max sat on the bedroom windowsill by the fire escape to smoke his usual evening cigarette. When he finished, he turned to Freida Sima and announced that there was still something missing in his life. "Before we get too old to travel", he said, "let's go to California." He missed his boys, he told her, and wanted to get to know his grandchildren. Freida Sima had already been to California while Max was still working and even their daughter Shirley had been to California the year before, returning with marvelous stories about her brothers, their wives and children, and Max's "revolutionary" sisters Rose and Vera, who lived there as well. But Max hadn't been back to California since his first wife had died, nor had he seen his sisters for years, and it was time to renew those family connections.

Both California in general and Los Angeles in particular had undergone many changes since Max had left as a widower with four sons in mid-1928, and moved back to his parents in New York City. During the quarter-century that had passed, the State's population had more than doubled, particularly in the years following the Second World War. The first decades of the century had seen the rise of the film studio system in southern California, and by the time Freida Sima and Max planned their trip, Hollywood was not only a center of radio production, but also of a new medium, television, which was becoming more and more popular throughout America.

Soon after moving to Brighton Beach, Freida Sima and Max had bought their first television set. Always looking for something interesting, Max was not satisfied with an ordinary set but had bought something new, a television with a long cable attached, threaded into a cylinder the size of one's fist, at the end of which was a button one pressed to change channels. What an innovation! Max would turn on the television, cross the living room to sit in his big easy chair, and change channels without having to get up and walk over to the television set. "*A Mechayeh!*" he would say to Freida Sima, who couldn't understand why her husband, the man who would get up every half hour without fail to smoke a cigarette out on the fire escape, needed a contraption on a long string in order to change his channels. After all, he only watched one channel all day long, CBS, which showed his favorite programs: the Ed Sullivan Show, I Love Lucy, The Jack Benny Show, Red Skelton, Johnny Carson, and of course, the seven o'clock news.[180] But he loved it, as did the young cousins who came to visit and were fascinated by the contraption. Sitting next to Max, they would change the channels over and over until he would throw up his hands and say "*Genug!*" ("enough!"), sending them to the kitchen to Freida Sima to have something tasty to eat, and let him watch television in peace.

That week they already sent a letter to "the boys" in Los Angeles announcing their intention of coming for a visit. A few weeks later, Freida Sima and Max closed up the Brighton apartment, and they flew out to California. Within days, Max had regained the tan that he had when Freida Sima had met him in February 1928. "What a *mechayeh* Bertie!" he would say to her over and over, gratified to be surrounded by family. They stayed at one son's home, visited the others, took trips to the coast with Max's sisters, played with the grandchildren, and felt that they were truly in seventh heaven.

Throughout her stay in California, Freida Sima kept in touch with her family in New York by mail, the same way that she had kept in touch with her family in Europe before the war, and in Israel after the war. Only this time, when she wrote to Shirley, she did so in English, unlike all the other letters she had written in her life, which she had penned in Yiddish. By now, everyone in the family owned a telephone, but she never even dreamed of calling New York from Los Angeles, or vice versa. By the mid-1950s one could already place a long-distance call from Los Angeles to New York, but the process was expensive and unwieldy. Long-distance direct dialing would only become possible in most areas years later. Telegrams were used in emergencies, and usually meant serious illness or death. Freida Sima therefore sat down once a week without fail, and wrote a letter to Shirley, keeping her up-to-date about their adventures in Los Angeles and the goings-on of her family.

In a letter from March 1954, she wrote about how much she and Max enjoyed the warm weather, as opposed to the New York cold. Commenting on Shirley's letter where she said that it had even been possible to open the window in New York the previous week, Freida Sima responded: "Here it is summer outdoors. By us this week it is exceptionally good, real July days, but December nights." Describing what it was like for Max to reconnect with friends and relatives that he hadn't seen in years, she wrote: "Having here old and new acquaintances, we feel very much content."

---

180 Some of these shows, such as Red Skelton, had previously been broadcast on a different channel during the early 1950s. Others, such as the Johnny Carson show, changed names (to "The Tonight Show") and moved to other channels during the late 1950s.

That short sentence held a world of meaning for Freida Sima. When she and Max were in New York, they were in "her" territory, which then became their mutual world. California was an unknown entity for Freida Sima, and she had been unsure about what would happen when Max would be back with his sons, visiting places where he had lived long before she knew him, and meeting people from his past. But she soon realized that there was no cause for concern. The boys treated the two of them like royalty. Max's sisters, and especially his older sister Rose with whom he had come to America almost half a century earlier, had a special place in his heart, and vice versa. The two of them were always talking Communism and even now, a year after Stalin's death, they were still arguing the fine points of the revolution, and the status of the working man in America. "How Shirley would have loved to hear these discussions", she thought, although Shirley was slowly becoming less and less Socialist and more and more traditional these days, a far cry from what she had been like as a teenager.

Shirley and Chaskel

"Now if only our Shirley would get married again and have children", Freida Sima thought, remembering how she had remarked to her daughter on the court steps after she had received her civil divorce: "At least you won't die an old maid!" Although she was very supportive of her daughter and loved her tremendously, like many of the Eisenbergs, Freida Sima rarely showed Shirley her soft side. And although she spoke to others with pride about her accomplished daughter, she never told Shirley directly how proud she was of her accomplishments, as it might give her a swelled head.

Well maybe there was hope for Shirley's future, she now thought. Shortly before she and Max had left for California, Shirley had confided that she was interested in her boss at Patra, the travel agency where she worked. Shirley had always been a "revolutionary", but this time, Freida Sima thought, she might have gone too far. Not only was her boss, Chaskel Tydor, a Holocaust survivor and widower, but he was twice her age, and an Orthodox Jew with two adult children whose mother had been killed by the Nazis. Chaskel has spent the war years in Auschwitz and Buchenwald, and his children, who had been sent out of Germany before the war, ended up being rescued to the United States.

Chaskel and Freida Sima had many talks since they met the first Passover that Shirley was working in Patra, when Freida Sima came down to the office with Kosher for Passover food for her daughter. Chaskel had told her a bit about his own experiences, and she had even met his children, Camilla and Manfred, when they came to visit him at the office. Camilla was married with a baby boy and lived in Rochester. Manfred was studying engineering at MIT. Coming from a similar European background, Freida Sima and Chaskel enjoyed chatting in Yiddish. Max had also visited the office several times since Shirley had begun working there, and enjoyed conversing with her boss. Chaskel had even sent Max a long and humorous letter in Yiddish when he heard that Shirley's father had been in the hospital, which earned him Max's respect and even affection. "For a religious Jew he isn't too bad", Max had once said to Freida Sima, a high honor from her Communist and atheist husband.

Friendship with her parents aside, why would Chaskel be interested in Shirley, a girl of twenty-five who was an avowed socialist, and far from observant? She was only a bit older than his daughter! And she was his secretary. Of course her Mordche had been an older widower with four big boys and a communist-atheist when she met him, but that was different! Or was it?

Three months later, when they returned to New York, Shirley whispered to her mother that she and her boss had secretly begun to "keep company". His children knew and approved, but his older family members might look at it askance, as might their co-workers. Chaskel, therefore, decided to take things slowly and keep their relationship private for a while. When Freida Sima and Max went back to California the next winter, she hoped that they would return to a wedding announcement, but it took another year until Chaskel felt it right to ask Max for his daughter's hand. Coming to dinner in Brighton Beach, the fifty-four year old dressed formally in a suit and black *yarmulkeh,* and deferentially requested "Reb Mordche's permission" to make Shirley his wife. "Let us call the girl and ask her", quoted Max in Hebrew, the Biblical response given to Abraham's servant Eliezer, when he requested to take Rivka back to Canaan, to become Isaac's wife. Communist and atheist that he was, Max Kraus had been brought up in an Orthodox home, had attended years of *cheder* in his native Kiev, and could quote the Scriptures with the best of them.

The match between Shirley Kraus and Chaskel Tydor was an unusual one but Chaskel Tydor was also an unusual man, somewhat different than the average Holocaust survivor, including those who came to the United

States. He had been liberated from Buchenwald when he was over forty, older than most concentration camp survivors. He had spent the entire five and a half years of the war in Nazi camps, something few people had survived. After the war, he organized the first *hachshara* (pioneering) kibbutz in liberated Germany, composed of members of all political and religious groups who wanted to come to *Eretz Yisrael,* from the far left to the ultra-Orthodox. Finally, in September 1945, he brought the first group of survivors-pioneers to Palestine to continue their training, had participated in the Israeli War of Independence, and only came to America in 1950, initially as a temporary work visit. It was only as the years progressed that he realized that he would be remaining in America for longer than he had originally planned, as his brother-in-law, Patra's owner, desperately needed his help in running the New York branch of the travel agency. Unlike most Holocaust survivors who tended to marry other survivors, he was actively interested in marrying an American woman, whom hoped would have more in common with his fully Americanized children.

In certain things he was similar to Freida Sima's family who had survived the war in Europe. Like Leibish, Srul, Elish and Naftula who had been in labor camps in Transnistria or Rumania, he had spent the war in Nazi camps in Germany and Poland. He had lost a wife, just as Leibish and Frieda had lost two daughters. Like Tuleh and Sheindl, he had first moved to Palestine after the war, and had only come to America for the sake of family: his children, who had not wanted to leave America after so much wartime wandering, and his brother-in-law, who needed his help in the New York office.

Similar to Freida Sima's family who had survived the war in Europe, and many of the survivors who were able to lead positive and useful lives after the war, Chaskel Tydor exhibited the ten traits and qualities that William Helmreich points out in his study of Holocaust survivors in the United States: flexibility, assertiveness, tenacity, optimism, intelligence, distancing ability, group consciousness, assimilating the knowledge that they survived, finding meaning in one's life, and courage. As one survivor stated, those who succeeded in building new lives usually did so by deciding to make up their mind "never to look back, only forward."[181]

But in other things he differed slightly from most of Freida Sima's siblings. Although he had been born in Eastern Europe, and his family

---

181   William B. Helmreich, *Against All Odds: Holocaust Survivors and the Successful Lives They Made in America,* New York: Simon and Schuster, 1992: 269.

was also originally of Chassidic origin like the Enzenbergs, his parents had fled Galicia at the outbreak of the First World War, and he had had grown up in Germany. As he continued to live there as an adult, his outlook was more western European than theirs. He was also quite learned, and strictly Orthodox, reminding her more of her brother Elish than any of the others. Freida Sima felt quite comfortable with his Orthodoxy, but how would Shirley adapt, in view of her upbringing and her socialist leanings? "That will be interesting to see", Freida Sima thought.

Two months later, the wedding took place in Chaskel's cousin's home in Queens, with Abie and Elish holding two of the *chuppah* (marriage canopy) poles. "Now I will have a married daughter in New York", thought Freida Sima, already planning visits to the "young couple" and hoping to soon have a grandchild from them. But Chaskel and Shirley had other plans. Before marrying, they had decided to leave both Patra and New York for a while, in order to begin life together as a couple, away from any family or work pressures from their previous office.

Following a six-week honeymoon abroad, the couple moved to Deer Lodge, Montana where Chaskel had gotten a job managing a mining company. "My daughter finally remarries and then moves halfway across the country!" thought Freida Sima ruefully. But Shirley was a good correspondent, and wrote weekly letters to her parents, telling them about life in the "wild west", not only in Deer Lodge, but in Rapid City, South Dakota, where Chaskel's mining company also had a branch. "Well they certainly are not bored", remarked Freida Sima to Max, as she read him descriptions of Shirley and Chaskel's visits to Mt. Rushmore, to Indian reservations in the area, to ancient caves in South Dakota, and stories of their weeklong trip to Seattle, Washington for the High Holidays, where Chaskel had friends. Such adventures they were having in a place where one had to drive more than fifty miles to see a movie. And that was considered a "local drive"!

But their biggest adventure was yet to come. Right before Freida Sima and Max left for another winter in California, Shirley's letter arrived, informing them that she and Chaskel would be returning to New York in late spring, as she was due to give birth that summer. Montana and South Dakota had indeed been a wonderful adventure, she wrote her mother, but she wanted to be in New York when she gave birth, as well as afterwards. She and Chaskel had therefore decided that their western sojourn had come to an end, and Chaskel would now look for a job in New York. Besides, there was no Orthodox Jewish community in Rapid City, and no other Jews at all in Deer Lodge. Now that Shirley had married Chaskel, she was living a fully observant lifestyle, something that was possible, albeit difficult, out west, when they were just a couple. Raising a child there, however, without an Orthodox Jewish infrastructure, was not an option, she wrote. "An Orthodox Jewish infrastructure?!" thought Freida Sima when she heard this from Shirley, "Oy my *tochter* (daughter), you have really come a long way from the days you would go with your father to the Workmen's Circle and sing The *Internationale*".

Raising a Grandchild

Three months after returning to New York, Shirley gave birth to a daughter whom she and Chaskel named, Esther Judith, in memory of Chaskel's mother and sister who had perished during the Holocaust. The family took an apartment in Queens and Freida Sima came for a few days to help with little Judy after the birth. As days turned into weeks, Max joined her, and they fell into a routine of spending weekdays in Queens and returning for weekends to Brighton. Shirley was grateful to have her parents' help, as Chaskel had begun working as General Manager of a new travel agency, "General Tours", and was putting in long hours at the office while Shirley stayed home with the baby. "Let me help you in the kitchen so that you can get some sleep", Freida Sima suggested to Shirley, as Judy was keeping her up most nights. Shirley acquiesced with alacrity, and Freida Sima once again found herself cooking for a family and not just for herself and Max.

This routine continued for close to two years, apart from the months that Freida Sima and Max spent in California each winter. But by the time Judy was two and a half, Shirley was climbing the walls. "Ma, if I don't go back to work, I'll go out of my mind!" she told her mother. Freida Sima was not surprised. Knowing her daughter's temperament, she found it hard to believe that Shirley had managed to stay home for over four years after she and Chaskel had married. Besides, Chaskel was working such long hours since he had become a partner in General Tours, that Shirley barely saw him during the week, another reason that she wanted to go to work for him in the travel agency, just as she had done in Patra. For the present, she promised her mother, she would only work part-time, at least until Judy would begin elementary school.

"So what should we do Mordche?" Freida Sima asked her husband, aware of how crazy he was about his youngest grandchild, the only one they had in New York. Since Judy was born, he would sit for hours and compose Yiddish poems for her, oblivious to the fact that as of now, she spoke only English. "Just wait a bit", he would tell Freida Sima. "Soon she will be able to read what I am writing, and will appreciate it." Little did he know that only four decades after his death would his granddaughter find his handwritten Yiddish poems and be able to read, understand, and indeed appreciate them. During his lifetime, however, one song he composed actually became a family icon. Sung to the tune of "My Bonnie Lies Over the Ocean", with a pronounced Yiddish accent, it was a parody of the post-Kennedy era. "In Texas the people pay taxes/ They *shrei* (scream) *oy Gevalt, oy vey is mir* (woe is me)/ But Johnson he says 'nothing doing/ You pay up *dem* taxes *zu mir*' (to me)."

Freida Sima and Max had to make a decision. On the one hand, they wanted to help Shirley, and they loved helping her with their granddaughter, who was already promising to be as lively as Shirley had been at that age. But in the early winter of their lives, they also wanted some time for themselves, which full-time babysitting would prevent. They therefore agreed to babysit for a good deal of the year, taking Judy with them to Brighton Beach for the entire summer vacation, when nursery school and kindergarten would be closed, but winters would remain their own. "Just remember that we don't have *koyach* (strength) for more than one", said Freida Sima to her daughter. "If you want to have more children, you have to raise them yourself."

"Was that the only reason that you and Daddy didn't have any more children?" I once asked my mother. "No", she answered honestly, "but it was definitely a factor in my decision." Chaskel wanted more children but Shirley decided against it. With a husband twenty-five years older than she, Shirley was afraid of being left a young widow with several small children, making it impossible for her to work outside of the house to support them while they were young. Two decades of watching her mother run a boarding house to support her family, with all that it entailed, were enough to convince her that she should always keep up a profession that would enable her to work outside the house, and ensure that she would still have privacy at home. If the price for that would be having only one child, it was one more child than she had originally counted on, having figured that as Chaskel might not be interested in having more children, as he already had older children and grandchildren by the time she married him. She would, however, try to compensate for what her mother had said to her, by telling me when my first daughter was born: "have as many children as you want, I promise to help you with all of them."

Instead of going to California every year, which Freida Sima felt was a burden on Max's boys, they decided that from then on, they would travel to the west coast every second winter, and would spend alternate winters in Miami Beach, where many of their friends were now going. From the early 1960s onwards, they began renting a *Koch-alein,* a one room with kitchenette, on Collins Avenue, one block from the beach. The warm weather was beneficial to Freida Sima who was already beginning to suffer from arthritis in her legs. One winter in Miami, they hosted five-year-old Judy for a week while Shirley and Chaskel, both full-time travel agents once again, were on a business trip in the area. Taking her to a Yiddish festival that the elderly "snowbirds" held in a local park, granddaughter and grandfather ended up on the first page of the Florida Herald, one singing and the other dancing.

By the mid-1960s, Miami Beach was becoming a mecca for retirees and "snowbirds", looking to escape the cold north winters, and among them were many Jewish former immigrants from Eastern Europe, like Freida Sima and Max. Originally a rescue station for shipwrecks and later a coconut plantation, the man-made island was then turned into farmland for avocados and other crops until one of the investors, John S. Collins, saw the potential of turning the beach into a resort. The interior land mass was eventually cleared of undergrowth and mangroves, a two and a half mile long wooden bridge was built to connect the island to the mainland, hotels, mansions and bath houses were built, along with an aquarium and golf course.

During the 1920s, wealthy industrialists from the North built their winter homes in Miami Beach. A hurricane in 1926 put an end to the Miami building boom, but in the 1930s, in spite of the Depression, Miami Beach still attracted tourists, mainly in small-scale rooming houses for seasonal rent. During the Second World War, half a million Army Air Corps cadets passed through Miami Beach when it became a major training center. Later on, many of these servicemen decided to return to the area and make it their permanent home.

By the end of the 1950s, Miami, like the rest of South Florida, underwent a population explosion, doubling its population from what it had been a decade earlier. After Castro's revolution of 1959, a wave of Cuban refugees entered south Florida, changing the demographic makeup of the entire area. In 1965, 65,000 Jews were living in Miami Beach, a far cry from the 7,200 Jews who had been living there twenty years earlier.

Jews had not always been permitted to reside in all of Miami Beach. In 1915 when the area began to be developed as a resort, Jews were not allowed to live north of 5th Street. At various points, when Jews were already permitted to live in other areas on the island, hotels would post signs that stated "Gentiles only". This discrimination continued even after Miami Beach elected its first Jewish mayor in 1943, and Jews were only officially allowed into all the hotels after 1949, when a State law was passed, forbidding such practices.

By the time Freida Sima and Max were traveling to Florida every second year, there were only a few areas in Miami Beach where Jews were still not living, and even that would change by the end of the 1960s. Many of the Jewish retirees who wintered in Miami Beach were former union activists from the garment district and other professions, and they would spend hours on the porches and benches of the area discussing labor related issues and arguing politics. Max felt right at home, just as he had enjoyed his discussions and arguments with his friends at the *Arbeiter Ring,* the Workmen's Circle, in New York, during the 1930s. Now he spent hours sitting on the park benches with his new friends, fighting the revolution again and again, this time, however, only with words. It was indeed a wonderful retirement, and Freida Sima blessed the Almighty daily for having given them enough health and resources to be able to do this year after year. On alternate years Freida Sima and Max would fly to Los Angeles, where they continued to enjoy their grandchildren.

By this point, Judy had begun elementary school, and Shirley was talking about returning to work full time. As Freida Sima and Max had agreed to live with them for much of the year, Shirley and Chaskel had decided to move to a three bedroom apartment in Woodside, Queens that was closer to Manhattan where they both worked. For part of the year, Freida Sima and Max would be there for Judy when she came home from school, and Freida Sima once again took over the domestic arrangements of the household, leaving Shirley free to work even longer hours with her husband. Happy in her natural domain, the kitchen, Freida Sima spoiled Chaskel with Galician delicacies that he hadn't tasted since his youth. He, in turn, treated his *shviggerleben* and *shverleben* (beloved mother-in-law and father-in-law), as he called them, with so much deference and love, that Shirley often joked that he only married her as her mother was already "taken".

Max spent his spare time in Woodside reading, writing poetry, and returning to his profession, painting the apartment, the furniture, and for the first time in his life, even pictures on velvet which they later hung in their Brighton Beach living room. Chaskel and Shirley had bought unfinished wooden furniture for Judy's bedroom and Max had offered to paint it according to his little granddaughter's specifications. "Zeide I want everything turquoise", she informed him, and then changed her mind and added "but also pink and yellow." The result was a multicolored tableau reminiscent of Miami's Art Deco district. "All that is missing are the flamingos!", Freida Sima used to say when she entered Judy's room, enjoying her husband's handiwork alongside the inflatable pillows, footstools, chairs and giant paper daisies lining the walls, that Shirley had bought her daughter at "Azuma", the avant garde store in Manhattan that had everything.

Her "revolutionary" Shirley had a wild streak that an observant lifestyle had not diminished, and the very Orthodox Chaskel had learned to turn a blind eye to his wife's tendencies in that direction. He hadn't even said a word when Shirley took her daughter to Greenwich Village parades and for visits to her former revolutionary comrades home who were now living in an upstate barn that functioned more like a commune. Well, her Shirley had been exposed to worse, Freida Sima recalled, thinking of her daughter's communist upbringing, and look at how she had turned out, so she wasn't particularly concerned about the small inconsistencies in her granddaughter's upbringing.

During the summer months Freida Sima and Max returned with Judy to Brighton, where Max taught her to swim and play cards and Freida Sima taught her how to find bargains at the local *shul* bazaars. On Sundays at noon, the three would sit together, listening to the Yiddish journalist and commentator Shlomo Ben Israel (Gelfer), on WEVD. On Mondays, Max would take Judy to the corner library, where he tried to interest her in books about socialism, a topic he considered appropriate for a girl who had just turned seven. On Tuesday nights they would sit in the park between Brightwater Court and the boardwalk, watching the fireworks. And on Friday night, Max would put on a *yarmulkeh* and make *kiddush* for his Orthodox granddaughter, just as he wore a *yarmulkeh* all week long in Queens, in deference to his Orthodox son-in-law. "Who would have believed that my atheist would sit at the table and sing *zemiros* (Sabbath songs) with his *einikel* (grandchild)", thought Freida Sima one Friday night, looking at grandfather and granddaughter.

Now it was time to introduce the next generation to the Family Circle. Once a month the whole family would drive to the Inwood Jewish Center where the meetings were held, and now, Judy was old enough to come along and meet her cousins. The family no longer lived within walking distance from each other as they had in the past, and the third generation had not grown up together. Of course they would meet at family *simchas* such as bar mitzvas and weddings, but it was not the same as it had been when the cousins would go in and out of each other's homes on a constant basis.

Freida Sima remembered how Shirley would sleep over at Muriel's when the two were little. One day when she was four or five, Shirley came home and told Freida Sima how she had woken up early in the morning and gotten scared when she saw her Uncle Abie put these strange black ropes and boxes around his arm and on his head. Running back to the bedroom she had woken up Muriel and told her that her father was tying himself up, and she should come and help save him. "Oh that's just Daddy putting on *tefilin*", Muriel reassured her. "He does it every morning!" Poor Shirley had been so alarmed by what she had seen, as she had never seen anyone put on *tefilin* before, certainly not her atheist father. She also hadn't had a privilege of going to Hebrew school on a regular basis because of the cost during the Depression, nor had she had piano lessons like her cousins. And now she had a religious husband who put on *tefilin* every day, and she, too, had become observant. Her daughter Judy not only knew what *tefilin* was, but at eight she could already *daven* from a *siddur* (prayer book), just as Freida Sima learned to do at that age in Mihowa. And to top it off, Shirley finally had her own piano which she played by ear, and Judy was taking weekly lessons. Things had definitely changed for the family!

During the 1960s there had been quite a number of events where the family gathered together, some happier ones, others less. Throughout the decade the Scharf-Eisenberg Family Circle had lost members of the older generation, and everyone gathered at the plot at Wellwood Cemetery for the funerals, and later to mourn in *shiva* homes. Uncle Joe passed away in 1964, Aunt Sadie's husband, Uncle Sam, in 1967, cousin Abe Scharf, son of Uncle Shmilitzie, in 1968, and Uncle Moshe Leib in 1969.

But there were also *simchas* when the family got together to celebrate, and the next generation met each other. Srul's Yulbert had married Hedy Pahmer, a student, in Israel and moved to New York, Abie's Sheila married Barry Saltzman, a meteorologist, and Sheindl's Marta married Shimon Lowy, an engineering student from Israel. When Elish's Max married Abby Storch from Baltimore, later in the decade, the entire family chartered a bus to travel there together for the wedding. The Israeli branch of the family had *simchas* as well, when Leibush's Dori married Aryeh Hildenbrand. Then there was Norman's bar mitzvah, the first Bar Mitzvah in the immediate family that decade, after Max, Freddie and David's Bar Mitzvahs during the

1950s. The family was also expanding by birth. During the 1960s Yulbert, Marta, Sheila, Muriel, and Leibush's Dori all had children, adding another generation to the family.

In addition to *simchas,* some of the next generation of Scharf and Eisenberg descendants also got to see each other at various family related venues. On Sundays they would meet at Elish's store on the Lower East Side. Freida Sima would bring apple latkes and coleslaw, Sheindl would bring potato latkes and eggplant salad, and everyone would eat and talk, in between the occasional walk-in customers. Abie, who had retired from Eckstein Brothers, believed that one should continue working six days a week if possible, and would set up a table outside Elish's store on Sundays, selling wallets to passerbys in between *shmusing* (chatting) with the family.

A salesman by birth, Abie spent the other days of the working week running the Printogs outlet, a well-known dress company owned by his cousin Milton Handel, *Tante* Mollie's son. Abie sold all the women in the family beautiful geometrically-patterned Paganne dresses that Printogs manufactured, but only "seconds", because how in the world could he let anyone in the family buy something retail?! Even if it was a bit small, a bit too large, or a color that you hadn't originally wanted, Abie could convince you that it was not only a bargain, but that it was better than what you had been looking for in the first place! At family weddings, all the women would wear Paganne gowns, and Milton could not only be proud of the beautiful dress lines he carried, but of his "super salesman" who ensured that the family would be well-dressed walking advertisements of his creations.

Shirley was a good example, her mother thought. Although she didn't wear her Paganne creations to work, she definitely put them on whenever she had a work-related cocktail party or other occasion. And lately she had a lot of those. She was definitely working too hard, keeping the same long hours as Chaskel, and Freida Sima had pointed it out on more than one occasion. "But now I head my own division of General Tours, Ma, 'Golf Tours International'", she told her mother. As if Shirley knew which side of a golf club was up, Freida Sima thought. But her daughter had always been ambitious, and soon learned what she needed to know in order to send her clients on golfing adventures.

Although Shirley and Chaskel occasionally managed to take off a long weekend and go on excursions to Atlantic City or a New Jersey kosher farm with Freida Sima, Max and Judy, they would usually work twelve-hour days on a regular basis as the office expanded. "At least we are here eight months a year to make sure that Judy is all right", remarked Freida Sima to Max more than once, to which he would answer: "too bad California is so far away and we can't take her with us to meet her cousins." But there were other cousins in New York, at least from the Scharf and Eisenberg side, with whom the family would occasionally get together. Occasionally, but not regularly, as they had in the previous generation. The family no longer lived down the block from each other, or even in the same city. As for the brothers and sisters, although six out of eight Eisenberg siblings now lived in New York, they no longer lived in walking distance from each other, as the family had in the past. And as for the next generation, they were scattered even further, sometimes out of the city, the State, and in a few cases, even out of the country.

The geographical distance that began to separate members of Freida Sima's extended family during the 1960s was typical of a process that the immigrants of her generation were undergoing. After they immigrated to America at the beginning of the century, many had lived near each other, and continued to do so throughout much of their adult lives. Their children had often grown up within walking distance, and spent a great deal of time in each other's homes. After the war, new family members who had come to America from Europe or Israel often tried to live near their relatives. Many succeeded in recreating the same type of closeness that their pre-war families in America had achieved.

Years later Norman recalled his experiences as a young child in the mid-1950s: "We lived in the Bronx…and I remember as a very young child how my family would walk to see Uncle Abe and Aunt Minnie on Saturday afternoons. We were Sabbath observers, couldn't take the bus, and it was a very long walk, several miles. After stopping at Uncle Abe we would sit on a bench in front of the park on Broadway or visit some of the other relatives. There were many relatives living in the Inwood section of Washington Heights."[182]

Another cousin, Gary Gorran, *Tante* Mollie's grandson, also recalled the physical proximity of the family those days, which often made the emotional connection easier and more natural: "I also recall sitting on the benches outside Fort Tryon Park on Broadway and Thayer Street with my Grandmother Mollie and the rest of the family, just relaxing and watching the

---

182 Norman Eisenberg, Scharf-Eisenberg family circle email group correspondence, Jan. 10, 2014.

people and the cars go by. Those indeed were wonderful days, but the world has changed and we all move on."[183]

Indeed the world had changed and the family, like many others, had moved on. In more cases than not, the American-born children of the immigrant generation no longer lived in close proximity to their extended families, and their parents eventually followed suit. One reason was sociological-demographic. The various neighborhoods in which the Jewish immigrants had originally lived when they arrived, such as Harlem or the Lower East Side, or those to which they had moved when they married, such as the Bronx, or Washington Heights, were undergoing demographic changes, as immigrants and migrants belonging to other ethnic groups began to move in. Not only did the American-born children of the original immigrant generation not consider living there after they married, but by the 1950s and 1960s, their parents were also considering a move.

Another reason was biological. In their older years, immigrant parents often moved closer to their children, or even moved in with them. As the children usually did not live in the areas where their parents had been living, this move severed the parents' geographical ties with their own generation. Freida Sima and Max had moved to Brighton Beach of their own volition, partly because of their love of the sea but also because of the changing nature of their South Bronx neighborhood. Now they were spending much of their time in Queens with Shirley and her family, far from Freida Sima's siblings who were still congregated in the Bronx and Washington Heights. The rest of the family was undergoing a similar process. As additional areas of the Bronx began to change, and their children married and moved away, they, too, began to consider relocating to a different area of New York City. The first to do so was Elish who moved with his family to Queens in 1968, only a short ride from where Shirley and Chaskel lived. Although Elish continued to work long hours in his store, the two families, along with Freida Sima and Max, often got together on Saturday nights, starting a new family tradition in Queens.

Freida Sima and Max were somewhat different than other members of the family, if only because Max had retired, and together with Freida Sima, was actually enjoying his retirement years. Much of the Eisenberg family appeared to have adopted a work ethic in which a person was expected to continue working for as long as he or she was able to healthwise. Abie was

---

183   Gary Gorran, Scharf-Eisenberg family circle email group correspondence, Jan. 14, 2014.

over seventy, but continued to sell dresses at Printogs during the week and wallets on Sundays. Benny was running his butcher store and had no intention of stopping. In Israel, Srul felt the same way about his lumber yard, as did Elish and Sheindl, who although still young, had no intention of retiring when they reached sixty-five. Leibish, on the other hand, had never fully recovered from his wartime experiences and losing his two older daughters. Working in a dairy, at a job he did not enjoy, it was expected that he would leave work as soon as he reached retirement age. Only Tuleh, the youngest of the Eisenberg boys, spoke longingly about retirement and what he and Toni would then be able to do together. He and Toni planned to travel, as they did in the late 60s when they went to Israel, and on another trip that they took when they went back to Rumania to visit Czernowitz and Mihowa. He even brought back a jar of water from the well on the family's farm, and gave a portion of it to Elish and Sheindl as a memory of "home".

The End of an Era

Like Tuleh and Toni, Freida Sima and Max also enjoyed traveling, looking forward every year to their trips to California or Florida. Their California adventures, however, came to an abrupt end in early 1969, when Max had a stroke in California, and was hospitalized with partial paralysis. Although he recovered the use of his limbs, he was quite weakened, and Chaskel came to Los Angeles to bring his in-laws back to New York. For the next eighteen months Freida Sima and Max remained in Queens, going back to Brighton Beach only once when Shirley, Chaskel and Judy visited Israel. Max seemed to gain strength, although he needed a wheelchair to leave the house as his walking had grown unsteady. "May it never get any worse", prayed Freida Sima nightly.

Her prayers were not answered. On Rosh Hashana 1970, while Chaskel was in the hospital after leg surgery, Max complained of chest pains. "Oy Mordche, *sha shtill* (be quiet)", responded Freida Sima almost automatically, only realizing the next morning when she called an ambulance, that these were not his normal complaints. Max had suffered a heart attack complicated by emphysema, caused by sixty years of smoking. "Give me a cigarette", he told Shirley from his oxygen tent, determined to enjoy life, or at least his definition of it, to the very end. Freida Sima spent every day in the hospital, while Shirley ran between hospital and home, where Chaskel was in a wheelchair with a full leg cast.

Two and a half weeks later Max suffered a second heart attack. Freida Sima was at his side at the hospital and called Shirley to come from home before it was too late, but she arrived ten minutes after Max passed away. "I had been afraid to go near him because I had a cold and didn't want him to catch it", Freida Sima recalled years later. "But now he couldn't catch it anymore. So I went over to where he was lying in the hospital bed, and before they came to take him away, I gave him a last kiss on his forehead. And that was that. It was over. My Mordche was gone."

When Freida Sima came back to Queens that afternoon, she went straight to the kitchen, put on her apron, and spent the next four hours preparing quantities of fish. It was not only an escape from reality, while doing what she knew best, it was also an act born of practical knowledge. Knowing that her stepsons would be coming in from California for the funeral the next morning, she wanted them to have something to eat. The kitchen was her domain, the place she felt safest, and her apron was her armor. Whether it was to celebrate or mourn, the family always needed to eat.

As Max died on *hol hamoed* (intermediate days of) Sukkot, the funeral was held the next day, but *shiva* only began a week later, after the holiday. Herb and Harry flew in from Los Angeles for the funeral and back that same evening. Ben suffered from fear of flying since the war, couldn't bring himself to board a plane, and spoke to the family in New York by phone. Stewart came to New York two weeks later.

It was an end of an era for Freida Sima, one that had lasted for over forty-two years. She had lost her Mordche, the love of her life, the man who had swept her off her feet from the first handshake. For the first time in four decades she no longer had to be vigilant round the clock about her husband's health, watching his diet, making sure his feet had not gotten diabetic sores, reading him articles from the Yiddish press as his eyes had gotten worse in the years before his death, due to diabetic retina problems. For the first time in years, she began listening to her own body, feeling her joints as her arthritis made it harder and harder for her to walk. As conventional treatments had not helped, she turned to alternative medicine. In addition to massive vitamin therapy, she began going to a "healer", Yehuda Isk, a middle-aged Israeli who had come to New York and was reported to have "electric hands". "It helps, but not enough", she told Shirley, who was worried about her mother's health. Freida Sima, who Max had always said woke up smiling and would start singing like the birds, no longer sang. "I don't even have anyone to argue with anymore", she once said to her daughter, recalling the battles that she and Max would have about politics, religion, and anything under the sun, just so that they could make up afterwards. Where she would once respond to Shirley's emotionalism with down-to-earth and even ironic comments, she rarely voiced them that year, preferring to withdraw more into the kitchen or just sit and read the newspaper.

Shirley was worried. "Maybe it would do my mother some good to get away for a while, to go someplace warm", she suggested to Chaskel. But Freida Sima had no intention of traveling to Florida or California on her own. "Those days are over", she told her daughter. "Without your father, there is no *ta'am* (sense) in going anywhere, and I don't want to go alone." Not wanting her mother to have to have to prepare for Passover that year, Shirley and Chaskel took her to a kosher hotel in Acapulco for the holiday, in the hope that she would begin to recover. As much as Freida Sima enjoyed traveling, she was relatively subdued during the ten days that they were at the resort, causing her daughter great concern.

When they got back to New York, Freida Sima began spending more time with her sister, Sheindl. Sheindl had been widowed the same year and the two sisters now mourned together. Naftula had been buried in Israel, and Sheindl was planning to go back to Israel during the summer to spend time with the family there. "Maybe Mother should do the same thing", Chaskel suggested, and so, the summer after Max died, Freida Sima and Judy spent July together at a small family-run hotel in Herzliya. Together with Sheindl they travelled to Holon to visit Naftula's grave, and in the afternoons and evenings enjoyed visits from Srul, Leibish and other Israeli relatives.

At the beginning of August they were joined by Shirley and Chaskel who took Freida Sima on excursions to various sites which she had not been able to see on her previous trips in the 1950s: the Western Wall, Rachel's Tomb, Hebron and the Golan Heights, all areas that had become part of Israel as a result of the Six Day War in 1967. Standing at the impressive plaza before the Western Wall, Shirley turned to her mother. "So what do you think of the *Kosel Ma'arovi* (Western Wall), Ma, isn't it something?" she asked. "What do I think? I think that it's a *Kosel Ma'arovi* like any other *Kosel Ma'arovi*!" Freida Sima answered in her usual ironic style, a sign that she had begun to come back to herself during the summer.

Shirley and Chaskel had also prepared a surprise for Freida Sima: from Tel-Aviv they flew to Athens to embark on a Greek Island cruise. This was Freida Sima's first experience of "vacationing in Europe", as all the years she had refused her daughter's offer of a European excursion. "At least take advantage of the fact that your daughter and son-in-law are travel agents!" Shirley used to say to her, to which she would answer that she never understood why people wanted to visit Europe. After all, she had run away from there as fast as she could. This time, however, Shirley reminded her that a Greek Island cruise was different than the usual "trip to Europe", and she should just sit on deck and enjoy herself. To her surprise, she did.

When she came back to New York in late summer it was time to prepare for the holidays, and Max's unveiling. Once again the family gathered at the Family Circle Plot at Wellwood, and as was family custom at the time, they brought liquor and cake to the parking area where the family all made a *lechayim* after the ceremony. "Why do we do this?" asked twelve year old Judy, as it was the first time she had ever been to a cemetery. "Some have a custom of making a *lechayim* and wishing each other a long life after they leave the cemetery, in the hope of keeping away the *malach hamoves,* the 'angel of death'", her father answered. "More likely, the *schnaps* is more in the hope of keeping away the cold", added Freida Sima wryly, in view of the chilly October weather.

All year long Freida Sima had waited for the unveiling as if that, and not Max's death the previous year, was the true end of a major portion of her life. Now that it was over, she found herself somewhat at a loss over what to do to keep herself busy. Shirley and Chaskel were working long hours, Judy was soon to begin high school and would only be home in the late afternoon, and most of the day the house was empty. Freida Sima had taken over caring for the entire domestic sphere of the Queens apartment, and had only gone back to Brighton Beach for a few days during the summer. "I don't know if is worth keeping up", she once said to Chaskel, but her son-in-law insisted that she shouldn't give up the apartment, and took over paying the rent. Being of the same generation as Freida Sima, there were times that he understood her mindset better than her daughter. "Your mother should never feel that she has to live with us because she has nowhere else to go", he told Shirley when she questioned his decision. "She should always feel that she has a choice, that she has a place of her own, and that we are grateful to her for making her home with us and taking care of us so well."

Freida Sima knew she was appreciated, but felt that there was something missing in her life. She had never undergone an identity crisis. Ever since she was a young girl she had thought of herself as being independent, rarely defining herself as someone's daughter, wife or mother, but rather as a person of her own worth. If she ruled the kitchen, wherever she lived, it was not as someone who served others, but rather as part of an absolute identity of her own. Maybe that was why she refused to let anyone else into her kitchen, nor had she taught her daughter or granddaughter how to make any of her delicious recipes. "Everyone had their job", she would say to her daughter. "Yours is to work, Judy's is to go to school, and mine is to run the kitchen." There would be time enough to teach them how to make all her delicacies when she would no longer be able to stand on her feet.

Freida Sima's identity being her kitchen activities may have had an additional contextual meaning, in view of the metaphorical meanings of food and hunger. Jewish immigrant writer Mary Antin argued that "food is knowledge", and ethnic writers often expressed their great desire for learning in terms of "hunger".[184] Freida Sima's hunger for a formal education, which was never assuaged or fulfilled, may have metamorphosed itself into turning the kitchen into her unchallenged domain. Food is sustenance, and it is also a symbol, an image and a metaphor. Food feeds one's body, but also one's memories, evoking time and place, recalling experiences of the past, thus creating a symbolic structure of cohesion with one's loved ones. Food was knowledge, and also tradition and love. And above all, food was power. Just like education and knowledge.

But none of that had to do with her feeling that something was missing in her life. Part of it, of course, was missing Max, whom she thought of constantly, but it was more than that. It was missing her greater family in general. She would speak to them on the telephone, but it wasn't the same. If only they lived closer so that she could see them more often!

Within the next few months she got her wish. The Bronx was changing and another one of her brothers decided to move. Soon after their son David married Breindle Knobel, Benny and Bertha moved to Queens, not far from where Elish, Lola and Norman were living. Later that year, David and Breindle also moved nearby. Although none of them lived within walking distance

---

184 Mary V. Dearborn, *Pocahontas's Daughters*, New York and London: Oxford UP, 1986: 80.

from Freida Sima, "my walking days aren't what they used to be anyhow", she thought, grateful that they were now only fifteen minutes away by car or bus. In fact, when Judy would ask her: "Baba, maybe you want to get married again? What kind of a husband would you like?" she would answer her granddaughter jokingly "The most important thing is that he has to have a car! I can't walk anymore!" Tuleh and Toni couldn't be swayed to leave the Grand Concourse, even though their Dora was no longer home, having married Solomon Polachek that year, nor would Abie and Minnie leave Washington Heights. Sheindl, however, was considering moving to Queens in the near future.

Freida Sima finally had more family living nearby, and on Saturday nights they would occasionally meet at Elish's home for *Melaveh Malke*, the post-Sabbath meal in which the "Sabbath Queen" was ushered out until next week. Within a few months the family was looking forward to another wedding, when Norman became engaged to Gail Lefkowitz. Freida Sima offered them her apartment in Brighton Beach. "It's empty almost all year anyhow", she told them. But they decided to wait and only marry the following year. "At least there is another family wedding to look forward to", she thought, happily awaiting another family celebration.

Just when Freida Sima began to feel comfortable once again, surrounded by family, Shirley dropped a bombshell on her mother. Several years earlier, on a trip to Israel, Chaskel had bought an apartment for the family in Ramat-Gan. The apartment was still "on paper" and would take years to build. Besides, no one talked about moving there soon, but only in the distant future, maybe after Chaskel retired. All of a sudden, in the summer of 1973, Shirley mentioned that the apartment would be completed in a few months and began talking about moving to Israel the next summer. "I'll believe it when I see it", thought Freida Sima, convinced that her daughter couldn't be serious about leaving her job, leaving New York, and moving to Israel.

But when Shirley began to make lists of moving companies and inquiring about 220 voltage appliances that would suit the Middle East electric current requirements, Freida Sima began to fear that she might actually be serious. Although the Yom Kippur War of October 1973 put these plans on hold for several months, in the long run, the war strengthened Shirley's resolve to convince Chaskel to retire and for the family to make *aliyah*. "So what will be with me?" asked Freida Sima when she saw her daughter begin to order kitchen equipment to be sent in a "lift" to

Israel. "What do you mean, Ma, what kind of question is that? Of course you are coming with us!" Shirley replied. "And I thought I no longer had anything to look forward to", responded Freida Sima, only now beginning to realize that she had at least one more great adventure ahead of her in the years to come.

Chapter 9 Freida Sima Makes Aliyah – Ramat-Gan and New York (1974–1984)

Introduction

In July 1974, Freida Sima packed her bags, and returned to Brighton Beach. Over the years she had spent occasional days in the apartment that she and Max had enjoyed together, but since his death, Woodside, Queens had become her home base. Although arthritis made it increasingly difficult to walk, the kitchen remained her domain. It gave her pleasure to feel appreciated, and that she was! Shirley and Chaskel worked long hours in the travel business, and young Judy enjoyed the benefits of a "full time Baba". It was like raising another child, thought Freida Sima, remembering Shirley's teenage years. But at least this one wasn't running off to the "Young Socialists", as Shirley had once done, but rather to Orthodox Jewish youth activities or Soviet Jewry rallies.

More of the family was moving to Queens, and again she had close family nearby. Elish and Benny lived ten minutes away by car and Sheindl was about to move to the area as well. The Bronx and Washington Heights weren't far, and the family still got together on various occasions. Although Srul and Leibish lived in Israel, Freida Sima had visited them when she and Judy spent the summer there after Max's death. Sheindl had also come that summer, taking them to visit Naftula's grave in Holon. When he got sick in America, Naftula had dreamed about being buried in Israel, and Sheindl had spent her savings to fulfill his last request. "But I'll be buried with the family at Wellwood", she promised Freida Sima.

"And where will I be buried?" mused Freida Sima, thinking of why she was in Brighton. After Max's death, Shirley and Chaskel had bought an apartment in Israel "for the future", and suddenly the future was now. Several months after his 70th birthday Chaskel had sold his travel agency partnership, and in a few weeks the family would be making *aliyah*, expecting Freida Sima to join them soon after. Meanwhile, they had packed up everything that they were taking from their apartment, and it has gone to the port where it was placed in a "lift" that was being sent to Israel by boat. In mid-July the family would leave the Woodside apartment and move into Freida Sima's Brighton Beach apartment until they left for Israel in early August.

When Shirley asked her mother whether there was anything from Brighton that she would want to send to Israel with the "lift", Freida Sima felt the ground slipping away from under her. How could she choose from among her possessions what to take and what to leave? Everything in the apartment had a story behind it, either her story, Max's story, or their story as a family. Leaving things behind would be like wiping out her past, as these had been the backdrop of her entire married life. At the end, she decided to take only two items: the large mirror that Max had bought her when they moved to Brighton that spanned the length of her bedroom dresser, and a small bookcase that used to hold Shirley's textbooks and Max's Yiddish and Russian Communist literature. "Beauty and Brains", she thought, and she could hear her husband's voice in her head, saying "What 'Beauty and Brains'?! Vanity and the Revolution!" "Vanity it may be, Mordche", she thought, but one day that mirror will be on your granddaughter's dresser, or that of her children, and the bookcase will hold the books of another generation, in another country, in another century.

The Yom Kippur War nine months earlier had somewhat changed the family's timetable. The apartment that Chaskel had bought in Ramat-Gan "on paper" was supposed to have been completed by the winter of 1973, but because of the war it was only ready now, six months later. Shirley had been warned that "ready" was a relative term in Israel, and that it would still take several months for the apartment to be fully inhabitable. Besides, they had neither furniture nor electrical appliances which were still enroute by boat from New York. Until the "lift" with their possessions would arrive in late October, the family would live in a nearby *maon olim,* an immigrants' residence from where Shirley could oversee the apartment's final design.

"It's not for you Ma", Shirley told her, and Freida Sima immediately thought of the *ma'abara* where her family had lived when they immigrated to Israel from Rumania. Shirley reassured her that it was a nothing like a *ma'abara,* but rather a room and a half in a multi-story building, complete with bathroom and kitchen facilities. By the end of October they should already be in their own apartment, Shirley said, and Chaskel would come back to New York in November to see his children, finish some business matters, and accompany Freida Sima to Israel. "So at the end, Sheindl, you will be in

Wellwood, and I will be in Holon", she thought, not dreaming what surprises the last years of her life still had in store for her.

Aliyah

Freida Sima loved America, her home for the past sixty-three years. Had it been up to her, she would never have left the United States, would never have left New York, and in view of the fact that her siblings were slowly moving nearby, would never have left Queens. But she also had no illusions about what it would be like to remain in America, whether in Woodside or in Brighton Beach, without her daughter. Until now she had been lucky with her health. A few years earlier she had suffered a mini-stroke that had affected her walking for a few days, and she had bouts of arthritis, but she knew that as she aged, it would be unrealistic to stay in New York after Shirley moved. "It's not as if I don't have brothers in Israel", she reminded herself, although she would miss her siblings in America. Not only them, but also her three remaining Aunts, *Tante* Rivka, *Tante* Mollie, and Aunt Saide, along with her cousins, nieces and nephews.

She thought back to the last family gathering which had been at Norman and Gail's wedding in June 1974, where everyone had come to celebrate the *simcha*. What a beautiful wedding it had been, even more so for Freida Sima, as she thought it would be the last time she would ever see some of her American relatives. She had even taken a group picture with her sister, brothers and their wives, which she was certain would be her last memento of some of them. But she was in for a surprise. Before Shirley, Chaskel and Judy left for Israel, the family prepared a gala send-off for them at "Café Baba" in Queens, where everyone signed the menu as a parting gift. Once again they took pictures, ate, sang, and danced, Benny with his little grandson Ya'akov in his arms, a redhead like her Shirley, like her mother Devorah had been. "Oy, Mama, what would you say about your family today", she thought. Besides, how could she complain. So much of the family was scattered throughout the world. Abie's Muriel and her children lived in Israel, while Abie was in New York; Srul's Yulbert and his children lived in New York, and his Freddie and children lived in Denmark, while Srul was in Israel. Sheindl and Naftula's daughters and their families lived in Israel, and Sheindl went back and forth constantly. So Freida Sima would see them, and there were always letters, as in the days when the Family Circle would write to Mihowa.

The next few months passed all too fast. Two weeks before she left, she gave up the Brighton apartment, dividing her furniture among relatives. Leaving the building for the last time, she looked up and down Brightwater Court, imprinting the picture on her mind. To the right was the library where Max used to take Judy when she came for the summers. To the left she saw the park where they would sit on Tuesday nights and watch the fireworks set off from the water. Straight ahead was the boardwalk, on which she and Max would walk, and then sit on the benches in the pavilions overlooking the beach. "Make memories when you are young", she would always say to Judy, "because when you get old, that's what you will have. And then you will sit and take the memories out of their box one by one, going over them in your head, spending time with them again, and reliving your life. So make sure that your memory box will be full." Freida Sima hoped that she was at the age when she could still have a last adventure, but at the same time she made sure she had pictures in her mind to fill up that memory box in her head and heart.

From Brighton Beach she went to Washington Heights where she spent the next two weeks living with her cousin, Max Scharf, Minnie's brother. Abie and Minnie lived in the same building, and she ate her meals with them, savoring her last days in America with her close family, and reminiscing in the evening with the first brother she had brought to that country fifty-four years earlier. During the day, however, he was still at work, selling their cousin Milton Handel's dresses at his Printogs factory outlet. After all, Abie was only seventy-five, a "youngster" in family terms, and emphasized on every occasion that he still had many years of work ahead of him.

Right before she left for Israel, the family threw a last birthday party for her in America. Surrounded by her brothers and sister, she cut the cake that Abie and Minnie had ordered, on which the words "Happy Birthday Sister-Mother" were written in chocolate icing. She had indeed been both sister and mother to her American family before the war, when their mother was far away, and afterwards, when she was gone forever. That's what it means to be the oldest of ten children, she thought, and of all her siblings, the one who suddenly came to mind was little Mendel, the brother born between Abie and Benny, who had died of an accident when he was two.

Freida Sima's immigration to Israel differentiated her from the majority of Eastern European Jews who had immigrated to the United States during the first years of the 20th century. As a whole, they were extremely patriotic, viewing America as the country that given them a new life. They were also usually quite Zionist-oriented, had supported the establishment of the State of Israel, and often belonged to Zionist organizations and donated to Zionist charities. But that was where most of them drew the line. "Of course I love Israel", remarked Freida Sima more than once when asked how she felt about making *aliyah*. "But America gave me a home, and God bless Franklin Roosevelt", she would add as an aside, echoing the feelings of myriads of American Jews who had been spared the European Holocaust because they had immigrated to America before and after the First World War, and whose proudest day in the United States was when they obtained American citizenship.

She and her family were, however, part of a growing group of American Jews who had decided to make *aliyah* after the Six Day War.[185] Since the State's establishment in 1948 there had been a small but steady flow of American immigrants to Israel. During the 1950s, some 6,000 American Jews had moved to the Zionist State, of which only 1,000 remained in the country. It was only after the Six Day War that a large wave of North American Jews decided to make Israel their home. Motivated by idealistic considerations, they came with visions and dreams, and included not only the Orthodox, but also more politically liberal and culturally progressive American Jews. Between the summer of 1967 and the outbreak of the Yom Kippur War in the autumn of 1973, over 60,000 Jews from North American moved to Israel. However the October war, as it was known in the Arab world, had been devastating to Israeli morale and caused many potential American immigrants to reconsider their plans.

When Freida Sima came to Israel in early November 1974, she was already considered an anomaly, an elderly American Jews, born in Europe, who had immigrated to Israel of her own volition. "I could understand if you were the mother of a *refusenik* from the Soviet Union who had been permitted to finally leave the country, but why in the world did you leave America to come here now?!" was a question that she heard more than once during her first months in Ramat-Gan. At least it was better than what her granddaughter had been asked at school, she thought, recalling Judy's stories of her new classmates treating her so kindly as most were certain that her

---

185 Liel Leibovitz, *Aliyah: Three Generations of American Jewish Immigration to Israel,* New York: St. Martins Griffin, 2007.

father had lost his job, or even worse, necessitating the family's attempting their luck elsewhere. After all, why else would a family from America make *aliyah* at a time that a devastated Israel was licking its wounds after a war in which they had lost 2,569 soldiers, had over 7,500 soldiers wounded, and another 301 taken into enemy captivity.[186]

Before she turned around, Freida Sima was once again running the family kitchen, this time in the Ramat-Gan apartment. In addition, she was going to ulpan along with Shirley, to learn Hebrew. For Shirley, the language major, learning Hebrew turned out to be a lost cause ("I guess I've got a mental block, Ma!" she would tell her mother) while Freida Sima, used to the Yiddish alphabet since childhood, had no trouble reading texts or sounding out the newspaper headlines. Understanding modern Israeli Hebrew, however, was another matter, and she never picked up enough to follow the news programs. When Judy came home from school asking why she was watching an Arabic program on television, Freida Sima responded that it was all the same to her, she couldn't understand either language when it was spoken so fast!

Immigration is never easy, even under the best of circumstances. Every successful immigration process requires the newcomer to confront and overcome unfamiliar spatial, temporal and social challenges in order to successfully integrate into their new surroundings. Freida Sima's immigration to Israel was a "deluxe immigration" as she once called it, but it was still a challenge. Although Shirley and Chaskel tried to make the transition as easy as possible for her, it brought back memories of what she had gone through almost sixty-four years earlier. Once again, leaving your old life behind. Once again, learning to adapt to a new country, a new language and a new culture. Once again, having to make new friends, get used to different family members, live your life according to a different rhythm. Just as when she had left Europe for America, Freida Sima now felt that she was again embarking on a great adventure. But while life in America had been a step forwards in so many things, compared to the life in the *Kresy*, or that in Mihowa, life in Israel often appeared to be a step backwards, reminding her of what America had been like a quarter of a century earlier.

Shopping was a daily and often complex task. There were few supermarkets in the country, the first having been the Supersol supermarket which opened in north Tel-Aviv in August 1958. At a time that North America

---

186 Abraham Rabinovitch, *The Yom Kippur War: The Epic Encounter that Transformed the Middle East,* New York: Schocken, 2005.

and Europe were already enjoying advanced consumerism, the opening of the large American-style self-service store was met with a massive protest demonstration, claiming it would harm the small grocery and provision stores, some backed by the Histadrut labor federation.[187] By the time Freida Sima made *aliya* there were a number of supermarkets in the country, but none were located in the area where she lived. Instead, she usually left the daily shop to other family members, although she occasionally accompanied Shirley and Chaskel on their "food rounds" as she called it. Bread, milk, eggs, cheese, noodles and basic cleaning supplies were bought at the corner grocery. Fish at the fish store, blocks away. Chicken at the butcher, a fifteen minute drive from home. And what chickens! No frozen Empire chickens here, but old-fashioned fresh plucked chickens, like the kind she used to get from the *shochet* in the Bronx when she was first married. And they weren't even that clean, requiring her to stand over the stove and singe their feathers as she hadn't had to do for decades.

Produce was excellent but seasonal, something that people in America, used to having fruits and vegetables delivered from different climates, had long forgotten. Twice a week Chaskel would go to the *Carmel Shuk,* the open market in Tel-Aviv, where one could buy fruit, vegetables, spices and even clothing, and bring home produce exploding with flavor. When she questioned him about prices, he would always tell her that he had bargained down the prices, and had paid some ridiculously low sum for the plump tomatoes, juicy oranges, sweet fuzzy peaches or crisp apples in his shopping basket. "How could that be?" she thought, only later overhearing him tell Judy: "I get the best for your Baba, but if she heard what it really cost, she would have *harzveitig* (conniptions), so I take off half when I tell her."

The food in Israel was good, but the variety was minimal. Instead of a dairy section filled with shelves overflowing with different flavors of yoghurts, during the mid-1970s the Israeli yoghurt selection consisted of "plain", "coffee", and "apricot". Bread came in two varieties, "black" and "white", and was delivered to the grocery at 5:30 AM uncovered, unwrapped and in a large carton box which was left outside at the mercy of the elements, until the owner opened up an hour later. Toilet paper was mostly of the scratchy "crepe" variety, available in grey and light purple. There were three categories of frozen foods: ice cream, Sunfrost frozen carrots, peas or corn, and Broadway

187 Noam Dvir, "A Brief History of the First Hebrew Supermarket", *Ha'aretz English Edition,* April 4, 2010.

pizza, the only frozen "ready-made" food available in the country at the time. "Good that I am used to cooking almost everything from scratch", thought Freida Sima, putting aside thoughts of Thomas's English Muffins and Eggo frozen waffles that she used to enjoy for breakfast.

At least the baked goods were delicious. Freida Sima had never learned to bake much before marriage and as Max was a diabetic, she had not baked since, wishing to keep any extra carbohydrates or foods made with sugar out of Max's way. This state of events didn't change much after his death, as there had been no kosher bakery in Woodside, and it was only on rare occasions that the family had cake in the house. Now she was living two blocks away from some of the best bakeries in the area, and every Friday Chaskel would bring home delicacies that she remembered from her childhood. Freshly baked rugelach, sponge and marble cakes with a crunchy chocolate topping, sweet challah with raisins and also something new, bourekas, a Mediterranean delicacy of puff pastry filled with mashed potatoes or cheese. "*Rachmunes!* (Have Mercy!)", she once told Chaskel. "If you keep this up I won't be able to fit into any of the dresses that I brought from New York!" But she continued to enjoy a piece of cake with her afternoon coffee, letting out the ties of the old-fashioned lace-up corset that she still wore every day, to fit her slightly expanding girth.

Freida Sima also had to get used her Israeli brothers whom she had never really gotten to know as adults. In terms of their outward appearance, the Enzenberg/Eisenberg family was divided into two groups: those who looked like Devorah, with white skin and broader features, and those who looked like Nachman who were taller, and had a thinner face. The first group included the three sisters – Freida Sima, Marium, and Sheindl – and two of the brothers, Benny and Leibish who were both clean shaven. The second group included three of the brothers – Srul, Elish and Tuleh, all of whom sported mustaches. Abie, who also had a mustache, was shorter in stature, and had a combination of both parents' features.

In terms of personality and inclination, however, each of the brothers and sisters was different. Freida Sima was naturally cheerful and calm, the homemaker and the mother figure in the family. Abie was the enthusiast, the salesman, family man and staunch union man. Benny was more stubborn and emotional. Unlike most of the older and economically left-wing Scharf-Eisenbergs, he was also more right of center. Elish was the intellectual and the peacemaker, Tuleh the most fun-loving, and Sheindl the most fiercely emotional.

Srul and Leibish, however, were unknown entities to their older sister. As she got to know them better, she discovered that Srul was a calm and shrewd businessman, the only Israeli she had ever heard of who sent money abroad to help his children and not vice versa. Despite their wartime experiences, their difficult early years in Israel, and that fact that both of their sons and their families lived abroad, he and Anna were quite resilient, and calmer than the usual level of Eisenberg sentiment that Freida Sima was used to among her American siblings.

When it came to emotion, Leibish was the opposite of Srul, sensitive and often exuding a type of melancholia that sometimes bordering on despondency. More than thirty years after the war's end, both he and Frieda carried their wartime experiences with them on a daily basis as a constant dark cloud over their heads. Leibish had always been a dutiful son, extremely close to his mother, and had never recovered from his parents' death. That blow was compounded by the tragedy of losing his two young daughters in Transnistria. Although he had raised a third, well-adjusted daughter after the war, life in Israel had been very difficult for his family in all senses. Many of his early meetings with Freida Sima were punctuated by descriptions of his wartime experiences, with tears welling up in his eyes when he talked about their parents and his little daughters. Now that he was retired, and living only a twenty-minute walk away, Leibish made it his business to come over at least twice a week during the day to spend time with his older sister. Srul, who belonged to the Abie Eisenberg "work until you drop" school of thought, was still running the lumberyard, and would visit mostly in the evenings.

Although Srul and Leibish came to see their sister constantly, it was sometimes difficult for Freida Sima to follow their Yiddish, as they peppered it with Hebrew expressions, just as she interspersed hers with English ones. Initially, they also had less to talk about, missing mutual past experiences, as they had parted at fifteen, five and three. It took several months for Freida Sima to become completely comfortable with them, at which point they already had more in common to talk about. It was easier when the American family came to visit, and Abie and Minnie did, already that first spring. Muriel also came to visit often, as did Dora, Leibish's daughter, and her growing family that now encompassed three children, and Sheindl's daughter Marta, who told her that her mother planned to visit Israel that coming summer.

Sheindl's preparations for her upcoming visit became a family story that Freida Sima laughed about for years. Marta and Shimon had asked Sheindl to bring them a few baby items from America, and at the last moment they decided to add something for the adults as well. Thrilled to buy supplies for her new grandson, Sheindl hurried with the list to her local drugstore and asked the pharmacist to bring her the necessary baby supplies. The last thing on the list was a bottle of Chivas Regal and not being familiar with the drink, she asked the pharmacist to bring her "a bottle of Chivas for the baby". Needless to say the pharmacist was somewhat surprised that Sheindl planned to feed her grandson blended scotch whiskey. "How was I supposed to know it was liquor?!" she exclaimed to her sister that summer, "I know from *schnaps*, not from Chivas!"

But Freida Sima's joy at her siblings' visits suddenly turned to grief when she received news of her brother Tuleh's death in America. Tuleh had become ill soon after his sister had left for Israel, but the first that Freida Sima heard of it was after his death, five weeks later. Like many Israeli homes at the time, the apartment in Ramat-Gan had no telephone, and Shirley only received the news when the *shiva* was almost over. She therefore decided that they would tell her mother only after the thirty-day mourning period, so that she would only need to sit *shiva* for an hour and not an entire week. "And now we are only seven", thought Freida Sima, as Judy helped her cut her blouse and sat with her for the hour while she cried over her youngest brother, the one whom she had only gotten to know as an adult when he came to America, twenty years earlier. Seven months later she mourned once again when she learned of her *Tante* Mollie's death, the aunt who had taken her to her *chuppah*, and had been a substitute mother to her during her first years in America.

Life in Israel

The months passed and Freida Sima made friends among the neighbors, some older Europeans like her, others younger English speakers. To keep her mother from being lonely, Shirley founded an English-speaking seniors club nearby, and Freida Sima made even more friends there. Her brothers in Israel found it amazing that she took so well to unfamiliar Israeli food. Walking in one day, and seeing her enjoy a plate of extra-sharp humus and techina, Leibish admitted that even after twenty-five years in the country he had never once been tempted to try them.

244

Freida Sima even learned to cook a few local dishes, although her specialties remained the American-Jewish foods at which she excelled. On Friday after school, Judy and her girlfriends would stand in the kitchen, eating Freida Sima's *schnitzel* straight from the pan. "Leave some for Shabbos *kinderlach* (children)", she would laugh, but in truth she was pleased. She hadn't lost her touch. The girls would always insist on "Just one more piece, Baba". In Israel, she had once again lost her name, and become everyone's Baba, except for Srul and Leibish, for whom she was *shvester* (sister).

Now that she lived in Israel she could also visit places that she hadn't seen before on her three trips. During her first two summers in the country, the whole family went on a three-day tour through the Galilee and the Golan Heights, visiting the areas where major battles had taken place during the Yom Kippur War and marveling at beauty of Mt. Hermon in the distance. From their first year in Israel onward the family spent Rosh Hashanah at a Tel-Aviv hotel to enable Freida Sima to go to *shul*, as the local *shul* that Chaskel attended was too far away for her to walk to comfortably. They also spent the entire week of Pesach at the Holyland Hotel in Jerusalem, sparing Freida Sima the necessity of changing over the kitchen to Passover dishes, and cooking for the holiday.

Freida Sima was indeed aging and her body was changing. One day she found herself getting a headache, something she rarely had in her life. "Take an aspirin, Ma", Shirley told her, giving her a Bayer Aspirin that she had brought from America. Shortly after swallowing the pill, Freida Sima got an allergic reaction that put her into bed for a day, in a semi-comatose state. Shirley and Chaskel frantically called their local physician to examine her, and although he was concerned, he advised them not to take her to a hospital, as Israeli hospitals at the time were not known for devoting their best resources to geriatric patients. "Wait it out until morning and see", he suggested, and indeed the next morning Freida Sima opened her eyes and slowly got out of bed. "Are you alive Ma? Would you like me to bring you some toast and tea?" asked her daughter. "Better you should bring me a tasty piece of herring or lox so I should die with a good taste in my mouth", responded Freida Sima with her usual dry sense of humor.

Although she could not understand the hourly news broadcasts on the radio, Freida Sima did her utmost to keep abreast of current events. "So what's new in the world?" she would ask her son-in-law and granddaughter as they watched the evening news on Israel's one-and-only television channel. In the aftermath of the Yom Kippur war, Israel of the mid-1970s was a country in transition, and Freida Sima followed as much as she could of the process with fascination. Fascination, at times however, turned into dread and trepidation, particularly during the numerous terrorist attacks which took place during her first months in the country.

1975 was indeed a year of terror. In March, four months after Freida Sima's arrival, eight el-Fatah terrorists seized the Savoy Hotel in Tel-Aviv, taking thirteen Israeli civilians hostage. Later in the day, elite Israeli army forces stormed the building, killing seven of the eight terrorists, and freeing five of the hostages. Eight other civilians were killed along with three of the soldiers. In May of that year, two rockets fired by Arab guerillas struck Jerusalem, only 500 meters from the Israeli Knesset (Parliament) building. A month later, in June a terrorist cell from Lebanon crossed the border, infiltrating the Kfar Yuval moshav, killing a resident and holding the rest of the family hostage until they were overcome by an army infantry unit. In July, a refrigerator bomb planted by the PLO (Palestine Liberation Organization) exploded in Zion Square in Jerusalem. Fifteen Israelis were killed and seventy-seven were injured in the attack.

"It is hard to be a Jew", thought Freida Sima, evoking the common Yiddish phrase, "but it is even harder to be an Israeli." Although she had been a reluctant immigrant, each attack strengthened her resolve that Israel needed more support, more immigrants, and more backing by American Jews. Her next year in Israel was somewhat easier. The first months of the year were relatively peaceful, and in June 1976, Shirley, Chaskel and Judy made plans to attend a cousin's wedding in London. Still using travel agents' tickets, Shirley and Chaskel were supposed to fly to London via Paris on Air France, while Judy flew directly to London. At the last moment there was a problem with the tickets and instead, Shirley and Chaskel boarded an El Al flight to Paris that took off half an hour later. What they did not know until they landed, was that the Air France flight they missed had been hijacked to Uganda, where the Israeli passengers and French crew were being held hostage. Freida Sima, who had chosen not to travel to the wedding because of her problems walking, only heard the news when she received a phone call from London, in which she learned that they had all arrived safely. "Thank heavens we finally have a telephone", she thought, as the family had only gotten their telephone a few weeks earlier. A week later, on July 4th, she joined in the country's euphoria when the Israeli hostages and the French air crew being held in Entebbe were liberated by Israeli forces.

The next few months brought a number of changes for Freida Sima. One evening in early 1977, she slipped in the house and broke her foot. Her pain threshold was severly tested that evening when the family brought her to the local hospital's emergency room. As there was only a skeleton crew of medical personnel on duty that evening, due to a hospital strike, the young orthopedist said he could not set her leg as he had no anesthesiologist to to put her out while he did it. "Just do it the old-fashioned way doctor", she told him, "don't worry, I won't make a sound." While her granddaughter gave her a rag to bite on, and held her leg above the knee, the somewhat hesitant orthopedist pulled her bones back into position and put her leg in a cast which he told her to keep on for the next six weeks. "I don't know how you didn't scream the hospital down. It must have hurt incredibly!" he said to her afterwards. But even at eighty-two she was still a tower of strength, never complaining even when she was in pain.

She recovered fully, but her daily rehabilitation exercises were a reminder of her growing fragility, which was never far from her mind. That year she was particularly grateful that the family was going to a hotel for Pesach, as she was not yet able to spend long periods of time standing on her foot. Like the rest of the country, she sat glued to the hotel television in the lobby on April 7th, watching Maccabi Tel-Aviv's basketball team win its first European championship, and was just as excited as she had been the previous July when one week after the Entebbe rescue, Miss Israel, Rina Mor, had been crowned Miss Universe. "Just look at how the world loves us when we are strong and successful", she said to Shirley, not even realizing that she was already speaking of herself as "us", the Israelis, and categorizing everyone else, including American Jews, as "them".

That same night would also mark the beginning of a major change in the Israeli political arena, affecting Freida Sima's along with everyone else in the country. Late at night, after Maccabi's victory, Israeli Prime Minister Yitzhak Rabin resigned from the premiership of the Labor Party, following the discovery of his wife's illegal dollar account in the United States. At the time, Israel did not have a free foreign currency policy, and the only way for an Israeli to legally obtain dollars, was to buy a limited amount from the bank when traveling abroad. Within less than six weeks new elections were held, and Likud leader Menachem Begin was elected Prime Minister of Israel, ending almost thirty years of Labor party rule.

Six months later, the unbelievable occurred. After months of clandestine negotiations, Egyptian President Anwar Sadat visited Jerusalem and addressed the Israeli Knesset, only four years after Egypt had attacked Israel during the Yom Kippur War. "Can we trust him?" Freida Sima asked her daughter, echoing what most Israelis were thinking at the time. Standing at the terrace of the Ramat-Gan apartment, Freida Sima watched Sadat's plane fly inland from the coast to the nearby Ben-Gurion airport. "Who would believe that we are watching this happen in our lifetime", she said to her daughter. Indeed it appeared to her as a time of miracles, something she never could have dreamed of when she visited Israel for the first time in the early 1950s.

When Judy came home from university that day and described how all the students at the campus had stood outside to watch Sadat's plane arrive with its Israeli military escorts, Freida Sima told her to remember that moment so that one day she would be able to tell her own grandchildren about it. "Just like you told me about when the Titanic's survivors reached New York or how you attended Sholom Aleichem's funeral", Judy responded, making Freida Sima feel like a walking history lesson. "And who knows, maybe next year we can start running Israeli tours to the pyramids", added Shirley, still a travel agent at heart.

As negotiations with Egypt continued throughout the beginning of 1978, the pyramids appeared to be slipping further and further away. In March, a group of Fatah members hijacked a bus on Israel's coastal road. After a lengthy chase and shootout, thirty-seven Israelis were killed and seventy-six wounded. Three days later Operation Litani began, with Israeli Defense Forces invading South Lebanon and expelling PLO forces from the area, pushing them north of the Litani river. In April, Israel won the Eurovision song contest with *A-Ba-Ni-Bi,* a song based on an Israeli version of "pig Latin". "Why does the world love us this time?" Freida Sima asked her family, tongue in cheek, understanding by now that any Israeli victory in a judged contest was rooted primarily in politics and rarely in skill or beauty. "Is it because we are still negotiating a peace treaty with Egypt, and they are trying to encourage us to give up more territory than we are willing to?"

Throughout the summer of that year the country's mood changed daily, depending on the news from the intense peace negotiations that were continuing between Egypt and Israel. Freida Sima's family's mood also changed that summer, as in early July she slipped a second time and broke her hip. In those days, Israeli doctors rarely operated on octogenarians who had undergone such accidents. Instead, she was placed in a full leg cast for three months, and sent to a rehabilitation facility where the doctors informed Shirley that there was almost no chance her mother would walk again. Freida Sima responded in her usual no-nonsense way, telling her daughter: "no one is going to tell me that I'm not going to walk again." And she did, surprising her doctors, her daughter, her convalescent home room-mates, everyone but herself. True, it was with a walker, and for only short distances. But she was not about to spend the rest of her life in a wheelchair, unable to run her kitchen.

Even in her convalescent home Freida Sima had avidly followed the news, and her first question to Shirley who came every morning to spend the day with her mother in rehab was "What's going on in the world?" Despite being confined to a wheelchair for most of the day, Freida Sima had kept up with current events, reading the *Jerusalem Post*, the daily English-language newspaper that Shirley brought her, following the events unfolding at Camp David and after, when Anwar Sadat and Menachem Begin's were awarded the Nobel Peace Prize for their bold step at breaking the status quo between their two countries. She even managed to attend Judy's wedding in a wheel-chair, a week after her cast was removed, although her granddaughter's young friends had to carry her up two flights of stair in her wheelchair, as the hall had no elevator.

Post-rehabilitation reality, though, was somewhat different than her hopes. After she came back home from rehab, Freida Sima's physical lim-itations made it more difficult to run the kitchen than she had imagined, and from early 1979 onward Shirley did most of the work while she gave instructions from a chair in the dining area. But it didn't stop Freida Sima from celebrating the Israeli Peace treaty with Egypt that spring, and enjoying Israel's victory at the European Eurovision song contest five days later with the song *Hallelujah*. "Again they love us", said Freida Sima to her daughter, to which Shirley responded "It's all politics, Ma. Don't take it too seriously, it won't last." Three weeks later a terrorist attack on Nahariya left four Israeli civilians dead, three from one family. The terror attacks had recommenced.

The months passed and Freida Sima found herself more and more limited, unable to venture out of the building except with assistance. If that wasn't depressing enough, Srul and Leibish had abruptly stopped visiting. True, they still called her daily on the phone but even those calls were strange. And where had her niece Muriel disappeared to? Only after a month did the pieces fall into place. One day in mid-August, Judy came into her bedroom to tell her that Srul and Leibish had come to visit. Starting with "Baba, your brothers are here", she continued with the same fateful words that she had used when she prepared her for Tuleh's death: "before you come out, maybe change your blouse, that one is too nice".

Abie. Her Abie that she had brought to America. The little brother that she had played with, the one who had been with her the longest. The only one who remembered the *Kresy*, the brother who at seventy-five had told her that he still had years of work in him, and would never retire as long as he could still stand on his feet. Her Avrum had been run over early one morning on his way home from *shul*. Abie had lingered for ten days in a coma, but died of his injuries without opening his eyes. Muriel had flown to America as soon as she got news about her father. Srul and Leibish knew, and had sat *shiva*, but once again the family wanted to spare her an entire week of *shiva*, particularly in view of her physical limitations. Had her brothers come to visit with their mourning beards, they couldn't have hid the tragedy; hence they only came to be with her now that the *shloshim,* the thirtieth day after a death, marking the end of the initial mourning period, was over, and to sit by her side while she sat her hour of mourning.

Tuleh was gone, and now Abie was gone as well. She heard that Elish had closed the blinds to his store which remained in darkness, as he could not bear to look outside and not see his brother standing with his table on the sidewalk, selling wallets. Muriel returned to Israel, telling her aunt how Benny was also filled with grief. "I should have died instead of him", he kept saying. Sheindl was also wrapped in misery, having lost her big brother who had kept everyone together after Freida Sima had left.

Srul and Leibish mourned their brother, but they hadn't lived with Abie since they were fourteen and eleven, and had never really gotten to know him much as adults. For the first time in her life, Freida Sima felt alone in her grief, unlike after Tuleh had died, as Srul and Leibish could tell her about their life with Tuleh in Europe before, during and after the war. Now she was the one who could tell them about life with Abie in America, but it wasn't the same as being with family who had lived through the same experiences with him. While she refused to succumb to depression, she often felt herself overwhelmed, and would sit for hours on the kitchen terrace, looking out of the window and thinking. Shirley noticed, and for the first time she asked her mother if she wouldn't be happier in America. Giving a deep sigh, Freida Sima patted her daughter's hand and remained silent. How could she tell her only daughter that her heart was torn between to irreconcilable desires: to be with her family in Israel, and to be with her family in America.

250

There were times that she felt almost imprisoned in the apartment, particularly on the days that she had yahrzeit for her parents, her siblings or her husband. Ever since she had learned of her parents' and Marium's death, she could not bear to look at a burning yahrzeit candle. As soon as she would light one, she would try to find a reason to leave the house, and would stay out the next day for as long as possible, until the candle burned down. Now that she could not leave the apartment on her own, that was no longer a possibility. And there were too many yahrzeits. Devorah, Nachman, Marium, Mordche, Tuleh, Abie.

Throughout their lives, people are defined by many factors: their geography, profession, heritage, beliefs, ethnicity, religion and gender, to mention just a few. A person can be characterized by his actions or lack thereof, the company he keeps, or the comportment of his descendants. But none of this is necessarily his or her identity. Identity is located the center of one's being, it is the sum total of one's "self" and plays a central role in a person's motivation, cognition, perceptions, emotions and thought. It is the major component of one's self-definition, how people perceive themselves and not necessarily as how they are perceived by others.

As Sydney Stahl Weinberg writes about the immigrant generation of women: "While women of the younger immigrant generation were caring for families and trying to make ends meet, they were tooo busy filling the needs of othes to wonder about the direction of their own lives. But with the passage of years, children grow up and husbands die. After being the center of the family for so long, most women eventually had to come to grips with losing the focus that had shaped their lives. Often widowed, with children dispersed, middle-aged and elderly women had to find a different purpose to give their lives meaning."[188]

For decades Freida Sima was secure in her identity. She was a Jew, an American, a woman, a wife and mother. But most of all she was a nurturer, a provider of food which was what she perceived herself as being. The home was her castle and the kitchen was her power chamber. She was of the generation and background where food was equated with love and care, but for her, food preparation was also equated with her identity, her most inner being. For years she had refused to let anyone into "her kitchen", each time with another excuse or explanation. "Everyone had their job", she used to say, "and this is mine". Shirley's job was first to go to school, and later to work

---

188 Weingberg, *The World of Our Mothers*: 247.

alongside her husband. Then it was Judy's job to go to school, and there would be time later to teach her how to take care of a kitchen. Meanwhile it was Freida Sima's domain, and she would not relinquish it to anyone for any reason. Only a few weeks before she had broken her hip, she had let Judy help her clean a chicken for the first time, until then having preferred to let her nineteen-year-old granddaughter set the table, or wash the dishes as her domestic contribution to the household.

Now all that had changed and she felt her identity in jeopardy. Freida Sima was still a Jew, but she was no longer in America. Her Mordche was gone for more than a decade, and although she was still a mother, the roles had been reversed with daughter caring for mother since the accident. "If you can't be, then at least do", Freida Sima used to say to herself since Max's death when her title changed from wife to widow, taking her culinary responsibilities even more seriously than before, if that was even possible. But even that was now gone. The kitchen was no longer her exclusive domain. Although she grudgingly admitted that her daughter was not a bad cook, she sensed that Shirley didn't have the instinctive feel for cooking that Freida Sima had from the first day she had taken a knife and chopping bowl in her hands. "A good cook is born, and all the cookbooks in the world won't change that", she once said to Judy, looking pointedly at Shirley's "Fanny Farmer Cookbook" and the "Joys of Jewish Cooking" on the shelf. But in truth, Freida Sima was talking more about herself than her daughter, as she felt her identity slipping away, day by day.

One day, when Shirley asked her again if she wouldn't be happier in America, she finally gave her answer. "I want to be buried next to your father", she said. For Shirley that was enough. Leaving for what she thought would be a two-week trip to New York to check out residences for Freida Sima, Shirley found herself spending over four months abroad, moving between homes of friends and family while trying to secure a place for her mother in a senior citizen's home. The bureaucracy was fierce, and the question was where she would find the most suitable solution for her mother. Should she consider putting her in the same facility as Aunt Sadie, who had been living in a senior complex out on Long Island for several years? How would the two get on if they once again lived next door to each other? Would her mother be better in a Residence somewhere in Queens, now that Elish, Benny, Sheindl, Minnie and Minnie's brother Max were all living there within a ten-block radius? Only Toni, Tuleh's widow, remained in the Bronx, not far from one of the best Senior Homes, the Daughters of Jacob, located not far from the Grand Concourse where Toni still lived. The determining factor would be the bureaucracy involved, and the proximity to family who could easily visit. Long Island was too far away for most of them to come by public transportation, there was nothing available in Queens, and the Bronx facility therefore appeared to be the Residence of choice.

During the long and complex process of finding a suitable solution for Freida Sima, Aunt Sadie's daughter, Molly Sanders, tried to lift Shirley's spirits. In November 1980 Molly wrote her younger cousin, giving her advice on how to get through the process in one piece: "Shirl, it's not easy and my heart goes out to you. We are all full of that Jewish guilt that was laid on us. Mom's home is wonderful and they have all sorts of good things which she hasn't had in years, but they all long for the early days of their youth when they were fruitful and the head of the family. She just told me my Pop is lucky he's gone since he died at home and she'll die in a Home. Try not to feel guilty because you've been a <u>great</u> [emphasis in the original] daughter and Chaskel has been a marvelous son-in-law, and there comes a time one must have a life of their own."[189]

In this case, however, it was Freida Sima who wanted a life of her own, one where she would not be "a useless appendage" to her daughter, as she would often call herself since becoming incapacitated. Molly Sanders had succinctly summarized the dilemma of an entire generation of aging American Jews, and one that was even more painful to the former immigrants among them who had deeply internalized the American work ethic, and the necessity for productivity to ensure their survival. "They all long for the early days of their youth when they were fruitful and the head of the family".

One method of dealing with that longing was "the Abie Eisenberg school of thought", to which most of the Eisenbergs/Enzenbergs subscribed, where one worked for as long as one humanly could. In a sense Freida Sima ascribed to the same philosophy, viewing her vocation as the provider of sustenance, albeit an unpaid profession, but a profession nonetheless. Idleness was uselessness, something that was more than a deadly sin, but a harbinger of death itself.

Max had been an exception, being ill with diabetes, and besides, he wasn't an Eisenberg by birth. Leibish was an Enzenberg by birth, but with a difficult life, wartime memories and melancholy that he could not shake

---

189   Correspondence Molly Sanders to Shirley K. Tydor, Nov. 20, 1980.

off, and a tedious job that he worked at from lack of choice, so it was understandable that he wanted to retire. But in general, life was for work, not for fun, and heaven help anyone who acted otherwise. Years later Judy and Dora would reminisce about Dora's father, Tuleh. When Judy remarked that he was that the only Eisenberg who had no problem stating that he wanted to stop working and enjoy life while he still could, Dora added how ironic it was that he was also the first of the surviving siblings to die.

After months of utilizing every connection she could think of, Shirley secured a place for her mother in the Daughters of Jacob Home for the Aged in the Bronx. Founded in 1897, it was one of the oldest and best known Jewish Senior Residences in New York City. For the first three decades of its existence, the Home had been supported by Jewish women's organizations, and at the thirtieth anniversary dinner of its founding, it was described as an institution which is "a monument for the capacity of women for service to the Jewish community."[190] Located a little over a mile away from Beck Street where Freida Sima had first lived when she married Max, she would not only be closing a circle by moving back to America, but completing an even tighter circle by moving back to the Bronx, not far from her old neighborhood.

Freida Sima reacted to the news of her impending move with equanimity. During Shirley's four-month absence, she had moved into a temporary Senior Care Facility in Ramat-Gan, as Chaskel, in his late seventies, was unable to provide her with the necessary care on his own, and there was no full-time home health care in Israel. At the same time she had wanted to see what a Senior Care Facility would be like, figuring that the American version would certainly be more advanced than its Israeli counterpart. Never one to whitewash her terminology, she would laugh when Chaskel and Judy called it a "Senior Citizens Facility" saying, "What "Senior Citizens". It's a Home, a *moishav zkeinim* (Old Age Home)". Judy, who was to accompany her grandmother to America, helped her pack up her possessions, assisting her in choosing what to take and what to leave behind. "You are going to America Baba", Judy reminded her, "and if there is anything you need, it can be bought there."

In late March 1981 Judy brought Freida Sima to America. Shirley met them in the airport with an ambulette that could accommodate her mother's

---

190 "Home for the Aged, Erected by Daughters of Jacob, Observes 30th Anniversary", *JTA* Dec. 16, 1926, <http://www.jta.org/1926/12/16/archive/home-for-aged-erected-by-daughters-of-jacob-observes-30th-anniversary>, retrieved on Jan. 15, 2016.

travel wheelchair and they travelled to Toni's apartment in the Bronx where they would be staying until Freida Sima entered the Daughters of Jacob home a few days later. Years later, Shirley recalled the moment she knew that she had done the right thing for her mother. A few hours earlier, American President Ronald Reagan had been shot and wounded, and the ambulette's radio was turned to a news station. Enroute to the Bronx, when Shirley tried to speak with her mother, whom she hadn't seen in months, Freida Sima put her fingers to her lips. "Sha! I'm listening to the news, they shot the President!" It was the first time in years that her homebound mother, who had been feeling more and more cut off from the world, could listen to the radio, and understand every word.

The Daughters of Jacob

When she came back to New York in 1981, Freida Sima did not return as an immigrant but as an American citizen. Nevertheless, she underwent a transition, once again having to deal with new spatial, temporal and social challenges. Her surroundings were different than before, a "Home" instead of "her home", just as Molly Sanders had described her mother as having said. She had her own clothing, but had left her jewelry for her daughter in Israel as she was afraid of it being stolen in the Residence. She had no familiar furniture, but Shirley had arranged for her to have her own telephone so that she could be in constant touch with friends and family. There was no one in the Home whom she knew, but she had a roommate, and made friends easily. Within a short time was involved in social activities.

This was the third time in her life that she had moved close to six thousand miles away from where she had been living. The first time, it was with the hope of getting an education and starting a new life in America. The second time, it was not by choice but out of necessity, as she realized it would not be possible for her to remain in America without her daughter. This time it was by choice, but it was a hard choice. She loved Israel, but if she was going to be housebound, she preferred to do it in a country where she understood the language and where there was better developed geriatric care than in Israel of the early 1980s. When Shirley asked her how she felt about the move, her only comment about it to her daughter was: "By the third time you go from country to country, at least you know that you are going to live through it."

Freida Sima spent the next three years at the Daughters of Jacob Home, running the social committee on her floor, and enjoying daily phone calls and weekly visits from her family in America. Shirley flew in at least four times a year, using up all her old perks from the travel business to see her mother, and Judy made the trip twice to spend time with her grandmother. During Freida Sima's first eighteen months at the Daughters of Jacob, Aunt Sadie was still alive, living in a Senior Citizen's Residence on Long Island, and the two women talked daily, reminiscing about the days when they were both young girls in New York.

Concerned that her mother would be bored, Shirley has suggested ordering her a large print subscription to a newspaper, but Freida Sima told her that she couldn't read much lately, although she could see well enough to navigate her way around her floor of the Home. "Good that I know to *daven* and say *yizkor* by heart", she told Shirley when she visited a week before the holidays. At eighty-six she was already showing signs of macular degeneration, the disease that would rob her daughter of her own sight thirty years later. "How can I be old when I still have two aunts!" she told Shirley, thinking about her *Tante* Rivka and Aunt Sadie.

The American family visited her constantly, but the older generation was slowly disappearing. Within eight months she lost her sister-in-law Toni, *Tante* Rivka, Aunt Sadie, and finally her cousin Max Scharf, Minnie's brother. By mid-February 1983 she was the oldest member of the Scharf-Eisenberg family still alive. Other than her eyes and her feet, there was nothing seriously wrong with her. "My head still works and I want to live long enough to see another generation", she would say to her brothers and sister when they would visit her. That autumn she had no visitors from Israel as Shirley had broken a hip and Judy was on bed rest in early pregnancy. Freida Sima was thrilled. "Finally, a new generation to look forward to!" she told everyone who would listen.

In April 1984, three days after Judy gave birth to her daughter in Israel, Freida Sima had a slight stroke and was moved temporarily to Montifiore hospital for treatment. Speaking to Shirley on the phone, she learned that the baby was named Rivka for Max's sister Becky and Freida Sima's *Tante* Rivka. Dori, Tuleh's daughter, came to the hospital, and took pictures of Freida Sima which she sent to Israel. Around the same time, Shirley took pictures of the baby in Israel to send to her mother. Convalescing with the baby at her parents' home, Judy called the Bronx hospital to speak to her grandmother. After over a dozen rings, the phone was answered by what sounded like a very old and sick woman who whispered "I'm dying" and hung up. White with fright, Judy turned to her mother, and Shirley spent the better part of an hour trying to reach Freida Sima, who was in the hospital rehabilitation room and laughed at her daughter's fears. "Judy must have dialed the wrong number", she said "as you can hear, I'm fine and dandy, and I hope I won't be dying for a very long time!"

Freida Sima returned to the Daughters of Jacob Home in early May, and slowly began returning to her normal activities. Shirley had seen her mother in March and in view of her hospital stay, wanted to visit her again in May. But she was torn between her yearning to visit her mother in New York, and her desire to be with her daughter in Israel to help with the new baby. Freida Sima solved her daughter's dilemma by reassuring her that she was fine, telling her to stay in Israel to help raise the new generation. "Come and visit me later this summer", she told Shirley. "Meanwhile stay where you are and make sure my great-granddaughter is being brought up right."

Shirley had tried to describe her baby granddaughter to her mother over the phone. "She's got dark eyes and dark hair like Judy and white skin like you", she had said, to which Freida Sima replied that in their family, red hair seemed to skip a generation or two, and maybe one day Judy would have a redheaded grandchild. Each morning Freida Sima eagerly waited for the mail delivery, hoping to receive the airmail envelope from Israel with pictures of the baby. But it was not to be. Early Friday morning, June 15, she woke up complaining of chest pains, and four hours later she closed her eyes forever. Freida Sima was gone.

Elish, who was her family contact person listed at the Home, was the first they informed, and he immediately called Shirley in Israel to tell her about her mother. It was slightly past noon in America, and seven hours later in Israel, a few minutes before Shabbos. For the first time in her life, Shirley, who never *benched lecht* early on Friday night, had done so in order to walk over to Judy, two blocks away, and see the baby. Hearing the phone ring as she walked out the door, she absentmindedly thought "who in the world would be calling me five minutes before Shabbos?" and walked down the stairs, not even bothering to mention it to anyone that evening.

Early Shabbos morning Judy awoke to a loud knock at her front door, and opened it to see Srul's wife Anna standing there. When Elish hadn't been able to reach Shirley, he had called his brother Srul, who had not yet made Shabbos, and still answered the phone. Knowing that Shirley would have to leave for New York immediately after Shabbos, Anna had walked all the way from Yad Eliyahu to Ramat-Gan in order to tell Judy about her grandmother, and let her decide how and when to tell her mother. When Judy went over to Shirley with the baby later that morning, she didn't have to say a word. "It was written all over your face", Shirley later told her. That night, Shirley and Chaskel caught a midnight flight to New York, arriving on time for Freida Sima's funeral on Sunday morning. Shirley sat *shiva* at Elish's home, together with him, Sheindl and Benny, who had now become the oldest member of the Sharf-Eisenberg family.

When Shirley got up from *shiva* the following week and went to the Daughters of Jacob Home to pack up her mother's possessions, the first thing she saw was the airmail envelope with pictures on her mother's night table. It had arrived in Monday's mail, the day after Freida Sima was buried next to her beloved Mordche at Wellwood cemetery. Next to the envelope was her mother's *Techina*, the woman's book of Yiddish prayers that Freida Sima had gotten in 1916 from her *Tante* Mollie, a last vestige of her mother's desire for an education. The bookmark was still set to a prayer that Freida Sima had often said as she grew older: "Prayer for a woman who has to live with her children in her old age".

The end of a person, however, is not always the end of a story, and an end can also be a beginning, as we will see in the final chapter of this book.

Chapter 10 An End that is also a Beginning

Introduction

When Freida Sima died in June 1984, she left behind an extensive and widespread family: a daughter, son-in-law, granddaughter and family in Israel, four stepsons and their families in California, a sister, two brothers and three sisters-in-law in New York, and two brothers and two sisters-in-law in Israel. Four weeks to the day after Freida Sima's death, her sister-in-law and cousin Minnie passed away. Since returning to America, Freida Sima and Minnie had spoken daily by phone. Shirley remarked to Minnie's daughters that their mothers had obviously been unable to live more than a month without calling each other.

The same ironic sense of humor that exemplified many of the Eisenbergs and their descendants, had accompanied my grandmother throughout her life. When someone would complain to her about being bored, my grandmother would retort: "You are bored? *Zug Viddui* (say the "Confession"), *Lein Krishma* (recite the "Shema" prayer), there is always something to do!" Never squeamish about any subject, the closest she would lament about getting old was to say "Love? Once we used to do it all night…now it takes all night to do it!"

After her death, that ironic humor expressed itself in her siblings. At Srul's grandson's wedding dinner, men and women were separated by a wooden *mechitza* (partition) as per ultra-Orthodox custom. When the sisters-in-law expressed their dismay that they couldn't sit with their husbands, eighty-four year old Benny and seventy-seven year old Elish put their shoulders to the *mechitza's* last section, dancing it to the music until perpendicular to the rest of the partition, opening a passage between the two sections of the divided room. Within minutes, the family pushed together tables from each side and spent the wedding together. Religious services aside, nothing would keep the oldest Eisenbergs away from each other during a three-hour-long wedding dinner.

Over the next decade, however, that older generation of Eisenbergs began to disappear. Benny died four years after Freida Sima, followed by his wife Betty. Frieda and Anna passed away in Israel, a year apart. Srul and Elish died two months apart, and Leibish followed a year later. Sheindl and Lola, the last surviving family members, lived near each other in Queens and were in almost daily contact until Lola's death in 2004. Sheindl, the youngest and only one of the original Eisenberg siblings still alive, then became the senior member of the extended family.

All of the family stayed in touch with her on a constant basis, but only Shirley still called her Sheindl, as had Freida Sima who never used her sister's Rumanian name, Jenny. "The last of the Eisenbergs!" her great nephews, Elish's grandsons Daniel and Stevie, used to say when they would call Sheindl every Friday to wish her a good Shabbos. After Shirley broke a hip at eighty and told her aunt that she was feeling old, Sheindl would laugh. "Old? You are old? I am old, you are still young!" But years earlier, after Elish's death, Sheindl had confided to Shirley that it was not easy for her to be the youngest of ten children as she got older. "First I was in *ovel* (mourning) for my parents and Marium, then for my husband Schaje, then for my husband Naftula, then for Tuleh, for Avrum, for *dayn Mameh* (your mother), for Benny, for Srul, for Leibish, and finally for Elish. If you outlive everyone, you spend the last years of your life being in *ovel* all the time, instead of being happy that you are alive", she told her niece.

Sheindl, the last of the Eisenbergs, lived until she was over ninety-six years old. The remnants of the jar of water from the family well, which her brother Tuleh had brought back from Mihowa more than forty years earlier, was poured over her grave at the end of the funeral, symbolically linking her to her European home. In addition to her personal details, Sheindl's tombstone proclaimed her to be a "Holocaust Survivor" and "Keeper of the Family Lore". Now that she was gone, it would be up to the next generation of Eisenbergs and their descendants to tell the stories, and by doing so, to keep the memory and the voices of the family alive.

The Making of "My Name is Freida Sima"

The desire to keep my grandmother's memory and voice alive initially inspired me to write an article about her for The Jewish Press. I approached the paper's editor, Jason Maoz, with the idea, and his enthusiasm motivated me to write a series, chronicling her life and that of her family, and through them, much of the 20th century Jewish world.

For fourteen months these articles appeared as a monthly front-page feature. The opening pictures made the characters come alive for the readers. Each article's dedication to a family member's memory reminded us that no one is an island. The stories touched people's hearts, recalling their own ancestors. The series generated responses worldwide, strengthening my feeling that I was doing something worthwhile, not only in my grandmother's memory, but for everyone's grandmothers and grandfathers who deserved to be remembered.

Soon I realized the articles were just the beginning. I wanted to do more. With my family's encouragement, and the helpful comments and support of the Jewish Press's editor, I decided to expand them as the basis for a book about my grandmother Freida Sima. This was the culmination of a lifelong venture of getting to know her and my extended family, while learning more about the world in which they lived.

Keeping my grandmother's memory and voice alive was definitely a major objective in turning the articles into a book. But it was not the only reason that I began this project. My grandmother had always been a big part of my life, having raised me from childhood, a continuous presence in word and deed. This book was therefore not part of what Marcus Hansen has called the "principle of third-generation interest" where: "what the son wishes to forget, the grandson wishes to remember"[191], but an ongoing family story of several generations.

"My Name is Freida Sima" is both a personal history, and an attempt at understanding the history of an entire generation of young Jewish immigrants, particularly women immigrants, at the turn of the 20th century. At the same time, it is also the story of different voices and shifting identities, those of Freida Sima and her contemporaries, and also those of others connected with the making of the story and the writing of this book. While most of the chapters were written in Freida Sima's voice, they also give expression to other voices, such as that of her mother Devorah, who describes the segment about her trip to America in the early 1930s, or her youngest sister Sheindl, who is the primary voice recounting the European family's experiences during the Holocaust.

---

191   Marcus Lee Hansen, *The Immigrant in American History,* Harvard: Harvard UP, 1940: 7.

Although I appear as a character in several chapters of the book, they are still written in Freida Sima's voice and from her perspective, as she, and not I, is the story's focus. Only the methodological introduction, delineating the book's scope and framework, and part of this final chapter, dealing with the period after Freida Sima's lifetime, are written in my voice. Not because Freida Sima's voice was completely silenced after her death, for indeed it was not. However, from then on it was not heard directly, but only through others, in this case, through me. Thus I became part of the story, not only as an individual, but as the transmitter of my grandmother's voice to future generations.

The different voices are only one part of this story. Another is the shifting identities of the characters being described. The Freida Sima who left the *Kresy* in late 1910 was not the same Freida Sima who celebrated her twenty-first birthday in New York in 1916. Nor was she the same Freida Sima who emerged during the early 1920s, or whom we encounter during the first years of her marriage in the 1930s. The same holds true for quite a number of other family members appearing in the book, particularly, but not only, those who came to America in their youth. But the shifting identities in this book do not end with the story's protagonists. As I researched the background of family stories, unearthed hitherto unknown family members, and rekindled connections between various individuals in the extended family, I felt my own identity, along with theirs, shifting and expanding in order for us now encompass each other as well.

Throughout my formative years, I had known of the existence of this big Scharf-Eisenberg clan to which I belonged, but rarely experienced it en masse, other than at family *simchas,* or the few Family Circle meetings that I attended before moving to Israel. I had always been somewhat envious of my mother and grandmother's stories of growing up while being enveloped by so many layers of family. Although there was surely a less positive side to always being surrounded by what may have sometimes seemed like too many interested relatives, they had never experienced the sense of being alone and missing family, that was all too familiar to me during my youth. I yearned for a family that was also a community, like my grandmother's stories of Mihowa where she used to say that during her childhood there were five hundred Jews and fifty families, but only ten or so last names as they were all related.

As time passed, the age gap between cousins seemingly narrowed and mattered less, and I slowly got to know some of them better when they visited Israel or when I visited America. The advent of internet communication was another boon in closing the gap between members of our geographically widespread family. More than once, I heard news about my family in Israel from cousins in America, even before I heard it directly from my local relatives. On the sadder side, it enabled us to instantly notify family members about accidents, illnesses, deaths and funerals, unlike the days, weeks, and sometimes even months it had taken previous generations in the family to receive such notifications only a few decades earlier.

As I slowly progressed in the researching and writing of "My Name is Freida Sima", I often had the feeling that in addition to a book, it had also turned, at least for me, into a project of family reunification. I hoped that the epilogue to the story of Freida Sima's generation would become a prologue to our new connections as a family, in a sense continuing her saga. What initially was a case study of a young Jewish female immigrant in the early twentieth century soon became a family adventure that restored some of my family to me. Step by step, I found it putting me back in the life that my grandmother and mother had described when the *Tantes* and Uncles all lived down the block and were always going in and out of each other's houses. Only now, I found myself going in and out of my cousin's homes and lives virtually, with late night e-mail questions to the Family Circle list or to individual cousins, exchanges of family pictures, and electronic video chats.

Almost all of them responded to my questions with alacrity and gave me unlimited love and support. "You've done us all a great service, because you have forced us to reflect on the past and its importance in our personal lives,"[192] wrote my cousin Dora Polachek. "It is a privilege and an honor to give you as much info as I can about our past and thank you for creating a written memorial for our entire extended family to enjoy now and for generations to come. Bless you for what you're doing,"[193] wrote my cousin David Eisenberg. For months I found myself obsessed with the project, lying in bed sleepless at night trying to recall incidents or stories that I wanted to add to a particular chapter I was completing, and waking up in the morning, impatient to begin working on the next one. Two years earlier, my cousin Norman Eisenberg had written to the Family Circle email group: "Life is much more complicated today. Unlike years past when the majority of the family lived within walking distance of each other and family circle meetings were held monthly at the Inwood Jewish Center where Uncle Abe was

---

192 Author's correspondence with Dr. Dora Polachek, Dec. 23, 2015.
193 Author's correspondence with Dr. David Eisenberg, Nov. 9, 2015; Nov. 15, 2015.

the mainstay of the *shul*, the family is spread out and we see each other infrequently. My hope is that we continue to share history together and enjoy each other even if it is only once or twice a year."[194] I now felt charged with a task, to write a book which would help the family share that history. What had begun as a project for my own enjoyment now became a mission for my entire extended family.

And as I continued writing the book, the family became even more extended. "How is it that we know so much about Baba Devorah's family and so little about Zeide Nachman's?" Norman asked me more than once, and I answered him that although I knew the names of Zeide Nachman's siblings, I had indeed met only one relative on the Enzenberg side who wasn't Nachman's direct descendent, but rather the granddaughter of his sister Marium Raisel. When the book was almost completed, almost by chance I stumbled across an entire branch of the Enzenberg family, grandchildren and great-grandchildren of Zeide Nachman's brothers, scattered around the world.

As one began sending me to another, I realized that I was now in the process of discovering an entire world of Enzenberg cousins and their descendents, whose parents and grandparents had often married first cousins just as I had seen on the Scharf side. What's more, when they ran out of Enzenberg first cousins, they then married Hallers, Rosenbergs, Steinbrechers, Handels, Bernthals, Hirschs and Weiners, just as the Scharfs had done over and over, proving what my grandmother had indeed said to me more than once: there may have been five hundred Jews in Mihowa (and some more in Behromet), but only ten or so last names as everyone was related to each other. From someone who had always felt that she was part of a pretty small family, by the time I finished writing this book, I realized that I had over four hundred second, third, and fourth cousins on my Grandmother Freida Sima's side alone – almost the size of the entire population of Mihowa when she was born there one hundred and twenty years earlier! – and now spent days and nights getting in touch with some of them, and then putting some of them get in touch with each other. Just as in the days of Mihowa and Behromet ("and don't forget Lopushna", as Muriel Eisenberg Arens said to me, reminding me of her mother Minnie's home town), we once again appear to be a family that is also a community of sorts, a twenty-first century style community in the Western World.

---

194 Correspondence Norman Eisenberg to Family Circle List, Jan. 10, 2014.

This community, however, got me to thinking. Where I had always known so much about the Scharfs and Eisenbergs, my grandmother's brothers and sisters, why had I never heard from her about most of my Zeide Nachman's siblings and their children? This became a particularly pointed question, as I learned during the writing of this book, how many of that side of the family had moved to America. From the time she moved to America, and soon after, my grandmother had quite a number of first cousins on the Enzenberg side in New York, many of whom had already changed their name to Eisenberg, as she and her siblings later did. But the only ones of whom I ever heard from her directly, or who I got to know personally during my childhood, were descendents of her father's sister, the *Mime* (Aunt) Marium Raisel. Other than hearing that her brother Abie had come to America with a first cousin, Nathan, why had I never heard from her about any of her other cousins, children of her father's brother Meier Moshe, who had come to America?

The answer appears to be a combination of the nature of large families, and the role of women in the Scharf-Eisenberg family. In large families, having myriads of first cousins is a natural state of affairs. My grandmother eventually had over sixty first cousins, close to half of whom lived in America. Under those circumstances there were those who tended to spend more time with their (very large) nuclear families. Therefore, while I am sure that my grandmother was in touch during her youth with her extended American family, by the time I came into the picture those connections with their descendents had grown thin, particularly as many of those first cousins were no longer alive.

A second reason was the central role that women appeared to play in the Scharf-Eisenberg family. Although Nachman was patriarchal and somewhat autocratic, Devorah was more often than not the family pillar of strength. So had been her mother, Malka, particularly after her husband's early death. The connection of family members to the women's side of the family appears to have been quite strong, even in America. Thus it would make sense that my grandmother, having been brought up with her Scharf uncles and aunts, would be closer to them than to the Enzenberg-Eisenberg side. Finally, it is interesting that she was definitely close to her aunt Marium Raisel Enzenberg Handel who moved to America, the only one of her father's siblings of whom she had a picture in her personal album. Again, possibly testimony to the strength and central role that women played in families, or at least our family, at that time.

When I began the process of writing "My Name is Freida Sima", I thought I would be taking a journey into the familiar territory of my grandmother's history in order to reconstruct her life. What I didn't realize is that I would also be embarking on a journey into more uncharted territory, a psychological journey into other people's stories and memories which would eventually mesh with my own recollections, and sometimes even a physical journey into the tangible remnants of various relatives' lives.

How does one reconstruct a person's life? What do they leave behind in order to enable us to reassemble the components of their identity? What is a difficult task when speaking of a person you actually knew, becomes an almost herculean undertaking when referring to someone born more than a century before your own birth. That was the position I found myself in at this project's outset, when I attempted to reconstruct the nuances of my great-great-grandmother, Malka Haller Scharf's personality. Who was the sixteen-year-old Malka Haller who married Avraham Scharf? What was she like? Did she have a sense of humor and if so, what kind? I knew that I could never reconstruct her voice in the literal sense, as there were no recordings from that period, but how could I reconstruct her as a person?

Reconstructing a person takes place in several stages. There is the factual description, of their sex, date and place of birth, education, profession, date and place of marriage, number of children, and date and place of death. These can usually be found in official or unofficial records, such as a family Bible. Charting the geographical locales where a person lived during their lives, can often be done through records and documents such as a census, passport, visa, or even family stories, like that of Nachman Enzenberg's forestry contract that moved the entire family to the *Kresy*, or the Scharfs and Enzenbergs of Mihowa having to take refuge in Poland during the First World War.

There is the visual. What did a person look like? If we are lucky, we have photographs which show what someone looked like at a particular time, what they wore, their hairstyle, facial expression, and possibly, depending on the type of picture, even a glimpse of their body language and general demeanor. There is the audial, what their voice sounded like, which one can only have if one has recordings of that person. There is the performative, how they moved, what their common gestures were, how they performed various acts. And finally there is their essence, the most difficult dimension to capture when reconstructing a person one did not know, as even the stories one hears about them are processed through at least two filters: that of the person telling the story, and that of the listener who is attempting the reconstruction.

Years ago I had read an anthropological study claiming that at most, a person's true memory could "live" for four generations. Their children would still know them well, their grandchildren to a lesser extent, but would remember their voice, what they looked like, and mutual experiences, and their great-grandchildren would at most have vague childhood memories of their great-grandparent, but would be able to connect those personal memories to stories told by others. After that, an ancestor might, at most, become a story, but with no personal memories attached. That is when their literal and figurative "voice", and any intimate memory of them, would be lost. Sometimes, their names might not even be known to their descendants. For that reason, the study continued, there are remote tribes who dig up their ancestors' remains after four generations and rebury their bones together with those of previous generations, because after that time, all of one's forebears blur into an ancestral mass. This blur was exactly what I feared when trying to decode the lives of family members more than four generations before mine, and what I tried to avoid by harnessing all the available resources that a person leaves behind after they are gone, in order to reconstruct their lives.

The first groups of resources that serve as clues to people's lives are the technical ones: official records and documents such as passports, visas, steamship manifests, citizenship papers, census records and the like. These I found through painstaking research and the assistance of many cousins who sent me copies of their parents' documents.

The next group of resources are stories, and in particular, the stories of previous generations. As the daughter and granddaughter of two women who loved to talk about their experiences, and those of their ancestors, I had the fortune of hearing countless stories describing the Scharfs, Enzenbergs and Hallers, going back at least five generations. Other members of the family augmented my knowledge with stories that they had heard from their cousins, parents or grandparents about our mutual ancestors.

Another group of resources are the tangible remnants of people's lives, the pictures and artifacts that they leave behind. I had been familiar with pictures of various family members since my youth, and especially the family group portrait, taken during Baba Devorah's visit to America, that had hung for years on my Grandmother's wall, was passed on to my mother, and which I inherited after my mother's death, along with her albums. Today it has a place of pride, not only on my family picture wall, but also on my technological picture wall, my computer screensaver which is composed of family photos.

Each time I progressed chronologically in the book, I added more and more family photos to my screensaver, some scanned from my mother's albums, and others which family members kindly sent me, picturing their parents' and grandparents' past. Ultimately, that screensaver became a photographic accompaniment to the chapters I was writing. Each time I stopped typing for more than sixty seconds, my ancestors' faces appearing on my screen, instantly guilting me back to working on their story.

Other photos were new to me, and added a depth to my understanding of the person portrayed and the event captured on film. As a cultural historian, I read each picture as a text, noting placing, background, lighting, props, clothing, hairstyles, body language and facial expression, and trying to learn what I can from them about the persons and situations being portrayed. When combined with the stories I had heard of Baba Malka, the picture of her which my cousin Sheila Saltzman sent me, gave me insight into an additional dimension of her personality. Sheila's sister Muriel Arens added a number of family vigniettes about Baba Malka, which together with the picture, gave me even more insight into the woman she had been. The wedding pictures of the various Eisenberg and Enzenberg siblings that their children and grandchildren sent me were often eye openers about both the people appearing in them, and an entire era. Sometimes the third generation or fourth, such as my cousins Baila Cohen, Nute Eisenberg, Thomas Enzenberg, Bob Friedman, Gary Gorran, Bernard Handel, Techiya Hildenbrand, Avraham Iwanir, Moshe Rosenberg and Moishe Rosman, were the ones to send me the photos along with the stories, providing me with a sight of and insight into our mutual ancestors' past.

Then there were the artifacts, the tangible items that a person leaves behind after they are gone. No artifacts were left from the earliest generations, those of Baba Chantzel and Baba Malka. But as the oldest daughter (Judy) of the oldest daughter (Shirley), of the oldest daughter (Freida Sima), of the oldest daughter (Devorah), of the oldest daughter (Malka), I had the privilege of inheriting one of the relics that survived the family's European cataclysm, Baba Devorah's *sheitl* (marriage wig) that Sheindl had kept in Transnistria after her mother died. That *sheitl* was one of the three possessions left from Baba Devorah and Zeide Nachman's lives. The second was Devorah's *siddur* (prayer book) held today by Sheindl's daughter. The third was the floor rag which Nachman had taken from Mihowa when deported to Transnistria and wore over his shoulders to keep out the cold, which is now in the possession of the Museum of Jewish Heritage in New York City.

Other artifacts that brought me closer to my grandmother's generation were her possessions and those of my grandfather. I have no idea what happened to her clothing and possessions in New York after her death, other than her *techina* which my mother brought home, that sits today on my desk, and that I often find myself usng. But before she left Israel for New York, my grandmother presented me with a number of personal items, telling me the history of each one and what they meant to her. The delicate pillowcases and doilies that she had crocheted as a young girl in America during the Great War as she worried about her family in Europe. The embroidered dish towels and wall hangings that she had prepared for her dowry during the 1920s. The black beaded bag that she had made, and whose line she had originally designed at the factory where she was forelady. The small metal purse in a black holder, with separate compartments for powder, lipstick, money and a handkerchief, that she and other girls took on dates during the 1920s. The tiny make-up compact on a chain, worn by girls on their wrists when she came to America, with place for powder and rouge. The long thin curved metal hook that opened up from a tiny case like a pocket knife, that she explained to me was a "button-hooker", used to close the tiny buttons on one's shoes during the first years of the 20th century. And of course the small turquoise nail kit that she received for her "sweet sixteen" the year after she came to America, and that she gave me for my sixteenth birthday decades later.

Those, together with her bookcase, mirror, picture album, two round gold boxes from her dresser with a matching picture frame holding a snapshot of my mother and her cousin Muriel, her *Arbeitsbuch* from Europe, a few letters, her will, her American citizenship papers and Israeli immigration documents, were the sum-total of her tangible life. I keep many of these items in a box on my dresser, and treasure them as a map charting the various stations of my grandmother's eighty-eight and a half years of life. One day they will belong to my daughters, who will hopefully pass them on to their future children as tangible evidence of what my Baba used to say to be about ancestry: "you don't come from a stone".

The next group of resources are memories. Several years ago, a friend of my mother who had written his memoirs, sent her a copy along with a letter that began with the words: "You are in control of a very perishable treasure, memories. If you don't try to save them, they will be lost forever.

The losers will be your children, their children, and grandchildren. Memory is a muscle. The more you use it, the stronger it becomes. You remember much more than you know."[195]

There were my own memories, incidents which I had witnessed, or those in which I had taken part, and that I remembered firsthand. Remembering them was a task in itself, as memories came back in pieces, not necessarily in the same chronological order as the book I was researching, or with any connection to the chapter I was writing. Memories, as we have seen throughout this book, can also be tricky, and even when precise, they do not necessarily stand on their own, but can trigger memories of previous generations. When on my late mother's birthday, one of my daughters recalled a song she used to sing to them, I suddenly remembered a half-Yiddish, half-Ruthenian tune beginning with the words "*Hoy Dash Kota Nash*" ("our cat") that my grandmother would sing to me as a child, bouncing me on her knee, which she had learned from her Baba Malka, and which my mother had also sung to my children as babies. Baba Malka had told my grandmother that her mother, Baba Chantzel, had also sung it to her as a child. From whom had Chantzel learned it? Probably from her own mother, my great-great-great-great Grandmother, whose name Baba Malka had neglected to mention to her granddaughter, and thus was lost to me forever.

This memory is known as a performative memory as it was accompanied by something tangible, a children's song, and a specific way that a child was held and bounced on one's knee, dipping them at a particular line of the tune. Other memories, accompanied by a performative action, can actually give us a glimpse into an ancestor's demeanor. When *benching lecht* on Friday night, I hold my hands in a certain way that I remember my grandmother doing, just as she learned from her mother and grandmother and so on. The inflection and tune that my great uncles Abie, Benny, Srul, Leibish, Elish and Tuleh used when they make *Kiddush*, was that which they surely learned from their father, my Zeide Nachman, and which Nachman had learned from his father, his father from his grandfather, and thus back in time. Some of my cousins today still make *Kiddush* the same way. Although I will never know my Baba Malka, or Baba Chantzel, I know exactly how they *benched lecht* 160 years ago, just as my Eisenberg cousins make *Kiddush* just like the Zeide Srul, father of Zeide Nachman, did in the middle of the 19th century. While we may never actually capture an ancestor's essence

---

195 Correspondence of Victor Geller to Shirley K. Tydor, Sept. 2007.

from long ago, we can occasionally sense a bit of that essence wafting into our life like an elusive scent or melody, as it lives on in some of our performative traditions and gestures.

Then there is the vocabulary that our ancestors leave us as part of a verbal inheritance, one composed of expressions that would have been instantly understood by members of their generation, but are often an enigma to those two generations later. Anyone living in New York at the beginning of the twentieth century would have understood the terms buying "on time" (installment plan), "Allrightnik" (immigrant who succeeded by exploiting other immigrants), "The pictures" (movies), "take you around" (hug), "icebox" (non-electric refrigerator), or my grandmother all-time favorite: "no kick coming" (nothing to complain about). All were familiar to me, as I grew up hearing them from my grandmother, but they are indeed unknown expressions to my children who could not place them in any time framework, nor have they ever heard them being used.

A last resource for reconstructing my ancestors' lives was their final resting places and tombstones. At a certain point, the pictures of all the family tombstones in the Scharf-Eisenberg Family Circle plot at Wellwood Cemetery were open on my computer desktop all day long as I referred to them continuously in the same way that historians constantly refer to a crucial collection of archival documents. These tombstones were not only a way of tracing people's Hebrew names and those of their parents, but also the chronology of their lives and deaths. There were days that I spent hours switching back and forth between the Wellwood pictures and the family tree appearing on the "Geni" genealogical site in order to figure out some of the more complex family relationships or trying to understand how I was related to someone buried "right across the way" from my grandparent's.

But what of the relatives who were not buried at Wellwood? Here I often felt as if I had turned from historian to sleuth as I galvanized all the human and cyber resources as my disposal in order to track down where certain relatives were buried. Who of the European relatives had died in Mihowa and who elsewhere? Who had died in Europe and who in America? In some cases, even grandchildren were initially unsure where their grandparents had been were buried. Two of the most elusive relatives whom I ultimately managed to trace, were my grandmother's uncles Srul Nachman Handel and Shmilitzie (Shmuel Yitzchak) Scharf. After involving, connecting and reconnecting over half a dozen relatives during the process, Uncle Srul Nachman's grave surfaced in New Jersey, while I learned that Uncle Shmilitzie had moved to Israel during what turned out to be the last year of his life, and was buried in the same Tel-Aviv cemetery as my parents. On my next visit to the cemetery I found his grave, leaving a stone on it as per Jewish custom, and reciting a prayer in his memory. A week later, my cousin Gary Gorran sent me a family picture in which Uncle Shmilitzie appears, the first time I had ever seen his face. As I add family pictures to my screensaver in the order that I take or receive them, the picture of Uncle Shmilitzie's tombstone appears right before his picture at Gary's bar-mitzvah, proving that in cultural and visual history, life can sometimes appear after death.

Soon after, as I began learning of my myriads of Enzenberg relatives, I discovered that my grandmother had several first cousins on that side buried in Israel. One of them, Tziril Enzenberg Muschel, daughter of Meier Moshe Enzenberg, had immigrated to America as a young girl and had only moved to Israel shortly before her death. Learning that Tziril had no living descendents, I once again returned to the cemetery to find her grave, leave a stone on it as per Jewish custom to mark that someone had been there, and recite memorial prayers in her memory. Another circle closed.

And what of those relatives who graves could not be found? Among these were the graves, whether mass or individual, of family members who had died in Transnistria, such as my great-grandparents Devorah and Nachman, my great-aunt Marium, and my mother's first cousins, my great-uncle Leibish's two little daughters, Malka and Rivka. Malka and Rivka are commemorated on a tiny tombstone built between their parent's graves, and years ago, my mother requested to commemorate the rest of the family on her tombstone when her time would come. Today, my mother's tombstone bears not only her name, but reads: "In memory of her family, her grandfather Nachman Enzenberg, her grandmother Devorah Enzenberg, her mother's sister Marium Enzenberg Rosenberg, and her father's sister Mata Karasik, who perished in the Holocaust".

Even those whose grave is somewhere outside Moghilev can still have a cemetery listing. When going through my grandmother's documents I found a personal *yahrzeit* (death date) calendar from the Family Circle's funeral home, listing the dates of her parents' deaths, one day after the other in the Hebrew months of Adar, and giving the English dates from 1945 and onward on which she should light a memorial candle. Decades earlier, as a very young girl, I had seen the *yahrzeit* calendar and noticed that it ran only until 1984. "What will you do after that Baba?" I asked her. "Let's first see if I'm still here" she answered, shrugging her shoulders at the time. Was she prophesizing her own fate? My grandmother died in June 1984, three months after her parent's *yahrzeits* that year, her life ending together with the last of the dates listed on her parents' *yahrzeit* calendar.

An End that is also a Beginning

Life is often described as a circle with a beginning and an end, one that opens and closes, ending just as it began. Here, too, let us end the tale of Freida Sima in the same way as it began, with her names.

Throughout my grandmother's life she had many names, each one expressing a different part of her life and essence. Each name represented a distinct identity that she embodied at different times in her life, and for different people: her parents, her siblings in Europe and America, her nuclear family, her extended family, her co-workers, her friends. Her legal papers in Europe bore one name, her American documents another, and her Israeli immigration papers a third.

I sometimes wondered by which name she thought of herself when alone, her inner identity that remained at the nexus of her being throughout all the metamorphoses that she experienced during the eighty-eight years of her life. Did she think of herself as *tochter* (daughter), as her parents called her, or *shvester* (sister), as she was called by her European and later Israeli siblings? Was she Bertha, the name her aunts suggested and the one that she ultimately chose as her American identity? Where did "Bert" or "Bertie" come in, the name by which my Zeide Max called her throughout their forty-two years together? What about "Boytee", which she heard for over seven decades from her American family? And finally, where did her birth name, Freida Sima, come into all of this?

Sometime in my teens, possibly around the time of my grandmother's eightieth birthday party that I describe in this book's opening chapter, I remember asking her for a reason I can no longer remember, "Baba what's your name?" "Whaddya mean 'what's my name'? she said, looking at me strangely, "My name is Bertha Kraus!" "That's not what I meant Baba", I responded. "Oh you mean in Jewish? My real name? Freida Sima. My name is Freida Sima".

Does that mean that she thought of herself as Freida Sima? I will never know. But she definitely considered it to be her "real name", "the real McCoy", to use one of her favorite American expressions from the days of flapper slang. It was, however, a name that she rarely remembered anyone using during her lifetime. It was given to her by her young, tall and handsome father Nachman, when he received an *aliyah* to the Torah and blessed the new mother and baby only hours after she was born. It was used for the first few months of her life until she became ill, after which everyone began calling her "Babaleh", "little grandmother", to fool the angel of death. It appeared in German letters on the opening page of her *Arbeitsbuch,* the legal working document that she received from the Austrian government when she turned fourteen, and it appeared in Hebrew letters on her *ketubah,* her marriage contract to my grandfather. It was used by her Uncle Joe when he made the blessings for the new mother and baby for her, after my mother was born. And it was used by my father each time he received an *aliyah* and made a *misheberach,* a blessing for the whole family, mentioning his wife, children, and in-laws by name. Although my grandmother was rarely present on the occasions when this name was voiced, it remained her "real name", the one that was engraved on her heart and soul.

In 1974, the year that my grandmother moved to Israel, the Israeli poetess, Zelda[196] wrote in Hebrew about the different names that people are given throughout their lifetime:

Everyone has a name, given to him by God, and given to him by his parents. Everyone has a name, given to him by his stature and the way he smiles, and given to him by his clothing. Everyone has a name, given to him by the mountains, and given to him by the walls. Everyone has a name, given to him by the stars, and given to him by his neighbors. Everyone has a name, given to him by his sins, and given to him by his longings. Everyone has a name, given to him by his enemies, and given to him by his love. Everyone has a name, given to him by his holidays, and given to him by his work. Everyone has a name, given to him by the seasons, and given to him by his blindness. Everyone has a name, given to him by the sea, and given to him by his death.[197]

My grandmother knew that she had many names, and wanted to be sure that she would be given the correct name by her death, her "real name",

---

196   Zelda Schneerson-Mishkovsky, 1914–1984.
197   Zelda (Mishovsky), *Al Tirchak* (Do Not Go Far), Tel Aviv: Hakibbutz Hameuhad, 1974.

her Jewish name, the one that she was given at birth. It was the name she reminded us more than once, that we should put on her tombstone – the last time, she assumed, it would ever be used or appear anywhere.

Life, however, is full of surprises. When I first contemplated the idea of writing her life story, I thought of a suitable title even before composing the opening pages. From the first moment, the title and the book were one. My grandmother was Freida Sima, and no matter what name she went by at a certain time, it was how I would refer to her throughout the book.

Two years after my grandmother's death, I named my second daughter after her. At the time, though, I thought "Freida" to be too old fashioned, and decided to use a Hebrew equivalent. Thirty years after her death, I had matured enough to realize the name's beauty and significance, and to understand the subtle subtext behind each occasion she had reminded me "my (real) name is Freida Sima". I hope I have done justice to her life story and that of her family, the entire extended Scharf-Eisenberg clan, with this book. And I hope that by writing it, I have finally given her back her name.

Maps

Map of the Bukovina

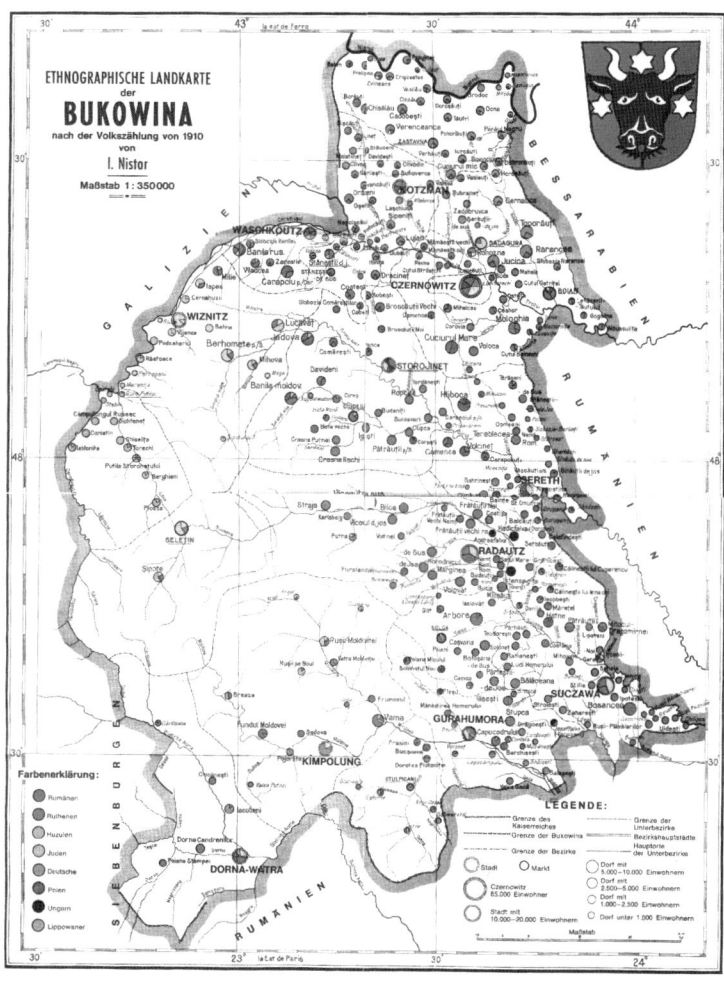

Dr. I. Nistor, Der Nationale Kampf und der Bukowina mit besonderer Berucksichtigung der Rumanen und Ruthenen, Bucaresti: Der Romanischen Akademie, 1918.

MAP OF RUMANIA, BUKOVINA, BESSARABIA, AND TRANSNISTRIA

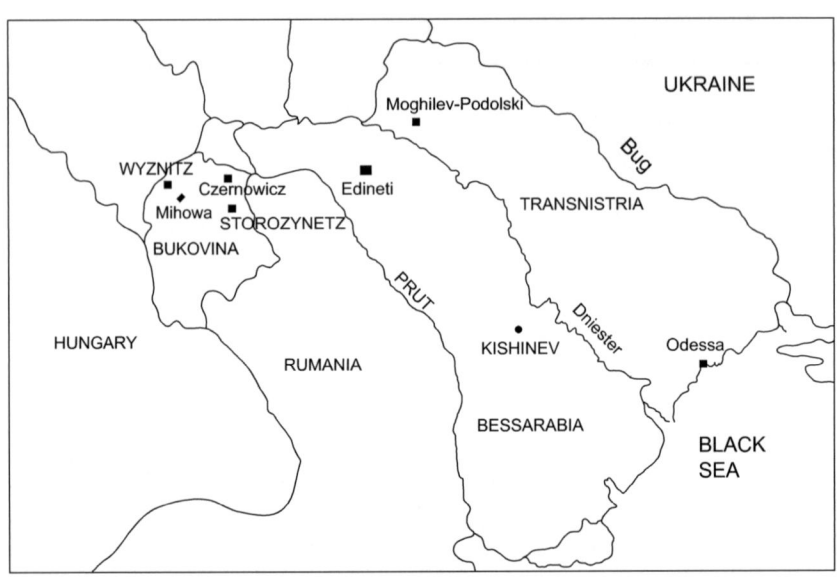

Family tree

Scharf–Eisenberg Family Tree

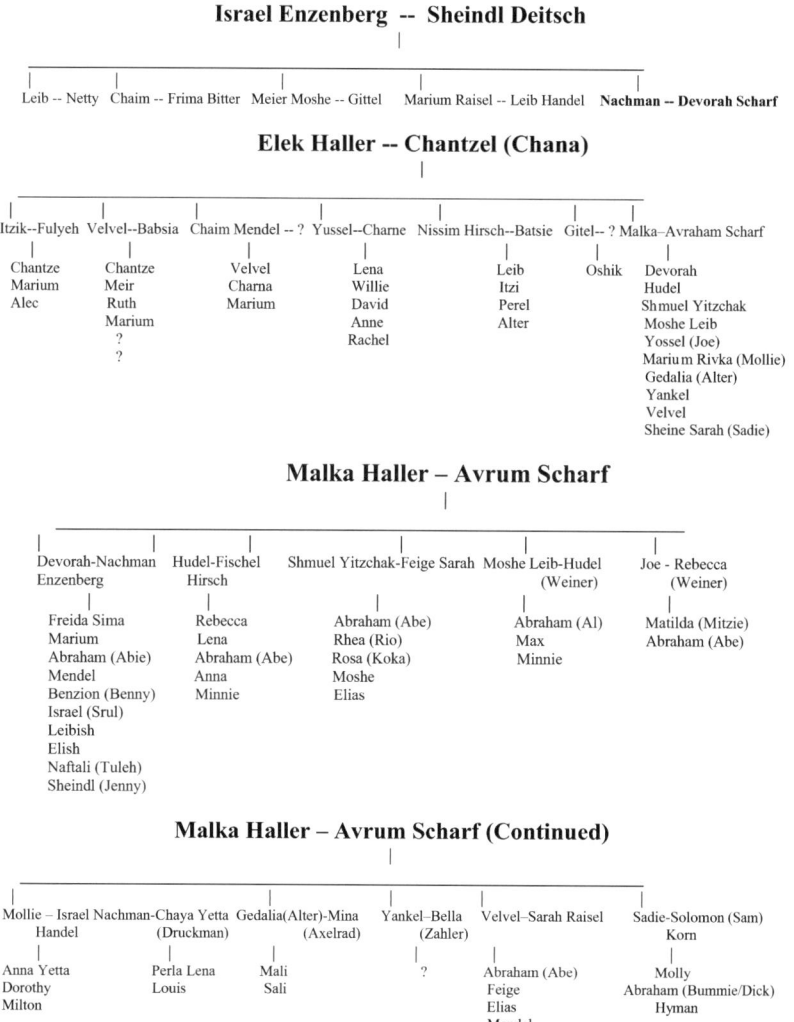

Israel Enzenberg -- Sheindl Deitsch

| Leib -- Netty | Chaim -- Frima Bitter | Meier Moshe -- Gittel | Marium Raisel -- Leib Handel | **Nachman -- Devorah Scharf** |

Elek Haller -- Chantzel (Chana)

Itzik--Fulyeh	Velvel--Babsia	Chaim Mendel -- ?	Yussel--Charne	Nissim Hirsch--Batsie	Gitel-- ?	Malka–Avraham Scharf
Chantze	Chantze	Velvel	Lena	Leib	Oshik	Devorah
Marium	Meir	Charna	Willie	Itzi		Hudel
Alec	Ruth	Marium	David	Perel		Shmuel Yitzchak
	Marium		Anne	Alter		Moshe Leib
	?		Rachel			Yossel (Joe)
	?					Marium Rivka (Mollie)
						Gedalia (Alter)
						Yankel
						Velvel
						Sheine Sarah (Sadie)

Malka Haller – Avrum Scharf

Devorah-Nachman Enzenberg	Hudel-Fischel Hirsch	Shmuel Yitzchak-Feige Sarah	Moshe Leib-Hudel (Weiner)	Joe - Rebecca (Weiner)
Freida Sima	Rebecca	Abraham (Abe)	Abraham (Al)	Matilda (Mitzie)
Marium	Lena	Rhea (Rio)	Max	Abraham (Abe)
Abraham (Abie)	Abraham (Abe)	Rosa (Koka)	Minnie	
Mendel	Anna	Moshe		
Benzion (Benny)	Minnie	Elias		
Israel (Srul)				
Leibish				
Elish				
Naftali (Tuleh)				
Sheindl (Jenny)				

Malka Haller – Avrum Scharf (Continued)

Mollie – Israel Handel	Nachman-Chaya Yetta (Druckman)	Gedalia(Alter)-Mina (Axelrad)	Yankel–Bella (Zahler)	Velvel–Sarah Raisel	Sadie-Solomon (Sam) Korn
Anna Yetta	Perla Lena	Mali	?	Abraham (Abe)	Molly
Dorothy	Louis	Sali		Feige	Abraham (Bummie/Dick)
Milton				Elias	Hyman
				Mendel	

Family tree page 2

Devorah Scharf – Nachman Enzenberg

Freida Sima ----- Max -------- Sadie	Marium--Feivel	Abie--Minnie	Mendel	Benzion---Betty
| (Oberund)	|			| (Lobel)
Shirley-Chaskel-Bertha	Herbert - Molly	Zilly	Muriel- Moshe Arens	Bernice-Oscar Finkelstein
Tydor (Greiver) Stewart - Reba	Baby?	Sheila-Barry Saltzman	David-Breindl (Knobel)
| | Ben - Anne				
Esther Judith Camilla Harry - Shirley				
Manfred				

Devorah Scharf – Nachman Enzenberg (continued)

Israel (Srul)-Anna	Leibish-Frieda	Elish-Charlotte (Lola)	Tuleh – Toni	Shaja - Sheindl(Jenny)-Naftali -Berta
(Rosensweig)	(Sheitl-Weiss)	(Wagner)	(Cumpana) Steinbrecher	Bernthal
Yulbert-Hedy (Pahmer) Rivka		Max-Abby (Storch) Dora-Solomon Polachek	Marta-Shimon Lowy Yehudit-Benny Hort
Marianne- Freddie-Rina Malka		Norman-Gail (Lefkowitz)	
(Dror) Dora-Aryeh Hildebrand				

Gittel Haller – Meier Moshe Enzenberg

Tzirl-	Feige (Fanny)-	Reisel-	Sime (Sadie)-	Nathan-	Malka-	Sheindl-	Leib-	Shmuel	Ethel-	Lotte (Litzi)-
William	?	Zeide	Gershon	Rose	Yitzchak	Shmuel	Leah		Joe	Efraim
Muschel	Masur	Haller	Levine	Iwanir	Rosenberg	Leibovich	Leibovich		Samet	Fischel
										Iwanir
Herbert		Yetty	Esther	Gilbert	Yetti	Esther	Pinchas		Gilbert	Avraham
		Henya	Irving	Irene	Gusta		Yossel		Irene	
		Peppy	Gilbert		Zev		Gittel			
					Yosef					
					Eliezer					
					Pinchas					
					Rosa					
					Menachem Mendel					

Glossary of Non-English Words

A Gut Shabbos – a good Sabbath
A Sheine Meidel – A pretty girl
Aber ich bin a yid – but I am a Jew
Agunah – grass widow
Aliyah – literally "elevation", "going up", called up to read the Torah; moving to Israel
Alter – the "old one"
Alter Heim – Old Country
Arbeitsbuch – work pamphlet, "working papers"
Auf der flucht – "in flight"
Badeken – veiling of a bride
Balabusta – housewife
Bashert – destined one
Bench Lecht – to light candles
Bochur – single young man
Brisses (singular, *Bris*) – circumcision
Chai – eighteen
Chas veshulem – Heaven Forbid
Cheder – religious elementary school
Chosen – bridegroom
Chuppah – wedding canopy, figuratively, the wedding ceremony
Daven (davened) – pray (prayed)
Dayn Mameh – your mother
Dor Holech vedor Ba – One generation goes and another comes
Einiklach (singular *Einikel*) – grandchildren
El Mole Rachamim – a memorial prayer
Eretz Yisrael (*Yisroel*) – The Land of Israel
Fapitzed – fancy, dressed up
Freier – freethinker
Frum – religious, devout
Genug – enough
Get – religious divorce
Getoig – an "evil eye", literally a "good eye"

Goldeneh Medineh – the Golden Country (America)

Goyim – Gentiles

Gut Yiddishe Tochter – Good Jewish daughter

Gut Yuntif – Happy Holiday

Gymnasium – high school

Hachshara – pioneering

Halt Yiddishkeit – literally: observe Judaism, figuratively: to remain religious

Harzveitig – conniptions

Hazonnes – liturgical music

Hol hamoed – intermediate days of Sukkot or Passover

Kaddish – a memorial prayer

Karka – literally: land, figuratively, burial plot

Katchke – duck

Keneine Hora – May the Evil Eye stay away

Keren Kayemeth – Jewish National Fund

Ketubah – marriage contract

Kiddush – ceremony of prayer and blessing over wine

Kimpeturin – a woman after giving birth

Kinderlach – children

Kishke – derma

Klita – absorption

Koch-alein – self-catering establishment

Kosel (Kotel) Ma'arovi – Western Wall

Koyach – strength

Kresy – marshlands of Eastern Galicia

Kriya – literally: tearing, figuratively: rending garments in mourning

Kriyas Shma (Krishma) – reciting the *Shma* prayer

Lachter – candlesticks

Landsleit – fellow town members

Landsmanschaften – mutual aid societies, benevolent societies

Lebedig – lively

Lechaim – to life (a toast)

Leffel – spoon

Lein – recite (literally: read)

Levaya – funeral

Loshon Kodesh – Hebrew, literally: the "Holy Tongue"

Ma'abara (plural: *Ma'abarot*) – Immigrant transit camps

Malach Hamoves – The Angel of Death

Mameh – mother
Maon Olim – immigrants' residence
Mazel – fortune, luck
Mazeldik chayn – lucky charm
Mechayeh – pleasure
Mechitza – partition
Mein – my
Mein Tochter – my daughter
Melamed – teacher
Melaveh Malke – post-Sabbath meal
Mikva – ritual bath
Mime – Aunt
Minhag America – American tradition
Minyan – religious quorum of ten men
Misheberach – blessing
Mitzvah – good deed, commandment
Moishav Zkeinim – Old Age Home
Moshiach – The Messiah
Nadan – dowry
Narishkeit – nonsense
Ovel – mourning
Oy Gevalt – "oh no"
Oy vey is mir – woe is me
Parnosseh – livelihood
Paskening shailos – determining religious matters
Potch – slap
Putsch – political overthrow
Rachmunes – mercy
Rebbe – Hassidic rabbi
Refusenik – a Soviet Jew who had been refused permission to leave the country
Ribono Shel Olam – Master of the Universe
Schmaltz – fat
Schochet – ritual slaughterer
Sha shtill – be quiet
Shabbos Bereishis – The Sabbath of Genesis (when the Torah portion of Genesis is read)
Shadchan – matchmaker

Shamash – beadle
Shehechiyanu Vekimanu Vehigiyanu Lazeman Hazeh – the blessing "for having given us life and allowing us to reach this day"
Sheitl – wig
Sheva brochos – seven blessings, recited at the marriage ceremony and for the following week
Shidduch – matrimonial match
Shiva – literally: seven, figuratively: the week of mourning
Shloshim – literally: thirty, figuratively: the thirtieth day after a death
Shmusing – chatting
Shomer Shabbos – Sabbath obeservant
Shrei – scream
Shtetl (plural: *Shtetlach*) – small villages
Shuk – market
Shul – synagogue
Shver – literally: difficult. Also: father-in-law
Shverleben – beloved father-in-law
Shvester – sister
Shviggerleben – beloved mother-in-law
Shvitz – literally: sweat, figuratively: public baths, sauna
Siddur – prayer book
Simcha – celebration, happiness
Ta'am – sense
Tachana Sofit – final destination
Tallis – prayer shawl
Talmid chochom – scholar
Tante – aunt
Tateh – father
Techina – Women's Yiddish prayer book
Tefilah – prayer
Tefillin – phylacteries
Tichel – kerchief
Tochter – daughter
Treife Medineh – an unkosher country
Tzena – austerity program
Tzrifim (singular: *tzrif*) – shack
Tzurris – trouble
Veter – Uncle

Viddui – confession
Yahrzeit – anniversary of death
Yarmulkeh – skullcap
Yeshiya – salvation
Yidden – Jews
Yizkor – memorial prayer
Zadekes – saint (female)
Zedakah – charity
Zeide – grandfather
Zemiros – Sabbath songs
Zorgt Nisht – don't worry
Zug – say
Zu mir – to me

Bibliography

Archives

Archives of the First Mihowa Berhometh Bucowiner Society K.U.V. 1925–1988:
RG 1801, YIVO Archives, Center for Jewish History, New York City, N.Y.

Scharf-Eisenberg Family Circle Archives, New York:
Scharf-Eisenberg Family Circle Certificate of Incorporation, Department of State in Albany, July 2, 1943.

Wellwood Cemetery Archives, Farmington, New York:
Agreement between Abe Eisenberg, representing the Scharf Eisenberg Family Circle and Moses Jaffe, President of the Wellwood Cemetery Association, Inc., March 12, 1941,

Bernard Handel Collection:
Louis Handel, "The Story of My Life", Correspondence Louis Handel to Lauren Gold, 1975, in the possession of his son, Bernard Handel.
Louis Handel, "My Life Story Continued", 1975, in the possession of his son, Bernard Handel.

Riverside Cemetery Archives, Saddle Brook, New Jersey:
Material pertaining to the burial of Israel Nachman Handel, 1939.

Testimony
Jenny Bernthal, USC Shoa Foundation, The Institute for Visual History and Education (Spielberg) – March 30, 1998.

Internet Resources
The Statue of Liberty and Ellis Island Foundation: <http://www.libertyellisfoundation.org/passenger>.
Czernowitz 1930 Census: <http://czernowitz.blogspot.co.il/2014/05/census-of-romania-for-year-1930.html> retrieved, Dec. 2, 2015.

Data about Myhove, Ukraine: <http://data.jewishgen.org/wconnect/wc. dll?jg~jgsys~community~-1046548>, retrieved, Dec. 2, 2015.

Jewish Population in the United States, 1654-present: <https://www.jewish-virtuallibrary.org/jsource/US-Israel/usjewpop1.html> retrieved, Dec. 6, 2015.

History of Charms Candies: <http://www.nj.com/news/local/index. ssf/2012/08/glimpse_of_history_sweet_treat.html> (retrieved Dec. 17, 2015).

Bukovina Society of the Americas, <http://www.bukovinasociety.org/> retrieved, Dec. 17, 2015.

Correspondence

Author's correspondence with Dr. David Eisenberg, Nov. 9, 2015; Nov. 15, 2015.

Author's correspondence with Bob Friedman, Feb. 9, 2016.

Author's correspondence with Bernard Handel, Dec. 29, 2015; Jan. 21, 2016.

Author's correspondence with Techiya Hildenbrand, Nov. 21, 2015.

Author's correspondence with Irving Levine, Feb. 18, 2016.

Author's correspondence with Dr. Dora Polachek, Dec. 23, 2015.

Author's correspondence with Sheila Eisenberg Saltzman, Sept. 20, 2015.

Author's correspondence with Jeffrey Sanders, Oct. 11, 2015.

Correspondence Victor Geller to Shirley K. Tydor, Sept. 2007.

Correspondence Molly Sanders to Shirley K. Tydor, Nov. 20, 1980.

Norman Eisenberg, Scharf-Eisenberg Family Circle email group correspondence, Jan. 10, 2014.

Gary Gorran, Scharf-Eisenberg Family Circle email group correspondence, Jan. 14, 2014.

Interviews

Author's telephone interviews with Muriel Eisenberg Arens, Sept. 22, 2015; Nov. 6, 2015; Nov. 12, 2015.

Author's telephone interview with Dr. Max Eisenberg, Nov. 18, 2015.

Author's telephone interview with Abraham Iwanir, great-nephew of Nachman Enzenberg, Jan. 28, 2016.

Author's telephone interview with Moshe Rosenberg, great-great nephew of Nachman Enzenberg, Jan. 29, 2016.

Films
Hester Street, directed by Joan Micklin Silver, 1975.

Books and Articles

"A Hazkoro fir Isidor und Ida Strauss" ("A Memorial Prayer for Isidor and Ida Strauss"), *Shas Techina Rav Pninim,* New York: Hebrew Publishing Company, 1916: 257–258.

Aleichem, Sholom (Somon N. Rabinovich), *Tevye the Dairyman and the Railroad Stories,* Library of Yiddish Classics, Hillel Halkin, tr., New York: Shocken, 1987.

Alexander, Ruth M., *The "Girl Problem": Female Sexual Delinquency in New York, 1900–1930,* Ithaca: Cornell University Press, 1995.

Alpern, Joil, *No One Awaiting Me: Two Brothers Defy Death During the Holocaust in Romania,* Calgary: University of Calgary Press, 2001.

Ancel, Jean, *The History of the Holocaust in Romania (Comprehensive History of the Holocaust),* Lincoln and Jerusalem: University Press of Nebraska and Yad Vashem, 2012.

Anthias, Floya, "New Hybridities, Old Concepts: The Limits of 'Culture'", *Ethnic and Racial Studies* 24:4 (2001): 619–641.

Antin, Mary, *The Promised Land,* Boston: Houghton Mifflin, 1969.

A Timeline of Evolution Retirement in the United States, Workplace Flexibility 2010, Georgetown University Law Center, <http://scholarship.law.georgetown.edu/legal/50>, retrieved, Jan. 1, 2016.

Baumel (Schwartz), Judith Tydor, "In Everlasting Memory: Individual and Communal Holocaust Commemoration in Israel", *Israel Affairs* 3:1 (1995): 146–170.

Bavel, Jay van, "The World Population Explosion: Causes, Backgrounds and Projections for the Future", in: *Facts, Views and Visions, Issues in Obstetrics, Gynaecology and Reproductive Health* 5:4 (2013): 281–291.

Berg, A. Scott, *Lindburgh,* New York: Berkeley, 1999.

Berger, Joseph, "City Room: Long Lost, Little Known", *The New York Times,* March 27, 2011.

Braham, Randolph L. (ed.), *The Destruction of Romanian and Ukranian Jews during the Antonescu Era,* New York: East European Monographs (Columbia UP), 1997.

Bridges, William, *The Bronx Zoo Book of Wild Animals,* New York: New York Zoological Society, 1968.

Brownstone, David M., *Island of Hope, Island of Tears: The Story of Those Who Entered the New World Through Ellis Island – in Their Own Words,* New York: Barnes and Noble, 2000.

Bynum, Caroline Walker, *Holy Feast and Holy Fast: The Religious Significance of Food to Medieval Women,* Berkeley, Los Angeles, London, University of California Press, 1987.

Cahan, Abraham, *Yekl: A Tale of the New York Ghetto,* New York: D. Appleton and Company, 1896.

Cannato, Vincent J., *American Passage: The History of Ellis Island,* New York: Harper Perennial, 2010.

Carr, E.H., *What is History?* Cambridge: Cambridge U.P., 1961.

Chartier, Roger, *Cultural History: Between Practices and Representations,* Ithaca: Cornell UP, 1988.

Chiel, Chris and Decker, Julie, *Quonset Huts: Metal Living for the Modern Age,* Princeton: Princeton Architectural Press, 2005.

Chodorow, Nancy, *The Reproduction of Mothering: Psychoanalysis and the Sociology of Gender,* Berkeley, 1978.

Cohen, Rose, *Out of the Shadow,* New York: George H. Doran Co., 1918.

Corbea-Hoisie, Andrei, „Bucovina", The YIVO Encyclopedia of Jews in Eastern Europe, <http://www.yivoencyclopedia.org/article.aspx/Bucovina> retrieved, Dec. 4, 2015.

Costa, Dora, *The Evolution of Retirement: An American Economic History 1880–1980,* Chicago: University of Chicago Press, 1998.

Daniels, Roger, *Franklin D. Roosevelt: Road to the New Deal 1882–1939,* Champaign: University of Illinois Press, 2015.

David Henige, *Oral Historiography,* London: Longman, 1982.

Diner, Hasia R, *Lower East Side Memories: A Jewish Place in America,* Princeton: Princeton UP, 2002.

Dobelstein, Andrew, *Understanding the Social Security Act: the Foundation For Social Welfare in America in the Twenty-First Century,* Oxford and New York: Oxford University Press, 2009.

Duncan, Susan Kirsch Duncan, *Levittown: The Way We Were,* Huntington: Maple Hill Press, 1999.

DuPont, Brandon, Keeling, Drew, Weiss, Thomas, Passengers Fare for Overseas Travel in the 19th and 20th century, paper presented for the Annual Meeting of the Economic History Association, Vancouver BC Canada, Sept. 21–23, 2012.

Dvir, Noam, "A Brief History of the First Hebrew Supermarket", *Ha'aretz English Edition,* April 4, 2010.

Enzenberg, Jakob, "Mihowa", in: Hugo Gold (ed.), *Geschichte der Juden in der Bukowina,* vol. II, Tel-Aviv: Olameinu, 1962.

Epstein, Lawrence J., *At the Edge of a Dream: The Story of Jewish Immigrants on New York's Lower East Side 1880–1920,* San Francisco: Jossey-Bass, 2007.

Erikson, Erik H., *Childhood and Society*, New York: W.W. Norton and Company, 1993.

Erikson, Erik H., *Identity, Youth and Crisis,* New York: W.W. Norton and Company, 1994.

Eshkoli, Hava W., "The Transdnistrian Plan: An Opportunity for Rescue or a Deception", in *American Jewry during the Holocaust: A Report for the American Jewish Commission on the Holocaust,* ed. Seymour M. Finger, New York: Holmes and Meier, 1984: 237–260.

Ewen, Elizabeth, *Immigrant Women in the Land of Dollars: Life and Culture on the Lower East Side 1890–1925,* New York: Monthly Review Press, 1985.

Ferrer, Margaret Lundringan and Navarra, Tova, *Levittown: The First Fifty Years,* Mount Pheasant, S.C.: Arcadia Press, 1997.

Field, Bruce E., *Harvest of Dissent: The National Farmers Union and the Early Cold War,* Lawrence, KS: University Press of Kansas, 1998.

Fisher, Julius S., *Transnystria: The Forgotten Cemetery*, New York: South Brunswick, London: Yoseloff, 1969.

Foley, John Miles, *The Theory of Oral Composition: History and Methodology* Bloomington: University of Indiana Press, 1988.

Freedland, Michael, *Jolson: The Story of Al Jolson,* New York: Virgin, 1995.

Friedlander, Dov, "Mass Immigration and Population Dynamics in Israel", *Demography* 12:4 (Nov. 1975): 581–599.

Frommer, Harvey, Sheppard, Bob, *Remembering Yankee Stadium: An Oral and Narrative History of "The House that Babe Ruth Built",* New York: Stewart, Tabori and Chang, 2008.

Geller, Victor B., *Take It like a Soldier: A Memoir,* Jerusalem: Self published, 2007.

Ginzburg, Carlo, "Microhistory; Two or three things that I know about it", *Critical Inquiry* 20:1 (1993): 10–35.

Gonzales, Evelyn, *The Bronx,* New York: Columbia University Press, 2003.

Grinberg, Leon and Grinberg, Rebeca, *Psychoanalytic Perspectives on Migration and Exile*, New Haven and London: Yale, 1989: 130–132.

Gurock, Jeffrey S., *When Harlem was Jewish, 1870–1930*, New York: Columbia, 1979.

Hacohen, Dvora, *Immigrants in Turmoil: Mass Immigration to Israel and Its Repercussions in the 1950s and After*, Syracuse: Syrcuse University Press, 2003.

Hall, Stuart, "Who Needs Identity?", in: Stuart Hall and Paul du Gay, eds., *Questions of Cultural Identity*, London: Sage Publications, 1996: 1–17.

Hamby, Alonzo L., *Man of Destiny: FDR and the Making of the American Century*, New York: Basic, 2015.

Handlin, Oscar, *The Uprooted: The Epic Story of the Great Migrations that Made the American People,* Boston: Little Brown and Co., 1951.

Hansen, Marcus Lee, *The Immigrant in American History,* Harvard: Harvard UP, 1940.

Helmreich, William B., *Against All Odds: Holocaust Survivors and the Successful Lives They Made in America,* New York: Simon and Schuster, 1992.

Helmreich, William B., *The New York Nobody Knows: Walking 6,000 Miles in the City,* Princeton: Princeton University Press, 2013.

Herman, Felicia, "From Priestess to Hostess: Sisterhoods of Personal Service in New York City, 1887–1936" in: Pamela S. Nadell and Jonathan D. Sarna, eds. *Women and American Judaism: Historical Perspectives,* Hanover and London: Brandeis University Press, 2001: 148–181.

Heymann, Florence "Bottles in the Sea: Letters of Deported Jews in Moghilev (Transnistria) November-December 1941", in: Valentina Glajar and Jeanine Teodorescu (eds.), *Local History: Transnational Memory in the Romanian Holocaust,* Basingstoke: Palgrave Macmillan, 2011: 77–89.

Hobsbawm, Eric, *The Age of Capital 1848–1875,* London: Weidenfeld and Nicholson, 1975.

Hobsbawm, Eric, *The Age of Empires 1875–1914,* London: Weidenfeld and Nicholson, 1987.

Hobsbawm, Eric, *The Age of Extremes: The Short Twentieth Century 1914–1991*, New York: Vintage, 1994.

Hobsbawm, Eric, *The Age of Revolution; 1789–1848,* New York: Vintage Books, 1972.

"Home for the Aged, Erected by Daughters of Jacob, Observes 30th Anniversary", *JTA* Dec. 16, 1926, <http://www.jta.org/1926/12/16/archive/

home-for-aged-erected-by-daughters-of-jacob-observes-30th-anniversary>, retrieved, Jan. 15, 2016.

Ionid, Radu, *The Holocaust in Romania: The Destruction of Jews and Gypsies Under the Antonescu Regime 1940–1944,* Chicago: Ivan R. Dee, 2000.

Isaacs, Miriam, "Yiddish "then and now": Creativity in contemporary Hasidic Yiddish", in: Leonard Jay Greenspoon (ed.), *Yiddish Language and Culture Then and Now,* Omaha: Creighton UP, 1998: 165–188.

Kalush, William, and Sloman, Larry, *The Secret Life of Houdini: The Making of America's First Superhero,* New York: Atria Books, 2007.

Katz, Yossi, *The Battle for the Land*, Jerusalem: The Magnes Press, 2006.

Keegan, John, *The Second World War*, New York: Penguin, 2005.

Kelman, Ari Y. Kelman, *Station Identification: A Cultural History of Yiddish Radio in the United States,* Berkeley: University of California Press, 2009.

Klapper, Melissa R., *Jewish Girls Coming of Age in America 1860–1920,* New York: NYU Press, 2005.

Kracauer, Sigfried, *From Hitler to Caligari: A Psychological History of the German Film*, Princeton: Princeton UP, 1971.

Kugelmass, Jack, *The Miracle of Intervale Avenue: The Story of a Jewish Congregation in the South Bronx,* New York: Columbia University Press, 1996.

Leibovitz, Liel, *Aliyah: Three Generations of American Jewish Immigration to Israel,* New York: St. Martins Griffin, 2007.

Leider, Emily W., *Dark Lover, the Life and Death of Rudolph Valentino,* New York: Farrar, Strauss, Giroux, 2003.

Lerner, Gerda, *The Creation of Feminist Consciousness from the Middle Ages to Eighteen-seventy,* New York and Oxford: Oxford UP, 1993.

Leuchtenberg, William E., *The Perils of Prosperity 1914–1932,* Chicago: University of Chicago Press, 1993.

Lewis, Oscar, *Five Families: Mexican Case Studies in the Culture of Poverty,* New York: Basic Books, 1959.

Lewis, Oscar, *La Vida: A Puerto Rican Family in the Culture of Poverty – San Juan and New York,* New York: Random House, 1966.

Liebmann, Hersch, "International Migration of Jews" in: Walter Wilcox (ed.), *International Migrations v. II: Interpretations,* Cambridge: National Bureau of Economic Research, 1931: 471–520.

Madden, Stephen, Sullivan, Robert, Scott, Willard, *America's Parade: A Celebration of Macy's Thanksgiving Parade,* Springfield MO: Life, 2001.

Mandel, Irving Aaron, "Attitude of the American Jewish Community Towards East-European Immigration As Reflected in the Anglo-Jewish Press (1880–1890)", *American Jewish Archives* (June 1950): 11–36.

Mayhew, Billy, *It's a Sin to Tell a Lie,* Sheet Music, WB Music Corp., 1936.

McConnaughy, Corinne, M., *The Women's Suffrage Movement in America,* Cambridge: Cambridge University Press, 2013.

McElvaine, Robert S., *The Great Depression: America 1929–1941,* New York: Time, 1993.

Medoff, Rafael, *Militant Zionism in America: The Rise and Impact of the Jabotinsky Movement in the United States, 1926–1948,* Tuscaloosa: University of Alabama Press, 2006.

Mettler, Suzanne, *Soldiers to Citizens: The G.I. Bill and the Making of the Greatest Generation,* Cambridge: Oxford University Press, 2007.

Metzker, Isaac, *A Bintel Brief: Sixty Years of Letters from the Lower East Side to the Jewish Daily Forward,* New York: Schoken, 1990.

Mishkovsky-Schneerson, Zelda, *Al Tirchak* (Do Not Go Far), Tel-Aviv: Hakibbutz Hameuhad, 1974.

Monhollon, Rusty (ed.), *Baby Boom: People and Perspectives,* Santa Barbara: ABC-Clio, 2010.

Nistor, Ion, *Der Nationale Kampf und der Bukowina mit besonderer Berücksichtigung der Rumanen und Ruthenen,* Bucaresti: Der Romanischen Akademie, 1918.

Nullman, Macy, "Prayer and Education in the Life of Jewish Women", *Journal of Jewish Music and Liturgy* 19 (1997): 31–41.

Odem, Mary, *Delinquent Daughters: Protecting and Policing Adolescent Female Sexuality in the United States 1885–1920,* Chapel Hill: University of North Carolina Press, 1995.

Ofer, Dalia, "Life in the Ghettos of Transnistria", *Yad Vashem Studies* 25 (1996): 229–274.

Ofer, Dalia, "The Holocaust in Transnistria: A Special Case of Genocide", in Lucjan Dobroszycki and Jeffrey S. Gurock (eds.), *The Holocaust in the Soviet Union: Studies and Sources on the Destruction of the Jews in the Nazi-occupied Territories of the USSR 1941–1945,* Armonk, N.Y.: M.E. Sharpe, 1993: 133–154.

Okrent, Daniel, *Last Call: The Rise and Fall of Prohibition,* New York: Scribner, 2011.

Pinchuk, Ben-Cion, "How Jewish was the Shtetl?", *Polin* 17 (2004): 109–119.

Pinchuk, Ben-Cion, "The Eastern European Shtetl and Its Place in Jewish History," *Revue des etudes juives*, January-June 2005: 187–212.

Plakans, Andrejs and Halpern, Joel M., "An Historical Perspective on Eighteenth Century Jewish Family Households in Eastern Europe", in: Paul Ritterband (ed.), *Modern Jewish Fertility*, Leiden: Brill, 1981: 18–32.

Prange, Gordon W., *At Dawn We Slept: The Untold Story of Pearl Harbor v. 1,* Norwalk: The Easton Press, 1981.

Rabinovitch, Abraham, *The Yom Kippur War: The Epic Encounter that Transformed the Middle East,* New York: Schocken, 2005.

Recensamantul General al Populatiei Romaniei, 1930, vol. 2, Bucuresti, 1938. Census of Romania for the year 1930, Province of Bukovina by Departments and Districts.

Reeves, Pamela, *Ellis Island: Gateway to the American Dream,* New York: Gramercy, 1991.

Riis, Jacob, *How the Other Half Lives,* edited by Hasia Diner, New York and London: W. W. Norton and Co., 2010.

Ritterband, Paul, "Counting the Jews of New York 1900–1991: An Essay in Substance and Method", *Jewish Population Studies* (*Papers in Jewish Demography*) 29 (1997): 199–228.

Rosenberg, Samuel, *American Economy Development Since 1945: Growth, Decline, Rejuvenation,* Basingstoke: Palgrave Macmillan, 2003.

Rosin, Orit, "The Struggle for the Tzena: Housewives and the Government" (in Hebrew), *Israel* 1 (2002): 81–118.

Rosin, Orit, *The Rise of the Individual in 1950s Israel: A challenge to Collectivism,* Brandeis: Brandeis University Press, 1911.

Ross, Leonard Q. (Leo Rosten), *The Education of H*Y*M*A*N K*A*P*L*A*N,* New York: Harcourt Brace, 1937.

Sarna, Jonathan D., "The Myth of No Return: Jewish Return Migration to Eastern Europe, 1881–1914", *American Jewish History* 71:2 (Dec. 1981): 256–268.

Sarna, Jonathan D., *American Judaism: A History,* New Haven: Yale UP, 2005.

Schama, Simon, *Landscape and Memory,* New York: Alfred Knopf, 1995.

Schreier, Barbara A., *Becoming American Women: Clothing and the Jewish Immigrant Experience, 1880–1920,* Chicago: Chicago Historical Society, 1994.

Sefer Tzena Urena, translated from the Yiddish into the Holy Tongue by Rabbi. S. A. Hershkovitz, Bnai Brak, 1974.

Seidman, Joel, *The Needle Trades,* New York: Farrar and Reinhard, 1942.

Shas Tekhina Rav Pninim, New York: Hebrew Publishing Company, 1916.

Shimony, Tali Tadmor, Raichel, Nurit, "The Hebrew Teachers as Creators of the Zionist Community in (the Land of) Israel", *Israel Studies Review* 28:1 (Summer 2013): 120–141.

Shimony, Tali Tadmor, *Shiur Moledet: Chinuch Leumi Vekinun Medina 1954–1966 (National Education and Formation of State in Israel),* Sde Boqer: Ben Gurion University Press, 2010.

Shmeruk, Khone, "The East European Versions of the 'Tsene-Rene'" (Yiddish). *For Max Weinreich on His Seventieth Birthday,* London, The Hague, Paris, 1964: 319–336.

Shollar, Barbara, *Writing Ethnicity/Writing Modernity: Autobiographies by Jewish-American Women,* Ph.D dissertation submitted to the City University of New York, Ann Arbor: University Microfilms, International, 1992.

Silber, Marcos, "'Immigrants from Poland want to go back': The Politics of Return Migration and National Building in 1950s Israel", *The Journal of Israeli History* 27:2 (2008): 201–219.

Simkhovitch, Mary Kingsbury, *The City Worker's World,* New York: The Macmillan Company, 1917.

Sorin, Gerald, "Mutual Contempt, Mutual Benefit: The Strained Encounter Between German and Eastern European Jews in America, 1880–1920, *American Jewish History* 81:1 (Autumn 1993): 34–59.

Soyer, Daniel, *Jewish Immigrant Associations and American Identity in New York 1880–1939,* Detroit: Wayne State University Press, 2002.

Sternberg, Herman, "Geschichte des Schulwesens in der Bukowina" in: Hugo Gold (ed.), *Geschichte der Juden in der Bukowina,* vol. I, Tel-Aviv: Olameinu, 1958.

Tananbaum, Susan, review of *Jewish Girls Coming of Age in America, 1860–1920,* (review no. 612) <http://www.history.ac.uk/reviews/review/612>, retrieved, Jan. 4, 2016.

Tauranac, John, *The Empire State Building: The Making of a Landmark,* Ithaca: Cornell, 2014.

Waldinger, Roger D., *Through the Eye of the Needle: Immigrants and Enterprise in New York's Garment Trades,* New York: NYU Press, 1986.

The Weekly Midrash Tz'ena Ur'enah: The Classic Anthology of Torah Lore and Midrashic Commentary, translated by Miriam Stark Zakon. New York, 1994.

The Yiddish Writers Group of the Federal Writers Project, *The Jewish Landsmanschaften of New York,* New York: I.L. Peretz Yiddish Writers Union, 1938.

Tuchman, Arlene Marcia, "Diabetes and Race: A Historical Perspective", in: *American Journal of Public Health* 101(1) (2011): 23–33.

Turniansky, Chava, "A Haskala Interpretation of the Cene-rene", *Hasifrut* 2 (1971): 835–841.

U.S. Bureau of the Census, *A Century of Ppulation Growth from the First Census of the United States to the Twelfth, 1790–1900* (1909), Ann Arbor: University of Michigan Library, 1909.

Valery Raleigh Yow, *Recording Oral History: A Practical Guide for Social Scientists,* Thousand Oaks, CA: Sage, 1994.

Wegner, Beth, *New York Jews and the Great Depression: Uncertain Promise,* New Haven: Yale, 1996.

Weinberg, Sydney Stahl, *The World of Our Mothers: The Lives of Jewish Immigrant Women,* Chapel Hill and London: The University of North Carolina Press, 1988.

Weinryb, Bernard D., *The Jews of Poland: A Social and Economic History of the Jewish Community in Poland from 1100 to 1800,* Philadelphia: JPA, 1972.

Weissler, Chava, *Voices of the Matriarchs: Listening to the Prayers of Early Modern Jewish Women,* Boston: Beacon Press, 1998.

Wertzman, Vladimir F., *Salute to Romanian Jewish in America and Canada 1850–2010,* Xlibris: Bloomington, 2010.

Williams, Raymond, *The Sociology of Culture*, Chicago: University of Chicago Press, 1999.

Yablonka, Hanna, *Survivors of the Holocaust: Israel After the War*, New York: NYU Press, 1999.

Yezierska, Anzia, *Breadgivers,* Garden City, N.Y.: Doubleday, Page, and Co., 1925.

Zacutinsky, Rivka, *Techinas: A Voice from the Heart,* New York: Aura Press, 1992.

Zeitz, Joshua, *Flapper: A Madcap Story of Sex, Style, Celebrity and the Women Who Made America Modern,* New York: Broadway Books, 2007.

Zimilover, Seymour, "Radio Days: A Life Heard", *The Forward,* March 4, 2005, <http://forward.com/culture/3049/radio-days-a-life-heard/> retrieved, Dec. 22, 2015.

Photographs

Photo 1: Malka Scharf Haller (1859–1916).

Photo 2: Freida Sima Ensenberg, around 1916.

Photo 3: Freida Sima Ensenberg, around 1918.

Photo 4: Freida Sima Eisenberg, mid–1920s.

Photo 5: Nachman Enzenberg and Family, Mihowa 1920s.

Photo 6: Meier Moshe Enzenberg and Family, Mihowa.

Photo 7: Freida Sima Eisenberg, mid–1920s.

Photo 8: Beaded bag made by Freida Sima, early 1920s.

Photo 9: R to L: Abie, Freida Sima, and Benny Eisenberg, mid-1920s.

Photo 10: Benny Eisenberg as a young man.

Photo 11: Benny, Freida Sima, Abie Eisenberg and Minnie Scharf (seated), mid-1920s.

Photo 12: Freida Sima Eisenberg and Minnie Scharf, mid-1920s.

Photo 13: Freida Sima, Abie and Benny Eisenberg, late 1920s.

Photo 14: Chana, Abraham, Rose (right) and Vera Kraus.

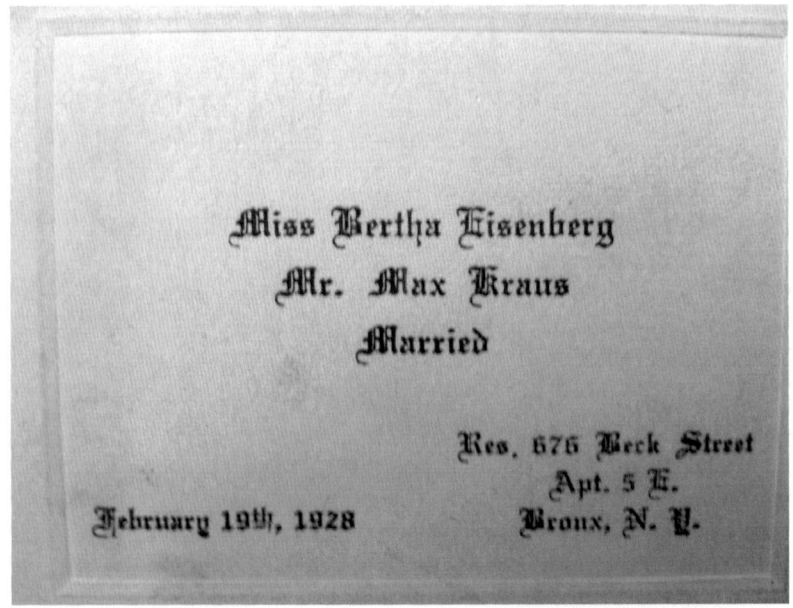

Miss Bertha Eisenberg
Mr. Max Kraus
Married

Res. 676 Beck Street
Apt. 5 E.
February 19th, 1928
Bronx, N. Y.

Photo 15: Freida Sima (Bertha) Eisenberg and Max Kraus, wedding announcement.

Photo 16: Freida Sima and Max Kraus, 1928.

Photo 17: Nachman and Devorah Enzenberg, 1919.

Photo 18: Devorah and Avrum (Abie) Enzenberg, 1919.

Photo 19: Enzenbergs in Mihowa during Abie's visit, 1928.

Photo 20: Devorah and Nachman Enzenberg, Mihowa 1928.

Photo 21: Freida Sima and Harry Kraus, 1928.

Photo 22: Stewart, Harry, and Ben Kraus, 1925.

Photo 23: Abie and Minnie Eisenberg wedding picture with Freida Sima and Max Kraus, February 1929.

Photo 24: Freida Sima, Max, Ben, Harry and Shirley Kraus, February 1929.

Photo 25: Marium Enzenberg and Feivel Rosenberg wedding picture, July 1929.

Photo 26: L to R: Mollie Scharf Handel, Devorah Scharf Enzenberg, Sadie Scharf Korn, Shmuel Yitzchak Scharf (inserted), Joe Scharf, Moshe Leib Scharf, Yankel Scharf (inserted).

Photo 27: Family picture, 1933

Top row left to right: Anne Handel [Rifkin] (Mollie Scharf Handel's daughter), Milton Handel (Mollie Scharf Handel's son), Dorothy Handel [Gorran] (Mollie Scharf Handel's daughter), Benny Eisenberg (Devorah's son), Betty Eisenberg (Benny's wife), Abe Scharf (Shmuel Yitzchok Scharf's [Devorah's brother] son), Jenny Scharf (Abe Scharf's wife), Al (Abraham) Scharf (Moshe Leib Scharf's son), Max Scharf (Moshe Leib Scharf's son).

Second row from top left to right: Lenny Korn (Sadie Korn's son), Sam (Solomon) Korn (Sadie Korn's Husband), Srul Nachman Handel (Mollie Scharf's husband), Abie Eisenberg (Devorah's son), Minnie Eisenberg (Abie's wife, first cousin, and Moshe Leib's daughter), Moshe Leib Scharf (Devorah's brother), Mitzi (Mathilde) Scharf [Hecht] (Joe Scharf's daughter), Abe Scharf (Joe Scharf's son).

Seated left to right: Max (Mordche) Kraus (Freida Sima's husband), Freida Sima (Bertha) Eisenberg Kraus (Devorah's daughter), Sadie Scharf Korn (Devorah's sister), Mollie Scharf Handel (Devorah's sister), Devorah Scharf Enzenberg, Hudel Weiner Scharf (Moshe Leib's wife, first cousin, and Rivka's aunt), Rivka Weiner Scharf (Joe's wife), Joe Scharf (Devorah's brother).

Children seated left to right: Abe (Bummie) Scharf (Sadie's son), Shirley Kraus [Tydor] (Freida Sima's daughter), Muriel Eisenberg [Arens] (Abie's daughter), Molly Korn [Sanders] (Sadie's daughter).

On Devorah's lap: Bernice Eisenberg [Finklestein] (Benny's daughter).

Photo 28: L to R: Abie Eisenberg, Max Kraus, Nachman Enzenberg (inserted), Benny Eisenberg, seated: Minnie Eisenberg, Freida Sima Kraus, Devorah Enzenberg, Betty, Eisenberg, Children Muriel Eisenberg, Shirley Kraus, Bernice Eisenberg, 1933.

Photo 29: L to R: Minnie Eisenberg, Devorah Enzenberg, Freida Sima Kraus, Betty Eisenberg, 1933.

Photo 30: Srul and Anna Enzenberg, wedding, January 1933.

Photo 31: L to R: Muriel Eisenberg, Shirley Kraus, Bernice and Sheila Eisenberg, 1938.

Photo 32: Abe Scharf, lawyer party, 1938.

Photo 33: Leibish and Frieda Enzenberg wedding, March 1939.

Photo 34: Elish and Lola Enzenberg, wedding, June 1939.

Photo 35: Freida Sima, Max, Shirley Kraus, and Shirley Goldberg, 1942.

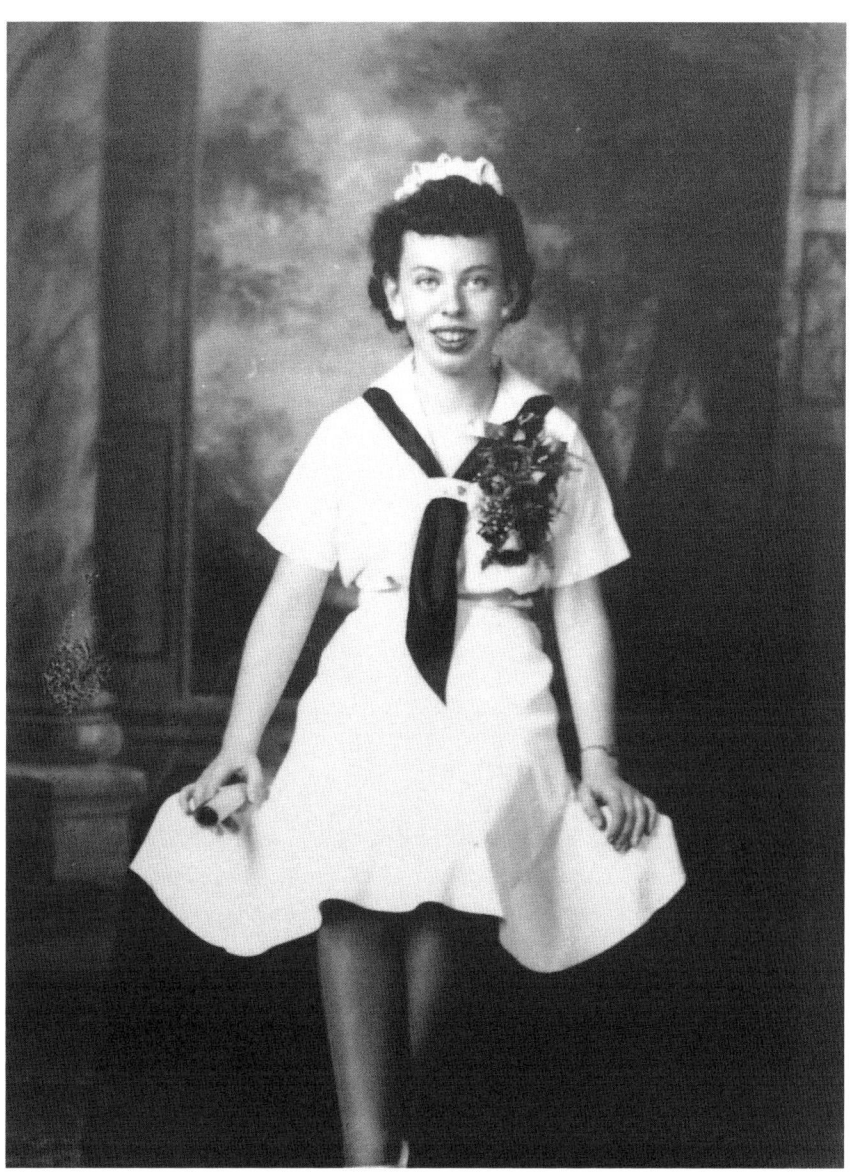

Photo 36: Shirley Kraus, junior high school graduation, June 1943.

Photo 37: Max, Freida Sima, Shirley, high school graduation, June 1946.

Photo 38: Enzenberg family picture during Freida Sima's trip to Israel, 1951.

Photo 39: L to R: Freida Enzenberg, Freida Sima Kraus, Toni Enzenberg, below: Anna Enzenberg, Israel 1951.

Photo 40: Shirley Kraus, Enzenberg, and Bernthal families in Israel, 1955.

Photo 41: Shirley Kraus and family in California, early 1950s.

Photo 42: Freida Sima, Max Kraus and family, 25th wedding anniversary, 1953.

Photo 43: Shirley and Chaskel Tydor wedding, November 1957.

Photo 44: Freida Sima, Max and Judy, 1960.

Photo 45: Freida Sima's 66th birthday, 1961.

Photo 46: Freida Sima and Max, California, 1954.

Photo 47: Freida Sima and Judy, Greek Island Cruise, August 1971.

Photo 48: Freida Sima's 79ᵗʰ birthday, "Happy Birthday Sister–Mother".

Photo 49: L to R: Tuleh, Sheindl (Jenny), Elish, Freida Sima, Benny, Abie, at Freida Sima's 79th birthday party.

Photo 50: L to R: Benny, Betty, Minnie, Abie, Freida Sima, Sheindl (Jenny), Lola, Elish, Toni, Tuleh, June 1974.

Photo 51: Family Party Café Baba before making Aliyah, July 1974, L to R: Top: Elish, Lola, Freida Sima, Sheindl (Jenny), Benny, Chaskel, Seated: Judy, Shirley, Toni.

Photo 52: Judy, Freida Sima, Abie, Freida Sima's 80th birthday party, Ramat-Gan 1975.

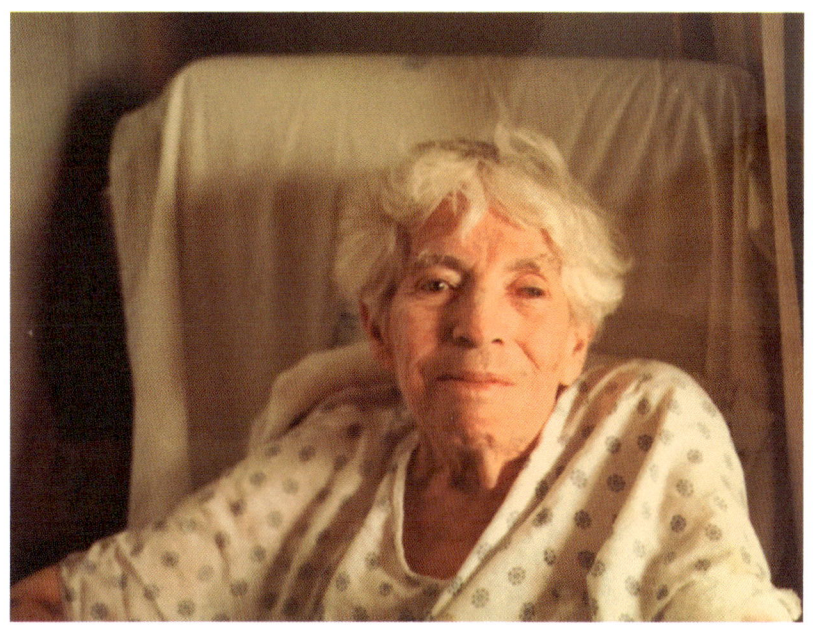

Photo 53: Freida Sima, May 1984.

Photo 54: Muriel Arens at Mihowa well, 1990s.

Photo 55: Extended Eisenberg–Enzenberg family in Israel, 2014.

Photo 56: Extended Eisenberg–Enzenberg family in America, 2015.

Photo 57: Extended Eisenberg–Enzenberg family in America (2), 2015.

Index names

250, 251, 253, 260, 265, 270,
307, 309, 311, 315, 316, 320,
324, 325, 346

Eisenberg, Benny (see: Enzenberg,
Benzion, Tzeendl), 48, 62,
87–89, 91, 92, 94, 102, 103,
124, 129, 135, 138, 141, 143,
154, 156, 157, 168, 169, 178,
189, 196, 201, 203, 227, 231,
235, 237, 238, 242, 250, 252,
258–260, 270, 307–309, 311,
324, 325, 345, 346

Eisenberg, Bernice (see: Finkelstein,
Bernice), 26, 135, 141, 142,
166, 324, 325, 328

Eisenberg, Betty (see Lobel,
Bruche), 129, 135, 141, 178,
260, 324–326, 346

Eisenberg, Breindle (see: Knobel,
Breindle), 231

Eisenberg, Daniel, 26, 260

Eisenberg, David, 23, 26, 178, 190,
223, 231, 263, 288

Eisenberg, Dora (see: Enzenberg,
Dora (Tuleh's)); Polachek,
Dora, 13, 26, 178, 194, 198,
201, 232, 254, 263, 288

Eisenberg, Elish (see: Enzenberg,
Elish), 53, 139, 149, 150, 171,
174, 177–179, 189, 190, 196,
202, 216, 217, 223, 224, 226,
227, 231, 232, 235, 242, 250,
252, 257–260, 270, 331, 345,
346

Eisenberg, Ethel (see: Samet,
Ethel), 52, 85

Eisenberg, Gail (see: Lefkowitz,
Gail), 26, 232, 237

Eisenberg, Hedy (see: Pahmer,
Hedy), 203, 224

Eisenberg, Lola (Charlotte)
(see: Enzenberg, Lola,
Wagner, Lola), 150, 171, 174,
178, 189, 190, 201, 231, 260,
331, 346

Eisenberg, Max (see: Enzenberg,
Max), 26, 174, 178, 189, 288

Eisenberg, Minnie (see: Scharf,
Minna (Minnie)), 7, 89, 103,
121, 123, 129, 130, 135,
139–141, 150, 157, 225, 232,
248, 243, 252, 256, 259, 264,
309, 310, 320, 324, 325, 326,
346

Eisenberg, Moshe, 26

Eisenberg, Muriel (see: Arens,
Muriel), 26, 78, 135, 136,
141, 145, 153, 166, 167, 187,
189, 190, 223, 224, 237, 243,
249, 250, 264, 268, 269, 288,
324, 325, 328, 347

Eisenberg, Nathan (see: Enzenberg,
Nathan), 52, 85, 265

Eisenberg, Norman, 24, 26, 178,
190, 201, 223, 225, 231, 232,
237, 263, 264, 288,

Eisenberg, Nute, 26

Eisenberg, Sadie (see: Enzenberg,
Sime (Sadie); Levine, Sadie),
52, 57

Eisenberg, Sam (see: Enzenberg,
Shmil (Sam)), 52

Eisenberg, Sheila (see: Saltzman,
Sheila), 26, 150, 166, 167,
179, 223, 224, 268, 288, 328

Eisenberg, Steven (Stevie), 260

Index places

Index organizations, institutions, issues

*Dedicated to my wonderful daughters, Beki and Rina,
who didn't know their great-grandmother Freida Sima
but have so much of her in them.*